FINANCING DEVELOPMENT IN LATIN AMERICA

FINANCING DEVELOPMENT IN LATIN AMERICA

Edited by
Jean-Claude Garcia-Zamor
Stewart E. Sutin

PRAEGER

PRAEGER SPECIAL STUDIES • PRAEGER SCIENTIFIC

Library of Congress Cataloging in Publication Data

Main entry under title:

Financing development in Latin America.

    1. Finance--Latin America--Addresses, essays,
lectures. 2. Loans, Foreign--Latin America--Addresses,
essays, lectures. I. García Zamor, Jean Claude.
II. Sutin, Stewart E.
HG185.L3F56   332.6'73'098   80-194
ISBN 0-03-051106-2

Published in 1980 by Praeger Publishers
CBS Educational and Professional Publishing
A Division of CBS, Inc.
521 Fifth Avenue, New York, New York 10017 U.S.A.

© 1980 by Praeger Publishers

0123456789   038   987654321

Printed in the United States of America

PREFACE

The objective of The Financing of Development in Latin America is to fill a void in current academic and business literature. A number of books and articles have been written about economic development in Latin America and international banking in general. Our book is intended to introduce the multifaceted subjects of finance and banking as they bear upon prevailing capital needs among the developing countries in the Western Hemisphere.

The scope of articles selected reflects the editors' perception that this book should be as broad as possible, although a totally comprehensive effort would have to cover at least twice as many subjects. At the editors' request, most chapters have been written in a basic and instructive fashion in order to enable nonspecialists and persons unfamiliar with either banking or finance to understand the issues addressed. The book is written primarily from the viewpoint of lenders or detached observers.

The editors wish to express their appreciation to the contributors, who were enthusiastic supporters of this project at the outset and who unselfishly devoted what little spare time they had during the past 15 months in order to complete their respective studies. We are additionally thankful to the Praeger staff for their early and unwavering support in seeing this project through to completion. All chapters represent the private efforts of the contributors, and the thoughts presented do not necessarily correspond with those of the institutions with which they are affiliated.

CONTENTS

INTRODUCTION

Jean-Claude Garcia-Zamor
Stewart E. Sutin

What is development and how does it relate to finance and the operations of international banks? This book does not dwell upon development, for much has already been written about its social and economic components. Instead, our effort is directed toward improving awareness of the role of finance in the development process in Latin America. Adequate financial resources, whether derived locally (through savings, investment, or trade surpluses) or from foreign borrowings or investments, are essential to the realization of growth targets established by national planners.

Among the more common economic programs in need of foreign capital are industrialization, infrastructural projects, import substitution, and export diversification. Capital goods and certain raw materials are often imported in support of these programs. Banks provide a substantial portion of the funds and services required for these features of development.

Public-sector institutions such as the World Bank and the Inter-American Development Bank offer the advantages of long-term repayments and are constituted, in terms of staff and mandate, to fund many programs that are impractical for private commercial banks to undertake. The latter offer the comparative advantages of rate sensitivity and relatively fast turnaround time from the point at which government officials make their needs known. In addition, the resources of public international banks are, by themselves, insufficient to meet existing demands. During the past few years, public and private institutions have shown interest in joining efforts through the cofinancing programs of the World Bank and the Inter-American Development Bank. At present, an interesting theme being studied pertains to the role of the International Monetary Fund and its relationship both to borrowing countries and to private commercial banks—not so much to the amounts of credit the fund can provide but to its role in the formulation of programs by which countries in balance-of-payments difficulties can restore equilibrium to their external accounts and can regain debt repayment ability.

PRIVATE SECTOR

The expansion of business activities in Latin America on the part of U.S. private commercial banks has been gradual. Prior to

World War I, international trade was not perceived as being important, with the exception of commerce related to a few commodities such as wool and cotton. Until that time, only a limited number of banks in the United States had foreign departments, and international banking was dominated by European institutions. English banks, for example, had a strong presence in Argentina dating from the early 1800s. World War I had the catalytic effect of drawing the United States into world affairs, inclusive of commercial relationships. Afterward, an increasing number of branches of U.S. banks opened overseas. By 1939, there were more than 100 branches worldwide, of which more than half were situated in Latin America.

The reconstruction period after World War II drew the United States to an even more central position in international trade. Exports increased to meet the needs of countries embarked upon rebuilding their economies. The dollar emerged as the major international currency. U.S. corporations expanded their level of activities internationally. All of these factors fostered the commitment of banks to international operations. By the mid-1960s, there were 170 branches established worldwide, of which 96 were in Latin America.

During the past 15 years, U.S. banks have escalated the scope and magnitude of their operations on a broad international scale. Coverage of Latin America has increased proportionately in this context. Continued expansion of branch facilities and placement of loans reflect this trend. A study recently concluded by the comptroller of the currency, the Federal Deposit Insurance Corporation, and the Federal Reserve Board provides data on the cross-border loans of large U.S. banks.[1] The aggregate of loans outstanding in Latin America as of December 1978 was $44.6 billion.* The largest outstandings were to Brazil and Mexico, with loans totaling $13.4 billion and $10.7 billion, respectively. Paraguay ($84.8 million) and Trinidad and Tobago ($87.2 million) had the lowest totals outstanding. Of the total loans, 36 percent were placed with private sector borrowers, and loans to government entities and banks were 29 percent and 35 percent, respectively.

Several varieties of so-called large ticket items consume a substantial amount of foreign capital. The Itaipu (Brazil-Paraguay) and Yacyreta (Argentina-Paraguay) hydroelectric dam projects are illustrations of major ventures. It is estimated that Yacyreta alone will cost over $5 billion by completion. Other types of government agencies that borrow directly from international banks include port authorities, shipping lines, telephone systems, and other public utilities.

---

*Excludes loans in offshore banking centers, such as the Bahamas, to avoid distortion.

Trade financings are accomplished in many ways. There is ample literature to describe the technical features of these operations. The Export-Import Bank of the United States (Eximbank) offers a variety of programs. Both buyers and suppliers credits may be arranged. Exporters may discount their trade bills at their line banks on either a recourse or a nonrecourse basis. Commodity financing may be arranged for exporters, brokers, or buyers. Only the larger banks generally engage in this type of operation, given the relatively more sophisticated level of expertise required.

PUBLIC SECTOR

The World Bank and its affiliate, the International Development Association (IDA), remain Latin America's most important sources of financing among the international and regional lending institutions. During fiscal year 1978, their loans to Latin America and the Caribbean amounted to $2.11 billion, of which $55.6 million came from IDA. Cofinancers committed resources totaling $773 million for 15 of the bank-assisted and IDA-assisted projects. Many of the loans were for projects in urban areas to develop industry, transportation, power, water supply, sanitation, and, more recently, health and education. However, agricultural lending projects led the way, both in amount ($655.5 million, or 31 percent of the total) and by number (12 operations, or 24 percent). The World Bank also offers loans and services to the private sector through its affiliate, the International Finance Corporation.

There are also several regional financial institutions lending money to Latin America. The most important one is the Inter-American Development Bank (IDB), which was established in 1959, with headquarters in Washington, D.C. The IDB currently has 41 member countries and is today the principal source of external public financing for most of the countries of Latin America. Its cumulative lending and technical cooperation for development projects and programs exceeded $14 billion at the end of 1978. The IDB also serves as a catalyst for mobilizing external private and public capital for Latin America's development through the sale of its own bonds and by promoting complementary financing and cofinancing arrangements with other financial institutions for development projects in the region. In 1978, the IDB's Board of Governors approved a fifth replenishment of the bank's resources amounting to $9.75 billion—$8 billion in the bank's capital resources and $1.75 billion in its Fund for Special Operations —to help meet Latin America's development requirements for the 1979-82 period.

The Central American Bank for Economic Integration (CABEI) was created in late 1960 through an agreement between four countries of the region: Guatemala, El Salvador, Honduras, and Nicaragua. Costa Rica joined in 1962. The CABEI had an initial capital of $20 million in 1963 and had raised it to $613.6 million by mid-1976. Of that amount, $520.9 million was obtained from external sources, almost two-thirds of which was through loans by the IDB and the U.S. Agency for International Development (AID). The CABEI's loans usually go to infrastructure and industry and in lesser proportion to agro-industry and low-cost housing. Total loans made by the CABEI amounted to $759.3 million in mid-1976.

The Andean Development Corporation (ADC) created in early 1968 by Bolivia, Chile, Colombia, Ecuador, Peru, and Venezuela, had about $142.9 million in mid-1976. These funds were obtained primarily through the issuance of long- and short-term bonds. The ADC also has obtained resources through lines of credit granted by the central banks of member countries to finance trade within the Andean region and from the U.S. AID, the Canadian International Development Agency, and other Latin American agencies in Mexico and Brazil. The ADC also has received funds earmarked for specific projects from Eximbank and commercial banks. The lending activities of the ADC have been directed basically to member countries, with special treatment for the developing countries of the region. Total loans made by the ADC amounted to $U.S. 174 million in 1976.

The Caribbean Development Bank (CDB) was created in 1969 in Jamaica and is presently headquartered in Barbados. Its membership comprises not only states and territories of the Caribbean region but nonregional member states as well. By the end of 1976, the CDB had an authorized capital of $187 million, of which $38 million was paid-in capital and the remainder callable capital. Its resources at that time totaled $210 million, with most of it coming from global loans from the Inter-American Bank; contributions from Canada, the United States, the United Kingdom, Venezuela, and Colombia; and a loan from the Federal Republic of Germany. The CDB lends to governments, public agencies, and private firms of member countries. Total loans made by the CDB amounted to $122 million at the end of 1976.

During the 1970s, a number of new financial institutions were also established in Latin America: the Venezuelan Investment Fund and the Inter-American Savings and Loan Bank, both located in Caracas; the Arab-Latin American Bank, headquartered in Lima; the Latin American Export Bank (BLADEX), with offices in Panama; plus a great number of finance corporations (financieras), some of which are analyzed in this volume.

NOTE

1. Federal Reserve, Country Exposure Lending Survey, June 21, 1979.

FINANCING DEVELOPMENT IN LATIN AMERICA

I

COUNTRY CONDITIONS AND EXTERNAL FINANCE

The flow of funds from international public and private sector institutions to Latin America has increased markedly during the past several years. This is somewhat reflective of both the petrodollar recycling process and the increased attention being given to development priorities by planners in a large number of countries. * In the context of increasing demand in Latin America for external financial resources, much attention has been given to analytical mechanisms by which foreign banks may evaluate the economic and political risk components of their overseas operations. Simultaneously, government officials in Latin America are increasingly aware of the need for appropriate fiscal and monetary policies in order to maintain internal equilibrium, ensure the availability of adequate international reserves to permit repayment of foreign debt, and inspire confidence among creditors. Trust and mutual respect between borrower and lender continue to be of paramount importance in any credit arrangement, but the vast sums of money involved require the adaptation of rather sophisticated mechanisms for the evaluation of a country's pay-back potential.

The chapters that follow treat a complicated subject matter from a number of vantage points. In Chapter 1, Stewart Sutin introduces international lending by private sector banks in the context of overall decision making on where a bank's loanable assets will be directed. He also reviews qualitative features of political risk evaluation. James Thornblade follows with a general presentation of economic checklist variables, one that is intended for readers unfamiliar with what components are customarily studied. Some thoughts are also presented regarding how various indexes may be interpreted. The study by Arturo Porzecanski relates general country risk considerations to experiences in Latin America. Commencing with an examination of specific debt-servicing difficulties that have occurred in several Latin American countries during the past 20 years, Porzecanski proceeds to sort out factors that contributed to those difficulties. Rodrigo Briones undertakes the difficult task of tying together country risk, social progress, and their relationship to the multinational corporation. Official policies that directly and indirectly influence a nation's external financial needs and the ability to repay debts incurred are given careful consideration in the chapters by Aida Pardee and Vito Tanzi.

-----

*Rising petroleum prices have generated large current account surpluses for members of the Organization of Petroleum Exporting (OPEC) countries and deficits among importers. Banks have served as a medium by which this imbalance in the external position of importing countries has been financed, using in part the deposits placed with them by petroleum exporters.

1

AN INTRODUCTION TO ASSET MANAGEMENT
AND ASSESSMENT OF POLITICAL RISK

Stewart E. Sutin

Private commercial banks involved in international lending have two prominent concerns: how much of a bank's asset base should be allocated to this function and what are prudent limits to consign to particular countries in which funds are placed. Asset management and country limit decisions are reached only after intensive study. This is an ongoing process in that changing political and economic conditions frequently require modifications of policy, plans, and targets. In recognition of the fluidity with which changes occur, bankers retain the flexibility to make judgment calls. This chapter is intended to identify considerations that are part of the decision-making process and to provide an introduction to a complex subject matter about which definitive studies have yet to be written.

The international presence of most banks resulted from an evolutionary process. Early overseas branch locations were often established to provide services and financing for trade in certain commodities. Two prominent U.S. banks, for example, inaugurated facilities in Buenos Aires between 1914 and 1917 to accommodate clients engaged in the importation of wool. Trade financing remains an important component of international banking. Nevertheless, the scope of operations has grown to include financing of such diverse activities as infrastructural development projects, balance of payments, working capital, expansion and modernization of plant locations, and ship charters. Loans are directed to private and public sector entities alike. International factoring, equipment leasing, money transfer, letters of credit, and cash letters are among the services provided to overseas clients. These loans and services are essential to the promotion of trade and development in Latin America. The nature of the industry has become increasingly complicated, and banks engaged in significant levels of international activity have had to adopt more sophisticated planning processes and technology to function in this marketplace.

Asset management as it relates to international lending covers a broad range of issues. Fundamentally, it is the means by which senior management and strategic planners provide direction and operating guidelines for line officers, with whom responsibility for the successful implementation of policy resides. The guidelines put forth may influence any facet of a bank's activities. One institution may refuse to offer fixed-rate financing under any condition, while another might have little hesitation to hold open this option to prime clients. Many banks will permit exposure in any one country only up to a certain percentage of their capital and reserves, thereby hoping to diversify risk. Others have refrained from participating in term loans where final repayments are scheduled beyond eight or ten years. There is also an increasing propensity for senior management to review interest rates on loan proposals relative to the level of risk involved in order to sustain standards for return on working assets. These are but highlights of asset management, and the variables that are studied along the way are numerous.

A manager might outline his bank's domestic and international client base and review those activities that have been consistent profit makers. Attention is given to the increasingly competitive nature of banking, evidenced by the large-scale entrance of foreign banks into the marketplace in the United States and the probability that large banks will more aggressively open so-called Edge Act facilities (those branches beyond one's state that concentrate on international banking) and subregional loan production offices. The contents of a marketing package, pricing of loans and services, and the ability to provide consistent high-quality service in the operational areas require constant examination. Availability of staff may be a factor in expansion of activities. Computer programs to chart overseas exposure and tax counseling are part of the planning process. Attention to international liquidity, the Eurodollar market, and the recycling of petrodollars is a demanding process. Banks also evaluate the relative merits of pursuing long-term objectives and the philosophy characteristic of the institution, perhaps in recognition of the potential short-term negative impact on earnings. If, for example, a bank has had a traditionally strong presence in a certain country and local competition escalates, with resulting declines in spreads, a management decision is required on whether assets are better placed in another market or whether competition should be met head on in order to sustain a market position.

A prudent asset allocation program is a precursor to establishing the guidelines for international lending operations. The next step is that of establishing lending limits for each country in which one does business. Some banks set nominal or target levels for short-, medium-, or long-term lending activities that can be exceeded up to preapproved margins with the consent of zone managers. Other banks have adopted the approach of setting firm country limits that can be only temporarily exceeded with the understanding that a new country study will soon be presented for evaluation. Banks also differ on who prepares the basic country study, with some institutions preferring to have the economics department do the basic analysis and others giving the responsibility for putting together the study to lending officers. In almost all cases, the lending officers and international economists interface at some point to compare notes. Accumulation of reliable, timely, and comprehensive information is a job in itself, but interpretation of that data and translating conclusions into the establishment of country limits is the true task.

The content, length, and methodology employed in doing country studies often vary markedly from one bank to another. Institutions tend to stay with approaches that have been successful in the past, with modifications made as experiences dictate. Use of a set format for presentation of information and recommendations is advisable to provide committee members who must decide upon exposure limits with reference points in familiar places and to ensure that predetermined key issues have been addressed. The main concern is that the two major types of risk, political and financial, are evaluated. Political risk may be defined as the potential loss or delay in payment brought about by expropriation, debt repudiation, or a breakdown of orderly processes. Financial or currency risk is associated with losses or delays in payment of loans caused by shortages of foreign exchange.

ANALYSIS OF POLITICAL RISK

Country studies may begin with an analysis of the political fabric in which the prospects for stability and retention of sound leadership are considered. The absence of either factor will ultimately affect economic variables and a nation's ability to amortize its foreign exchange obligations in a full and timely fashion. Throughout the process, one cannot overemphasize the importance attributable to a longstanding presence that a bank may have in particular countries and to the availability of in-house expertise to evaluate these factors. Banks unfamiliar with a certain marketplace have proportionately more homework to do in order to properly appraise all risk components. It does not necessarily follow that retention of low country limits is the best route to minimizing risk. One bank with, for example, a $300-million exposure limit for a country but with an ability to closely monitor day-to-day events and place or withdraw assets accordingly might well have less true risk than another bank with a far lower limit, especially if events in that country are not closely tracked by the latter institution.

It is not realistic to seek out a condensed recipe on how to measure political risk, complete with a standard laundry list of attractive catch phrases. It is best not to have too many preconceived notions. Access to reliable sources of information and an unprejudiced review of data obtained are of foremost importance. A failure to recognize one's political, ideological, cultural, or business opportunity biases may be detrimental to exercising clear and effective judgment. An understanding of certain concepts, such as the prospect for long-term political stability, is far more important than knowing such minute details as the biographies of cabinet members in a particular country.

The ingredients for political stability are apt to be notably different from one country to another. One nation may be stable because of a durable and autocratic chief executive, while another may be near revolution despite the presence of a similar political environment. In Latin America the precursors of change are often found in novels and political essays, as well as in increasing resentment toward political leaders. One may hypothesize that the origins for the social revolution that took place in Mexico during this century are traceable to that nation's prerevolutionary literature. The antecedents for Peru's political evolution may be found in the writings of Victor Raul Haya de la Torre and Juan Carlos Mariategui. Reliance upon a checklist of sociopolitical indexes as a means to anticipate political change presupposes that such occurrences adhere to consistently logical progressions. The fundamental benefit derived from such a list is that it may serve as a mechanism for stimulating thought rather than for answering questions.[1] The experiences in Mexico and Peru suggest that sweeping changes in political leadership and government programs are dynamic multidimensional processes that can be foreseen and understood through exercising sound judgment and familiarity with these countries. Precipitous political change rarely occurs without the emission of early warning signals.

Political risk, as defined earlier, is a de facto part of lending in that the potential for losses or delays in payment exists whenever a bank moves money across borders. The issue is not avoidance of risk, for only an insurance policy can accomplish that objective, but assessment of the probability factor for loss or delay. An ability to anticipate political disorders may permit a bank to scale down its exposure to a particular country and thereby proportionately reduce the impact of debt-servicing difficulties that might arise. Reduction in foreign loans outstanding to Nicaragua during the change in government in 1979 was due to the perception that it would take time for order to be restored and for evaluation of the manner in which that nation's fiscal and monetary affairs would be managed. The basic concern is not change in leadership per se, but in whether the fallout from those events will have an immediate or eventual effect on the repayment of international loans.

An objective and well-informed study of a nation's political environment is dependent upon accessibility to vital information in a timely fashion and on one's powers of interpretation. Subscriptions to several publications that closely monitor events in the Americas are essential. It might be advisable to include on that list at least one publication per country that is known to be critical of the government in power. An exchange of viewpoints with officials from international banks, State Department desk officers, academicians, and responsible and well-informed persons from that country should enable one to sustain a balanced analytical framework.

Objective and accurate interpretation of political phenomena has staffing and methodological implications. At least one authority contends that banks may find it advisable to establish political departments in addition to the economic research units that are now constituted. [2] It may be unnecessary to have a separate staff to evaluate political conditions, but line officers should certainly have the knowledge and expertise to do the job. The ideal situation might be to maintain a balance between regional specialists, seasoned bankers with no particular regional affinity, and economists. Additionally, an in-house checks and balances system might be established in which persons with no vested interest in doing business in a particular country, perhaps domestic loan officers, are called upon to assume the role of protagonist. This might assure the desired level of impartiality and offset the potential for a bank's becoming so close to a country that an objective appraisal of changing conditions becomes difficult to achieve.

Apart from a conceptual awareness of what constitutes political risk, one should exercise caution in generalizing about Latin America in toto. Each country has a distinct cultural heritage, history, level of development, and personality. Cultural norms and mores vary from country to country. Racial and ethnic composition of the people, sense of nationalism, attitudes toward foreigners, and population growth and distribution are but a few perceptible differences. While a common heritage among certain nations may be traced to the various European countries that colonized the Americas, most countries have evolved in varying ways. Argentina is a complex amalgam of peoples where large-scale immigration during the past 150 years has profoundly influenced development. Ecuador, more traditional by nature, has grown beyond the classic stereotype of an agricultural economy subsequent to the onset of its petroleum exports. Peru and Bolivia both have substantial indigenous or Indian populations, yet there are notable differences between these countries. Some nations have democratic governments but are scenes of occasional outbreaks of politically inspired violence. Other countries are ruled by military juntas or persons who have remained at the helm of authority for years, yet have populations that do not necessarily prefer immediate changes in the system. In summation, an important step in measuring the political risk associated with lending in a country is the determination to become acquainted with its historical, cultural, and political realities. References to "these Latin countries" are inappropriate and ill founded.

Another topic deserves a place within the political risk section of a country study: that of international relations. On the positive side, a peaceful, if not amiable, relationship with neighboring countries enables a government to place development spending in a priority position, to keep defense allocations to a minimum, and to aggressively promote trade relationships. Indeed, diversification of trade partners and expansion of exports have a direct tie-in to a nation's foreign exchange generating capacity, an immediate source of funds for repayment of international obligations. On the other hand, uneasy or strained relationships that occasionally reach near-war proportions, as in the case of the Beagle Island dispute between Argentina and Chile, could accelerate defense spending and drain international reserves. In the particular case in point, both countries were already well on the road to economic recovery, and the capable economic planning teams of the respective governments did not allow the financial and monetary systems to deteriorate. A similar confrontation between countries less fortunate could have unleashed a series of events culminating in massive drains in international reserves and debt-servicing difficulties, even if war were averted.

A long-term prognosis of political risk is a difficult proposition but is somewhat manageable if the objective is to assess the probability of cataclysmic change rather than the modifications in a nation's leadership caused by an election or coup d'etat. In this regard, corporate investors are more apt to be concerned about the degree of actual or latent xenophobic sentiment that might trigger expropriation of their subsidiaries. Bankers have an interest in this area as well, in that loans to those expropriated enterprises might not be repaid. This did indeed happen in the case of Cuba after Fidel Castro assumed control of the government; he nationalized certain foreign-owned enterprises and, in a number of cases, repudiated their debts.

The repayment record on official debt has been outstanding in the Americas even though renegotiation and occasional rescheduling of maturity dates have been required from time to time. To find exceptions to this pattern, one has to comb the archives dating from the nineteenth century, when certain municipalities defaulted on international loans and were not bailed out by the national governments. In addition, Cuba reputedly did not honor payments on certain bond issues that originated from pre-Castro administrations. In the context of billions of dollars of fully repaid debt, this fine record gives a measure of comfort to those banks engaged in long-term lending, particularly where the obligors are state-owned enterprises. On the basis of this performance in repayment of international obligations, one might feel that a bank could increase its long-term lending position to privately owned entities in proportion to its expertise and its assessment of any given country, for that is the area of relatively increased risk. Conversely, when confronting uncertainty, exposure to that country should be low, with loan emphasis given to the public sector or in support of international trade where the repayment record has been particularly solid. In brief, one should be cognizant of gradations of risk.

ADDITIONAL CONSIDERATIONS

Factors that might influence the volume and type of lending conducted in international markets are not solely associated with political or economic risk or even asset management in general. As just suggested, loans to the private sector require attention to details somewhat distinct from so-called sovereign risk lending. Customarily, a country study evaluates political and economic risk and concludes with recommendations on proposed short- and long-term limits. It would also be interesting to include a section on marketing strategy, inclusive of the outlook for growth and profitability for each major activity in which the bank intends to engage.

Once a determination is made to expand lending activities beyond the sovereign risk level, a myriad of credit and other questions arise (see Chapter 15). An understanding of the strength, independence, integrity, and efficiency of a nation's judicial system is essential in lending to the private sector, unless activities are restricted to those companies with attachable assets in various international sites or if offshore guarantees are offered. Should a loan workout situation emerge, the ability to obtain and enforce a local judgment may be crucial. It is hardly advisable to assess this issue after the fact. How familiar are we or should we be with the Napoleonic Code? Is an English language promissory note originated in one's home office acceptable documentation under another jurisdiction? Is a tested telex adequate proof of obligations incurred by correspondent banks? Retention of reliable and well-respected local counsel is advisable if one lends in the private sector, if for no other reason than to assemble a documentation package.

Besides strictly legal matters, a lender should understand the business morality, customs, and ethics prevailing in a given environment. One cannot overstate the importance of assessing the character of the borrower and the intent to repay creditors. If for any reason a banker has difficulty in understanding or accepting customs pervasive among businessmen in a given area, it might be prudent to scale down marketing plans, if not country limits, accordingly.

Bank checkings with other institutions are important if conducted with the proper objectives in mind. A follow-the-leader approach may well bring one to the right conclusion for the wrong reasons. The argument that other banks are conducting profitable business in a certain country is insufficient reason for increasing country limits; those institutions might have had a long presence in that country and a thorough awareness of all associated risks. The most immediate benefit of bank checkings, which should be done regularly and not only for annual review purposes, is to reveal accessibility of that country to international credit. Diminished availability of such credit facilities could have a major impact on that nation's foreign exchange position and could eventually affect debt-servicing capacity.

Even though flexibility is advisable in international lending, certain potential pitfalls deserve a moment of attention. For example, it is difficult to accept the validity of establishing country limits without a bank's line officer having visited that country with sufficient time to properly evaluate the area. The emergence of an attractive financial opportunity is, by itself, insufficient justification to commit to a loan before that study can be completed. Backing into country exposure carries an added measure of risk.

Finally, bankers should be aware, in general terms, of how the proceeds from their sovereign risk loans are applied. It is all but impossible to establish an audit trail to follow the flow of funds, except possibly in cases of trade or project financings in which disbursements can be made directly to the exporters or contractors. More commonly, the funds are credited directly to the Central Bank, with only a general indication of how they will be utilized. Nevertheless, it is worthwhile to observe the aggregate annual international borrowings of a country and to compare them with the perceptible level of infrastructural improvements. A rational public works program and a relatively efficient public sector is a manifestation of a sound official management—one that is more apt to cope with servicing international debt. This indirect means of assessing how drawdowns on international credit facilities are used is a practical means of relating participation in government lending to assessment of risk.

CONCLUSIONS

In appraising the political and economic risks associated with international lending in Latin America, it is noteworthy that the repayment record for official debt has been excellent over the years (see Chapter 3 for details). Governments in the Western Hemisphere have traditionally been careful to maintain high credit standings. Reschedulings of debt, when they have occurred, have usually been the result of a combination of factors rather than any one circumstance. Declining prices and demand for a nation's exports, an overly ambitious public works program, or the temporary breakdown in political processes have been among the more important underlying causes.

It is important to assess a nation's fiscal and monetary planning teams and the degree to which they are supported by the entrenched political leadership. A well-managed economy can better contend with unexpected difficulties and make necessary adjustments quickly and efficiently. To a certain extent, each country will arrive at its own definition of prudent policy in that there is a constituency to be served and development priorities have to be established. The latter programs have to take into account orderly repayments of international obligations, if for no other reason than to assure continued accessibility to credit. The contention that international lending is a high-risk business by definition is unsupportable by weight of evidence.[3]

The preceding commentary has not focused attention upon economic variables or country rankings, but a general appraisal of risk and asset allocation considerations would not be complete without offering a few words of caution in this area. The choice of economic indexes and the weighing of each variable's importance are difficult but necessary processes. Yet one should be cognizant of the lag time associated with obtaining this data. Lending to a country based upon a compilation and evaluation of such indexes alone is not dissimilar from establishing a credit facility to a corporation based strictly on its financial statements, with no evaluation of managerial competence and the changing marketplace. Data are important as reflections of certain domestic and international conditions worthy of study. Yet reliance upon data alone renders one vulnerable both to misinterpretation of country conditions and to delays in sensing when marked improvements or crises are in progress. An objective of this chapter has been to stimulate thought and to alert readers to the need for exercising judgment and broad analytical capacities at all times when engaging in international lending. A stilted, inflexible, and static country review process may be detrimental to creditor and borrower alike.

The wisdom of adhering to a multidimensional evaluation process is perhaps best summarized by Irving S. Friedman, who writes, "Country risk analysis may include (but is definitely not limited to) a numbers crunching or computer simulation exercise."[4]

NOTES

1. A comprehensive list of sociopolitical variables is available in Antoine W. Van Agtmael, "Evaluating the Risks of Lending to Developing Countries," Euromoney, April 1976, pp. 16-30.

2. S. M. Yassukovich, "The Growing Political Threat to International Lending," Euromoney, April 1976, pp. 10-15.

3. For a concise expansion on this theme read Charles Ganoe, "Loans to LDC'S: Five Myths," The Journal of Commercial Bank Lending, November 1977, pp. 18-27.

4. "Country Risk: The Lessons of Zaire," Banker, February 1978, p. 29.

2
A BASIC APPROACH TO COUNTRY EVALUATION: A CHECKLIST OF VARIABLES

James B. Thornblade

In recent years private organizations have become rapidly involved in financing and investment in developing countries. As a result there has been a growing demand for some analytical tools that provide a basis for more accurately assessing country risk.

Regardless of the scope of an organization's activity, it is useful to establish a checklist of economic data to help in determining the risks of international exposure. For example, a common decision for international loan officers in sovereign risk lending is whether or not to take a share of another bank's Eurocurrency credit. This relationship among banks has the disturbing potential for generating follow-the-leader behavior. Therefore, it is healthy to have a diversity of approaches to assessing country risk to increase the probability that someone in at least one financial institution will be able to say in respect to a country and its economic prospects, "The Emperor has no clothes on."

Ideally every company with significant foreign exposure should go through the exercise of establishing its own checklist of economic performance. It would be disturbing if banks were to make decisions on participation in international loans purely on the basis of a country rating that had been bought or cajoled from another source, such as a bank, consultant, international institution, or government agency. Although there would seem to be duplication when international officers in different corporations search after the same data, there is an important learning process in the individual effort to "nail down the numbers." Several banks believe that the area loan officers must, with guidance from the economics department, thoroughly familiarize themselves with the economic conditions in countries that they present to corporate customers. It then becomes the lending officer's responsibility to formally analyze and rate these countries.

Before turning to a discussion of the variables that might be included in a checklist, a few methodological points should be mentioned. First, a quantitative checklist does not take into account subjective evaluations of the quality of economic and business management, the educational and skill level of the population, or the political risk that economic leadership may abruptly change. A good performance as measured by economic statistics can deteriorate rapidly if human resources are unable to cope with a period of adverse world economic developments or if competent economic management is suddenly displaced by a political revolution. We shall return later to a brief discussion of how to make these important, but more subjective, assessments of political risk.

Second, the risk-ranking system discussed here concentrates on broad or macroeconomics and financial factors that may affect the general ability to service external debt in an orderly fashion. It was designed with the medium-sized bank in mind, where the issue is the arm's-length involvement in a large syndicated Eurocurrency term loan. This assessment does not cover factors that a company would consider in deciding whether to set up an operation in the country. These more market-oriented, micro factors might include wage rates, other employment conditions, location incentives, restrictions on foreign ownership, and market indicators, such as number of cars per 1,000 population. All this is not to deny that these more specific factors affecting operations in a country may reveal much about current and future general economic performance and political stability.

Third, the variables will generally be drawn from standard international sources. If every international company had a presence in the major borrowing countries and national data were comparable, then the checklist could be constructed from a wider range of economic data. In fact, this chapter is primarily directed at the many organizations that do not have a network of international offices and hence must rely on a few international sources (International Monetary Fund [IMF], World Bank, Organization for Economic Cooperation and Development [OECD], and the like).

Fourth, our emphasis in country ranking has been on analytical, not absolute, variables. A few measures of sheer economic size, for example, GNP or total exports, may be useful in a checklist, but in general the variables selected are corrected for size. Thus we look at reserves relative to imports, IMF credit usage relative to Fund quota, and so on. The absolute size of the current account deficit is less interesting than the size of the imbalance in relation to GNP and the factors influencing that deficit over time, such as export growth and the ability to restrict imports.

Fifth, there is the question of country coverage in devising an economic checklist for all countries. Very small countries or nations with significant institutional and political restrictions or severe data limitations (members of the Council for Mutual Economic Assistance [Comecon]) should probably not be included in a checklist overview. At the other end of the spectrum, major industrialized countries are included. There are some sound arguments in the theory of economic development for not including Germany in the same checklist ranking as Bolivia. However, a good test of the choice of variables used in assessing debt-servicing risk would be to include high income OECD countries. Furthermore, there is no reason why these countries should always place high in a ranking. Based solely on economic factors, an overly mature creditor nation, like Denmark, may indeed represent a higher debt-servicing risk than well-managed, fast-growing, developing countries, like Malaysia or Brazil.

THE BASIC PRINCIPLE: EXTERNAL
BORROWING FOR PRODUCTIVE PURPOSES

To provide a framework for the checklist we should briefly review a fundamental principle of economic development; that is, external borrowing should directly or indirectly finance projects that increase the economy's productivity. There can be some external financing of luxury items and some balance-of-payments financing (preferably during a cyclical low in net foreign exchange earnings). Beyond a reasonable point, however, if external debt does not enlarge the productive capacity of a country—and indirectly the export- or import-saving capacity or both—debt-servicing problems will arise.

Admittedly there is no easy way to make an assessment of the productivity of investment with the checklist. Nonetheless, a reasonably thorough assessment can be obtained by combining the checklist system, a quantitative approach, with a more impressionistic analysis in a country study that includes the prospects for major projects, the quality of central government and project management, and the outlook for continuity and completion of investments. This broader study would raise issues of political stability.

The checklist indirectly measures the history of a country's productivity with the variables falling into three groups: measures of level of development, rate of development, and net international liquidity. Generally, a high level of development implies past success in increasing productivity. This means that the economy is probably diversified and the management and education level fairly sophisticated. A high rate of recent economic growth suggests current success in allocating external borrowing for productive purposes. A relatively high level of net international liquidity indicates that the country is already competitive in the world economy. It may also suggest that loans flow into the country in such volume and terms (longer maturities, lower interest rates) that the country readily meets its import needs, and thus its net international liquidity position improves.

COUNTRY RISK: LEVEL OF DEVELOPMENT

It is generally agreed that there is lower sovereign risk and hence that commercial bank financing is generally more appropriate for countries at higher levels of development. More advanced economies tend to have more sophisticated management, diversified and hence more stable production, and greater leeway to restrict consumption and imports in the event of temporary external financial difficulties. It is not surprising, therefore, that one of the most common variables in a checklist to assess country risk is the per capita income level. The conceptual problems in comparing per capita incomes across countries are too well known to repeat here. The most obvious deficiency is the lack of information on the distribution of income, which the World Bank has estimated for some developing countries but which is not readily available even for industrialized countries. An interesting alternative measure of basic well-being or living standard is the Physical Quality of Life Index (PQLI) developed by the Overseas Development Council in Washington. It combines in an index measures of infant mortality, life expectancy, and literacy rate in over 100 countries, with Sweden representing the highest standard. Although in general PQLI and per capita income levels are closely correlated, there are some anomalies. Thus, for example, while the quality of life in Brazil with its great economic and social disparities is significantly lower than that in small homogeneous Costa Rica, Brazil's per capita income is slightly higher.

Other important factors reflect level of development and impinge more directly on the balance of payments. A measure of the composition of imports is useful. A higher percentage of imports devoted to food generally reflects a lower level of development, although there are exceptions. Incorporated in the ranking is the share of total imports accounted for by petroleum; a large share reflects not so much level of development as the absence of local energy sources or inefficient use of energy. Thus, Brazil has one of the highest petroleum import shares in the world, not only because of the paucity of local oil resources but also because in that large country there is no extensive railroad system. In analyzing the importance of both food and fuel in total imports, we are talking about the lack of compressibility of imports, an important concept in analyzing debt servicing introduced by D. Avramovic in the 1960s.

Another important factor that reflects level of development also determines the stability of foreign exchange earnings; it is the commonality composition of exports. The higher the proportion of exports accounted for by the top three commodities, the more vulnerable orderly debt servicing is to adverse world market or production conditions. Obviously, there may be some commodities with very little downside price risk. Oil, diamonds, and gold are examples. Adjustments should be made to rank more favorably an export mix dominated by oil. There are, however, data problems with both of these indicators, since international trade classifications are still quite unsatisfactory. A recent World Bank study suggests that it is extremely difficult to compare trade categories.

Finally, we add here total GNP, which is a function of population size as well as level of development. It is useful to have at least one measure of absolute economic size, since, everything else being equal, a larger economy offers more opportunities and provides greater diversity and hence greater stability.

COUNTRY RISK: RATE OF ECONOMIC DEVELOPMENT

Indicators of the rate of economic growth are an important complement to measures of the level of development. The ideal country risk involves high levels and rates of economic development (Japan, for example). In some cases, debt-servicing risks may materialize in high-income countries with low rates of growth (Denmark and the United Kingdom, for example). In a few instances the risk of lending to countries at lower levels of development may be perceived as lower if the country is growing rapidly (Brazil, for example). As the World Bank president, McNamara, has indicated, the difficult risk assessments lie with the group of middle- to upper-income developing countries ($500 to $2,000 per capita income). For this group, indicators of economic growth are an important differentiating factor.

The obvious place to start is with real GNP growth or growth of real GNP per capita. Again there are many well-known drawbacks to the use of comparative GNP growth rates, yet along with per capita income it is one of the most frequently included variables in a checklist. Another variable that reflects productivity, as well as balance-of-payments factors, is export growth, which is often closely correlated with GNP growth. In periods of external financing problems, export-led growth is generally to be preferred to growth induced by domestic demand.

The ratio of investment to GNP is included in the group dealing with economic growth since it represents a current commitment to future growth. A high rate of investment will generate greater pro-

ductivity and economic diversification, assuring a more stable environment for debt servicing. In the event of debt-servicing difficulties,
countries with ambitious investment programs can always cut back
their programs and thus bring fairly quick relief to the external account.

A negative factor related to economic growth is the rate of inflation. Rapid growth of real GNP tends to generate a higher inflation
rate, as in Brazil. Obviously one would give a lower risk rating to
countries that have achieved rapid growth and experienced only moderate inflation, although often the lower inflation reflects price controls or subsidies, which ultimately create distortions in the economy.
In general, the Latin American economies have experienced significantly higher inflation than other developing countries. Above average inflation need not imply problems in servicing external debt,
particularly if there is a flexible system of minidevaluation and in-
dexation to maintain export and investment incentives, as has been
the case in Brazil. However, high and accelerating inflation can be
a signal of poor economic management, which may reflect adversely
the ability to manage external debt.

COUNTRY RISK: NET INTERNATIONAL POSITION

The third and final group of variables on the checklist for country risk deals directly or indirectly with the net international indebtedness of a country. A large net external asset position may sometimes be a negative indication of a country's commitment to sustained
real growth. It suggests that the government has insufficient planning and vision to convert financial resources into expanded production.

On the other hand, there is no doubt that in assessing country
risk bankers often feel more comfortable with the developing countries that have larger net liquid international asset positions. A less-
advanced economy is more volatile and prone to inappropriate management decisions, and thus a large cushion of international reserves
is useful in carrying the country through a painful balance-of-payments adjustment.

The ideal variable would be one that measures the total net international asset position of a country, with assets and liabilities
given diminishing weight with increasing maturity. Thus, short-
term external assets count for more than longer-term investments.
On the other side in calculating the net position, short-term liabilities
weigh more heavily against a country than longer-term debts.

On the asset side there is the familiar ratio of international
reserves to imports, often expressed in months of imports. Using

only this measure of assets understates the position of the industrialized countries and some members of the Organization of Petroleum Exporting Countries (OPEC) that have accumulated significant non-liquid assets. International reserves data are found in the IMF's International Financial Statistics. The usual rule of thumb is that a country ought to maintain foreign exchange reserves equal to three months of imports. A lower reserve level is not a problem in advanced industrialized countries because they usually have a more diverse and steady stream of export earnings and easy access to international borrowing. In contrast, several Latin American countries have felt it prudent to hold substantially more than three months of reserves as a buffer against swings in export earnings. Chile and Brazil are recent examples.

As a check on the reserve position one might also monitor the net foreign asset position of the consolidated banking system, which is given in International Financial Statistics. A low or negative net asset position in conjunction with a respectable reserve position suggests that a country is "window dressing," that is, building up liquid assets by means of short-term external bank liabilities.

On the liability side is included the degree of IMF credit drawn by a country. This is the ratio of the International Monetary Fund's holding of a country currency to its quota and, in particular, the broader ratio that includes oil facility and compensatory financing, not just credit tranche drawings. Christopher McMahon of the Bank of England has suggested that a high level of IMF credit usage might actually be viewed favorably in that it suggests that a country will finally be forced by the IMF process to take tough stabilization measures. This has been the case in Peru.

One of several measures of the general external debt burden is the familiar debt-service ratio (the sum of interest and amortization payments divided by exports of goods and services). Shorter average debt maturity and higher interest rates increase the debt-service ratio. This variable is more directly related than any other to the basic question of ability to service debt and yet it correlates poorly with most rankings of overall country risk. The marketplace has given relatively low risk evaluations (as manifested by lower spreads on Eurocurrency loans) to many countries with high debt-service burdens. The explanation is that the debt burden must be evaluated in the context of the other variables that reflect level of development, rate of growth, and net liquidity.

To supplement the debt-service ratio in analyzing the external debt burden one also might include the ratio of interest payments to exports, which reflects the long-term cost of carrying the external debt. The structure of the debt is reflected in the degree of bunching, that is, the percentage of total principal coming due within the next three or five years. A high current debt-service ratio due to near-term bunching of principal payments may not constitute a serious problem if market conditions are favorable for a major refinancing to stretch out the debt repayment profile. Such restructuring has occurred in Mexico, Brazil, and Argentina. To get another perspective on the debt burden one could also compare across countries the debt outstanding with total GNP or export earnings.

There is one other indicator that is influenced by the level of development and rate of growth and that affects the net external position. This is the current account balance adjusted for GNP size. Roughly speaking, current account deficits mean rising external debt. For most developing countries the current account will remain in deficit since there is a natural tendency in the early and industrializing phases of development for investment to exceed domestic savings. Reflecting the basic theme that foreign borrowing should be invested productively, a chronic current account deficit is not a worry as long as the economy shows substantial real growth. A danger signal is a sharp rise in the payments deficit relative to GNP.

SOURCES OF INFORMATION

In order to be able to put together a complete profile of data that is comparable across a wide diversity of countries, the checklist system is based on a few international sources. For information on the dollar GNP and real growth the source is the World Bank Atlas and supplementary data published by the Economics and Social Data Division of the Bank. The time lag in getting data on GNP and the structure of national accounts varies tremendously with the level of statistical capability in the national government. The World Bank derives preliminary estimates of GNP growth and the dollar size of the economy about six months after the year in question, but published data may not be available until nine to twelve months after the year in question. For many countries, the Bank estimates are highly tentative, subject to substantial revision, and detailed GNP accounts from the national governments may not be available for at least two or three years. Data on export and import trends and composition, balance of payments, reserves, net external assets of the banking system, inflation, and IMF credit used all come from the IMF's International Financial Statistics.

Data on international reserves and position in the International Monetary Fund are available through the IMF with a lag of only a few months. Statistics on external merchandise trade are derived more quickly and reliably than either GNP accounts or the balance of payments, since most governments closely monitor commerce through international ports. As a result, aggregate figures on exports and imports are available within three to six months for most countries. The more complete balance-of-payments accounts, which include service transactions and financial flows, are available within six to eighteen months, but fortunately the information for virtually all Latin American countries appears in the IMF's International Financial Statistics within six months.

Information on external debt is difficult to get on a complete and up-to-date basis. The basic source is the World Bank External Debt Division, but the data are at best a year old and cover only publicly guaranteed external debt. At this writing World Bank has begun to issue a limited amount of data on private external debt. Alternative sources of information on debt are prospectuses for syndicated loans and direct contact with the central bank in the country. It should be stressed that there is no meaningful external debt information for the high-income developed countries, since they are generally not creditors to the World Bank and the international economy.

THE WHOLE IS GREATER
THAN THE SUM OF ITS PARTS

There are for each item on the checklist problems of measurement, comparability, and even causal relation to debt-servicing capability. A country ranking based on any one of these variables would be quite unsatisfactory, but we have found that in combination the variables on the checklist generate an overall result that makes a reasonable starting point in assessing country risk.

To derive an overall ranking, a country is rated according to its rank on each variable, from one to n, n being the total number of countries. The individual rankings are then multiplied by weights and the products are added together to get a composite score that determines the final overall rank. It is relatively simple to change the weights to reflect different aspects of country risk.

In particular, the weights can be shifted to highlight differences between long- and short-term risk. When assessing the risk of one- to two-year trade financing, greater (or exclusive) weight should be given to availability of IMF credit, the level of reserves, the net foreign asset position of the banking system, and possibly also the inflation rate (which may reflect near-term monetary and fiscal management) and the bunching of debt repayment. Factors that influence the medium-term risk (three to six years) are GNP and export growth, the inflation rate, the share of investment in GNP, and various indicators of debt burden. Longer-term characteristics, looking beyond six years, include total GNP, per capita GNP, the Quality of Life Index, the share of oil in total imports, and the composition of exports.

One might want to give a dominant position to one variable. Thus, for example, there is a tendency in many international organizations first to classify all countries by per capita GNP level. Countries with per capita GNP exceeding $2,000, for example, might automatically be considered low or medium sovereign risks, despite poor performance on the basis of other variables. However, in the case of OPEC countries where high income levels have been achieved in a comparatively short time, it can be argued that one should not underestimate the risk of political and social instability.

This leads to two notable omissions in the checklist: projections of future economic performance and political risk. One ought to be able to roughly estimate future growth rates of GNP, exports, and consumer prices at least in terms of whether performance will be better or worse than recent trends. However, we firmly believe that the country ranking must be used in conjunction with a more subjective and impressionistic country essay. Rather than projections being built into the checklist, the outlook should be included in the country essay and emphasized especially where future performance is expected to deviate, favorably or unfavorably, from recent experience.

One facet of projecting future economic performance is particularly useful, although very difficult to implement. It involves estimating for at least five years into the future a country's external financial requirements. One starts with a projection of imports that depends on the domestic growth rate and the effect of major projects on capital equipment requirements and with an estimate of exports based on the world growth outlook and, where relevant, commodity price trends. To the resulting merchandise trade balance, one adds estimates of net service earnings, particularly interest payments on foreign borrowing. The result is the current account balance, to which one adds amortization payments on existing debt to arrive at the gross external financial requirement.

Of great interest to the private international banking community is an adjusted financial requirement for private foreign financing (see Chapter 3). This is derived by subtracting from the gross financial requirement the net inflow of foreign direct investment, foreign grants, and gross disbursements of loans from foreign governments and multilateral organizations (World Bank and the like). Finally, the requirement for foreign private finance can be further altered, in the short run, by a policy of drawing down (hence reducing a country's financing needs) or of building up international reserves.

Projections of external financing requirements are made even more difficult by the interaction between the components of the analysis. Thus, for example, an initial current account deficit will trigger additional borrowing, which will increase future interest payments, which in turn will add to future current account deficits. This exercise is difficult but has certain parallels with cash flow projections done when analyzing a company. It is important to determine whether the estimated external financing requirements can be met from the world market, given conflicting demands from many countries for financing.

Political risk is a far more troublesome problem, as highlighted by the case of the Iranian revolution. There is no question that a political upheaval, particularly one affecting the export capacity of a country, can cause a rapid deterioration in several of the variables discussed. Furthermore, the marketplace has been pushing out the length of loans, and political risk takes on great importance beyond a five-year horizon. However, there is no satisfactory quantitative indicator of political risk that could be included in the checklist described here. Rather one should probably aim for a qualitative rating based on an impartial survey of political experts. If the survey results indicate significant political risk, that result should weigh heavily against economic indicators, particularly for periods beyond three to four years.

It was stressed at the beginning of this chapter that a checklist is only a first step in assessing country risk. Why undertake an intercountry comparison of selected data at all? We have found that a country comparison that is relatively free of subjective input stimulates a more incisive debate about country risk and international lending priorities. For example, countries falling in the bottom quarter or third of a ranking might, in an initial review, be held to a zero increase in lending. In order to get an increase in lending for a country that ranks low, the area officer would have to develop a special study, using the checklist variables as a framework for discussion.

Banks today are subject to a considerable amount of irrational and rational criticism about their lending to developing countries. One of the main faults of the less-reasoned criticism is the tendency to lump together all Third World countries on the basis of income level without regard to the more complex factors affecting risk. In response to criticism, there is much talk in banking circles about being selective in lending to developing countries. A checklist provides a systematic first step in the process of selective international lending.

3

THE ASSESSMENT OF COUNTRY RISK: LESSONS FROM THE LATIN AMERICAN EXPERIENCE

Arturo C. Porzecanski

The role of commercial bank lending in the financing of Latin America's economic development has increased dramatically during the past decade. Throughout most of the 1960s, foreign commercial banks constituted a relatively minor source of finance, and thus obligations to them represented only about 10 percent of the region's public medium- and long-term external debt. In contrast, over 60 percent of all obligations were with government agencies and private suppliers in the industrial countries. During the 1970s, however, lending by banks in the United States, Canada, Japan, and Western Europe to Latin America rose to the point where, by the end of 1978, about 45 percent of the public medium- and long-term external debt was accounted for by obligations to foreign commercial banks, and official bilateral and suppliers credits constituted only 25 percent of the total. The exposure of banks to Latin American governments and government-guaranteed private entities through medium- and long-term indebtedness alone was estimated at $45 billion as of the end of 1978, compared with just $1 billion throughout the early 1960s. The overall exposure of banks in the industrial countries to private sector and government borrowers in Latin America on a short- and long-term basis, meanwhile, neared $100 billion.

As Latin America's single most important creditor group, commercial banks are now more frequently and deeply affected by whatever debt-servicing problems arise in the area. The increase in risk entailed by the growth of exposure in Latin America has thus made it imperative for prudent banks to institute systems that can warn of potential debt-servicing difficulties. Lately, many banks in the United States are under added pressure to expand and upgrade their country risk assessment methods because regulatory agencies (namely, the Federal Deposit Insurance Corporation, the Office of the Comptroller of the Currency, and the Federal Reserve Board) have instructed bank examiners to include in their reports "an evaluation of a bank's procedures for monitoring and controlling exposure to country risk, the bank's system for establishing limits to lending in a country, and the bank's methods for analyzing country risk."[1]

When compared with more traditional areas of internal bank management, however, country risk assessment often stands out as a relatively primitive art. Since even academic researchers armed with the most sophisticated statistical techniques disagree on the crucial determinants of debt-servicing problems, it should not be surprising to find that the approach to country evaluation varies a great deal among commercial banks—and, it might be added, among government lending agencies and international development institutions. Given this state of affairs, it is easy for the uninitiated to lose sight of the essentials and to fail to note the main lessons from past experience.

To help clarify the issues, the following provides a back-to-basics review of the fundamentals of country risk assessment accomplished through an analysis of recent Latin American history. First, the region's experience since 1960 is surveyed and the principal episodes of debt-servicing difficulties are discussed. Second, the main factors that appear to have precipitated these episodes are identified. Finally, some general comments are made on the key economic policy failures and other exogenous events that frequently were at the root of debt-servicing crises.

THE LATIN AMERICAN CASE

In order to analyze the Latin American experience with debt-servicing difficulties, one must first define what potential difficulties should be of concern to commercial bankers. The most obvious is the risk of nonrepayment, namely, the risk that a government, acting as a borrower or guarantor, will repudiate its debts or wantonly ignore its lawful obligations. As far as debts to commercial banks are concerned, however, in the past two decades there has been no instance of default on public or publicly guaranteed debt in Latin America that was not preceded by arrangements to forestall it or followed by negotiations to settle the obligations in question. Consequently, for practical purposes, the more realistic risk is that debts to commercial banks will not be repaid according to the terms of the original loan agreement. This involves what is commonly known as a rescheduling of obligations, whereby the grace period or maturity structure of the contract are amended to favor the borrower, and some other terms (usually the interest rate) are changed to compensate the lender.

There are two additional types of risks, both of which can lead to an undesired increase in bank exposure. One is the risk that because the borrower cannot meet the terms of a first loan agreement, a second loan becomes necessary to facilitate compliance with the terms of the earlier one. This is what is termed a refinancing, and although it often involves an increase in exposure, the increase can be prevented only if amortization payments due are refinanced and if disbursements are tied to scheduled repayments of principal on the original loan. The other risk is that a general-purpose loan would have to be granted to assist a creditor in meeting a variety of obligations, including those arising from a prior loan. These are known as balance-of-payments-support loans and are the hardest to pinpoint in history because it is difficult to determine whether or not participation was forced on lenders by an explicit or implied threat of nonrepayment of previously contracted debts. Nevertheless, they represent a frequent type of risk that up to now has been inadequately documented.

The Latin American countries provide some interesting examples to illustrate these kinds of risks. During the early and mid-1960s, Argentina repeatedly restructured its external debts to commercial banks, government agencies, and suppliers. The first instance occurred at the beginning of 1961, when two $75-million loans, approved in 1959 by groups of U.S. and European banks, and obligations to official (and mostly European) lenders were rescheduled. The bank loans, which had an original maturity of three years with one year's grace, were extended to five years, with the result that amortization payments due in 1961/62 were halved and became payable during 1963/64. A meeting held in Paris with official creditors, meanwhile, stretched out $120 million in obligations from an earlier (1956) refunding agreement that matured in 1961/62. The result was a lowering of this amortization burden by 55 percent in 1961 and by 50 percent in 1962.

However, debt-servicing difficulties reappeared in 1962, and by August of that year the Export-Import Bank of the United States (Eximbank) was rolling over maturing principal on some of its Argentine exposure. Shortly thereafter, a meeting was held in Paris with European and Japanese government representatives, who agreed to reschedule $15 million and refinance $128 million in payments falling due in 1963/64 on account of past purchases of capital goods. As part of the same debt-relief package, an arrangement was concluded in early 1963 with the U.S. and European banks that had participated in the already rescheduled 1959 loans, with the result that $37.5 million in obligations due in 1963 were postponed until 1965. Finally, the Eximbank formalized its refinancing of debts in mid-1963 with the granting of a facility to cover $65 million due in 1962 and about $2 million owed during the 1963/64 period.

The need for additional debt relief arose again in early 1965, and consequently a meeting with the country's main official creditors was held in Paris in June of that year. The resulting agreement refinanced about 60 percent of the debts contracted by Argentina with suppliers and governments during 1963/64 (that is, $76 million), with the new amortizations due in 1968-72. In addition, U.S. and European banks agreed to a request to postpone 80 percent (or $30 million) of payments falling due that year on the ill-fated 1959 loans, which thus became payable in 1966.

The specter of severe debt-servicing problems did not reappear again until early 1976, when most of Argentina's creditor banks were made aware that the country was at the brink of default and could not be expected to service its foreign debts unless a certain minimum amount was raised in international financial markets. What followed was a typical balance-of-payments-support operation, which included a four-year, $500-million loan arranged by a syndicate of U.S. banks as part of a $900-million package of credits from commercial sources in Europe, Japan, and Canada, as well as the United States.

Brazil also experienced serious debt-servicing difficulties in the early 1960s. A $200-million loan granted by a consortium of U.S. banks in 1954 was rescheduled in 1958 and had to be rescheduled again in late 1960 to allow for the payment of the first ($25 million) maturity in early 1961. Also, commercial arrears were accumulated in 1960. But the country's external financial position remained problematic, and thus in 1961 generalized debt relief was sought from official as well as private commercial sources. Brazil's official European creditors met in May of that year to consider the refinancing of debts arising from guaranteed suppliers credits and eventually agreed to provide new loans for $135 million to cover payments falling due during the 1961-65 period. The U.S. and Japanese authorities, as well as numerous individual suppliers, also renegotiated amounts due. For instance, the Eximbank refinanced $213 million of 1961 maturities. The group of U.S. commercial banks, meanwhile, had to reschedule the $200-million loan for the third time, converting it into a five-year loan with two years' grace and sparing Brazil repayments of $75 million in 1961 and $50 million in 1962. At the same time, in what was a typical balance-of-payments-support operation, a consortium of U.S. banks granted two loans amounting to $48 million for a three-and-one-half-year term.

Debt-servicing problems persisted in 1962/63, however, as evidenced by a renewed accumulation of commercial arrears and a unilateral, $19-million refinancing of 1963 Eximbank debts. Thus in March of 1964 the country's main official creditors met in Paris to try to regularize the situation. A formal agreement was reached in July on the refinancing of up to 70 percent of the obligations maturing between January 1964 and December 1965 on guaranteed suppliers credits, with the new funds (an estimated $62 million) to be amortized within a six-year period starting in 1967. The Eximbank was present at the meetings and pledged a consolidation credit of $66 million, which was later accompanied by two smaller refinancings totaling $26 million.

Brazil's debt-relief negotiations spilled over into 1965, when refinancing agreements were concluded with the Export-Import Bank of Japan and with a number of individual suppliers in the United States and Canada to resolve the arrears problem. In addition, two balance-of-payments-support loans were negotiated: the first with a syndicate of U.S. banks from which $80 million was obtained for a four-year period and a second with individual banks in Europe in a package cumulating to $58 million. Since the country's external payments situation improved considerably shortly thereafter, both loans were serviced without incident and no new debt-relief operations became necessary.

Chile faced major debt-servicing difficulties in the early and mid-1960s and again in the early 1970s. In 1959, the country obtained a four-year, $55-million loan for balance-of-payments-support purposes from a group of U.S. banks, but in order to service it, additional short-term loans had to be contracted throughout the 1961-63 period with European and U.S. banks. Debt-servicing problems began to deepen in 1962, however, and commercial arrears started to accumulate. In 1963, the Kreditanstalt and a group of German commercial banks extended an $11-million consolidation credit to the Central Bank of Chile to cancel commercial arrears with German exporters. But the situation did not improve in 1964: additional arrears were incurred, another German refinancing loan was approved, and two one-year loans for $10 million each were granted by U.S. banks.

The prospect of renewed difficulties in 1965 led the Chilean authorities to seek generalized debt relief, and in January of 1965 the country's official creditors met in Paris to discuss the request. Their decision was to renegotiate 70 percent of principal payments due in 1965/66 on guaranteed suppliers credits contracted prior to the end of 1964 as well as on some government loans. Overall, debt relief totaled some $93 million, with the Eximbank accounting for $40 million. Although most of the debts were refinanced (with the new loans repayable starting in 1968), about 70 percent of the obligations contracted by the Chilean public sector with the Eximbank ($16.4 million) and with Belgium and the Netherlands ($1.4 million) were rescheduled. Similarly rescheduled were some $14.5 million in debts due in 1965/66 to the German Kreditanstalt, which were excluded from the Paris discussions. Finally, a four-year, $45-million loan was obtained by Chile from a group of U.S. banks in early 1965 for balance-of-payments-support purposes, including the prompt repayment of an outstanding $10-million short-term loan.

Acute debt-servicing problems reappeared several years later, when in November of 1971 payments on the bulk of the country's foreign debt were suspended and Chile requested a meeting in Paris with official creditors. The discussions, which started in February of 1972, were protracted largely because of the issue of compensation for nationalized properties. Eventually they ended with a recommendation to refinance 70 percent of amortization and interest payments (namely, $181 million) due on account of guaranteed suppliers credits and official loans. However, because all of the necessary bilateral agreements were not completed promptly (especially with the United States), numerous obligations again went unpaid. Also refinanced were sizable debts to commercial banks in the U.S. and Europe. The former consolidated obligations outstanding as of March 1972 into three five-year loans: one for $52.2 million covering public sector debts, another for $90.5 million on account of obligations accumulated by Chile's nationalized copper companies, and a third for $17.8 million to cover various private sector debts. Other arrangements included refinancings with European banks for a total of about $60 million, with the international consortium Atlantic Community Development Group for Latin America (ADELA) for $13.8 million, and with some suppliers and governments not included in the Paris discussions.

External financial difficulties only grew worse in 1973. Numerous obligations went unpaid while government representatives met twice in Paris seeking a renegotiation of debt-service payments falling due in 1973/74, but the meetings failed to produce new agreements. Not until December 1973 was an arrangement finally concluded with the United States to implement commitments made in Paris at the beginning of the previous year for approximately $90 million, including an Eximbank refinancing of $53 million. By early 1974, therefore, it was clear that the virtual suspension of payments to suppliers and foreign governments in 1973 had increased Chile's heavy 1974 debt-service burden by an extra 50 percent, and in the context of a difficult balance-of-payments situation, this led the authorities to seek new debt relief. In March 1974, officials from 14 countries met in Paris and agreed to refinance approximately $380 million, representing 80 percent of maturities on suppliers and bilateral credits falling due in 1974. The Eximbank's portion was $113 million. The remaining 20 percent (or $96 million) was rescheduled, with 5 percent payable immediately, 5 percent in 1975, and 10 percent in 1976.

In 1975 Chile's continued heavy debt-service burden, particularly in view of obligations arising from compensation for previously nationalized properties, again was judged to be beyond the country's payment capacity. The authorities thus sought a further renegotiation with foreign governments with regard to debts maturing in 1975, and by May of that year seven countries had agreed to provide relief by refinancing 70 percent (namely, $147 million) of payments due and by rescheduling the remainder ($63 million) in three installments of 10 percent each due in 1975-77. Obligations to six other countries for $29 million subsequently were restructured on the same basis. The Eximbank, which represented the United States at the former gathering of governments, provided relief worth $33 million. Later on, various other obligations to foreign (government-related) entities, such as those pending since 1973 with banks in the Soviet Union and in Eastern Europe, were successfully renegotiated.

Peru first encountered debt-servicing difficulties in 1968, at which time the authorities sought to restructure obligations to commercial banks and outstanding suppliers credits. The process began in June of that year with a 90-day rollover of numerous debts contracted by a state-owned steel mill and continued with negotiations held with U.S., Canadian, and European banks aimed at refinancing loans, both their own and those granted by various suppliers. Some banks refinanced only their previous loans: for example, a group of U.S. banks refinanced $68 million on account of two loans granted in 1966 and 1967, respectively, and a California-based bank refinanced $8.4 million for principal and interest due on a 1965 loan. Other banks granted loans to refinance both obligations on their books and suppliers credits, as illustrated by a New York-based bank that made a $16.5-million loan (of which $5.4 million constituted a refinancing of its own obligations) and by a Canadian bank that approved a $10.5-million loan ($3.9 million of which refinanced principal payments due on a past loan). Finally, other U.S., Canadian, French, and British banks consolidated and refinanced suppliers credits amounting to over $17 million. Most of these credits matured during the 1970-73 period. In addition, the Peruvian authorities negotiated the refinancing of guaranteed suppliers credits with individual European governments. The Belgian, French, German, Italian, and Spanish authorities agreed to refinance some $48 million, representing over 60 percent of principal and interest payments maturing in the latter half of 1968 or during 1969. Several Japanese suppliers refinanced obligations in excess of $6 million.

The ink was hardly dry on these debt-relief agreements when in mid-1969 the Peruvian authorities began to raise the issue of refinancing or rescheduling obligations falling due in 1970-72. The negotiations that followed with commercial banks were protracted and those with foreign government agencies did not yield an agreement with uniform terms and conditions, although a meeting in November 1969 did conclude with the recommendation to refinance at least 60 percent of government and government-guaranteed suppliers credits maturing in 1970/71. Debt-relief arrangements were finally concluded during the second quarter of 1970, when three Canadian banks consolidated and refinanced their 1968 loans ($19.7 million); U.S., French, and

British banks rescheduled loans totaling nearly $100 million (granting debt relief of approximately $12 million in both 1970 and 1971 plus over $7 million in 1972); and European government agencies refinanced payments of over $50 million. Most of the new agreements essentially stretched out repayments until 1975.

A year later, that is, in mid-1971, the Peruvian government began to explore the possibility of obtaining some debt relief on obligations maturing in 1973. Once again the negotiations were long and carried over into 1972, especially since European lenders and guarantors were understandably reluctant to go along with yet another rearrangement of maturities. In the end the consortium of U.S. banks whose loans had been renegotiated twice before, as well as the group of Canadian banks that had been involved in the 1970 refinancing, agreed in early 1972 to reschedule 85 percent ($30 million) and 75 percent ($5 million), respectively, of total obligations maturing in 1973. In addition, since only a Spanish government agency consented to a $3.1-million refinancing of outstanding suppliers credits, certain commercial banks in the United States and Germany were prevailed upon to consolidate and refinance maturing obligations to suppliers.

The possibility of serious debt-servicing difficulties did not arise again until mid-1976, when Peru's traditional creditor banks were approached for the purpose of arranging a sizable loan. Many of the banks were reluctant, but when the Peruvian authorities agreed to a conditional two-tranche disbursement schedule—with the second tranche to be granted only upon evidence of satisfactory economic performance—the negotiations came to a successful conclusion. The resulting balance-of-payments-support loan was for $330 million and was arranged by banks in the United States, Canada, and Europe.

A year later, however, Peru was still in dire straits. Unable to raise new funds to the degree that was required, the authorities had to devote much of 1978 to an extensive restructuring of the country's foreign debt. It began early in the year with the rescheduling of $65 million in obligations due to the Soviet Union and continued in mid-1978 with a postponement until 1979 of $185 million in payments owed to foreign commercial banks. Later on, two major agreements covering 1979/80 maturities were concluded with Peru's principal government and commercial bank creditors. Meeting in Paris, representatives of 14 governments agreed to refinance or reschedule about $550 million, with the equivalent of 90 percent of payments on bilateral and government-guaranteed suppliers credits falling due in 1979/80. Similarly, the banks decided to refinance some $360 million (or 90 percent) of 1979 maturities and pledged to refinance up to 90 percent of obligations maturing in 1980 (up to a maximum of $349 million). Additional restructuring with Eastern European, Latin American, and other government agencies, as well as certain minor reschedulings, are estimated to have provided a further $320 million in debt relief.

The only other Latin American country with a relatively rich history of debt-servicing problems is Uruguay. During the 1959-62 period, the country's balance-of-payments performance was very poor and required sizable compensatory inflows of foreign capital. The Uruguayan authorities relied extensively on short-term bank loans and lines of credit to meet their needs for external finance. Only in 1963, when their access to additional short-term facilities proved to be limited, did they obtain a five-year loan for $39 million from a group of New York banks in what was a balance-of-payments-support operation. In 1964, Uruguay began to fall in arrears under some suppliers credits and open account obligations to several petroleum companies. Although the country's external situation began to improve in early 1965, a series of bank failures led to heavy withdrawals of dollar deposits from the Uruguayan banking system, emergency intervention by the central bank, and the missing of a payment due to the country's New York creditor banks.

The exchange crisis of mid-1965 set the stage for negotiations with foreign banks and suppliers for the consolidation and restructuring of existing short-term obligations. By the end of the year, the Uruguayan authorities had been able to refinance 85 percent of outstandings to U.S. banks through a $48-million loan to be repaid over a four-and-a-half-year period, as well as $10 million due to Canadian and European banks. U.S. and British suppliers, in turn, agreed to a gradual elimination of arrears during 1966 and 1967. This debt relief proved to be short-lived, however, because Uruguay continued to rely too heavily on bank lines and suppliers credits with short maturities to meet its foreign currency needs. Thus in late 1967 negotiations were again reopened with creditor banks, eventually leading to a refinancing of 1968/69 maturities amounting to $27 million.

The country did not encounter debt-servicing difficulties again until 1971/72, when approximately $26 million in liabilities to suppliers were incurred because the Uruguayan monetary authorities did not release sufficient foreign exchange to cover import payments as they became due. In 1973 these arrears were formally assumed by the central bank and began to clear up. During this time, borrowings from and repayments to foreign commercial banks proceeded without major complications. It was only in 1975, in fact, that a seven-year, $130-million loan was arranged by a consortium of mostly U.S. banks for what can be considered balance-of-payments-support purposes. Although there is no direct evidence that the creditor banks were unwilling participants in the transaction, the loan was fully secured by a pledge of gold—a fact that suggests that without the collateral, the country would have encountered considerable resistance.

In addition to the cases discussed so far, there have been a few other more isolated or less serious incidents of debt-servicing difficulties elsewhere in Latin America. For example, foreign suppliers and banks were affected by Colombia's accumulation of commercial arrears in 1965/66. And commercial banks were not spared involvement in the difficult external payments situation that Mexico went through in 1976. As part of a package of emergency financing obtained by the Mexican government from the U.S. Federal Reserve System, the U.S. Treasury, and the International Monetary Fund, banks (largely from the United States) were prevailed upon by the Mexican authorities to grant a loan totaling $800 million.

A more recent incident involves Nicaragua, which stopped servicing its government and government-guaranteed debts to commercial banks in late 1978 following an outbreak of internal violence that triggered capital flight and closed the doors to most of the country's traditional sources of foreign finance. Ever since early 1979, negotiations with U.S. and other banks have been in progress to restructure obligations falling due in 1979 and 1980.

PRECIPITATING FACTORS

A case-by-case analysis of the debt-servicing problems summarized on the preceding pages reveals that, in virtually every instance, a rather clear-cut reason drove policy makers to seek direct or indirect relief from obligations to foreign governments, suppliers, or commercial banks: a perceived inability to make ends meet. Or, put in other words, it was the perception that foreign exchange resources would not be sufficient to cover immediate or near-term foreign exchange needs that led to requests for debt rescheduling or refinancing or for emergency loans in support of the balance of payments. Consequently, the country risk faced by banks in their international lending activity is basically a foreign exchange risk, as opposed to the essentially political risk encountered by multinational corporations and banks with equity investments abroad. In the latter case considerations of a noneconomic nature usually explain, for instance, the decision of foreign governments to nationalize certain properties. In the former case, it is human judgments about likely balance-of-payments trends that play the dominant precipitating role.

It should be noticed that special emphasis has been placed here on the perceptions and judgments of policy makers and not merely on the blind interaction of economic forces. The reason is that, as is illustrated later on, there have been several instances where government authorities plainly miscalculated the extent or timing of foreign exchange shortages. And there have been other cases where policy makers clearly did not have the same view of the costs and benefits of falling in arrears or renegotiating external obligations that their counterparts did at other times or in other countries. Thus, given that policy makers have neither perfect foresight of future balance-of-payments trends nor identical ways of dealing with them, there is no valid basis for the expectation of an exact, systematic relationship between specific economic conditions and instances of debt-servicing difficulties.

However, since it is impossible to read the minds of policy makers, a historical analysis of precipitating factors can only quantify the actual, ex post circumstances that may have prompted their decisions. In order to do so, an objective indicator of foreign exchange shortage, the gap between the supply and demand of foreign exchange prior to recourse to foreign borrowing, must be constructed. The evolution of such an indicator can perhaps suggest instances when policy makers may have had an objective basis for seeking debt relief.

Most developing countries register current account deficits; that is, they import more goods and services than they export. This is what usually gives rise to their borrowing needs and thus to the accumulation of external debt. While interest costs are included in the current account, amortization payments are considered to be a capital account transaction and must thus be added to the current account deficit to measure a country's gross borrowing requirements. This concept quantifies how much foreign exchange must be obtained from various sources if outflows stemming from current account and debt-repayment transactions are to be covered.

There are four main ways by which a country can meet its gross borrowing requirements. First, it can stimulate inflows of private direct investment, that is, the setting up of branches or subsidiaries by foreign corporations or the purchase of shares in local industry. Second, it can obtain project-related loans from international organizations (such as the World Bank and the Inter-American Development Bank) or from official bilateral sources (the Eximbank, the Agency for International Development, and their counterparts in other countries). Third, it can utilize previously accumulated reserves of foreign exchange. Finally, it can obtain funds via borrowing from commercial banks, foreign suppliers, and the International Monetary Fund. Consequently, from the point of view of the international banking community, a country's actual borrowing requirements are really the difference between its gross borrowing requirements and its net inflows on account of direct investment, multilateral and official loans, and international reserves usage. For example, if a country's projected current account deficit is $500 million and amortization payments falling due are an additional $200 million and if this $700 million outflow can be offset by direct investment inflows of $100 million, project loans of $150 million, and reserves usage of $200 million, then actual borrowing needs (from banks, suppliers, and the International Monetary Fund) can be said to total only $250 million.

This rather simplified view of the balance of payments of a typical developing country implicitly assumes that there are no sizable short-term capital inflows or outflows to augment or reduce borrowing requirements. As will be seen, however, this is an assumption that does not always hold. Indeed, capital flight has at times triggered an earlier or more severe foreign exchange crisis than the other more permanent sources of foreign currency outflows (that is, the current account and amortization payments) would have suggested.

In order to reconstruct the foreign exchange situation faced by government officials in a sample of Latin American countries—most of which encountered debt-servicing difficulties sometime during the 1960-79 period—their borrowing requirements have been quantified and are shown in Table 3.1. It should be noted, first of all, that actual (as opposed to projected) current account, direct investment, and project loan figures have been utilized in every case. This follows from the inability to obtain the ex ante estimates made by policy makers in each country with regard to these external flows. Therefore, the figures fail to capture the overly pessimistic or optimistic assessments that at times prompted policy makers to initiate debt-relief negotiations prematurely or belatedly.

Second, the amortization figures employed refer only to repayments of government and government-guaranteed medium- and long-term obligations, since no consistent statistical series on private sector and short-term debt repayments exist. Only in the case of Chile do the amortization statistics include repayment of private sector medium- and long-term indebtedness. This means, in general, that the countries' debt burdens are underestimated—and, consequently, so are their annual borrowing needs. The available amortization data are also deficient in that they measure only what was paid, as opposed to what was due. Therefore, estimates of obligations falling due but not fulfilled because of arrearages or debt rescheduling have been incorporated into the statistics on amortization payments. Nevertheless, the lack of complete information on amounts rescheduled indicates that instances of debt renegotiation do distort the available debt-servicing data and result in a further underestimation of the foreign exchange gap faced by policy makers.

Finally, the potential usage of international reserves as a financing item has been quantified by making two basic assumptions about Latin American central bank authorities: (1) that they have a reserves target of two months' import cover and (2) that gold holdings are not part of reserves because they usually are not or cannot be utilized for intervention purposes. In other words, policy makers are assumed to be willing to utilize their reserves of foreign exchange as long as they are in excess of one-sixth of the coming year's total import bill and, by the same token, are assumed to want to rebuild

TABLE 3.1

External Borrowing Requirements and Foreign Debt-Servicing Difficulties

Year	Argentina (1)	(2)	Debt Relief	Brazil (1)	(2)	Debt Relief	Chile (1)	(2)	Debt Relief	Colombia (1)	(2)	Debt Relief	Ecuador (1)	(2)	Debt Relief
1960	3.5	*	—	5.1	4.6	A/BS	5.3	2.1	—	3.8	0.5	—	2.3	*	—
1961	5.9	3.9	BS/OS	3.4	2.7	BS/BP/OF	8.6	6.2	—	4.2	2.2	—	3.4	0.7	—
1962	4.7	3.1	BS/OSF	5.2	4.0	A	8.9	6.7	A	4.4	3.2	—	2.0	*	—
1963	0.5	*	—	2.2	2.0	A/OF	9.0	7.2	A	4.0	2.3	—	1.7	*	—
1964	1.7	0.6	—	1.2	0.7	A/OF	6.2	5.1	A	3.7	1.8	—	3.2	0.4	—
1965	0.5	0.5	BS/OF	0.5	*	BP	4.6	3.3	OSF/BP	2.3	1.0	A	2.7	*	—
1966	0.8	0.2	—	1.7	*	—	5.6	4.2	A	7.3	5.2	A	2.6	*	—
1967	1.4	0.9	—	1.5	*	—	4.1	2.2	—	3.2	0.6	—	4.5	0.2	—
1968	2.2	*	—	2.4	1.6	—	6.5	2.1	—	4.2	1.5	—	7.6	3.3	—
1969	2.6	0.1	—	1.6	0.6	—	3.6	*	—	4.4	0.5	—	6.9	3.6	—
1970	2.0	0.6	—	2.7	0.5	—	5.1	2.0	—	6.2	1.7	—	8.3	1.7	—
1971	2.4	0.8	—	3.9	0.9	—	5.7	3.7	A	7.6	4.2	—	11.7	*	—
1972	2.0	1.8	—	3.6	0.2	—	5.2	4.6	A/BF/OF	4.1	0.9	—	5.9	0.3	—
1973	*	*	—	3.4	*	—	6.2	6.5	A	2.3	*	—	2.0	*	—
1974	1.0	*	—	7.7	1.6	—	5.2	9.5	A/OSF	4.6	0.4	—	1.1	*	—
1975	5.3	3.2	—	6.3	1.9	—	13.0	14.4	A/OSF	1.8	*	—	5.8	*	—
1976	*	*	BP	5.1	2.3	—	5.1	5.9	—	*	*	—	1.1	*	—
1977	*	*	—	4.2	*	—	9.8	8.8	—	*	*	—	6.7	0.5	—
1978	*	*	—	4.9	0.8	—	11.9	10.2	—	0.4	*	—	4.3	*	—
1979	*	*	—	6.3	0.5	—	10.9	7.1	—	1.0	*	—	6.5	*	—

	Mexico			Nicaragua			Peru			Uruguay			Venezuela		
	(1)	(2)	Debt Relief	(1)	(2)	Debt Relief	(1)	(2)	Debt Relief	(1)	(2)	Debt Relief	(1)	(2)	Debt Relief
1960	4.2	1.2	—	3.0	*	—	1.8	1.3	—	6.6	8.3	—	*	*	—
1961	3.1	0.2	—	2.5	*	—	1.7	2.4	—	1.5	2.5	—	*	*	—
1962	3.0	0.5	—	3.3	*	—	2.6	1.6	—	4.4	5.4	—	*	*	—
1963	2.8	0.2	—	3.6	0.2	—	4.2	4.1	—	0.9	0.1	BP	*	*	—
1964	4.3	1.4	—	4.7	*	—	0.6	*	—	2.4	2.8	A	*	*	—
1965	4.0	1.5	—	4.9	*	—	4.4	2.0	—	0.4	0.5	A/BF	0.3	*	—
1966	3.4	1.2	—	9.4	*	—	5.9	4.8	—	*	*	A	*	*	—
1967	4.4	2.4	—	12.8	3.7	—	6.8	7.0	—	2.8	1.6	—	2.4	*	—
1968	4.5	2.5	—	7.3	2.0	—	3.5	2.7	BF/OF	0.8	0.2	BF	2.4	*	—
1969	3.5	1.3	—	8.7	1.3	—	1.5	0.5	—	3.4	2.1	—	0.8	*	—
1970	4.7	2.5	—	8.8	1.4	—	*	*	BSF/OF	4.9	4.7	—	*	*	—
1971	3.7	1.6	—	8.0	1.7	—	3.1	*	—	4.1	4.0	—	1.3	*	—
1972	3.7	1.5	—	0.5	*	—	3.0	*	BS/OF	1.5	1.0	—	*	*	—
1973	4.4	2.1	—	11.4	5.6	—	7.1	2.3	—	2.1	0.2	A	*	*	—
1974	5.4	3.3	—	18.6	13.0	—	9.3	4.6	—	7.9	6.0	—	*	*	—
1975	6.1	4.3	—	13.3	8.3	—	13.0	4.0	—	10.8	10.3	BP	*	*	—
1976	5.8	3.9	BP	4.3	*	—	10.4	7.3	BP	6.4	6.0	—	*	*	—
1977	5.7	3.7	—	10.5	6.2	—	10.4	8.8	—	7.4	5.6	—	7.5	*	—
1978	6.7	5.2	—	3.3	*	A	8.5	5.0	BSF/OSF	3.6	*	—	13.0	*	—
1979	4.6	3.3	—	9.7	13.4	A	9.0	4.8	—	5.6	2.1	—	7.4	*	—

Note: (1) = current account deficit plus amortization payments, as a percent of GDP; (2) = (1) less net direct investment inflows, non-compensatory official and multilateral loans, and "excess" foreign exchange reserves (as defined in the text), as a percent of GDP; A = arrears; OF = refinancing of official debt; OS = rescheduling of official debt; OSF = OS and OF; BF = refinancing of bank debt; BS = rescheduling of bank debt; BSF = BS and BF; BP = bank balance-of-payments-support loan; and * indicates that the amount is zero or negative.

Sources: For external borrowing requirements, International Monetary Fund, International Financial Statistics; Inter-American Development Bank, External Financing of the Latin American Countries; Banco Central de Chile, Boletín mensual; and World Bank, World Debt Tables. Information for debt relief was compiled by the author from various sources. The figures for 1978/79 are estimates subject to revision.

39

their stock of foreign currency reserves whenever import coverage falls below two months.

Turning to an analysis of Table 3.1, it will be noticed that the two measures of borrowing requirements here discussed are expressed in relation to the gross domestic product (GDP) of each country. The purpose of this is to place the various financial gap statistics in perspective, thus allowing for some degree of comparability over time and across countries. In essence, this assumes that a $300-million gap is far more difficult for a small or poor country to fill than it is for a large or higher-income country.

A word of caution is in order about the pinpointing of debt-servicing incidents as they appear in the table. The discussion in the first section of this study should have made clear that such an exercise is an approximation and can be misleading. In many cases, between six and eighteen months elapsed from the start to the successful conclusion of a debt relief arrangement, yet because of insufficient information only the latter date is usually recorded. In addition, in some instances policy makers sought debt relief a year or two ahead of a projected difficult external financial situation—which sometimes never materialized—while others met it head on, often through heavy reliance on short-term borrowing, and only sought relief once the foreign exchange gap proved too large or too persistent to be bridged without it. Consequently, matching debt-servicing incidents with particular calendar years should only be interpreted with adequate allowance for the various leads and lags that may have occurred.

In the case of Argentina, for example, the debt-servicing difficulties encountered in 1961/62 appear to correlate well with the country's sizable foreign exchange gap (3.9 percent and 3.1 percent of GDP, respectively). In 1961 Argentina had a current account deficit ($585 million, the equivalent of 4 percent of GDP) that was by far the largest ever registered (in absolute as well as relative terms) throughout the 1953-74 period. It was followed in 1962 by yet another deficit ($273 million, or 2.1 percent of GDP) and, more important, by a massive flight of capital. Indeed, if such speculative capital outflows were to be included in the calculation of the 1962 borrowing requirements coefficient, they would increase it from 3.1 percent of GDP (as shown in Table 3.1) to about 5.5 percent of GDP. These adverse trends generated a foreign exchange imbalance that inflows on account of direct investment, project loans, and reserves usage could not possibly bridge. Argentina's reserves of foreign currency dropped, in fact, from over $400 million at the end of 1960 (providing four months' import cover) to half as much a year later and to only $50 million by late 1962. In light of political instability and a deteriorating domestic financial situation, the authorities were unable to raise sufficient foreign funds in international capital markets and had to seek relief from external obligations.

In contrast, the 1965 renegotiation of foreign debts seems odd in view of a foreign exchange gap of only 0.5 percent of GDP. But this follows from a severe distortion of the underlying current account data, which registered a $223 million surplus (or 1 percent of GDP) on paper. The reason is that in late 1964 and early 1965, in anticipation of untenably strong demand for foreign exchange, the Argentine authorities blocked profit remittances, restricted private transfer payments, cut tourist exchange allocations, and curtailed merchandise imports via the imposition of a 100 percent advance deposit. Debt relief negotiations were thus initiated to obtain sufficient foreign financing to meet a backlog of transactions that in the absence of controls would have generated a borrowing requirements gap of over 2 percent of GDP. Yet the successful conclusion of debt relief arrangements and the lifting of exchange controls in the second half of 1965 coincided with a domestic recession that depressed import demand and was followed by an unscheduled change of government that inspired public confidence and triggered a reflux of capital. Consequently, Argentina's balance of payments showed dramatic improvement (for example, reserves of foreign exchange rose from under $50 million in mid-1965 to $600 million two years later), which if foreseen by the authorities would have obviated the need for any debt relief.

Finally, the relevance of lags in some instances is exemplified by events in Argentina during 1975/76. A foreign exchange gap equivalent to 3.2 percent of GDP developed in 1975 as a result of a major deterioration of the balance of payments. Unable to obtain sufficient long-term financing to cover it, the authorities turned to short-term borrowing (largely via swaps), raising approximately $1.4 billion (equal to 3.8 percent of GDP). While this may have seemed a good alternative to debt renegotiation, it merely postponed the problem until the second half of 1976, when the obligations began to fall due. It was at that point that the Argentine government approached foreign banks for a sizable balance-of-payments-support loan with which to cancel debts incurred a year earlier. This need for foreign financing is not revealed by the 1976 coefficients shown in Table 3.1, however, because the underlying data include only repayments of long-term obligations. When proper allowance is made for the burden imposed by short-term debts, Argentina's borrowing requirements in 1976 exceed 4 percent of GDP.

The importance of taking into account policy reaction leads and lags, speculative capital flows, and forecast errors cannot be overemphasized. The Brazilian authorities sought debt relief from official lenders in mid-1964 and balance-of-payments-support loans from commercial banks in early 1965 for a reason not fully conveyed by the foreign exchange gap calculations shown in Table 3.1: The need to liquidate payments arrears and swap obligations totaling $830 million

(3.4 percent of GDP) in the context of depleted foreign currency reserves (averaging $100 million in 1964) and what was anticipated to be a balanced 1965 current account performance. Yet merchandise imports fell 13 percent in 1965 (following a drop of 16 percent in 1964) and exports rose by 12 percent, and thus the current account turned strongly positive, registering a surplus of $284 million, the largest (in absolute as well as in relative terms) recorded in at least three decades. This surplus led to a sudden accumulation of foreign exchange reserves, which quadrupled (to over $400 million) by the end of 1965. Had the Brazilian authorities been able to anticipate this quick turnabout, they would have had no objective reason for seeking extraordinary financial support from U.S. and European commercial banks.

Other incidents of this nature are not uncommon. Unexpected capital outflows played the leading role in triggering a major deterioration of Mexico's balance of payments in mid-1976 and were solely responsible for the Nicaraguan foreign exchange crisis that broke out in the second half of 1978. In addition, the accumulation of short-term debts and the need to repay them were aggravating factors in the Uruguayan debt refinancings of 1965 and 1968.

The only instances of debt relief that cannot be explained by making reference to the country's excessively large borrowing requirements are those of Peru in 1970 and 1972. In both cases the Peruvian authorities sought (and eventually achieved) a renegotiation of future obligations largely as a gesture of displeasure with the international organizations, official agencies, and commercial banks that had adopted a cool attitude toward new loans to the government of Peru because of its policy of nationalizations without adequate compensation. In other words, political rather than economic considerations are the relevant ones here. But this is an exception not likely to be repeated in the Latin American context now that most countries have nationalized or otherwise gained better control over foreign-dominated activities considered to be in the national interest.

The general conclusion to be drawn from Table 3.1—after making some ad hoc adjustments for the inadequacy of the available data as well as for the relevant leads, lags, and ex ante perceptions of policy makers—is that large foreign exchange gaps are a necessary condition for the emergence of debt-servicing problems. A critical minimum value for gross borrowing requirements adjusted for inflows on account of direct investment, project loans, and reserves usage appears to be 2.5 percent of GDP, although a higher threshold (of approximately 4 percent of GDP) seems relevant whenever estimates of short-term debt repayments or of short-term capital outflows are included.

However, an equally important conclusion to be derived from the table is that a large foreign exchange gap is a necessary but by no means sufficient condition to signal the onset of debt-servicing difficulties. A casual review of Mexico's external borrowing requirements or of those of Chile since 1977 or of other countries at various points in time should be sufficient to illustrate the point. The reason is that an analysis of borrowing requirements focuses only on a country's demand for foreign finance and fails to measure the supply side of the relationship, namely, the willingness of the commercial banking community (and the International Monetary Fund) to provide the required sums. This is where confidence (in the government, the economic team, and their policies) enters as a key determinant of the viability of any given foreign exchange gap. Experience demonstrates that a generalized perception of creditworthiness can validate a country's large borrowing requirements, whereas in the absence of confidence even a relatively small foreign exchange gap may prove untenable.

THE FUNDAMENTALS

Having established that debt-servicing difficulties arise when a country's borrowing requirements are large and exceed what lenders are willing to provide, our attention must focus on the fundamental economic and political factors that determine the severity of external imbalances and that give rise to confidence crises that curtail access to international capital markets.

With regard to the Latin American experience of the past two decades, the available evidence suggests, first of all, a strong relationship between the direction of demand-management policies and the condition of the current account of the balance of payments. Overly expansionary monetary policies, often caused by fiscal imbalances, have tended to generate excess demand for goods and services, including imports, to the detriment of exportable surpluses. Such stimulative monetary and fiscal policies generally have been a reflection of attempts to accelerate economic development and to relieve social pressures by increasing current and capital outlays of the public sector, while failing to transfer sufficient resources from the private sector to the government through taxation and other legitimate means. In addition, credit to the private sector has sometimes grown excessively in an effort to stimulate investment and production, generating, in the short run, inflationary pressures that have weakened the balance of payments.

Second, distortions in the structure of prices prevalent in the economy have often caused or contributed to balance-of-payments problems in Latin America. For instance, low administered prices of food and energy have at times imposed disincentives to domestic producers and have spurred undue reliance on imports. Ceilings and restrictions on the payments of interest have discouraged domestic savings and encouraged capital outflows in response to international interest rate differentials. And, to be sure, inadequate exchange rate policies, in view of existing and anticipated current account deficits, have been a notorious source of external imbalances. These and other distortions usually have come into being because governments wished to minimize the cost to consumers of certain vital commodities, but they tended to worsen over time because of the difficulty of effecting changes in pricing policies because of political considerations.

Third, current account difficulties have been fostered by strategies of economic development entailing a poor allocation of available resources. Policies of so-called import substitution, which established import-competing industries through tariff protection and fiscal and credit incentives, actually promoted greater dependence on certain import categories (for example, raw materials and capital goods), increased the cost of industrial inputs to local producers of other commodities, and represented an inefficient use of scarce capital and managerial talent. At the same time, policies that failed to promote exports (whether of traditional or nontraditional goods) resulted in a lackluster export earnings performance that created foreign exchange bottlenecks to rapid economic growth.

Finally, political instability and inept economic management have been major determinants of short- and long-term capital outflows. Political systems or economic policies that generated a great deal of uncertainty led to speculative attacks on the prevailing exchange rate that sometimes succeeded in depleting, in a matter of weeks or months, even large precautionary reserves of foreign exchange.

Surprisingly, perhaps, the Latin American experience fails to suggest that factors such as the paucity of natural resources, a low level of per capita income, or adverse exogenous developments related to international trade can trigger an external payments crisis. It is what governments are able to do with the available natural and human resources that seems to matter. It is also the ability of countries to live within their means, however modest or ample they may be, that is relevant. And it is the willingness to adjust to a sudden decline in the volume or world price of exports or to an unexpected increase in the price of imports that seems to be critical. All of the above are related to the quality of economic management and to the flexibility inherent in the political system.

Concerning what influenced the degree of confidence in a country and its government on the part of the international financial community, there are at least three somewhat intangible factors that appear to have played a leading role. First, confidence required that there be a consensus among creditors that the authorities of the borrowing country would "play by the rules," namely, that they would honor contracts and pledges in both letter and spirit. Actions considered to be arbitrary, whether against individuals or domestic corporations or especially against multinational enterprises, tended to destroy confidence by raising doubts about the borrower's respect for the laws and the eventual fulfillment of other kinds of obligations.

Second, financial institutions seem to have been favorably impressed by coherent foreign borrowing programs. They included, for instance, centralized control over the amounts, terms and purposes of new loans; careful coordination between borrowing and stabilization or economic development plans, so that the end use of foreign credits was evident and supplementary fiscal, monetary, and other measures were adopted; and a healthy reliance on a variety of lenders (suppliers, multilateral development institutions, and so on).

Third, sensible economic policies and good economic performance prospects appear to have been additional keys to gaining and retaining the confidence of creditors. For example, hostile relations between the government of a country and its private sector or between national authorities and the officials of international organizations (particularly the International Monetary Fund) were taken to be bad omens. On the other hand, good relations plus the prospect of high rates of economic growth and of low, or at least predictable, rates of inflation were considered to be sound reasons for being confident.

SUMMARY AND CONCLUSIONS

The history of Latin America during the past two decades reveals that countries can encounter debt-servicing difficulties and that these disrupt the timely flow of repayments or result in undesired increases of exposure to countries deemed not creditworthy. Argentina, Brazil, and Chile experienced severe difficulties in the early 1960s, Uruguay and Peru in the mid- or late 1960s, Chile again in the early 1970s, and Peru and Nicaragua in the late 1970s. However, some other countries have come close to having serious difficulties or have had isolated problems some time during the 1960-79 period. The accumulation of arrears, the arrangement of reschedulings and refinancings, and the need for new loans to repay a variety of prior obligations were the manifestations of debt-servicing difficulties or the forms of debt relief. The parties affected were commercial banks, multilateral financial institutions, suppliers, and government agencies, that is, all sources of external finance available to the developing countries.

With only two exceptions (and both in the same country, Peru), all episodes of debt-servicing difficulties have taken place in the context of large external imbalances. There are instances when the effect of one upon the other is not apparent now, because the conditions of the times and the expectations of policy makers cannot be recreated or ascertained. In addition, the limitations of the available data on short-term obligations and on speculative outflows of capital tend to minimize the vital role they played in triggering or aggravating external imbalances.

However, the evidence also demonstrates that not all instances of large current account imbalances or heavy amortization burdens necessarily lead to debt-servicing crises, not even if a country's reserves of foreign exchange are low and inflows of capital via private direct investment or project loans are inadequate. The confidence displayed by international lenders and their willingness to step forth with the required sums have often broken that seemingly inevitable link and have given countries time to improve their external performance. Consequently, debt-servicing difficulties have arisen only when a country's borrowing requirements have been large and have been considered excessive by the international financial community.

No assessment of country risk is complete, therefore, unless it focuses both on likely external payments trends and on the potential reaction of creditors to them. The former entails an analysis of demand management, resource allocation, and other policies that will affect the current account of the balance of payments. It must also take into consideration future political developments and government attitudes toward interest rates and the exchange rate, for they influence the direction and magnitude of private sector capital flows.

Predicting the lenders' degree of confidence in a certain country is, admittedly, a difficult task. One must judge, for example, whether the government involved is likely to draw up and persevere with economic development or stabilization plans, to maintain a favorable climate for private sector and foreign investment, to refrain from borrowing at terms and from sources that are inappropriate from a long-run perspective, or to rely on competent individuals to manage the economy. And yet, taking these confidence-building factors into consideration is truly the only way to assess country risk.

NOTE

1. Federal Reserve Board, Press Release, November 8, 1978, p. 3.

4
COUNTRY RISK EVALUATION:
INTERNATIONAL AND SOCIAL CONTEXT

Rodrigo K. Briones

INTRODUCTION

Over the past three decades the concept of economic development has been subject to considerable change. Traditionally, in any society economic development has been associated with increases in both per capita income and employment opportunities and with changes in the structure of production. This well-known approach, called the trickle-down theory because of its direct and indirect effects on an economy, makes casual reference to noneconomic social indicators such as income distribution, population growth, and other variables related to poverty in Third World nations.* However, despite high rates of economic growth in developing countries over the past two decades, <u>absolute poverty</u>, defined as a per capita annual income below $50, has not been eradicated. According to the International Labour Organization (ILO), some 700 million people throughout the world are "destitute" and about 1.2 billion are "seriously poor."[1] Likewise, the ability of developing countries to provide food, health, shelter, and protection to the bulk of their populations has been inhibited, if not reduced.

During the late 1960s, the United Nations became increasingly aware of social deterioration and therefore undertook a modern approach to development whereby economic conditions such as per capita income growth and changes in a nation's production structure were considered along with direct actions aimed toward reducing widespread

---

*The Third World includes the 42 poorest countries known as the "least developed," 63 non-oil-exporting developing countries, and 13 members of the Organization of Petroleum Exporting Countries (OPEC).

poverty, inequitable distribution of income, and unemployment.[2] Hence, the concept of development expanded from its traditional western historical roots to a more adequate explanation of the current economic and social situation of Third World nations. Furthermore, development was conceived of as a multidimensional process whereby economic growth was considered an impossible task without social progress, which in turn was measured by improvement in the living conditions and basic necessities of the world's poor. Moreover, according to the United Nations, the world's current social situation has been characterized "by an interaction among factors . . . where badly distributed income leads to malnutrition and inadequate housing, which lead in turn to poor health, which influences school attendance and effectiveness, which result ultimately in low incomes."[3]

Even though the traditional concept of economic development (the trickle-down approach) dealt with strategies geared toward rapid economic growth as part of the framework of a market economy, it also dealt with social progress and the ideal of humanitarianism. In a 1937 message urging passage of the Fair Labor Standards Act, President Roosevelt said: "The time has arrived for us to take further action to extend the frontiers of social progress. . . . One-third of our population . . . is ill-nourished, ill-clad and ill-housed. . . . A self-supporting and self-respecting democracy can plead no justification for the existence of child labor, no economic reason for chiseling workers' wages or stretching workers' hours."[4] Therefore, the concept of social progress was present in a market and industrialized economy more than 40 years ago. Social progress in industrialized nations was not fully achieved through high rates of economic expansion only; social legislation based on a combination of moral and ethical principles that contributed to the development of social services (for example, education, health, and the like) also enhanced social progress. However, many citizens in industrialized nations still conceive of economic development as being composed of rapid rates of aggregate economic growth with little relation to socioeconomic indicators.

The availability of funds to foster social progress depends in large part upon the choices made by each government. Fiscal tools such as taxation and social security can be used to implement the government's preferences. Moreover, it is the responsibility of the government to guarantee the satisfaction of the population's basic needs (for example, health, education, and housing). However, 1976 figures available for government expenditures in some Latin American countries do show relatively minor changes in the allocation of funds for social services as compared with 1973 expenditures (see Table 4.1).

The answer to low government expenditures in social services lies in a wide spectrum of economic and political issues that are

TABLE 4.1

Government Expenditures for Some Latin American Countries
(in percent of gross domestic product)

Country	Year	Per Capita GNP (in U.S. dollars)	Total Government Expenditures	Government Expenditures on Social Services					
				Total	Education	Health	Social Security and Welfare	Housing and Community Services	Other
Bolivia	1973	—	11.5	4.5	3.3	1.0	0.1	0.1	*
	1976	390	13.8	5.5	3.6	1.1	0.4	0.4	*
Chile	1972	—	39.8	25.5	5.9	4.2	11.7	3.7	*
	1974	1,050	31.9	15.2	4.0	2.6	5.8	2.7	0.1
Dominican Republic	1973	—	15.3	6.7	2.5	2.1	0.7	1.4	*
	1976	780	15.9	6.6	1.8	1.4	1.0	2.2	0.2
Ecuador	1973	—	11.9	4.0	3.3	0.6	0.1	*	*
	1976	640	13.6	4.3	3.1	1.0	0.2	*	*
Guatemala	1972	—	9.7	4.0	1.9	0.9	0.6	0.5	0.1
	1976	630	10.0	4.6	1.6	0.8	0.9	1.2	0.1
Honduras	1972	—	15.3	6.3	3.4	1.5	1.1	0.3	*
	1976	390	18.8	8.2	3.9	2.8	0.9	0.5	0.1
Mexico	1972	—	13.4	5.8	2.2	0.7	3.0	*	*
	1976	1,090	16.5	7.3	2.9	0.7	3.6	0.1	*
Nicaragua	1972	—	14.9	5.7	2.5	0.6	2.3	0.1	0.2
	1976	750	15.8	8.7	2.7	0.7	3.2	2.0	0.1
Panama	1973	—	19.4	7.3	4.3	1.6	0.7	0.4	0.3
	1976	1,310	19.7	7.2	4.4	1.6	0.4	0.5	0.3
Peru	1973	—	17.9	5.8	4.1	1.0	0.1	0.6	*
	1976	800	19.0	5.5	3.9	1.1	*	0.5	*
Uruguay	1973	—	23.4	13.5	2.8	1.0	9.6	0.1	*
	1976	1,390	23.3	15.7	2.7	0.9	12.0	*	0.1
Venezuela	1972	—	22.3	8.6	3.8	1.4	2.3	0.7	0.4
	1976	2,570	30.1	9.2	4.0	1.5	2.7	1.3	0.2

*Insignificantly small.

Sources: United Nations, Patterns of Government Expenditure on Social Services (ST/ESA/87/Addi), 1979. Per capita GNP figures were obtained from World Bank, World Development Report (Washington, D.C., August 1978).

deeply rooted in recent changes in the world economy (for example, the oil crisis). These changes and their direct effect on nonoil developing countries aggravated already existing balance-of-payments difficulties and low domestic savings, contributing to significantly increased borrowings from international and private lenders. Despite the fact that no numbers are precise, the best estimates show that total foreign debt of developing countries may have well exceeded $250 billion at the end of 1978 compared with some $75 billion in 1972.

Therefore, in assessing Latin America's future outlook, it is crucial to understand the concept of creditworthiness and its effect on social progress. Creditworthiness from the point of view of international lenders refers to the ability of a nation to favorably adjust its overall performance in the face of domestic and international change and, above all, to generate sufficient foreign exchange earnings to fulfill its international financial commitments.

PRIVATE LENDERS AND MULTINATIONAL CORPORATIONS VERSUS SOCIAL PROGRESS: AN ASSESSMENT

Today's rapidly changing international environment, with business conducted across national boundaries, has resulted in the increasing use of country evaluation by private lenders and multinationals. Systems that provide assessments of country performance and international creditworthiness are being developed and currently being used as management tools by large firms in their overseas decision-making processes. Multilateral agencies (for example, World Bank, Eximbank, and so on) and medium-sized multinational firms are also devoting greater attention to country analysis and risk. In other words, both lenders and investors desire to minimize the international risk of credit and investment extensions.

In appraising credit risk, that is, the ability of an institution (for example, a government agency or a private company) to repay a loan on the basis of future income earnings and other financial instruments, many private lenders have developed a comprehensive system by which country risks incurred in most of their foreign activities can be estimated. For example, in measuring country risk, banks usually consider a wide spectrum of economic and financial information such as international reserves, balance-of-trade performance, economic growth, and so on.[5] Each of these financial and economic components is analyzed, checked, and weighted within standard procedures for individual countries. However, because a global perspective must be maintained from the point of view of the rating and the analysis, countries in different parts of the world are evaluated according to the same standards.

Once an analytical rate has been obtained for a specific country, this quantified measure is immediately adjusted for factors that are difficult (or almost impossible) to measure quantitatively, such as political stability, social pressures, and cultural factors. To illustrate, Bank of America's country risk rating has two main components. On the one hand, the analytical factor takes into account both the behavior of the domestic economy and the performance of the external sector. The judgmental analysis, on the other hand, explicitly includes the evaluation of social pressures, foreign investment regulations, and other noneconomic variables.

Therefore, a sound country risk measurement should answer the following questions:

1. Does a certain country have the capacity to implement policies by which the current expansion of both its local economy and balance of payments can be sustained or enhanced? This portion of the analysis should address itself to the quality of the country's management and its ability to adapt itself to political and economic changes. Furthermore, it should also deal with the effects of both economic and political measures taken or likely to be taken by a government.

2. Does a particular country have the potential to adjust itself to exogenous shocks? While it is difficult to predict the behavior of financial and economic variables for a long period of time (five years or more), this portion of the rating deals with the structure of the country and how it is affected by economic, social, and political problems that might result in difficulties for foreign investors and lenders, difficulties such as servicing foreign debt, expropriation, or remittances of profits).

Almost all major financial institutions have similar country risk systems, although with different degrees of sophistication. In assessing their overseas investments large multinationals are relying more and more on this type of approach.

In understanding country risk evaluation it is essential to appreciate the objectives of private lenders and multinational corporations. Both are profit seekers and therefore their immediate goal is to maximize the wealth of their stockholders. It is equally important to understand that private commercial banks participate in investments and projects that typically have high rates of return over a period of five to ten years and that therefore minimize their liability exposure. Unfortunately, social programs do not generate an overt immediate or midterm flow of income, and if they do generate income it is typically a long-run expectation. Furthermore, regardless of the high social and economic rate of return that a social investment project (for example, in education or health) may have in the long run, it generates a conflict between the lender and the lender's goals, that is, the maximization of the stockholders' wealth without undue liability exposure and risk. However, it is essential to understand that social progress has become an important component of country risk evaluation. More and more there is an awareness on the part of private creditors and multinationals of the sine qua non role that social progress assumes within the country's long-term risk evaluation concept by minimizing the potential for instability through long-term structural change.

It is true that the New International Economic Order, through an increased control of multinationals, has contributed to the recognition of the needs for social progress on the part of foreign creditors and investors. It is equally true that the essential nature of their activities has resulted in a self-commitment to a broader definition of development, one that includes economic growth and social progress.

LATIN AMERICA:
PERFORMANCE AND PROSPECTS

In 1978, the region's real rate of economic growth (measured by a weighted average of GNPs) was estimated to be 4.3 percent, or the same rate as in 1977. In 1979 the Latin American nations were expected to reach a rate of growth of roughly 4 percent, with inflation of some 50 percent, vis-à-vis a 43 percent rate in 1978. Therefore, higher rates of economic expansion, a slowdown in inflationary pressures, and a slight improvement in the region's overall trade balance were the main macroeconomic trends to be expected for that year. [6]

Furthermore, social indicators point to a more favorable global position for the Latin American nations compared with most countries in Asia and Africa. According to the Food and Agriculture Organization (FAO), per capita index numbers of food production for the period 1970-77 show an annual change of 0.5 percent, compared with an overall rate of 0.2 percent for the Far East, 1.1 percent for the Near East, and a decline of 1.4 percent for Africa. The life expectancy at birth for the period 1970-75 was 61 years for Latin America, 49 years for South Asia, and 45 years for Africa. Furthermore, total unemployment and underemployment rates for 1975 were within the range of 40 to 49 percent for Asia (excluding China and other centrally planned Asian economies), Africa, and Oceania, while Latin America had a rate of 34 percent. [7]

The Latin American nations have become more closely integrated into the world economy than at any time before in their recent history and thus more vulnerable to changes in the economic performance of industrialized countries. Therefore, in assessing the future outlook of Latin America in the early 1980s it is essential to devote careful attention to the behavior of world economic trends, above all those common to the industrialized nations (for example, the Organization for Economic Cooperation and Development [OECD] countries).

Although it is difficult to predict the exact economic future of OECD nations, some current socioeconomic and political issues combined with certain decision policies emerging today are likely to have a predictable future effect:

1. Currently, the main concern of OECD nations is inflation, rather than the traditional policies of coping with social maladies such as unemployment. Hence actions and policies designed to curb inflationary pressures will be actively pursued.

2. The answer to inflation, and particularly to stagnation of inflation (stagflation), lies in a combination of economic policies aimed to slow down, if not reduce, the real economic growth in industrialized nations in the near future.

3. A conservative mood in some of the major industrialized countries (for example, the United States) will result in a curb in the growth of government expenditures, thereby reducing the potential transfer of financial resources (official development assistance) to other nations. [8]

4. The resurgence of economic protectionism and higher energy costs will undoubtedly constrain the ability of industrialized governments to deal with developing countries within the context of the North-South dialogue and the New International Economic Order. Consequently, there are strong reasons to assume that mounting tensions will continue to prevail in international forums.

These issues combined with political-economic actions could adversely affect the external markets and foreign exchange earnings of Latin America as the world's industrialized economies head for moderate and uneven rates of economic expansion. There is no doubt that this scenario will affect developing countries, since high real rates of economic growth are required (for example, at least a 6 percent growth rate) to fulfill national development goals. [9]

The following socioeconomic and political adjustments are likely to be observed in Latin America in the next decade, given the scenario described above:

1. The slowdown of growth in world markets will undoubtedly have some effect on the industrialization and diversification efforts of Latin American nations. Therefore, increasing concern over nations with large balance-of-payments deficits will be a major influence on international lenders and multilateral agencies.

2. With the need for increased foreign borrowings to finance balance-of-payments deficits, the present debt service structure will

become by itself an increasing burden for Latin American governments in their allocations of foreign exchange, particularly in the face of the hopes and desires of their populations. [10]

3. As a result of increased protectionism in the industrialized world, the Latin American economies, above all those who are export oriented, will find it more difficult to penetrate the industrialized markets. Therefore, at the local level a more balanced approach between export promotion and import substitution should be achieved, particularly on a regional basis through integration policies.

4. In order to attract foreign lenders and multinationals a more favorable attitude toward foreign investment should be observed, whereby sound economic policies geared to an overall improvement in the creditworthiness of a country would be pursued.

5. Sound economic policies combined with improved creditworthiness should reduce inflationary pressures to more tolerable levels.

The necessary adjustments of the Latin American economies to international change could undermine social progress. Hence, the ability of the present economic system to bring about a more equitable distribution of the benefits of growth could be subject to considerable strain. Likewise, the region's current political momentum could result in a reassessment of government priorities.

While it is true that social progress could reduce the gap between what is economically wise (high rates of economic growth) and what is politically acceptable (increasing employment opportunities and increased government expenditures to finance social programs), it is equally true that the scenario described previously would generate strong pressures on the current socioeconomic system. Therefore, the state should continue to preserve its leading role in providing social goods and services to the community, while exercising sound financial policies.

The concept of creditworthiness would become an essential means by which international funds could be attracted to finance the region's increasing economic and social needs. Moreover, it should be expected that sound policies aimed at improving each country's creditworthiness would be followed. However, these policies should balance economic aggregates with social progress.

PRIVATE LENDERS, MULTINATIONALS,
AND MULTILATERAL AGENCIES: THEIR
ROLE IN SOCIAL PROGRESS

Obviously, Latin American nations will have to undertake greater efforts to foster social progress. Therefore, it seems appropriate to assess how private lenders, multinationals, and multi-lateral agencies can contribute to social progress.

The activities of multinational corporations have a direct effect on the economy of the host country through the transfer of technology and other investment-related flows. However, because of their physical presence multinationals are in a better position to make a direct contribution to social progress vis-à-vis private lenders.

Multinationals through taxes and social security payments are directly contributing to government revenues, which in turn can be used to finance social progress. Furthermore, through contractual obligations multinationals can be encouraged to finance social programs within the geographical areas in which they operate. Although contractual obligations are coercive in nature, perhaps these commitments could be more efficient and appropriate than taxes.

Multinationals quite frequently do not assess their socioeconomic influence on the host country. At least for public relations purposes, multinationals could develop a social-economic impact statement whereby both costs and benefits of their operations are assessed.[11] Furthermore, a social program inventory could be developed to include voluntary activities such as construction of emergency care units, maintenance of roads and schools, education subsidies, and nutrition programs. While this approach may seem utopic, undoubtedly it would help senior managements to take a more positive attitude toward the disbursement of funds for voluntary social activities.

It has been argued that multinationals do not have a direct effect on employment creation because of their capital-intensive nature.[12] For example, almost one-half of the U.S. direct investment position in Latin America ($28 billion, roughly 20 percent of total U.S. foreign investment in 1977) was in the petroleum and manufacturing sectors, which are capital intensive.[13] Moreover, because of higher salaries and fringe benefits, multinationals are sometimes in a better position to attract managerial talents than are local firms. Therefore, multinationals may be in a position to provide consulting services to government agencies or municipalities. The company sponsoring this program would provide the salary and selection procedures for consulting executives. Hence, managerial skills in the fields of finance, development, health, education, and related social services would be made available to governments. For example, the Economic Development Council of New York lends executives to the city of New York for a specified period of time. The executives are members of large banks and firms operating in New York City. The result of this interchange has been helpful in assisting city agencies and their goals.

Multinationals do generate indirect employment effects through purchases of goods and services from local producers. However, additional research should be conducted on the indirect socioeconomic effects of multinationals on the host country. Moreover, with increasing frequency, multinational companies are trying through country analysis to improve their ability to predict political and social change, thereby taking an objective approach to economic and social progress.

Finally, the increasing role of Third World multinationals "builds prosperity. . . . Third World multinationalism, only yesterday an apparent contradiction in terms, is now a serious force in the development process."[14] Through the generation of income and employment opportunities, Third World multinationals could also foster social progress.

The issues discussed above could also be extended to private commercial banks located in Third World nations. Private lenders and multilateral agencies (for example, World Bank, Inter-American Development Bank, and so on) can make substantial contributions to social progress through joint financing ventures. Private lenders can finance investment projects with high rates of return, and multilateral agencies can take a portion of the responsibility for social progress. Furthermore, commercial banks are in a position to support the financial needs of these organizations.

Although commercial banks will continue to play an increasing role in working toward a solution of the financial difficulties of developing countries, it is important to understand that joint ventures with multilateral agencies will liberate local funds that otherwise would not have been available. These funds could be used by the government to foster social progress.

NOTES

1. International Labour Office, Employment, Growth, and Basic Needs: A One-World Problem (Geneva: ILO, 1976). According to the World Bank, some 20 percent of the total world population earn an equivalent of $50 per year or less. World Bank, The Assault on World Poverty: Problems of Rural Development, Education, and Health (Baltimore: Johns Hopkins University Press, 1975).

2. United Nations, International Development Strategy for the First Development Decade.

3. United Nations, Commission for Social Development, Implementation of the Declaration on Social Progress and Development (E/CN.5/563), December 1978.

4. Harry N. Scheiber, H. G. Vatter, and H. V. Faulkner, American Economic History (New York: Harper & Row, 1976), p. 390.

5. For further information see John Wilson, "Measuring Country Risk in a Global Context," Business Economics 14 (January 1979): 23-27.

6. Bank of America, Economic Outlook 1979 (San Francisco: Bank of America, 1979).

7. United Nations, Commission for Social Development, Implementation of the Declaration on Social Progress and Development (E/CN.5/563), December 1978. The terms unemployment and underemployment refer to "persons who are in employment of less than normal duration and who are seeking or would accept additional work and persons with a job yielding inadequate income." International Labour Organization, Employment, Growth, and Basic Needs.

8. Official development assistance from OECD members as a percentage of GNP could reach some 0.37 percent in 1980 compared with a 0.52 percent ratio in 1960 and the UN target of 0.80 percent. World Bank, World Development Report (Washington, D.C.: August 1978), pp. 98-99.

9. A recent UN study on the experience of development plans during the first half of this decade shows that out of 34 countries only 13 were able to exceed their national development targets for economic growth with rates fluctuating within the 6 to 13 percent range. United Nations, Center for Development Planning, Projections, and Policies, "Implementation of Development Plans: The Experience of Developing Countries in the First Half of the 1970s," Journal of Development Planning 12 (1977).

10. The debt service (on public and publicly guaranteed medium- and long-term loans) as a percentage of goods and nonfactor services for all developing nations could reach some 21 percent by 1985, compared with an estimated 12 percent rate in 1975. World Bank, World Development Report (Washington, D.C., 1978), p. 31.

11. H. R. Geyelin, J. N. Behrman, D. H. Blake, and N. E. Moffett, Communicating the Socioeconomic Impact of Multinational Corporations in Developing Countries (New York: Council of the Americas, 1976), pp. 16-17.

12. W. Howard Wriggins and Gunnar Adler-Karlson, Reducing Global Inequalities, 1980s Project, Council of Foreign Relations (New York: McGraw-Hill, 1978).

13. Direct investment position is defined as the net book value of U.S. direct investors' equity in, and outstanding loans to, foreign affiliates. U.S., Department of Commerce, Survey of Current Business, August 1978.

14. David A. Heenan and Warren J. Keegan, "The Rise of Third World Multinationals," Harvard Business Review 57 (January-February 1979): 101-9.

5

FOREIGN EXCHANGE CONSIDERATIONS

Aida M. Pardee

Article IV of the International Monetary Fund's Articles of Agreement, which governs the kind of exchange regime countries may follow, correctly places emphasis on seeking equilibrium in the underlying economy as the means of achieving exchange rate stability. The Latin American nations, which as a group have experimented with every conceivable exchange rate system, have fared best not by any particular exchange rate strategy but by their underlying economic strengths.

Unfortunately, for most of these countries equilibrium has been a fleeting condition. More usual for most nations have been huge deficits alternating with huge surpluses, leading to wide fluctuations in exchange rates and international reserves. In part, this reflects their status as suppliers of basic commodities—sugar, coffee, tin, and petroleum—that have experienced wide swings in prices over the years. But in many cases, it also reflects the many political and economic instabilities that beset most of the nations.

THE OBJECTIVES OF FOREIGN EXCHANGE POLICY

Ideally, the exchange rate of a nation's currency should be at a level consistent with both domestic and external equilibrium. That is, the country should not be experiencing high unemployment or inflation at home or massive disequilibrium in international trade and capital accounts. A stable exchange rate is not a sufficient indication of equilibrium, since it may be that the stability is achieved only by heavy intervention (by the central bank) in the exchange market and by sudden changes in international reserves.

Equilibrium in the exchange market is only one of several objectives that Latin American governments have had in formulating exchange rate policy. Most countries have embarked on ambitious programs of economic development. In this context they have used exchange rate policy as a means of encouraging local industry to develop substitutes for imports while seeking to earn as much as possible from exports, either through the traditional agricultural or mining output or through expanding sales of new products.

Unified or multiple exchange rates may be used in an effort to influence relative prices. But taxes and subsidies or outright controls (including prohibitions) are also used. Even within the broad categories, exchange rate policies are often adjusted to favor certain types of imports of manufacturing goods or certain types of agricultural exports. In some cases, fiscal policy considerations are important, in that the exchange rate mechanism can be molded into a means of collecting taxes directly from exporters as well as importers in a manner more efficient than simply relying on corporate and personal income tax procedures.

The objective of price stability also interacts with exchange rate mechanisms in Latin America. Inflation-prone countries tend to be caught up in vicious circles. Domestic inflation leads to a weakening of the exchange rate, causing import prices to rise (particularly prices of much needed food products and raw materials, such as oil), in turn exacerbating the pace of domestic inflation. Efforts to halt the imported inflation by holding the exchange rate steady often fail because the rise of domestic prices continues to erode the country's competitive position. This often leads to the stagnation of key export sectors and to the proliferation of imports. In other cases, the external position becomes so strong that the main source of inflation is the balance-of-payments surplus through its effects on export earnings and the domestic money supply.

Finally, exchange rate policies may reflect nothing more than institutional traditions. Some countries have maintained fixed exchange rates for so long that it would be unthinkable for any government wishing to stay in power to change either the rates or the rules by which exchange dealings take place. In other cases, it is the exchange rate adjustment process that has become institutionalized. Since the political stakes are great in avoiding overt changes in policy, formal mechanisms are often kept in place to maintain the official exchange rate while background adjustments are made in specific rates for individual products, in taxes or subsidies, or in other policies. In some cases, governments allow parallel markets to flourish rather than change the official rate. The distinction between a parallel or gray market, which is accepted by the authorities, and an outright illegal black market is not always clear to the uninitiated.

One does not become an expert on foreign exchange policies and practices in Latin America by simply reading up on the formal regulations and by following the exchange rate movements as reported in the daily press. It is also important to establish regular contact with the local authorities and responsible firms that operate in the country to get a complete picture of how foreign exchange dealings are conducted. U.S. companies wishing to do business in the area are well advised to deal through commercial banks. Several of the major U.S. banks operating in the region are willing to assist in providing detailed information on the foreign exchange regulations in any nation. They will also convey their views on the outlook for a particular country's economy and assist in any foreign exchange transactions U.S. companies (or any other companies) may wish to make.

DIFFERENCES IN EXCHANGE RATE REGIMES

Every nation in the region has its own exchange regime, but it may be useful to generalize them into three categories: (1) fixed exchange rates, (2) the crawling peg, and (3) mixed exchange rates (fixed rates interposed with large adjustments).

Fixed Exchange Rates

First, several nations, mainly in the Caribbean and Central America, have fixed their exchange rates, either to the dollar, to sterling, or to special drawing rights (SDR). These are countries with historically low rates of inflation. Fixed rates are not easy to maintain, especially for countries that export primary products, so these countries typically have tight systems of controls, both on the terms of invoicing of exports and imports and on capital account transactions. With the exchange rate steady, favorable swings in the trade balance tend to be reflected in sharp rises in international reserves. Unfavorable trade developments lead to a runoff of reserves and an increase in indebtedness. Sometimes pressures become so great that a parity or even the fixed-rate regime is abandoned. This was the case in Mexico, which held a fixed rate for the peso from 1954 through late 1976 and then allowed the rate to float downward. The peso is still on a floating rate basis but has moved very narrowly since early 1977, with Mexico's reserve position, international borrowings, and other policy instruments all being adjusted in the background. In view of the huge common frontier with the United States, the Mexican authorities believe it is of the utmost importance to have a stable relationship between the peso and the dollar.

The Crawling Peg

The second type of exchange rate regime is that of the crawling peg, or systematic minidevaluations. This regime has been employed successfully for some years in Brazil, Chile, and Colombia and at various times elsewhere, as in Argentina and Peru. Crawling pegs are applied mainly by countries that have such high inflation rates that efforts at holding the rate would be futile. The mechanism is one of small and frequent devaluations to maintain some relationship between the exchange rate and domestic prices and costs. In this manner the authorities can avoid distortions in internal versus external prices and the repeated crises inherent in a less frequently adjusted parity. With a crawling peg, exchange controls can be liberalized and the international reserves position can be better managed.

Actual movements of exchange rates are often determined by formulas, but the authorities use considerable discretion as to when and by how much a minidevaluation will occur. Central bankers who administer such regimes always point out the advantages of their particular crawling peg system but are quick to argue that they would prefer to eliminate inflation or at least reduce it to a degree consistent with greater exchange rate stability.

Mixed Exchange Rates

The third type of strategy is a mixture of fixed rates with frequent exchange rate adjustments. Most countries seek to maintain a fixed exchange rate or, in cases of multiple exchange rates for different kinds of trade and capital transactions, a fixed structure of rates. But this approach has varying degrees of success over the years. In some cases, an exchange rate system may function smoothly for several years, but then a poor harvest, an earthquake, a political change, or other event beyond control may suddenly alter the underlying payments pattern. The government may decide that it is important to avoid drastic changes in the exchange rate and may choose instead to draw down international reserves and available credits, as well as to tighten exchange controls. Sometimes these actions are sufficient to overcome the difficulties, but in other cases, major stabilization measures may ultimately be required, including drawings on the International Monetary Fund (IMF) coupled with strict policy constraints. When such a package is announced, the exchange rate may be adjusted or the multiple exchange structure altered to bring rates more in line with the underlying conditions and practical possibilities. These are nerve-racking experiences for everyone involved, but the stabilization programs have helped turn around many situations that appeared to be hopeless. The successful incidents are often overlooked or forgotten in an age in which most countries of the world, not just those in Latin America, seem to be bumping along from crisis to crisis in the exchange markets.

EXCHANGE-RATE EXPERIENCE IN THE 1970s

The 1970s have been a period of considerable turmoil in the exchange markets, with vast changes in currency relationships. In 1971-73, we witnessed the breakup of the fixed-rate Bretton Woods System and two formal devaluations of the U.S. dollar, followed by the floating of the dollar against the currencies of most major industrial countries. Since then, there have been extremely wide swings in exchange rates in response to such events as the fourfold rise in the Organization of Petroleum Exporting Countries (OPEC) oil price in 1973/74, the worldwide recession in 1974/75, and the massive external imbalances between the United States, on one side, with a deficit and Japan, Germany, and Switzerland, on the other, with substantial surpluses in 1976-78. Beginning in 1979, a new round of oil price increases has had to be absorbed. This has been a very difficult environment for many countries in Latin America and the Caribbean, irrespective of their internal problems.

Table 5.1 summarizes the actual market exchange rates in terms of local currency units per dollar during the 1971 to August 1979 period. The differences are striking. Many of the countries included in the table held to the same exchange rate vis-à-vis the dollar throughout the period (the Bahamas, the Dominican Republic, Ecuador, El Salvador, Guatemala, Haiti, Honduras, Panama, and Paraguay). A similar number had only narrow movements (Barbados, Grenada, Guyana, the Netherlands Antilles, Nicaragua, Surinam, Trinidad and Tobago, and Venezuela). A few countries had periods of stability punctuated with one or more large changes (Bolivia, Costa Rica, Jamaica, Mexico, and Peru). Finally, there are the countries that have had continuous, and in some cases drastic, declines in their currencies against the dollar (Argentina, Brazil, Chile, Colombia, Peru, and Uruguay). The case of Chile is the most dramatic; its currency depreciated from 0.01 units to the dollar in 1971 to 39.0 units to the dollar in 1979.

Table 5.2 presents the year-to-year percent changes in the exchange rates listed in Table 5.1. Depreciations are recorded as positive rather than negative numbers; that is, since the rates are in terms of currency units per U.S. dollar, the depreciation of a currency means that it takes more units of that currency to buy one dollar. Appreciations of currencies against the dollar are indicated with a nega-

TABLE 5.1

Market Exchange Rates: Annual Averages, 1971–79
(in local currency units per U.S. dollar)

	1971	1972	1973	1974	1975	1976	1977	1978	1979*
Argentina	4.62	8.17	9.35	8.87	36.60	140.00	407.60	795.80	1,397.80
Bahamas	1.00	1.00	1.00	1.00	1.00	1.00	1.00	1.00	1.00
Barbados	1.96	1.92	1.96	2.05	2.02	2.00	2.01	2.01	2.01
Bolivia	11.88	13.23	20.00	20.00	20.00	20.00	20.00	20.00	20.00
Brazil	5.29	5.93	6.13	6.79	8.13	10.68	14.14	18.07	26.12
Chile	0.01	0.02	0.11	0.83	4.91	13.05	21.53	31.66	39.00
Colombia	20.08	22.02	23.81	27.11	31.20	34.98	36.99	39.25	42.80
Costa Rica	6.63	6.64	6.65	7.93	8.57	8.57	8.57	8.57	8.57
Dominican Republic	1.00	1.00	1.00	1.00	1.00	1.00	1.00	1.00	1.00
Ecuador	25.00	25.00	25.00	25.00	25.00	25.00	25.00	25.00	25.00
El Salvador	2.50	2.50	2.50	2.50	2.50	2.50	2.50	2.50	2.50
Grenada	1.97	1.92	1.96	2.05	2.17	2.61	2.70	2.70	2.70
Guatemala	1.00	1.00	1.00	1.00	1.00	1.00	1.00	1.00	1.00
Guyana	1.98	2.09	2.13	2.23	2.36	2.55	2.55	2.55	2.55
Haiti	5.00	5.00	5.00	5.00	5.00	5.00	5.00	5.00	5.00
Honduras	2.00	2.00	2.00	2.00	2.00	2.00	2.00	2.00	2.00
Jamaica	0.82	0.80	0.91	0.91	0.91	0.91	0.91	1.38	1.79
Mexico	12.50	12.50	12.50	12.50	12.49	15.43	22.57	22.77	22.81
Netherlands Antilles	1.88	1.80	1.80	1.80	1.80	1.80	1.80	1.80	1.80
Nicaragua	7.00	7.00	7.00	7.01	7.03	7.03	7.03	7.03	10.00
Panama	1.00	1.00	1.00	1.00	1.00	1.00	1.00	1.00	1.00
Paraguay	126.00	126.00	126.00	126.00	126.00	126.00	126.00	126.00	126.00
Peru	38.70	38.70	38.70	38.70	40.80	57.51	83.81	156.34	234.18
Surinam	1.88	1.79	1.79	1.79	1.79	1.79	1.79	1.79	1.79
Trinidad and Tobago	1.97	1.92	1.96	2.05	2.17	2.44	2.40	2.40	2.40
Uruguay	0.26	0.56	0.88	1.22	2.30	3.40	4.75	6.13	7.79
Venezuela	4.50	4.40	4.30	4.28	4.29	4.29	4.29	4.29	4.29

*End-of-August quotations with the exceptions of Brazil (July) and Uruguay (May).

Source: International Monetary Fund, International Financial Statistics.

TABLE 5.2

Changes in Exchange Rates
(percent change of local currency against U.S. dollar)

	1972	1973	1974	1975	1976	1977	1978	1979
Argentina	76.8	14.4	-5.1	311.6	282.5	191.1	95.2	75.6
Bahamas	0.0	0.0	0.0	0.0	0.0	0.0	0.0	0.0
Barbados	-2.0	2.1	4.6	-1.5	-1.0	0.5	0.0	0.0
Bolivia	11.4	51.2	0.0	0.0	0.0	0.0	0.0	0.0
Brazil	12.1	3.4	10.8	19.7	31.4	32.3	27.8	44.5
Chile	100.0	455.0	654.5	491.6	165.8	65.0	47.1	23.2
Colombia	9.7	8.1	13.9	15.1	12.1	5.7	6.1	9.0
Costa Rica	0.0	0.0	19.2	8.1	0.0	0.0	0.0	0.0
Dominican Republic	0.0	0.0	0.0	0.0	0.0	0.0	0.0	0.0
Ecuador	0.0	0.0	0.0	0.0	0.0	0.0	0.0	0.0
El Salvador	0.0	0.0	0.0	0.0	0.0	0.0	0.0	0.0
Grenada	-2.5	2.1	4.6	5.9	20.3	3.4	0.0	0.0
Guatemala	0.0	0.0	0.0	0.0	0.0	0.0	0.0	0.0
Guyana	5.6	1.9	4.7	5.8	8.1	0.0	0.0	0.0
Haiti	0.0	0.0	0.0	0.0	0.0	0.0	0.0	0.0
Honduras	0.0	0.0	0.0	0.0	0.0	0.0	0.0	0.0
Jamaica	-2.4	13.7	0.0	0.0	0.0	0.0	51.6	29.7
Mexico	0.0	0.0	0.0	0.0	23.5	46.3	0.9	0.1
Netherlands Antilles	0.0	0.0	0.0	0.0	0.0	0.0	0.0	0.0
Nicaragua	0.0	0.0	0.0	0.0	0.0	0.0	0.0	42.2
Panama	0.0	0.0	0.0	0.0	0.0	0.0	0.0	0.0
Paraguay	0.0	0.0	0.0	0.0	0.0	0.0	0.0	0.0
Peru	-4.8	0.0	0.0	5.4	41.0	45.7	86.5	49.8
Surinam	0.0	0.0	0.0	0.0	0.0	0.0	0.0	0.0
Trinidad and Tobago	-2.5	2.1	4.6	5.9	12.4	-1.6	0.0	0.0
Uruguay	115.4	57.1	38.6	88.5	47.8	39.7	29.1	27.1
Venezuela	-2.2	-2.3	0.0	0.0	0.0	0.0	0.0	0.0

Note: A rise means a depreciation of the local currency.

Source: Calculated from Table 5.1.

64

tive sign, since it takes less local currency to buy one dollar. This table highlights all the more the contrast between the many nations whose exchange rates have not moved at all and those whose rates have moved frequently and by large amounts. The exchange rate movements for the more inflation-prone countries show through more clearly, as in the case of Argentina, Brazil, Chile, and Uruguay. Even with the large numbers involved, progress can be observed from the crisis years of 1975/76 in Argentina and 1973-75 in Chile. At the same time, more recent payments difficulties show through for Mexico in 1976/77, Peru in 1976-79, Jamaica in 1978/79, and Nicaragua in 1979.

EXCHANGE RATES AND INFLATION RATES

Many economic variables influence exchange rates, but none is so powerful in the context of Latin America as the relative rate of inflation. A country that has a rapid inflation rate has little hope of maintaining a fixed or even a stable exchange rate for long. The relationship is nevertheless highly complex. Which prices should be compared—consumer prices, wholesale prices, or export prices? What are the relevant time periods—months, quarters, or years? And what about lead-lag considerations, as with vicious circles and their effects on the real economy? How do these elements relate to the broader economic and social objectives of governments? Some answers have been provided by various authors, and serious econometric studies have been made of most of the major countries in Latin America in recent years. For the purpose of this study, however, a few straightforward points can be made.

Table 5.3 presents the annual rates of inflation for the countries of Latin America and the Caribbean in 1971-78. The U.S. inflation rates are also listed for comparison purposes. Consumer prices are used, since it is the series most readily available in all nations. No country in this hemisphere has had what would be considered a satisfactory record on price stability in the 1970s, but some have fared better than others. The lower rates of inflation are found mainly in countries of Central America and the Caribbean. The higher rates are in South America, with the highest recorded by Argentina, Brazil, Chile, and Uruguay. It is noteworthy, however, that there has been dramatic improvement in several nations, such as Argentina and Chile. Patterns have changed over time. Of the 25 Latin American and Caribbean countries listed, 5 experienced double-digit inflation in 1972, but in 1974, after OPEC hiked the oil prices, all nations except Venezuela recorded price rises in excess of 10 percent. By 1976, the number of countries recording double-digit inflation had

TABLE 5.3

Rise in Consumer Prices
(in percent)

	1972	1973	1974	1975	1976	1977	1978
Argentina	59.5	62.7	22.9	182.5	443.2	176.0	175.4
Bahamas	7.0	5.2	30.9	10.3	4.3	3.2	6.0
Barbados	6.9	16.8	39.0	12.0	5.0	8.3	10.5
Bolivia	6.7	31.4	62.7	8.0	4.5	8.1	10.4
Brazil	16.4	12.8	27.6	28.9	41.9	43.7	39.7
Chile	79.1	351.9	505.5	374.6	211.9	92.0	39.9
Colombia	14.3	20.3	24.0	22.7	20.2	32.5	18.2
Costa Rica	4.6	15.3	30.1	17.4	3.5	4.2	6.0
Dominican Republic	7.7	15.2	13.0	14.5	7.7	12.9	3.5
Ecuador	7.8	13.0	23.3	15.3	10.7	13.0	11.7
El Salvador	1.5	6.3	16.9	16.9	7.0	11.9	13.2
Grenada	n.a.	n.a.	n.a.	n.a.	n.a.	n.a.	n.a.
Guatemala	0.6	13.6	16.6	13.1	10.7	12.6	7.9
Guyana	5.2	7.4	17.4	8.0	9.0	8.2	15.3
Haiti	3.2	22.7	14.9	16.8	7.0	6.5	-2.6
Honduras	5.3	4.5	13.4	6.4	4.9	8.3	6.2
Jamaica	4.6	19.8	24.4	16.8	9.6	11.4	34.9
Mexico	5.0	11.3	22.5	15.7	15.1	29.0	17.5
Netherlands Antilles	4.0	8.0	19.4	15.6	5.3	4.7	9.2
Nicaragua	n.a.	n.a.	n.a.	1.8	2.8	11.4	n.a.
Panama	5.3	6.9	16.9	5.4	4.0	4.5	4.2
Paraguay	9.2	12.8	25.1	6.7	4.5	9.2	10.7
Peru	7.1	9.4	16.9	23.6	33.5	39.0	57.8
Surinam	3.2	12.9	16.9	8.5	10.1	9.7	9.8
Trinidad and Tobago	9.3	14.9	22.0	17.0	10.5	11.9	10.2
Uruguay	77.5	96.8	77.1	81.5	50.5	58.1	44.6
Venezuela	2.8	4.2	8.4	10.1	7.7	7.7	7.2
United States	3.3	6.3	10.9	9.2	5.8	6.5	7.5

n.a. = not available.

Sources: Based on indexes published in International Monetary Fund, International Financial Statistics; and official statistics of the countries.

been reduced to 11; however, in 1978 it rose to 15. Such wide swings in inflation rates would inevitably affect exchange rate patterns.

As noted, the relationship between any price index and an exchange rate is a complex matter, but it is worthwhile to make some direct comparisons between internal price movements and exchange rate changes. This is attempted in Table 5.4, which compares inflation rates and percent changes in exchange rates for the years 1972-78. Since the exchange rate comparisons of Tables 5.1 and 5.2 are in dollar terms, each country's inflation rate had to be adjusted by the relative rate of inflation in the United States for the same years. The first step was to calculate the ratio of the increase in the consumer price index in the Latin American or Caribbean country over the increase in the consumer price index in the United States for each year. The results are shown in Table 5.5. Note that although some of the countries appear to be highly inflationary, the deterioration of the U.S. price performance in recent years is also evident in these comparisons. The next step was to subtract the annual percentage changes in exchange rates (Table 5.2) from the adjusted consumer price figure for each country (Table 5.5). These results are shown in Table 5.4. For a country whose inflation rate exceeded the relative rate of depreciation of the currency during a given year, the corresponding entry in Table 5.4 is positive. Where the inflation rate was lower than the rate of currency depreciation, the result is presented with a minus sign.

The results are striking, both for the region as a whole and for individual countries. Following the OPEC's increase in oil prices in 1974, nearly all countries suffered a sharp upsurge in consumer prices that was not matched by a corresponding decline in the exchange rate in that year. In effect, the inflationary buildup of 1973/74 was not allowed to be reflected immediately in the exchange rates. But by 1976, the situation was basically reversed, as most nations were experiencing a greater (percentage) depreciation of their exchange rates than the rise in their consumer price indexes. By then, creditworthiness questions were raising doubts in the minds of international financial market participants, and it had become quite difficult for many countries to continue to finance large deficits through external sources. The authorities of various nations began to allow exchange rates to depreciate more rapidly as means of reestablishing internal and external balance.

For the countries with the highest inflation rates, the data in Table 5.4 lose precision but still point to interesting developments. For example, Brazil's crawling peg has been keyed to annual inflation rates with the result that the differences recorded in Table 5.4 are very small. Chile, on the other hand, had a sharp net depreciation of its exchange rate in 1972-75 relative to domestic prices during the

TABLE 5.4

Net Excess of Adjusted Inflation Rates over Percentage Depreciation of Exchange Rates
(in percent per annum)

	1972	1973	1974	1975	1976	1977	1978
Argentina	-22.4	38.7	15.9	-144.5	126.4	-25.8	87.6
Bahamas	3.6	-1.0	18.0	9.4	-1.4	-3.1	-1.4
Barbados	1.5	7.8	20.7	4.1	0.2	1.2	2.8
Bolivia	-8.1	-27.6	46.7	-1.1	-1.3	1.5	2.7
Brazil	0.6	2.7	4.3	-1.7	2.7	2.6	2.2
Chile	-26.7	-124.0	-198.7	-145.6	34.5	15.3	-17.0
Colombia	0.9	5.1	-2.1	-2.7	1.5	18.7	4.9
Costa Rica	1.3	8.5	-1.9	-0.6	-2.2	-2.2	-1.5
Dominican Republic	4.3	8.4	1.9	4.9	1.8	6.0	-3.7
Ecuador	4.4	6.3	11.2	5.6	4.6	6.1	3.9
El Salvador	-1.7	0.0	5.2	7.1	1.1	5.1	5.3
Guatemala	-2.6	6.9	5.1	3.6	4.6	5.7	0.4
Guyana	-3.6	-0.8	1.2	-6.9	-5.1	1.6	7.3
Haiti	-0.1	15.4	3.6	7.0	1.1	0.0	-9.4
Honduras	1.9	-1.7	2.3	-2.6	-0.9	1.7	-1.2
Jamaica	-1.2	25.0	12.2	7.0	3.6	4.6	0.5
Mexico	1.6	4.7	10.5	6.0	-14.7	-25.2	8.4
Netherlands Antilles	0.7	1.6	7.7	5.9	-0.5	-1.7	1.6
Nicaragua	n.a.	n.a.	n.a.	n.a.	-2.8	4.6	n.a.
Panama	1.9	0.6	5.4	-3.5	-1.7	-1.9	-3.1
Paraguay	5.7	6.1	12.8	-2.3	-1.2	2.5	3.0
Peru	3.8	2.9	5.4	7.8	-17.8	-15.8	-39.7
Surinam	-4.9	6.2	5.4	-0.6	4.1	3.0	2.1
Trinidad and Tobago	8.3	6.0	5.4	1.2	-8.0	6.7	2.5
Uruguay	-43.6	28.0	21.1	-22.3	-5.6	8.8	7.4
Venezuela	-2.7	0.3	-2.4	0.8	1.8	6.6	-0.3

n.a. = not available

Sources: Calculated from Tables 5.2 and 5.5, with each element in Table 5.2 subtracted from corresponding element in Table 5.5.

TABLE 5.5

Annual Rise in Consumer Prices in Latin American and Caribbean Countries over the Rise in Consumer Prices in the United States
(in percent)

	1972	1973	1974	1975	1976	1977	1978
Argentina	54.4	53.1	10.8	167.1	418.9	165.3	163.2
Bahamas	3.6	-1.0	18.0	9.4	-1.4	-3.1	-1.4
Barbados	3.5	9.9	25.3	2.6	-0.8	1.7	2.8
Bolivia	3.3	23.6	46.7	-1.1	-1.3	1.5	2.7
Brazil	12.7	6.1	15.1	18.0	34.1	34.9	30.0
Chile	73.3	331.0	455.8	343.0	200.3	80.3	30.1
Colombia	10.6	13.2	11.8	12.4	13.6	24.4	10.0
Costa Rica	1.3	8.5	17.3	7.5	-2.2	-2.2	-1.5
Dominican Republic	4.3	8.4	1.9	4.9	1.8	6.0	-3.7
Ecuador	4.4	6.3	11.2	5.6	4.6	6.1	3.9
El Salvador	-1.7	0.0	5.4	7.1	1.1	5.1	5.3
Grenada	n.a.	n.a.	n.a.	n.a.	n.a.	n.a.	n.a.
Guatemala	-2.6	6.9	5.1	3.6	4.6	5.7	0.4
Guyana	1.8	1.0	5.9	-1.1	3.0	1.6	7.3
Haiti	-0.1	15.4	3.6	7.0	1.1	0.0	-9.4
Honduras	1.9	-1.7	2.3	-2.6	-0.9	1.7	-1.2
Jamaica	1.3	13.0	12.2	7.0	3.6	4.6	25.5
Mexico	1.6	4.7	10.5	6.0	8.8	21.1	9.3
Netherlands Antilles	0.7	1.6	7.7	5.9	-0.5	-1.7	1.6
Nicaragua	n.a.	n.a.	n.a.	n.a.	-2.8	4.6	n.a.
Panama	1.9	0.6	5.4	-3.5	-1.7	-1.9	-3.1
Paraguay	5.7	6.1	12.8	-2.3	-1.2	2.5	3.0
Peru	3.8	2.9	5.4	13.2	26.2	30.5	46.8
Surinam	-0.1	6.2	5.4	-0.6	4.1	3.0	2.1
Trinidad and Tobago	5.8	8.1	10.0	7.1	4.4	5.1	2.5
Uruguay	71.8	85.1	59.7	66.2	42.2	48.5	34.5
Venezuela	-0.5	-2.0	-2.2	0.8	1.8	6.6	-0.3

n.a. = not available

Source: Calculated from Table 5.3, using ratios of Latin American and Caribbean price indexes over U.S. price indexes.

time of extreme instability in the economy. This situation was partly reversed in 1976/77. Argentina went through a similar cycle, with extremely sharp currency depreciation in 1975/76 and a subsequent net appreciation of the currency relative to internal prices.

OTHER FACTORS INFLUENCING
THE FOREIGN EXCHANGE RATE

Beyond the relative inflation rate, many other economic variables enter into the process by which exchange rates are determined. The influence of these factors varies from country to country and over time. In recent years it has been common practice to focus on the current account position of a country as an important measure of its international standing. This is the net of all exports and imports of currently produced goods and services over the course of the year, roughly corresponding to what is computed in the gross domestic product and other measures of the real economy as distinct from financial flows. Table 5.6 presents the current account balances for most of the nations of Latin America and the Caribbean in the 1972-78 period.

Once again, the major events show through. The oil price hikes of 1973/74 led to a sharp rise in current earnings for the oil-producing countries, such as Venezuela and Trinidad and Tobago, and a surge in current payments by most of the others, who were consumers of oil. The jump in world coffee prices following the freeze in Brazil in 1975/76 gave a boost to current earnings of other coffee producers, most notably Colombia and El Salvador.

Current account developments do not always correspond to exchange rate movements, as in the cases of most of the countries on fixed exchange rates, but they can help in explaining drastic exchange rate changes, as with the severe deterioration of Mexico's current account balance before the September 1976 decision to allow the peso to depreciate sharply.

Part of the offset to current account imbalances can be found in capital flows. Indeed, for developing countries in need of additional savings, it is considered healthy to run a current account deficit financed by capital inflows from abroad. These inflows are to help finance infrastructural development and pay for needed imports and capital goods.

Table 5.7 presents the net balance on capital accounts for most of the countries in the region in 1972-77. Virtually all nations show a positive balance, indicating net capital inflows, as suggested before. But the process is not automatic, and nations may occasionally have difficulties in obtaining full financing. Countries like Mexico, Brazil,

TABLE 5.6

Current Account
(in millions of U.S. dollars)

	1972	1973	1974	1975	1976	1977*
Argentina	-226.9	710.5	117.8	-1,287.0	650.0	1,293.6
Barbados	-43.4	-52.9	-48.0	-41.2	-64.7	-45.6
Bolivia	-45.2	-20.9	116.9	-157.2	-101.4	-176.8
Brazil	-1,690.4	-2,157.7	-7,562.2	-7,008.0	-6,548.4	-4,839.3
Chile	-471.2	-279.0	-178.0	-564.6	187.1	-448.3
Colombia	-190.0	-54.9	-350.0	-109.3	206.7	429.7
Costa Rica	-100.0	-112.2	-266.2	-217.7	-201.5	-219.5
Dominican Republic	-47.5	-97.9	-241.9	-74.4	-243.8	-264.2
Ecuador	-77.4	6.5	37.7	-220.0	-6.4	-312.3
El Salvador	12.4	-43.8	-134.2	-92.9	-7.1	10.1
Guatemala	-11.5	7.7	-103.1	-65.7	-80.1	-57.1
Guyana	15.4	-63.5	-9.2	-23.4	-141.1	-95.7
Haiti	6.5	-0.8	-21.6	-26.3	-20.5	-52.2
Honduras	-12.7	-34.6	-105.6	-119.7	-108.6	-134.1
Jamaica	-196.7	-247.6	-91.9	-282.7	-302.7	-68.0
Mexico	-916.3	-1,415.0	-2,875.5	-4,054.0	-3,410.4	-1,771.1
Nicaragua	21.7	-66.0	-257.3	-185.0	-39.3	-193.6
Panama	-98.5	-111.1	-224.3	-168.5	-176.2	-161.4
Paraguay	-5.3	-16.0	-53.5	-89.4	-70.9	-61.7
Peru	-31.5	-261.0	-725.2	-1,540.8	-1,192.6	-918.9
Trinidad and Tobago	-161.5	-26.3	271.0	302.5	203.9	209.5
Ueuguay	58.8	37.2	-132.4	-189.5	-73.8	-97.4
Venezuela	-39.1	898.8	5,861.6	2,394.3	967.5	-2,052.5
Latin America	-4,281.2	-3,461.0	-7,097.7	-13,806.3	-10,525.0	-9,963.7

*Complete figures for 1978 are not yet available.

Note: "Current account" refers to the sum of the trade balance, net services, and unrequited transfers.

Sources: International Monetary Fund tapes; and Inter-American Development Bank, Annual Report.

71

TABLE 5.7

Net Balance on Capital Account
(in millions of U.S. dollars)

	1972	1973	1974	1975	1976	1977
Argentina	121.6	65.6	-68.6	202.8	482.6	607.1
Barbados	17.8	21.9	10.2	27.9	25.2	39.5
Bolivia	88.6	49.2	56.3	148.5	172.1	283.5
Brazil	3,628.4	4,116.4	6,663.8	6,426.5	8,319.5	5,889.0
Chile	331.1	401.7	128.7	361.8	129.3	638.6
Colombia	247.5	157.4	275.4	165.1	209.0	-117.9
Costa Rica	58.3	90.4	165.2	201.7	256.5	267.6
Dominican Republic	85.1	83.2	253.6	143.3	173.5	170.9
Ecuador	134.8	78.4	101.4	202.4	140.7	492.8
El Salvador	0.3	28.6	151.9	114.5	97.0	143.0
Guatemala	50.4	72.1	87.8	180.4	308.5	230.9
Guyana	15.4	28.0	48.2	65.2	57.4	66.1
Haiti	9.7	7.2	19.4	20.8	26.3	67.7
Honduras	20.3	42.7	90.4	173.1	149.9	194.7
Jamaica	170.8	213.4	176.8	291.9	80.9	65.6
Mexico	444.1	1,983.7	3,794.3	5,468.5	5,547.5	2,681.8
Nicaragua	5.1	127.1	240.9	224.5	31.1	222.6
Panama	179.0	214.1	336.1	262.5	346.0	209.8
Paraguay	19.9	48.4	77.3	113.5	107.1	194.7
Peru	127.0	398.2	1,196.6	1,222.6	1,141.8	1,006.4
Trinidad and Tobago	114.5	75.7	20.0	172.7	33.5	264.8
Uruguay	22.5	33.4	147.6	166.9	183.2	225.9
Venezuela	-263.8	176.4	-936.9	86.2	-2,968.3	196.1
Latin America	5,628.6	8,607.8	13,188.1	16,451.6	15,023.6	14,100.8

Note: The table refers to net result of capital inflows and outflows of the monetary and nonmonetary sectors.

Sources: International Monetary Fund tapes; and Inter-American Development Bank, Annual Report.

TABLE 5.8

International Reserves, 1972-79 End of Year
(in millions of SDRs)

	1972	1973	1974	1975	1976	1977	1978	1979 (June)
Argentina	429	1,093	1,074	386	1,384	2,742	3,962	5,977
Bahamas	34	36	41	46	41	56	47	83
Brazil	3,853	5,318	4,306	3,446	5,630	5,973	9,134	7,831
Chile	137	149	83	93	396	399	885	1,253
Colombia	299	443	367	445	997	1,499	1,885	2,539
Dominican Republic	54	73	74	99	109	152	122	173
Ecuador	132	200	286	244	443	552	528	485
El Salvador	76	51	80	108	177	191	223	239
Guatemala	124	176	165	260	440	568	587	619
Jamaica	147	106	156	107	28	40	40	39
Mexico	1,072	1,123	1,139	1,310	1,078	1,418	1,480	1,585*
Netherlands Antilles	65	59	69	79	99	100	71	57
Peru	446	471	791	399	284	329	334	343*
Trinidad and Tobago	54	39	319	642	872	1,221	1,387	1,353
Uruguay	187	199	189	186	271	378	348	336*
Venezuela	1,595	1,999	5,320	7,569	7,383	6,762	5,002	4,617

*As of May.

Source: International Monetary Fund, International Financial Statistics, October 1979.

and Peru became a matter of international concern toward the mid-1970s, and pressures were applied on the governments, from within and without, to reduce their current deficits and their needs for financing. Sometimes both current and capital accounts move in the same direction. At times of political crisis, a current account deficit may be accompanied by heavy capital outflows. This development puts added strain on the nation's reserve position and the exchange rate. In other instances the opposite occurs, when a sudden recovery of confidence leads to a surplus in current account concurrent with net capital inflows. This has been the case in Argentina since 1976; despite a continued sharp depreciation of the peso as a result of inflation, Argentina's reserves have risen dramatically.

International reserves are presented in Table 5.8. The original idea of holding reserves was to backstop a nation's currency, as through intervention in the exchange market. On this basis, one would expect the reserves to rise at times of strength for the currency and fall when the value of the currency declines, but for most nations in Latin America and the Caribbean reserves are also related to the capacity of a country to borrow. As a result, some countries have adopted a strategy of building up reserves, irrespective of current exchange rate policy, as a basis for improving their prospects for borrowing additional funds in the international capital markets.

All told, these are just a few of the many comparisons that could be made. They serve to illustrate the basic argument made here that foreign exchange policy should not be considered in isolation. Its success or failure must be weighed in the broader context of the internal and external economies and of the occasionally conflicting objectives of each nation's economic policies.

6

MOBILIZATION OF SAVINGS, CAPITAL MARKETS, AND FISCAL POLICY

Vito Tanzi

INTRODUCTION

Fiscal policy, alone or with the help of other policy instruments, can promote growth in a variety of ways. It can, for example, (1) increase the rate of saving of a country; (2) channel these savings into more socially productive uses; (3) increase what has been called productive consumption, that is, education and health; (4) discourage nonproductive and extravagant consumption and investment, such as purchasing of expensive cars and luxury housing; (5) reduce inefficiency throughout the economy and particularly in the public sector; (6) maintain a climate of economic stability; (7) remove bottlenecks of various kinds; (8) reduce or eliminate growth-retarding distortions introduced by the tax system and other public policies; and (9) eliminate or at least reduce distortions in the relative prices of the factors of production.

In past discussions of the role of fiscal policy vis-à-vis growth, the emphasis has generally been on (1) the tax structure that would be the least damaging (or the most favorable) to growth, (2) the role of the government in providing the basic economic and social infrastructures for development, and (3) the role of the government in mobilizing savings. In this chapter emphasis is mainly on the mobilization of savings.

In a remarkable book first published in 1911, Joseph Schumpeter wrote that "the increase . . . of savings is obviously an important factor in explaining the course of economic history through the centuries, but . . . development consists primarily in employing existing resources in a different way . . . irrespective of whether those resources increase or not."[1] As a consequence of the predominance, in recent decades, of macroeconomics and of growth models that have generally ignored the more mundane microissues of allocation of existing resources, Schumpeter's message was largely forgotten. In this period the developing countries (and the economists advising them) have been excessively preoccupied with the increase in the rate of saving (and investment) and not enough in a better employment of existing resources.

The general framework that has determined the role that the governments of these countries play and that has, consequently, influenced economic policy can be briefly outlined as follows. To increase the rate of saving, the governments must increase their own saving rate in current account (that is, the difference between their ordinary revenue and their current expenditure). This is to be done by increasing taxes and by limiting current expenditure. This increase is to be accompanied by an increase in public investment as public investment is almost always productive and private investment is not likely to be forthcoming at the desired level. At the same time, the governments are not urged to follow general economic policies that would stimulate the promotion and, what is perhaps more important, the efficient allocation of private savings. This implicit framework is obviously too aggregative, too simple, and politically naive.

First, in the recommendation to increase taxes, little attention has been paid to the tax structure, although if the wrong taxes are increased (as, for example, those on foreign trade), the effect of this increase on the rate of growth may be negative.

Second, and perhaps more important, little attention has been paid to the composition and allocation of investment. Somehow there has been the implicit—and, in many growth models and development plans, the explicit—assumption that the rate of saving (and the rate of investment) will determine the growth rate of a country. This, however, is obviously not true when the economy does not necessarily allocate investment toward the most productive uses. In economies with excessive rigidities and nonefficient allocative mechanisms (as is the normal case in most developing countries), a given rate of investment can be associated with a whole spectrum of rates of growth depending on the allocation of that investment. The better the allocation, the higher the rate of growth.

A third criticism of that implicit framework is that the distinction made between the supposedly growth-retarding current expenditure and the supposedly growth-promoting capital expenditure is really too sharp to reflect reality. Many types of capital expenditures are not very productive (cathedrals in the deserts), while many current expenditures (primary education, preventive medicine, and so on), may be very productive.

Finally, as the experience of many countries shows, the increase in total taxes is not necessarily associated with an increase in current account savings, since in many cases the least desirable current expenditures (defense, general administration, and so on) are the ones that increase when taxes are raised. Consequently, the increase in public investment is often financed through external financing or through internal money creation with obvious inflationary results, which, in turn, influence the particular use of savings.

For the reasons outlined above, it would be desirable if the governments of the developing countries became less concerned with macroeconomic variables and more concerned with a more efficient allocation of available resources. This objective can be pursued through policies that speed up the development of a capital market or, failing this, through a particular role for fiscal policy.

The productivity of public investments is closely related to both the level and the quality of investment in the private sector. In fact, one can think of public investment as a kind of input for private investment (and, of course, for private consumption). Generally one can argue that, with the exception of investment in public enterprises, the direct contribution of most public investment to potential output is not high. It is generally its effect on the productivity of private investment that makes public investment worthwhile. Consequently, fiscal policy in developing countries should not be limited to creating the economic and social infrastructures, although this is an important function, but should also be extended to ensuring that the level as well as the quality of private investment is as high as needed.

Private investment is normally stimulated by the maintenance of political and economic stability and by a climate that is conducive to the internal reinvestment of saving. This process is obviously aided by the parallel creation of the essential economic, financial, and social infrastructures. It would certainly be desirable for the developing countries to have financial institutions that worked smoothly and efficiently to promote economic development. Unfortunately, many developing countries do not have the benefits of such institutions and are not likely to have them for many years to come. There is then a particular and rather obvious role that the governments of these countries can take in alleviating some of the shortcomings associated with the absence of a capital market. To put this role in the proper perspective it is necessary to start by giving a brief account of the main functions that a well-working capital market would perform if it existed.

CAPITAL MARKETS AND THE
ALLOCATION OF SAVINGS

The main task of a well-working capital market is the transfer of claims on resources from some economic units (the surplus units) to others (the deficit ones). This transfer of resources is generally indirect in the sense that the savers, or surplus units, lend their savings to financial institutions, which then, acting as intermediaries, lend the funds to the investors. In this process there is no need for savers and investors to be acquainted with, or to come in direct contact with, one another. Once the investors have received control over these resources, they invest them in opportunities or projects from which they expect rates of return high enough to pay back the loans and the interest charges, as well as to make a profit.

In the process of acting as an intermediary between surplus and deficit units, a well-working capital market performs some important, and perhaps not so obvious, functions. These can ultimately be expected to raise the overall rate of saving for the country and, what is perhaps more important, the rate of return to investment, thus leading to faster economic growth.

The capital market provides an easy and normally relatively safe investment opportunity to both large and small savers. Large investors normally have an easier time finding attractive investments. However, when financial or investment opportunities are absent, small savers may be discouraged from saving and thus may remain in permanent poverty. If an investment opportunity is accompanied by an attractive real rate of interest, it is likely to result in higher savings. This stimulation of savings in response to high interest rates has been reported in a few countries (for example, Korea, Taiwan, and Indonesia) where reform aimed at raising those rates (from often negative real levels to positive ones) has been followed by increases in savings.

A well-working capital market brings together in a common pool the savings of thousands or millions of individuals. This pooling of resources is very important, as the nature of modern technology is such that many investment opportunities require financing that may often exceed the financial capacity of any one individual or of any small group of individuals, especially in countries with relatively low per capita incomes. Without this pooling, some productive but relatively large investments would not be made, while the resources saved might be fragmented in many less productive investments. Where the capital market is not well developed and where the government does not exercise this pooling-of-savings function, only the rich may be able to amass the resources needed to take advantage of investment opportunities. In these particular circumstances the rich may be viewed as a substitute for the pooling-of-resources function of the capital market. It could even be hypothesized that income redistribution may affect growth more by bringing about an atomization of savings than by reducing total savings, as some argue would result from reducing the income of those who supposedly have a greater marginal propensity to save. In other words, under such circumstances, one million dollars of savings in the hands of one person might be more productive than an equivalent amount scattered among thousands of people, as long as the person used that million in the most productive investment rather than in the most prestigious or conspicuous one.

If the argument outlined above is correct, it implies that a well-working capital market will eliminate the need for this pooling function on the part of the rich, making the rich less economically useful. This argument is reinforced if, by allowing the payment of higher rates of interest to savers, such a market does in fact bring about additional savings on the part of the masses.

By replacing the debt of the deficit units (the real investors) with that of the intermediaries, the capital market increases the liquidity of the assets held by the surplus units while the savings are made available to the deficit units for longer periods of time. In other words, it converts short-term into longer-term debt and relatively illiquid debt into relatively liquid debt. Also important in this context is the fact that the savers can now continuously convert their savings into financial assets rather than accumulate large amounts to be invested into real assets. Quite apart from what happens to the rate of returns on savings, the availability of safe financial assets in small denominations will facilitate the saving process.

By averaging the risk, the capital market decreases the possibility of loss to any one saver and thus increases his willingness to lend.

If the capital market is fairly well working, it guarantees that the investors who succeed in getting the funds are also the most productive; in other words, it not only transfers savings from savers to investors, but from savers to the potentially most productive investors, that is, those with the greatest entrepreneurial ability. As Ronald McKinnon has argued in a recent book, when the economy is fragmented "firms and households are so isolated that they face different effective prices for land, labor, capital, and produced commodities and do not have access to the same technologies." In particular, "fragmentation in the capital market . . . causes the misuse of labor and land, suppresses entrepreneurial development, and condemns important sectors of the economy to inferior technology."[2]

The basic point is that when the capital market is too fragmented and the rate of interest that a saver can expect from lending is too low, he will have the incentive to use his savings himself even when the rate of return that he can expect from his own investment is low. Thus a low rate of interest will not only discourage people from saving but, what may even be more important, it will also stimulate many unproductive uses for existing savings.* In this case, those

---

*One example of this misuse is the building of houses over several (or even many) years. Normally, the individual spends his sav-

who have entrepreneurial ability and who are able to direct savings toward more productive uses may not be able to do so for lack of investable funds.

Entrepreneurial ability is an extremely important and scarce quality, especially in developing countries, and should be fully utilized and not wasted. The degree to which available entrepreneurial ability is utilized determines to a large extent the quality of investment and, in some cases, even its quantity; the government has the responsibility to see that this scarce resource is utilized to the fullest degree.

An interesting aspect of this ability is that it is most likely not strongly concentrated in any particular income group of the population. There is, in fact, no strong reason to assume that those with high incomes also possess a monopoly of those qualities that Schumpeter associated with the successful investor, especially when those incomes are generated by inherited wealth. It is likely that often those who have financial resources do not know what to do with them, except perhaps to spend them, to invest in land and residential construction, or to take them out of the country. On the other hand, many people who because of their mental qualities and their general aptitudes could be successful entrepreneurs often have neither personal wealth nor access to resources through the capital market. An important function for fiscal policy would then be that of making financial resources available to these people.

A final point that is worth making concerns the relationship between the capital market and protection policy. In a recent important paper Robert E. Baldwin convincingly argued that the theoretical case for infant-industry protection had been oversold.[3] The details of Baldwin's arguments cannot be discussed here, but what he has done is essentially to show that four principal infant-industry cases are invalid. However, Baldwin's own argument against infant-industry tariff protection depends largely and critically on the ability of affected firms or workers to obtain access to credit—to make up for temporary losses for the former and to survive on very low wages "or even pay the firm with these borrowed funds to provide on-the-job training" for the latter.[4] What is implicit in Baldwin's argument is that the case for infant-industry protection may be largely a case for a well-working capital market. Or, what is the same, the argument for protection becomes stronger the less developed the capital market is and the more difficult it is to get credit.

---

ings on the construction of the house and then stops the work. A few months (or even years) later, when he has accumulated more savings, the work is continued; for these countries, which must have high rates of discount, this process is wasteful.

FISCAL POLICY AND THE
GENERATION AND ALLOCATION OF SAVINGS

If a country does not have a centralized economy and if it does
not have a well-working capital market, it should be the responsibility of the government to try to develop one. This, however, is a difficult task that requires a long time to be accomplished. In the inter-
vening period, the government can follow two alternative, second-best
solutions.

First, it can itself invest a rather substantial share of total
savings, as has been done in Latin America in the past two decades.
There the share of total investment carried out by the public sector
has often exceeded 50 percent. This is the route that has been supported in much of the writing on the role of government in economic
development. This support has been based (1) on the assumption that
the government should supply the entrepreneurial function that supposedly is missing in the private sector* and (2) on the need for the creation of infrastructures discussed above and on the implied assumption
of high productivity for public investment.

Second, it can itself provide a kind of proxy for this function of
the capital market. This leads back to the role of fiscal policy in the
developing countries. If the reasoning through much of this chapter
is valid, it would provide an argument for a planned budgetary surplus.
In other words, the government should aim to set its total tax revenues
and, the basic point here, its total expenditure (both current and capital) at a level that would yield an overall surplus, which could then be
made available on a competitive and nonconcessionary basis to the
private sector, as well as to public enterprises. This would provide
the government with a powerful and flexible tool that would facilitate,
to a considerable extent, the allocation of private investment along
more efficient lines.†

That such an approach is possible is shown by the Japanese example in the decade after the Meiji Restoration (1868) and in the period following World War II. Koichi Emi has described how during

---

*An obvious question is, If entrepreneurial ability is missing
among the population that constitutes the private sector, why should
it not be missing among the supposedly similar population that makes
up the public sector?

†The implication of this choice is that public capital expenditure,
not only current expenditure, should be limited in order to generate
the needed budgetary surplus to be made available to the private sector. Thus, the basic policy recommendation is not necessarily a
higher tax burden for the countries.

these periods "the function of public finance was extended to set up a new saving-investment scheme for the national economy" and how during the first of these periods this function was "gradually switched to the private banking system." He goes on to state that "at this stage, the purpose of government loans and investments shifted from the establishment of private enterprises to the proper function of creating public works and other social overhead capital.[5]

Surveys carried out in some Latin American countries have shown that the inability on the part of many enterprises and individuals to obtain credit is, perhaps, the most serious obstacle to investment and development. In these countries those who obtain the credit available often get it at concessionary or even at negative real rates of interest. On the other hand, many who would gladly have paid high positive rates are not able to obtain any credit. It is likely that the availability of credit is far more important than all the incentive schemes, especially for the creation of new enterprises.

Thus, the availability of credit financed by surpluses in the government budget is an integral part of fiscal policy; but, unlike tax incentives and controls, it puts in the hands of the government an instrument that is exceedingly flexible. Through the use of this instrument, resources can be directed toward productive investments carried out by private entrepreneurs and toward those with high social significance. In this way the government would, in fact, be acting as a proxy for the capital market; in addition to increasing the level of savings, it would stimulate entrepreneurship and thus affect the quality and not just the quantity of investment. It would, as shown above, also have implications for protective policy.

The objection to this scheme can be easily anticipated: it concerns the capacity of many governments to actually use these funds for the purposes indicated. As already discussed, given extra revenues, the political pressure on the government may lead to increases in nonproductive budgetary expenditure. Thus it is clear that "generation of 'public savings' . . . would require some very deliberate efforts on the part of the governments to economize on their administration and other current [and one should add capital] expenditures."[6] The basic point made here is that we cannot assume that public capital expenditure is always productive. Funds can be wasted in nonproductive capital expenditure as well as in current expenditure.

Many developing countries have had substantial deficits that have generally been financed either by borrowing from the public (and often from foreign institutions) or by borrowing from their central banks. This action has reduced the availability of resources available for investment in the private sectors and often has had inflationary consequences that have distorted the financial structure of the countries, generated serious balance-of-payment difficulties, and retarded the development of a capital market. A relatively tight fiscal policy, together with a liberal monetary or credit policy, is likely to create the most favorable economic atmosphere for economic development.

NOTES

1. Joseph A. Schumpeter, The Theory of Economic Development (New York: Oxford University Press, 1961), p. 68.

2. Ronald I. McKinnon, Money and Capital in Economic Development (Washington, D.C.: Brookings Institution, 1973), pp. 5, 8.

3. Robert E. Baldwin, "The Case against Infant-Industry Tariff Protection," Journal of Political Economy 77 (May–June 1969): 295–305.

4. Ibid., p. 301.

5. Koichi Emi, "Saving and Investment through the Government Budget," in Fiscal and Monetary Problems in Developing States: Proceedings of the Third Rehoboth Conference, ed. David Krivine (New York: Praeger, 1967), pp. 138, 142.

6. Ved P. Gandhi, "Are There Economies of Size in Government Current Expenditures in Developing Countries?" Nigerian Journal of Economic and Social Studies 12 (July 1970): 173.

II

CAPITAL-FLOW ALTERNATIVES AND DYNAMICS OF THE LATIN AMERICAN MARKET

Development goals and programs are defined on the national level. The ability of a government to realize its targets may be dependent upon accessibility to internal and external financial resources. This section commences with Steven Arnold's study of the Inter-American Development Bank, with particular attention to the theme of balanced development (that is, inclusion of social progress within development priorities). Hugh Schwartz relates finance to the growth of industrial companies and perceives that small and medium-tier entities often lack accessibility to sufficient credit facilities. A look at Brazil by William Tyler supports that hypothesis. The attraction that a country may hold for the foreign investor has a bearing upon capital flows. In his review of the paper industry in Brazil, Robert Reitzes depicts the highlights of a feasibility study that a corporate investor might undertake. The financiera is a financial vehicle with much potential for promoting development. Stewart Sutin describes how the financieras operate in Venezuela, Colombia, and Ecuador. The ability of a country to generate capital locally has implications for development. Juan Rada looks at the growth of the money market in Venezuela. Sheldon Gitelman's chapter offers still another perspective to Latin America's ability to generate funds flow through a commentary on the increasing commercial relationships with Africa.

7

THE INTER-AMERICAN DEVELOPMENT BANK APPROACH TO DEVELOPMENT FINANCING

Steven H. Arnold

INTRODUCTION

Since its creation in 1959, the Inter-American Development Bank (IDB) has grown from relatively modest beginnings to a role of importance in the financing of Latin American development. IDB membership currently includes 41 nations, both from within and outside the hemisphere. Loans for the most recent year (1978) exceeded $1.8 billion, of which about $700 million was on concessional terms. In terms of total development assistance funds available for Latin America, the IDB has steadily increased its share from about 13 percent in 1961–65 to almost 25 percent in 1971–75, with many Latin American nations now considering the IDB as their single most important source of public external financing for development.[1]

From the point of view of the IDB itself, its importance is measured not only by its volume of lending but also by what it regards as its unique approach to multilateral funding, an approach that has characterized the IDB since its beginnings. Challenging the more traditional approach, which focused largely on economic infrastructure, the IDB has expressed a strong commitment to balanced development,

Research for the present chapter was initially conducted as part of a study for the Congressional Research Service, published as U.S., Congress, House, Subcommittee of the Committee on Appropriations, Towards an Assessment of the Effectiveness of the World Bank and the Inter-American Development Bank in Aiding the Poor: Hearings, prepared by James H. Weaver, Steven H. Arnold, Linda D. Smith, and Elizabeth Shelton, 95th Cong., 2d sess., 1978, pt. 5. Parts of the present chapter are updated versions of the author's contribution to that publication.

TABLE 7.1

Distribution by Sector of Approved Loans from Ordinary Capital and Fund for Special Operations, 1961-62, 1966-77

(in percent)

	1961[a]	1962[a]	1966	1967	1968	1969	1970	1971	1972	1973	1974	1975	1976[b]	1977[b,c]	1978[d]
Directly productive															
Agriculture	16.7	22.2	30.5	27.0	20.2	28.2	35.1	15.7	16.8	20.4	20.4	25.1	31.2	21.4	13.4
Industry and mining	28.2	11.7	11.9	19.6	12.8	5.2	6.8	8.9	20.6	18.7	9.6	11.0	15.4	23.5	17.0
Subtotal	44.9	33.9	42.4	46.6	33.0	33.4	41.9	24.6	37.4	39.1	30.0	36.1	46.6	44.9	30.4
Economic infrastructure															
Electric power	6.4	5.3	7.9	15.7	32.0	18.3	18.1	19.7	28.3	25.2	35.4	21.0	14.6	19.6	40.7
Transportation and communication	0.8	1.3	7.5	16.5	16.0	35.6	25.5	27.9	15.2	15.7	18.0	23.7	16.9	11.3	10.4
Subtotal	7.2	6.6	15.4	32.2	48.0	53.9	43.6	47.6	43.5	40.9	53.4	44.7	31.5	30.9	51.3
Social infrastructure															
Sanitation	23.8	26.1	15.6	8.9	5.5	6.5	4.4	9.4	7.8	5.0	8.5	8.3	9.4	13.3	7.9
Urban	23.3	28.3	12.7	3.0	6.3	1.8	4.5	1.4	5.7	1.7	0.0	3.0	0.5	2.4	0.0
Education	0.0	3.8	7.9	7.0	2.3	2.6	2.2	5.1	2.6	10.6	1.8	5.5	6.0	5.1	4.5
Subtotal	47.1	58.2	36.2	18.9	14.1	10.9	11.1	15.9	16.1	17.3	10.3	16.8	15.9	20.8	12.4
Other															
Tourism	0.0	n.a.	0.6	0.0	0.0	0.4	0.2	5.2	0.1	0.4	2.7	0.2	1.9	3.1	1.7
Export finance	0.0	n.a.	0.8	1.1	3.2	1.2	2.0	4.1	1.8	1.1	1.0	2.0	1.9	[e]	2.4
Preinvestment	0.9	1.3	4.4	1.1	1.7	0.2	1.3	2.6	1.0	1.2	2.6	0.4	2.4	1.3	1.7
Subtotal	0.9	1.3	5.8	2.2	4.9	1.8	3.5	11.9	2.9	2.7	6.3	2.6	6.2	3.4	5.8

n.a. = not available

[a]Includes Social Progress Trust Fund.
[b]1976 and 1977 include interregional capital.
[c]Includes mixed loans for $15 million divided between industry and tourism and $6.1 million divided between agriculture and industry.
[d]Includes administered funds of $80.8 million.
[e]Negligible.

which includes a concern for social as well as economic factors. In following this more balanced approach, the IDB sees itself as having played a pioneering role by introducing agricultural and social sector loans to the field of development banking.

This concern for balanced development has remained an important article of faith throughout the IDB's history. At the same time, however, it is important to stress that this concept has never been precisely defined and has been subject to varying interpretations and emphases, which have led to important fluctuations in IDB policy. For example, while it is true that from 1961 to 1977 a higher proportion of IDB lending was placed in pioneering sectors (agriculture and the social sectors) than in the more traditional economic infrastructure sectors (transport, communications, and power), this does not reveal the rather wide swings in emphasis that have occurred over the years (see Table 7.1). In addition, if one includes the preliminary figures for 1978, then the enormous growth of one of the traditional sectors, power (energy), and the drop in funds for the agriculture sector for that year mean that in overall terms, the total loan amount allotted to the traditional sectors is now slightly greater than that in the pioneering sectors (see Tables 7.2 and 7.3). As a consequence,

TABLE 7.2

Distribution of Loans

	1961–77	1961–78*
Productive sectors		
Agriculture	23	21.7
Industry and mining	16	16.5
Social infrastructure		
Sanitation	10	9.5
Urban development	4	3.8
Education	4	4.4
Economic infrastructure		
Transportation and communication	15	14.3
Power (energy)	23	25.3
Other (export finance, preinvestment, tourism)	5	4.5

*1978 figures are from preliminary data from the Inter-American Development Bank.

Source: Inter-American Development Bank, Annual Report, 1977, p. 5.

TABLE 7.3

Distribution of Loans in Traditional versus Pioneering Sectors
(in percent)

	1961-77	1961-78*
Pioneering (agriculture and social infra-structure)	41	39
Traditional (economic infrastructure)	38	40

*1978 figures are from preliminary data from the Inter-American Development Bank.

Source: Inter-American Development Bank, Annual Report, 1977, p. 5.

the long-standing IDB claim that agriculture has been the single most important sector seems to be no longer true, as overall lending in the power (energy) sector now appears greatest (see Table 7.2). Whether or not the 1978 figures represent a trend or an aberration is difficult to say; moreover, dividing loans arbitrarily into pioneering and traditional can also be misleading, since sector classification may have little relation to the design, impact, or intended purpose and beneficiaries of a loan. However, it does at least raise questions regarding the overall directions of IDB lending, invites closer analysis of its directions, and demonstrates the difficulties in attempting to operationalize the IDB commitment to innovative development.

EVOLUTION OF THE IDB

A fuller appreciation of the philosophies, goals, and dilemmas of the IDB requires an analysis of the bank from its beginnings. In fact, one can argue that the IDB has passed through several distinct phases as it has attempted to deal with the operational problems inherent in attempting to implement its socioeconomic goal of balanced development. Although it is somewhat artificial to define such periods exactly, in general four reasonably distinct periods seem to emerge: the founding of the IDB, its early experimental years (1961-66), a period of reassessment (1967-71), and a new priorities phase beginning in 1971. In addition, it is possible that 1979 marks the beginning of yet another rethinking of the bank's position, although such a conclusion remains tentative.

Founding the IDB

The creation of the IDB was seen as a victory for the Latin Americans for two reasons: It increased the flow of resources to Latin America, and it placed these resources in an organization that was considered sympathetic to the Latin point of view regarding the unique development needs of Latin America.

Prior to the IDB's creation, Latin Americans were particularly concerned by the low volume of bilateral assistance that was forthcoming from the United States, which placed Latin America low in terms of its lending priorities.[2] In addition, they were not pleased with the policies of the major multilateral development agency, the World Bank, or International Bank for Reconstruction and Development (IBRD), which was becoming increasingly influential not only as a source of funds but also as a coordinator of development assistance from other sources. In the view of Latin America, the World Bank's choice of loanable sectors was far too conservative: its focus was on economic infrastructure and its interpretation of the IBRD charter excluded consideration of loans in social sectors. To compound the problem, the World Bank also tended to make its loans conditional on the acceptance by recipient countries of macroeconomic policies that, in the opinion of the bank, would ensure creditworthiness. Not only did the Latin Americans oppose this use of leverage on general principle as simply another form of intervention in their affairs, but they also opposed it on economic grounds, arguing that the conservative policies imposed could work against balanced development, particularly in the social sectors that the bank considered beyond its scope. Given this lack of confidence in the World Bank, the Latins were faced with the task of convincing the United States that a mechanism needed to be created that not only would increase the flow of resources to Latin America, but also would permit the inclusion of funding for the social sectors of the economy.

Acceptance of such a proposal by the United States in 1959 marked a major policy reversal. The United States had long opposed all such proposals (the first originating at the First Inter-American Conference in 1889/90), arguing that enough sources of dollars already existed to finance all sound projects.[3] Moreover, the United States argued that its aid programs were to be used to finance economic, not social, development, since it was believed that if the proper environment were provided through economic development, social development could be carried out through private means.[4]

The dramatic demonstrations in Latin America against Vice-President Nixon in May 1958 combined with the hemispherewide threat presented by the Cuban revolution had a profound impact on U.S. policy. Latin America quickly moved from a back burner to become a focus of attention for U.S. policy makers, who now realized that threats to the hemisphere were more likely to arise from internal discontent than from external invasion. The events in Latin America also dramatized the fact that in spite of the growth in the economic sector, many Latins were still desperately poor and were increasingly frustrated at their inability to share in the growth that was surrounding them.[5]

This led to the beginnings of a major reassessment of U.S. policy in an effort to channel Latin American aspirations into "productive and responsible" channels; later under President Kennedy this effort evolved into the Alliance for Progress in 1961. During this period of reassessment, one of the major initiatives proposed by the United States was the creation of an Inter-American Development Bank to give more tangible expression to the special relationship between the United States and its hemispheric neighbors.

Equally important, the United States now expressed a willingness to give assistance for social as well as economic programs to ensure that all could share in the growth that was occurring. First expressed in general terms by President Dwight D. Eisenhower in his Declaration of Newport on July 11, 1960, this policy was further clarified in the Act of Bogotá, approved by the Council of the Organization of American States on October 11, 1960. In essence, the Act of Bogotá listed the specific areas in which the United States was willing to give assistance, including rural credit, land use planning and improvement of living conditions, housing and community facilities, education and training, and improved public health. The act also noted the fact that the U.S. Congress had authorized a $500 million Special Fund for Social Progress for Latin America in August and welcomed the U.S. proposal that the fund be administered by the Inter-American Development Bank. Under this arrangement, the funds were to be made available, on flexible and concessional terms, to nations interested in "achieving greater social progress and more balanced economic growth."[6] This fund, which was renamed the Social Progress Trust Fund, eventually was increased to $525 million. And, although it was technically a U.S. fund administered by the IDB, for all practical purposes it served as the major source of concessional IDB lending until its resources became virtually exhausted by the end of 1965.*

---

*More precisely, Congress appropriated funds for $500 million in May 1961, of which $394 million was allocated by President John F. Kennedy to the Social Progress Trust Fund to be administered by the IDB. Subsequently, this fund was increased to $525 million.

First Lending Years (1961-66)

Buoyed by the support of the Social Progress Trust Fund, the IDB began with its first loans in 1961 to distinguish itself from the World Bank by strongly emphasizing the social sectors (particularly housing, education, and water and sewerage), as well as agricultural projects that experimented with agrarian reform. As a result, social sector loans accounted for over 47 percent of IDB lending in 1961 and 58 percent in 1962, while economic infrastructure for the same two years accounted for only about 7 percent of total lending (see Table 7.2).

These first efforts to create a new approach to multilateral lending were marked by considerable experimentation and mixed success. In the water and sewerage sector, the IDB developed a number of successful projects and has continued to be active in this area. Success was more uneven in agrarian projects focused on land settlement and land use, but such projects did signal the beginning of a commitment to agriculture that has remained a primary focus of IDB lending.

In the field of low-income housing, the IDB experienced the least success. Initially, the hope had been that IDB resources could serve as seed capital, creating savings and loan institutions managed by the benefiting low-income sectors to generate considerable additional resources to build homes on a large scale. In reality, however, houses were built, but the hoped-for multiplier effect failed to materialize because of inflation and a variety of institutional factors. As a result, it quickly became apparent that in the absence of such multipliers, the limited IDB resources (approximately $200 million) could do little to solve the region's vast housing shortages, and as a result the IDB withdrew from any major effort in the housing sector.

This experience with housing appears to have had a profound effect on the IDB not only in housing but also in its efforts to serve as a pioneer in the field of social projects in general. More important, the IDB became acutely aware of how limited its own resources were for meeting the apparently limitless needs of Latin American social development. This limitation presents the IDB with a major problem: In order to have any meaningful influence on development, the IDB's projects must generate considerable additional resources. At the same time, however, many of the bank staff are concerned that many social sector projects, particularly those focused on the poor, may follow the course of housing: although successful in themselves, they fail to serve as catalysts to stimulate other resources. In short, the experience with housing produced what has become a continuing and unresolved concern within the IDB: Can a strategy that emphasizes social goals and reformist programs be made highly productive from an economic point of view?

Reassessing Bank Priorities (1967-71)

The experimentation of the early 1960s was followed by a more cautious period of reassessment. The exhaustion of the resources of the Social Progress Trust Fund had occurred by the end of 1965, and a new problem arose—the difficulties inherent in the financing of social projects. Such projects often involved a high proportion of local costs, a fact that raised the issue of the wisdom of financing these costs with hard currencies. In addition, it also became clear that many social projects were unlikely to generate directly the foreign exchange necessary to repay the loans that financed the projects.

Such questions were less pressing during the period of the Social Progress Trust Fund, since it provided dollars and permitted repayment in local currencies. But with the exhaustion of this fund, its functions were then incorporated into the soft loan window of the bank, the Fund for Special Operations (FSO), and the problem was brought more clearly in focus. The FSO, as originally conceived, had been seen as a modest fund of concessional financing to help, in a limited way, nations that were not yet sufficiently creditworthy to accept extensive financing from the IDB's much more substantial hard loan window. Incorporating the goals of the Social Progress Trust Fund into the FSO represented massive new responsibilities, since the FSO would now also be responsible for social projects throughout the region.

To help meet this new role, the United States agreed to a major replenishment of FSO resources in 1967, but on different terms from those previously agreed to for the Social Progress Trust Fund. Distracted by the Viet Nam War and concerned about an increasingly precarious balance of payments, the United States attempted to ensure that the FSO would not represent an additional strain on the treasury. More important, the United States was opposed to using FSO dollars to finance increasing amounts of local costs, as it was felt that these would not be used to finance U.S. exports. As a result, it was agreed that with the exceptions of agriculture and education, the average percentage of dollars used to finance local costs would not exceed the average for 1966. At the same time, the Latin Americans agreed to double their own contributions to the FSO so that it would have local currencies to fund local costs.

FSO repayment procedures were also reexamined, with an eye toward placing the FSO on a sounder financial footing. Originally, the FSO had allowed countries to repay in local currencies. Given its increased responsibilities and the increasingly restrictive mood in the United States, however, repayment procedures were tightened so that by 1972 most countries were no longer allowed to repay hard loans in local currencies. (By 1974 all loans had to be repaid in currencies disbursed.) Not surprisingly, such tightening of repayment requirements increased the reluctance of Latin American governments to use IDB funding for many social sector projects. The new requirements meant that loans in hard currencies would have to be repaid in those currencies, even if the project itself did not generate the needed foreign exchange. Alternatively, the IDB could lend a nation its own currency to finance local costs, but governments considered this to be of dubious value, since they could normally generate such resources on their own and avoid the requirements of IDB financing.

Such policy changes clearly had an important effect on the pattern of sectoral lending. Social sector loans dropped from 36 percent of the total in 1966 to 19 percent in 1967 and then declined further to about 11 percent until 1971 (see Table 7.1). In contrast, economic infrastructure loans (electric power, transportation, and communications) expanded rapidly, reaching 48 percent of IDB lending in 1968 and continuing to be the dominant category of lending throughout the period. In essence, this change in lending patterns reflected a second major dilemma faced by the IDB—the problem of the compatibility of bank financing with the special needs of social projects.

Reconsidering Priorities (1971-78)

In 1971 a new president entered the IDB, marking the beginning of another attempt to conceptualize the mission of the bank. During the early 1970s, two general goals emerged, raising a third dilemma to be faced. On the one hand, the IDB restated its commitment to more balanced development, including a new and increasing emphasis on social projects and programs for low-income beneficiaries. On the other hand, however, there was also a major commitment to a sizable increase in total IDB lending, in order to increase the influence of the bank on Latin American development. This raised the question of the compatibility of the goal of balanced development with that of moving money.

The first effort at reemphasizing balanced development focused on countries, rather than individuals. Such a policy was formally approved at the Board of Governors' Meeting in Quito, Ecuador, in 1972, which called on bank management to implement immediately new measures to increase the benefits to the developing countries in the region by improving their access to concessional resources from the Fund for Special Operations.*

---

*The actions had actually been set in motion initially at the 1971 Board of Governors' meeting, but concrete action was not taken until 1972.

In response, the IDB created four categories of countries: Group A, which included the larger and relatively more developed countries (Argentina, Brazil, Mexico, and Venezuela); Group B, which included intermediate countries (Chile, Colombia, and Peru); Group C, which included countries that were not "least developed" in terms of income but that, owing to factors such as insufficient domestic markets, experienced economic difficulties; and Group D, which included those countries that in terms of income and other criteria were considered "least developed" (see Table 7.4). In creating these categories, the IDB had as its purpose the favoring of Group D nations and, to a lesser extent, the Group C nations in the granting of FSO concessional loans. In effect, virtually all loans to the Group D countries were now eligible to be financed from the FSO, regardless of the economic or social nature of the project. For the relatively more developed nations, on the other hand, the FSO loans remained reserved for highly important but slow-yielding projects, projects in relatively less developed regions of the country, projects of a social nature, or projects that directly benefited low-income sectors. This policy evolved further in favor of the poorer nations in 1975, when the IDB was able to persuade the Group A countries to take FSO loans only in their own currency, reserving the foreign exchange for the countries in the other categories.

In addition to this emphasis on low-income countries, this period also saw an evolving if less precisely articulated effort to refocus attention both on social projects and on projects in other sectors that have a direct impact on the lower-income population. Although there was no formal policy statement regarding these new concerns, they were featured in annual reports of the IDB and were at least symbolically expressed in the revision of the Charter in 1976 that added the promotion of social development alongside economic development as a primary purpose of the IDB.

In operational terms, there were signs that this concern permeated the actual loan procedures, but this was not a comprehensive effort. For funds supplied from the bank's hard window, no guidelines appear to exist regarding focus on social or low-income loans. Criteria for receiving loans from the concessional window (Fund for Special Operations), however, were considerably more complex and are continuously evolving. In general, it appears that the FSO window did attempt to encourage balanced growth both among and within nations Consequently, it justified the use of concessional lending in two general cases: (1) to minimize the impact of foreign debt on the balance of payments of the borrower (particularly Group D) countries and (2) to enable investment in social sectors (such as health, education, public health, urban and rural development, and preinvestment) that might not by themselves generate increased financial returns. In

TABLE 7.4

Inter-American Development Bank Country Classification

		GDP[a] (in millions of dollars)	GDP per Capita (in dollars)	GNP per Capita[b] (in dollars)
A.	Argentina	35,689	1,426	1,520
	Brazil	82,339	768	920
	Mexico	46,711	777	1,090
	Venezuela	17,824	1,486	1,960
B.	Chile	9,482	925	830
	Colombia	10,788	461	500
	Peru	9,275	594	740
C.	Barbados	175	721	n.a.
	Costa Rica	1,545	785	840
	Jamaica	2,187	1,086	1,190
	Panama	1,718	1,030	1,000
	Trinidad and Tobago	1,297	1,183	1,900
	Uruguay	2,652	959	1,190
D.	Bolivia	1,582	281	280
	Dominican Republic	2,920	618	650
	Ecuador	2,881	431	480
	El Salvador	1,779	433	410
	Guatemala	3,637	621	580
	Guyana	334	412	n.a.
	Haiti	688	150	170
	Honduras	1,000	369	340
	Nicaragua	1,390	643	670
	Paraguay	995	376	510

n.a. = not available

[a]Inter-American Development Bank official figures, 1976.
[b]World Bank official figures, 1974.

99

short, a country in Group D could normally qualify for FSO loans for projects in any sector, but the relatively richer countries could qualify only if the project was of a special nature or generally tended to benefit the relatively poorer individuals within the borrowing nation.

Since eligibility for FSO funding in all categories except Group D depends on demonstrating that projects will benefit social sectors or low-income groups, the IDB has given some attention to establishing criteria to operationalize this policy. To date, no specific criteria have been drafted that are concerned with social projects generally, nor are there any specific criteria regarding beneficiaries in urban programs. In the rural sector, however, which is one of the IDB's largest central concerns, there are fairly detailed criteria, created in 1973, which attempt to define cutoff points to determine what types of farms should be the beneficiaries of FSO projects. The IDA recognizes that any formula is somewhat arbitrary and therefore urges flexibility. In general, it attempts to reach those farmers who, in its opinion, are too poor to be able to operate with their own capital or borrow at commercial rates. At the same time, they should be strong enough to be able to use the FSO resources to eventually graduate to commercial credit and not be a continual drain on the bank's lending sources. In short, then, the IDB attempts to establish both a ceiling to exclude farmers who are not needy and a floor to exclude farmers who, in the bank's estimation, could not become economically self-sufficient even with concessional lending.

Given a variety of considerations, including the poor availability of some data, the IDB focuses upon the relationship between a farm's gross assets and the legal or prevailing minimum wage in the region in question. Specifically, it states that at least 75 percent of the land in the project area must be in farms with gross assets not exceeding 50 times the rural minimum wage if the farm produces crops or 100 times the minimum wage if the farm produces cattle. If possible, this asset ceiling is also checked against gross income measures, particularly in the case of cattle farming. The gross income ceiling is set at $5,000 or 10 times the minimum annual wage, whichever is the greater. Establishing the lower limits for acceptable farms is more variable, but in general projects exclude as nonviable any farms that do not generate income at least equal to that which a typical family could earn as salaried workers in the region.

While these criteria do effectively exclude the rich farmers, it is clear that low-middle- and possibly even middle-level farmers may be eligible under these guidelines. Following the 50/1 gross assets to rural wages guideline, maximum gross assets of eligible crop farms range from a low of $7,000 in Bolivia to a high of $35,000 in Costa Rica. For cattle ranches, of course, the 100/1 guideline means that the maximum could be even twice this high. Moreover, these figures may be even higher in real terms, since the underestimation of land value is widespread. Applying the income test as a check against this may of course help to lower eligibility levels, but the 10/1 ratio of gross income to prevailing rural wage rate is based on the assumption of a 10 percent return on investment. Since commercial farmers may earn a much higher rate of return (as high as 20 percent), it is possible that these farms could also be eligible under the FSO guidelines. This is not to imply that FSO funding is currently being used to finance commercial farms, but it does suggest that under certain assumptions the existing guidelines may conceivably permit this.

In addition to these eligibility guidelines, which apply primarily to countries in Groups A, B, and C, recent (1977) discussions have also clarified more precisely the beneficiaries issue in Group D countries. Prior to 1977, the beneficiaries issue had not been raised for Group D countries, since both economic (that is, infrastructure, industry, and so on) projects and the social projects normally funded by the FSO were eligible for loans. To ensure that no one benefited unfairly from such a procedure, however, the IDB established a two-step procedure for those types of economic loans that normally were financed by hard capital in the relatively more developed countries. Under this two-step procedure, the government of a Group D country received the loan at the FSO concessionary rates but could then, in turn, charge a higher rate of interest and establish harder terms if it felt that this was desirable. In effect, this two-step procedure attempted to ensure that for economic loans, the concessionary rates benefited the country but not the specific institutions or individuals concerned with the project since concessionary treatment was not required.

This two-step procedure has been and continues to be widely used. In November 1977, however, eligible loans using the two-step procedure were restricted to those economic projects in which benefits were widely distributed and for which it was not possible to establish a clear and identifiable link between individual beneficiaries and IDB financing (for example, energy and gas projects). If, on the other hand, it was possible to specify direct beneficiaries and these did not fit the general FSO criteria, the project would then be financed using ordinary or interregional capital funds. (Typical of such projects might be credit, irrigation, and tourism, if it could be shown that the project would directly benefit individuals above the FSO guidelines.) Ordinary and interregional capital was also to be used in the infrequent instances in which a project either involved high technological sophistication or was characterized by a high rate of return (for example, superhighways and oil refineries).*

In summarizing this analysis of IDB concessional lending, three conclusions stand out. First, although the general guidelines regarding lending are clear and have remained consistent since 1972, the specific policies within these guidelines have continued to evolve, with the IDB itself urging a flexible posture. Moreover, these guidelines are not so precise that they remove the need, in individual cases, for clarification and interpretation, which become part of the negotiation process as these loans are evaluated within the bank and by the board of directors. Second, it is clear that the main thrust of FSO lending has been to the poor countries, particularly Group D. Although there have been efforts to tighten up the FSO procedures by requiring repayment in the currency borrowed and by designating that some loans even in Group D countries will be eligible only for ordinary capital lending, the IDB does appear to be serious about ensuring that the developing nations receive the bulk of the concessionary financing, particularly of convertible currencies. Third, the IDB is also attempting to ensure that the FSO lending does have a social impact in all countries, either by having an effect on a wide spectrum of the population or by focusing on the poorer portion of the population. However, an analysis of the guidelines that do exist suggests that the lower limits tend to exclude the very poor (such as the landless and those considered to have no chance of becoming economically viable), while the upper limits may, in some cases, enable the inclusion of some middle-class or at least lower-middle-class beneficiaries.

This leads to two further conclusions regarding IDB policy in innovative sectors. First, a concern that such loans be productive is clearly evident, reflecting a policy rooted in the experience with housing in the early 1960s. Second, it is equally clear that loans in such sectors take a great deal of staff time and effort in terms of design, data generation, and implementation. In general, it is fair to say that such loans may require considerably more time and effort than more traditional loans, even though the loans themselves are often for smaller amounts.

This fact is particularly important when one considers that the IDB was also making a major effort to expand total lending volume during this period. The IDB staff faced contradictory objectives: in order to move money the incentive would be in favor of the large, tra-

---

*It was also agreed, in November 1977, to apply the two-step procedure to Group C nations if the country found itself in "exceptionally unfavorable" circumstances and if project benefits went to the entire country or a large segment of the population.

ditional projects, but in order to promote balanced development, the incentive would be toward the smaller, more difficult projects in social sectors or for low-income beneficiaries. In such a situation, staff members promoting balanced development would need to work harder simply to stay even. For example, between 1972 and 1977, the absolute amount of money destined for projects in which the poor were primary beneficiaries almost tripled (from $146 million to $422 million), but in terms of share of lending it increased only from 19 percent in 1972 to 25 percent in 1977 (see Table 7.5). This gives some idea of the difficulties involved in the effort to expand total lending and increase innovative projects simultaneously.

TABLE 7.5

Amount and Percentage of Inter-American Development Bank
Loans Classified as Benefiting the Poor

1972		1977	
Dollars	Percentage	Dollars	Percentage
146.2	19	422.1	25

Note: Loans in this category have at least 50 percent of the benefits going to the poor, as defined by the World Bank.

Source: Steven H. Arnold and Linda D. Smith, "The Impact of the Inter-American Development Bank upon the Poor in Latin America" (Paper presented at the Convention of the Latin American Studies Association, April 5-7, 1979), p. 44.

THE FUTURE OF THE IDB:
OLD DILEMMAS AND NEW DIRECTIONS

In December 1978 the board of governors approved a report that, among other goals, stated that approximately half of IDB future lending should benefit the poor. Although this goal remains characteristically vague in its definitions of such key words as benefits and poor, it does offer the potential of a major change in IDB lending, perhaps marking the beginning of another phase in IDB efforts to operationalize its long-standing goal of innovative and balanced development. On the other hand, it is also possible that such a goal may mean more a change of style than of substance, since the old dilemmas that have confronted the IDB in each phase of its development remain.

It is important, then, to examine each of these briefly in terms of the possible effects they may have on the future of the bank.

Maximizing the Impact of Resource Transfers

One of the earliest lessons learned by the IDB was that it will be relatively ineffective in the enormous task of contributing to the social and economic development of Latin America if it relies exclusively on its own resources. Consequently, the IDB has attempted to ensure that projects selected will stimulate additional capital formation through a variety of multiplier effects in order to give the IDB as large an influence as possible.

In the opinion of many on the IDB staff, this need for multipliers suggests a need for more traditional sector projects. Projects focusing on the poor are felt by many of the staff to have the potential problem of degenerating into welfare programs or at least into projects with a limited ability to generate additional capital. Drawing to an extent on its early experience with housing, the IDB staff tends to argue that the demonstration effects of such projects are usually very

FIGURE 7.1

Loans and Total Cost of Projects, 1961-77

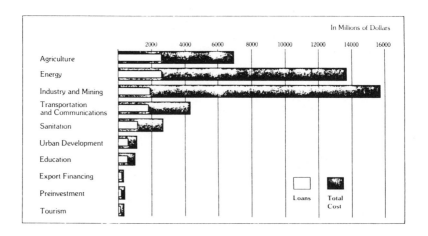

Source: Inter-American Development Bank, Annual Report, 1977, p. 5.

slight, so that they are unlikely to serve as catalysts to stimulate other resources. In contrast, large-scale projects in infrastructure and industry have a generally good record, both in generating additional non-IDB funds for the projects themselves (see Figure 7.1) and in stimulating additional growth and investment in the economy as a whole through the creation of linkages with other sectors.

These concerns have made the IDB relatively cautious in its expansion of social loans. In addition, it has also tended to exclude the very poor from consideration for loans, on the grounds that it is unlikely that the project would be productive. For example, FSO loans generally exclude not only the landless but also the poorest of the farmers on the grounds that their poor farms generally have so many problems (poor soil, droughts, location) that they are bad investments. In such situations, it is argued, bank lending would not stimulate enough productivity to allow the farmer to graduate to commercial credit but would, in fact, saddle the bank with a nonproductive welfare program.

Financial Issues

A second dilemma that first emerged in the mid-1960s concerns the special financing problems associated with social loans. For balance-of-payments reasons, donor countries may be reluctant to underwrite such loans, which typically involve high local costs that reduce the possibilities for promotion of donor nation exports. Similarly, poor nations may be unwilling to invest scarce hard currencies in projects that do not generate foreign exchange. The problem of balance of payments has become particularly acute in many Latin American nations in recent years, prompting the IDB to give renewed emphasis to such sectors as energy (to reduce imports) and projects that increase exports to earn foreign exchange. In many ways, then, the problems of finance appear to be becoming even more difficult than in the 1960s and may make both the IDB and the Latin American nations increasingly wary of projects aimed at the poor and the social sectors and inclined to favor traditional projects more likely to earn or save foreign exchange.

Project Implementation versus Moving Money

As the IDB experience of the 1970s has demonstrated, designing effective and innovative projects that meet the needs of the poorer sectors is a difficult and time-consuming undertaking. The rough rules of thumb developed for FSO loans in rural areas, for example, are only that and require considerable effort to gather data and design loans to ensure that the poor in fact do benefit. Such loans, which tend to be smaller in size than those for more traditional projects, clearly require more staff time per dollar loaned. This, however, is difficult to reconcile with the goal also held by the bank of expanding total lending. Currently, this conflict is made all the more acute by the present hiring ceiling for IDB personnel, which means that the staff will be asked to take on increasingly time-consuming tasks with little increase in support.

CONCLUSIONS: BANK OR DEVELOPMENT AGENCY?

The difficulties faced by the IDB in creating an innovative and balanced approach to development clearly demonstrate the problems that arise in attempting to adapt an international financial agency to the special needs of nontraditional projects. Since its beginnings, the IDB has confronted a succession of dilemmas—beginning with the problems of multipliers and productivity, extending to the problems of financing and balance-of-payments difficulties, and continuing with the trade-offs necessary between designing innovative projects and increasing the flow of resources—that have led to strong incentives to return to more traditional sectors of lending. Faced with such dilemmas and difficulties, the IDB has continued to finance social and other innovative projects, but it has on the whole remained skeptical of much of the current literature that concerns "redistribution with growth" and "basic needs" and that argues for a wholesale effort in such areas at the expense of more traditional projects.[7] At the same time, however, the new board of governors' directive to ensure that at least 50 percent of the loans benefit the poor gives a push in the direction of increased efforts at innovative projects.

In conclusion, it appears that the IDB faces yet another series of difficult choices over the next few years. The difficulties of innovation are many; yet, given the historic mission of the IDB and its current directives, it is unlikely that its dilemmas will be avoided by retreating into the role of a purely financial institution focusing on traditional projects. As a result, the next several years may be crucial for the IDB as it struggles to balance the requirements of innovative development and international finance.

NOTES

1. Inter-American Development Bank, Progress in Development (Washington, D.C., 1977), p. 4. It should also be pointed out

that in terms of total investments in Latin America, the IDB growth rate has been more uneven. In 1961–65, the IDB share was about 6.8 percent. This increased to about 10 percent in 1966–70 but fell to about 7.2 percent in 1971–75, reflecting a major increase in the activity of private international banks rather than a decline in IDB growth. Although precise data are not yet available, it is likely that the IDB share has increased since 1975, as the private banks have reduced their rate of expansion.

2. Latin America received only 6 percent of U.S. economic aid commitments in the 1957/58 fiscal year and only 1.4 percent of total commitments in the 1948–58 period. The best description of this and the creation of the bank is given in John White, Regional Development Banks: A Study of Institutional Style (London: Overseas Development Institute, 1970), pp. 144 ff.

3. A typical statement of this policy is found in U.S., Department of State, Department of State Bulletin 33 (1955): 1409.

4. For example, see Robert Hill, assistant secretary for Congressional Relations, in his April 14 speech to the Pan-American Day Banquet, Los Angeles, Calif., in U.S., Department of State, Department of State Bulletin 36 (May 6, 1957): 738.

5. On this point, see J. Lloyd Mecham, The United States and Inter-American Security, 1889–1960 (Austin: University of Texas Press, 1963), p. 384.

6. Act of Bogotá, sec. 2, para. 2.

7. For example, see International Labour Organization, Employment, Growth, and Basic Needs: A One-World Problem (New York: Praeger, 1977); and H. Chenery et al., Redistribution with Growth (London: Oxford University Press, 1974).

8
PROBLEMS OF INDUSTRIAL
FINANCING IN LATIN AMERICA

Hugh H. Schwartz

INTRODUCTION

Despite all the attention given to the industrialization of Latin America, no study is available that deals with the financing of industry in the region in a comprehensive way.[1] Even the basic data on which such an analysis would depend are generally not to be found in the principal publications dealing either with finance or with industry. This might lead one to conclude that there have not been any serious financing bottlenecks for Latin American industry or that there have been only the general financing problems that affect other sectors as well. Even if such were true in the past, there are reasons to believe that failure to take special account of industrial financing in the future would lead to unquestioned difficulties for efficient decision making. Among the reasons for this are (1) the increasing emphasis on Latin American ownership of Latin American industry, (2) the increasing tendency for Latin American industry to orient itself toward export markets, (3) the changing and currently relatively tightened international market for long-term funding (a phenomenon that has presented itself twice in the last five years), and (4) the inclination to increase the relative priorities given to other sectors, notably agriculture and energy.

It is far from easy to generalize about the financing of industry. Most of the literature on the topic relates only to the supply (or po-

The views expressed do not reflect the official position of the Inter-American Development Bank. Dino Siervo assisted in the preparation of an earlier draft on which this chapter is based. I am grateful to Simón Teitel, Nicholas Bruck, John Elac, Jorge Espinosa, and Ernesto Newbery for helpful comments.

tential supply) of funds available, along with the subsequent use of the funds actually supplied; the demand curve for industrial financing is ordinarily ignored, except for what can only be described as casual reference to major changes of an easily perceived nature. * As a consequence, much of the analysis of the problems of industrial finance is essentially an argument by analogy—analogy with another country or another period of time, though usually without attention to the extent to which particular differences in the supply and demand conditions affecting that other country or time period would lead one to expect differences in results. Rarely, moreover, is there an effort to estimate a supply curve for the various components of financing. Instead, the kinds and amounts of funds that have been supplied in the particular equilibrium realized by those firms sampled are usually just discussed sequentially and then added up.

The data on industrial credit outstanding, the proportion of industrial financing from particular internal or external sources, and even such generally unavailable data as those on industrial investment do not, by themselves, provide much in the way of guidelines as to the economic desirability of the situation documented.

Still other data are required, but until we have a suitable framework for dealing with the economic implications of developments in industrial financing we are unlikely even to ask for some of the most relevant information. Data on national rates of saving and investment need to be supplemented by explanations as to why particular conditions might suggest that higher—or lower—ratios are economically desirable and also by explanations of the degree to which, and the cost at which, a country's financial intermediaries can channel funds from savers to investors.

The data on the sources and uses of funds also require interpretation. The fact that the relative proportions of funding coming from the various sources differ from country to country, from time to time, or from industry to industry is not so important as the reasons for

---

*Demand is analyzed in an analytically rigorous manner only at the most aggregate level, as in the case of studies of the demand for money. A serious analysis of the demand for industrial financing would require data on the demand for various types of funds at different prices, and data of that type are seldom estimated and never published; indeed, even good data on market-clearing interest rates are not generally made available. A further disturbing note: while work must be undertaken at the level of individual industries, the interdependencies are so great for some industries that in those cases at least it would not be possible to gauge their demand for financing in an adequate way by a strictly partial equilibrium analysis.

the differences; note of the underlying supply and demand elements of the relevant markets may provide the basis for policy adjustments of the most economically justified type and degree, or it may result in the conclusion that the apparent abnormalities are temporary (or even desirable).

ASCERTAINING THE BASIC DATA AND THEIR IMPLICATIONS FOR THE ADEQUACY OF INDUSTRIAL FINANCING

Determining an Adequate Level of Industrial Financing

What is an adequate level of financing for industry, and how is adequacy to be judged? These questions cannot be fully answered without reference to the terms at which the financing is available, but some notion of what represents an adequate level of industrial financing is required in order to foster the kind of national development that is desired.

That part of gross domestic product (GDP) that is not consumed is by definition saved, and this domestic saving, along with such foreign resources as are made available, leads, with the help of financial intermediaries, to a particular level of overall and industrial investment. * Average savings rates are higher for the wealthiest than for the poorest Latin American nations, but the precise nature of savings behavior in the region is not yet well understood and is not likely to be better comprehended until savings data are far better than at present. All that can be said is that the rate of domestic savings seems to increase as does (1) the ratio of exports to the GDP, (2) the rate of growth of GDP, and perhaps (3) the real rate of interest or ease of access to alternative savings instruments that protect against inflation. [2] In addition, the level of savings is influenced by the distribution of income and by the allocation of investment in the past. Various studies indicate that domestic savings may be inversely related to capital imports; if this is true, it is worthy of special attention, given the significance of capital imports for industrial investment and, at the same time, the recurring complaint of difficulties in access to working capital, a substantial portion of which is used for purposes toward which additions to foreign capital are unlikely to contribute. Arguments can be advanced, however, as to why, in

---

*Of course, it is also possible, and has often been argued, that an efficient system of financial intermediaries may increase the proportion of GDP that is saved.

view of the economic potential of the economy, prevailing levels of savings and investment might be too low. To any strictly economic case for an increase in savings and investment there can, of course, be added such force as emanates from the political objectives of development.

Thus, the question of what is an adequate level of industrial financing is not an easy one to answer. If the effect of adding the demand for industrial financing that results from government policies to the demand that emerges from what might be described as basic market forces is to raise the price of investment goods in a country to levels relatively higher than those in the world market, then in the context of the given political framework the level of industrial financing might, under certain circumstances, be deemed inadequate. The level can be presumed to be adequate, though, when investment goods prices decline toward world levels in countries that have heavily protected import-substituting industrialization in capital goods. It is more difficult to offer conclusions about the adequacy of industrial financing if there are increases of investment goods prices under the same circumstances of import-substituting industrialization in capital goods, as is more often the case. How, then, might we begin to provide a rough first assessment of the adequacy of financing for industry?

Gauging the Adequacy of Industrial Financing

In a version of this chapter prepared five years ago for a meeting of the Economic Commission for Latin America, a considerable amount of data was presented in an attempt to indicate something about the adequacy of the level of industrial financing in the preceding period and the prospects for the years just ahead. The information related to savings and investment ratios (aggregates and, in some cases, subcategories), data on domestic financial intermediaries and on foreign funding (the latter from private as well as public sources), information on the industrial growth that had been achieved, and judgments as to the priority that had been accorded to industry in the various countries during the period under consideration.

It was conjectured that whatever might be said about the allocation of industrial financing, the level probably had been adequate in most countries. Note was taken of problems or trends that might alter that presumably favorable situation in the future, but, indeed, the dramatic rise in private bank credits and in Eurodollar loans to Latin America throughout the 1970s reveals that the supply of funding has continued to rise at a rapid (some would say excessive) rate, with industry clearly among the principal beneficiaries.

However, the assessments as to the earlier adequacy of industrial financing were not really well reasoned. Moreover, one of the misleading aspects of even presenting much of the kind of data referred to is that virtually all of the readily available information deals with the supply side and, at that, with the specific points on the supply curves reflecting the amounts that actually were made available. Few if any measures are provided of the demand for industrial financing that prevailed, and that is of no small significance, given the market imperfections that characterize so many financial markets. Furthermore, most of the public supply side data is too aggregate in nature to be easily juxtaposed with the relatively available information on the demand for industrial financing. In addition, in almost all cases in which such data on financial aggregates are presented, there is a tendency to lead the reader to particular conclusions concerning the adequacy of financing on the basis of insufficient or, at any rate, less than fully explained criteria or to invite the reader to come to his own conclusions—as if the facts spoke for themselves or the reader's criteria would necessarily be adequate to provide the standard of measurement.

Perhaps the best way to come to grips with the topic of industrial financing is by examining the data on sources and uses of funds for representative samples of manufacturing enterprises in each country. Such data should be analyzed with considerable care, of course. To begin with, many enterprises keep more than one set of books, and the resulting biases in the data undoubtedly are greater for some categories of entries than for others. Second, smaller enterprises often possess a limited knowledge of accounting techniques. Third, sources of funds studies relate almost exclusively to corporate enterprises, which means that data representing a substantial portion of manufacturing value added is not taken into account. Fourth, intercountry comparisons are treacherously difficult in view of (1) differences between countries in the relative prices of several major categories of goods; (2) differences in the composition of the industrial structure between countries, with a larger proportion of the sector consisting of activities ordinarily more dependent on internal financing in some countries than in others; and (3) differences in the adequacy of depreciation allowances to cover replacement costs and in the timing of special asset revaluation allowances to correct for the problem. Finally, to analyze the significance of differences in the proportions of the various sources of financing internal and external to the firm, it is necessary to refer to the relative supply of each of the possible funds for industrial financing, as well as to the demand for industrial financing in each of the countries being compared.

Relatively few compilations of sources and uses of funds data are available for Latin America. The U.S. Department of Commerce compiles such information for U.S. corporations in the region, but data for a representative group of industrial entities appear to be available for only four countries—Argentina, Brazil, Colombia, and Nicaragua. No such industrywide compilation ever has been made for Mexico, though balance sheet data is prepared periodically for small- and medium-sized enterprises. The first analysis of Latin American sources and uses of funds was prepared by the Economic Commission for Latin America (ECLA) in the mid-1960s and dealt with a limited group of corporations in Argentina, Brazil, Colombia, Chile, Ecuador, Uruguay, and Venezuela.[3]

The ECLA analysis concluded that Latin American enterprises provided a smaller portion of their funds from internal sources and were thus more dependent on outside financing than manufacturers in the United States or France and that this was truest of small enterprises. It is implied that these factors had negative consequences. It should be noted, though, that the basic data used by ECLA, drawn from a small number of firms over the course of only a few years, may not have been sufficiently representative to provide valid generalizations. In any event, the relatively large proportion of funds obtained from external sources might tend to suggest that access to financing was not all that difficult, at least on average, and that the study's conclusion that the ratio of credit to GDP was too low for developing countries should perhaps be reconsidered. * (None of this is to deny that the allocation of that credit may have been a problem, even if the level was not.)

The prevalence of short-term credits, high interest rates, and loans with little or no foreign exchange content led the ECLA group to conclude that the conditions for industrial financing in Latin America were highly unfavorable, though it stated that increased lending from bilateral and international development institutions was improving

---

*It was noted that U.S. firms in Latin America provided less of their own funds internally than did enterprises in the same industries in the United States and that they reinvested a smaller (though rising) proportion of their profits. Both factors were criticized in view of what was alleged to be a high rate of profits, but so was the tendency for the proportion of reinvested profits to rise. (The latter was attributed to special investment allowances that were termed responsible for the evolving excess industrial capacity—though responsibility for the excess capacity might well have been laid even more so to the protected, import-substituting industrialization that ECLA had endorsed in the past and at least as much to the subsidized interest rates that the Santiago-based institution endorsed throughout the 1950s and 1960s and specifically in the study under review.

matters. Of course, to consider the true duration for which loans were extended it is necessary to take account of the ease with which industrial loans ordinarily were renewed; moreover, the real (as contrasted to nominal) rates of interest were not generally high—indeed, they often involved disguised subsidies (which, combined with the use of various mechanisms to ration bank credit, must have tended to distort manufacturing investment). That the resulting allocation of industrial credit was not what at least some might have expected was acknowledged in two conflicting ways in the analysis. At one point there was a criticism of an alleged tendency for industrial credit to be granted to existing industries, while at another there was a favorable comment on the relatively large portion of long-term loans that went to "dynamic" industries (especially steel); no attempt to analyze the allocational efficiency of industrial credit was made, however.

Public institutions were taken to task for not being sufficiently in the vanguard in making industrial credit available, but no analysis was provided to indicate that industrial financing from the private sector was so unresponsive as to require greater public efforts than those that were undertaken, and there was no analysis of the rather major role of industrial financing in such countries as Mexico and Argentina, where the ratio of publicly financed industrial credit to GDP rose to levels higher than the ratio of all bank credit to GDP in some of the most industrialized nations. The study was rightfully critical of the limited role of the stock markets in financing industry in Latin America but gave little attention to the financieras and other new investment vehicles for channeling funds from one sector to another.

Finally, while the ECLA study made some adjustments to allow for the inadequacy of historic cost accounting in periods of inflation, it did not seem to recognize many of the serious problems undermining the use of sources of funds data for intercountry comparisons noted in the first paragraph of this section.

Sources of funds data and other microlevel information that might help ascertain the adequacy of industrial financing are difficult to come by. A limited amount of useful information is available for Brazil, Colombia, and Mexico, somewhat more for Nicaragua, and really extensive coverage only for Argentina. Since even the latter is characterized by limitations that prevent any meaningful resolution of the adequacy issue, only a few words will be noted concerning the other four nations.

In Colombia, loans from the banking system to industry dropped sharply as a percentage of all loans outstanding during a portion of the recent past, so the considerable amount of data available on balance sheets and sources and uses of funds would take on great importance were it not for the fact that some of the data is so obviously incorrect (implying, for example, that the rate of return of Colombian industry on equity averaged less than 1 percent during a decade when entrepreneurs seemed to be living quite well, the growth of industry averaged 8 percent, and considerable new capacity was financed).

Brazilian data cover only a small proportion of industrial enterprises but suggest that the proportion of funding that came from sources external to the firm increased greatly from the mid-1960s to the early 1970s, even as the sector was growing at a 10 to 14 percent rate and overall financing demands were increasing substantially. Approximately a third of the outside financing came from government development banks and less than a tenth from foreign capital. Stock issues accounted for almost a fifth, but most of this was negotiated privately rather than on the two principal stock exchanges.

In Mexico, bank credits to industry fluctuated in importance, following cycles opposite to those of the inflows from abroad. That at least suggests that financing for industry was not allowed to drop below a certain level. On the other hand, a number of indications suggest that there may have been deficiencies in the area of industrial financing. While financieras raised large amounts of money, most were relatively closed-end associations that did not make their funds available to enterprises that did not belong to their particular group. The ability to draw on outside financing varied considerably, not only from firm to firm but also from one branch of industry to another. And while a number of prominent large firms seemed to have even more success in obtaining debt financing than comparable enterprises in the United States, in the sizable group of small and medium-sized industries surveyed by Nacional Financiera, the debt-equity ratio was a surprisingly low 1:3.

The data for Nicaragua, based primarily on a 1971 Harvard Business School doctoral dissertation, appear to be relatively good and cover firms that account for half of the country's industrial production. Industrial financing seems to have been supplied primarily from the savings of enterprises or the resources of owners prior to 1960, but by the late 1960s outside sources were supplying approximately three-quarters of all funding. Moreover, medium- and long-term loans were twice as important as short-term credits. Much of the medium-term support came from private commercial banks, interestingly enough, as well as from financieras, while the relatively shorter term and more expensive suppliers credits accounted for only a tenth of the funding. In aggregate terms at least, most of the signs seemed quite favorable, though, again, no evidence of the demand for industrial financing is presented.

Far more data on the sources and uses of funds are available for Argentina than for any other Latin American nation, and the effect is to make clear many of the important, unanswered questions

TABLE 8.1

Sources of Funds in Argentine Manufacturing Enterprises
(in percent)

Source	1952–55	1960–62
Internal	60.0	40.0
Undistributed profits	47.8	14.0
Depreciation	12.2	26.0
External	40.0	60.0
Capital	9.4	9.0
Loans	15.8	12.0
Commercial banks		13.0
Banco Industrial*		-1.0
Suppliers	9.1	28.0
Reserves	5.7	11.0

*The 1952–55 commercial bank percentage includes credits from the Industrial Bank.

Source: Inter-American Development Bank, Analysis of the Possible Formation of a Regional Finance Corporation for the Expansion of Latin American Industry (Washington, D.C., August 1970), p. 60, citing the Economic Commission for Latin America industry study noted in the text and two Argentine government publications.

hidden in the more aggregate, sometimes single-year, data prepared for some other countries.[4]

Consider first the view of the sources of financing of Argentine industrial corporations that emerges from the 1966 ECLA study and the 1970 report by the IDB (see Table 8.1). The general impression that such data might produce and that is enunciated elsewhere is that the financing of Argentine industry was (and is) precarious, with a decreasing proportion of financing emanating from internal sources and an increasing proportion of external financing originating from short-term loans and suppliers credits.

Though not all that they might have been, the financing opportunities that actually confronted Argentine industry during the 1950s and 1960s must have been somewhat better than they have been portrayed. The fact is that Argentine manufacturers were often confronted with many serious problems aside from those involving financing, and even so Argentine industry managed to grow at an average of 7 percent annually, and Argentine industrial prices declined to an internationally more competitive level. All this was while the profitability of Argentine industry remained relatively high in both economic and financial terms.[5]

Judging by the generally favorable results, it would appear that the deficiencies of Argentine industrial financing may have been exaggerated. Perhaps the time has come to stop examining Latin American financial structures to see how closely they approximate those of other economies at different stages of industrialization and to begin analyzing the specifics confronting Latin American industry to see where and how serious the problems actually are, that is, to ascertain how much cost the various problems entail for their respective economies. This would help in determining which of the many suggestions and recommendations proffered by financial experts should be given most attention. It is suggestive, for example, that the sources of financing for Japanese industry have differed considerably from U.S. and European patterns.[6]

Examination of Argentine data suggests that the proportion of industrial financing that emanates from the respective sources varies so much from year to year in response to the shifts in the overall economy (and the changes in legislation on asset revaluation) that it is difficult to detect unequivocal evidence of trends. Some of the tendency toward an increase in internal funding appears to have taken place in periods of credit restriction (1962/63, for example), but after an interval of greater financing from sources outside the enterprises (1964-67), the proportion of funding accounted for by internal sources rose subsequently in a period of more expansionary credit policy; this may show that Argentina was reaching a status of industrial financing with characteristics similar to the most advanced industrial nations,[7] or it may merely reveal how complicated the factors are and how much is hidden by aggregates. In view of the usual assumption that a relatively high dependence on internal funds is a sign of financial and economic strength, it is to be noted that the rank correlation between the percentage of internal funds and the rate of growth of profits was relatively low. That is hardly surprising, though, given the level of disguised subsidy that accompanied Argentine indebtedness in the period prior to 1976.

There are at least three generalizations that can be made about Argentine industrial financing. First, among the categories of debts, suppliers credits have been more important than other sources of funding in most years. Second, short-term bank credits have been relatively much more important than long-term credits, but there is no information on the extent to which what appear as short-term loans are actually long-term loans, disguised, as it were, in order to enable banks or other lending institutions to protect themselves somewhat better in a situation in which both price levels and interest rates are likely to rise but by amounts not well predicted in advance. Third, large-sized enterprises have a substantial net credit position with respect to suppliers credits, but small-sized enterprises also have somewhat of a net creditor position and only the middle-sized firm group has a clearly net debtor position in suppliers credits.

There is another, rather important, observation that can be made about the sources of financing of Argentine industrial corporations, and that has to do with the extent to which the government encouraged, or at least permitted, the financing of private economic activity from funds earmarked for taxes and social security payments. This tendency began to take on major proportions in the 1950s, but has continued to grow, at least until the mid-1970s. Unpaid social security obligations rose from approximately 10 percent in 1950 to more than 50 percent in 1958,[8] and by 1966-68 postponed tax and social security payments (encouraged by continuing tax forgiveness arrangements) were nearly as large a source of corporate finance as bank credits.[9]

Tax evasion increased substantially between 1952 and 1957[10] and continued to rise at least through 1967.[11] The postponed tax and social security payments are accounted for in sources of funds data, but no sources of funds analyses even attempt to account for the sometimes appreciable amount of tax evasion. Surely tax evasion is in considerable measure a reflection of understated taxable income, and thus sources of funds analyses based on data filed with authorities substantially understate the amount and proportion of manufacturing enterprise funds that emanate from retained earnings.

Finally, we come to the outer manifestation of why the data we have are patently insufficient to resolve questions concerning industrial financing and why we must focus more on the particulars of supply and demand elements in each of the branches of industry. Until now, in referring to the proportion of industrial financing from specific sources, there has been little effort to indicate how representative the data averages are. In fact, as the disaggregation even at only the two-digit International Standard Industrial Classification (ISIC) level indicates, the proportion of financing that comes from any one source varies tremendously, not only from year to year but also from industry to industry.

In 1967-69, for which period the data are best, we find, for example, that retained profits accounted for as little as 11 percent of all sources of funds for small corporations in one branch of industry and up to as much as 49 percent in another, with the range from 21 to 52 percent for the large corporations group and from 20 to 60 percent

TABLE 8.2

Sources of Funds of Argentine Industrial Corporations: Range
between the Branches of Industry in the Percentages of Funds
Obtained from Alternative Sources, 1967-69 Average

	Large Firms	Medium-Sized Firms	Small Firms
Internal funds	29.1-67.2	31.0-68.7	26.8-70.4
Shareholder contributions	1.0-14.8	0.1- 9.4	1.7-35.5
Profits	20.9-52.4	20.4-59.9	10.7-49.3
Reduction of current assets	0.5-19.0	0.0-18.9	0.0-14.6
Sale of fixed assets	1.2- 8.6	0.6-12.8	0.8-10.8
External funds	32.8-70.9	31.3-68.9	29.6-67.2
Credits	13.0-62.5	n.a.	17.1-64.6
Suppliers	1.2-40.2	2.7-33.8	7.6-31.8
Banks	4.3-33.2	0.0-28.5	0.9-16.1
Financieras	0.2-21.5	0.3-17.5	1.0-19.4
Others			
Government	0.2-15.0	0.0-31.1	0.4-14.8
Others	0.4-26.4	0.0-11.3	0.5-33.2
Total short-term	12.1-59.3	2.6-47.5	17.6-62.6
Total long-term	0.5-20.9	0.3-27.6	0.0-15.4
Sale of assets not related to operations	0.0- 1.8	0.0- 1.6	0.0- 5.2
Advances			
Provisions			
Taxes	0.2-15.7	0.0-11.6	0.0- 7.1
Other	0.3- 5.8	0.0-12.5	0.0- 3.6
Contingencies	0.2- 8.0	0.1- 6.9	0.3- 5.6
Deferred profits	0.0- 7.3	0.0-17.4	0.0- 2.3

n.a. = not available

Sources: Mario S. Brodersohn, "Financiamiento de empresas privadas y mercados de capital" (Paper presented to the Buenos Aires Symposium of the Organization of American States Program for the Development of Latin American Capital Markets, May 2-5, 1972), tables 19-21. For the definition of small, medium-sized, and large firms, see Fundación de Investigaciones Económicas Latinoamericanas, La financiación de las empresas industriales en Argentina 1: 5-17.

TABLE 8.3

Inter-year Variation in the Proportion of Funds Obtained by Argentine Industrial Corporations from Alternative Sources: Range Obtained during 1956-69
(in percent)

Financing Sources	All Manufacturing	Branches of Industry			
		Foodstuffs	Textiles	Chemicals	Machinery
Commercial debt	4.6-22.9	7.8-18.2	5.3-16.2	10.4-17.0	5.8-35.2
Bank debt	8.9-21.2	4.2-33.2	0.6-25.4	3.4-19.6	9.5-26.2
Financiera debt	4.5-12.8	0.3-15.6	0.1- 6.5	3.8-10.2	0.5-26.5
Other debt	1.4-11.1	2.6-14.4	7.8-11.5	1.9- 5.5	1.6-17.0
Provisions	3.0-12.0	2.6-14.4	4.0-21.4	2.7-11.4	3.5-11.8
Total debt	40.1-58.7	27.7-63.9	33.8-57.4	30.4-49.8	49.1-71.2
Profits and shareholder contributions	34.4-56.7	23.0-64.5	38.7-64.9	34.3-56.1	8.3-48.0
Other	3.2-14.6	2.3-17.4	1.4-13.3	3.0-25.9	2.9-24.8

Source: Mario S. Brodersohn, "Financiamiento de empresas privadas y mercados de capital" (Paper presented to the Buenos Aires Symposium of the Organization of American States Program for the Development of Latin American Capital Markets, May 2-5, 1972), tables 10-14.

TABLE 8.4

Inter-year Variation in the Proportion of Funds Obtained by Four Branches of Argentine Manufacturing from Alternative Sources: Range Observed during Five Subperiods
(in percent)

Financing Sources	Year				
	1956-59	1960-62	1963-64	1965-66	1967-69
Commercial debt	16.2 -22.2	7.8-18.5	5.3-15.5	10.5 -35.2	5.8-15.0
Bank debt	10.5 -19.6	2.6-15.6	4.2-25.4	0.6 - 9.5	7.0-33.2
Financiera debt	0.3 - 4.5	3.3-10.0	7.9-26.5	0.1 -13.1	3.8-15.6
Other debt	(8.0)-17.0	n.a.	5.0-15.0	5.5 -11.5	1.6- 7.8
Provisions	(6.0)-10.0	n.a.	2.0- 8.5	(5.0)-11.8	2.6- 8.4
Total debt	49.2 -67.0	27.7-49.1	39.8-66.9	43.1 -71.2	30.4-63.9
Profits and shareholder contributions	27.4 -49.2	48.0-64.9	8.3-51.5	10.2 -52.9	23.0-56.1
Other	3.0 -17.4	1.4-11.6	2.3-25.9	4.0 -18.6	8.8-13.5

n.a. = not available

Note: Data for foodstuffs, textiles, chemicals, and machinery industries are considered in one grouping. Parentheses indicate approximate figure.

Source: Mario S. Brodersohn, "Financiamiento de empresas privadas y mercados de capital" (Paper presented to the Buenos Aires Symposium of the Organization of American States Program for the Development of Latin American Capital Markets, May 2-5, 1972), tables 11-14.

for the medium-sized group. [12] Bank credits accounted for 1 to 4 percent of all funds in some branches of some industries but more than 30 percent in others. Suppliers credits varied from less than 1 percent to approximately 40 percent, and postponed tax and social security payments varied from 0 percent to 10 to 15 percent in other branches of industry. Table 8.2 summarizes this information for 1967-69, and Tables 8.3 and 8.4 provide further data of a less detailed nature for 1956-69. [13]

The Fundación de las empresas industriales en la Argentina (FIEL) study provides brief explanations of a few factors affecting each of the branches of industry, but not nearly enough to gauge whether or not some of the shifts noted in the level, composition, and timing of an industry's funding placed it in a weaker financial position than another industry and, if so, whether or not the relative financial capacity of the respective industries was consistent with their economic potential. It may well be that in a completely market economy with relatively effective competition among the potential suppliers of finance to industry, such individual industry examination might rarely be necessary. In a situation characterized by large dominant banks, subsidized rates of interest, official allocation of credits between the sectors and branches of industry, and various weaknesses outside the banking sector, it is not possible to assume anything about the economic significance of the patterns of financing that have evolved for the various industries. One industry may find itself with levels and sources of financing in proportions easily defended in terms of national economic rationality; another may be drawing on an appropriate proportion of medium-term financiera funding, perhaps, but what seem to be less appropriate proportions in equity or from banks and too high (or low) an overall level of financing because of the terms available to it or the rationing of certain funds. Given the substantial number of imperfections and interventions in the money market and the differing situations of various groups of industry with respect to both sources of funds and prospects for using those funds to their financial advantage, analysis at the level of individual industries (or groups of similar industries) is indispensable to prescribing appropriate changes.

The role of the stock markets in financing Argentine industry has been generally minimal but may have been of consequence for a few industries at certain points in time (for example, 1960/61). Financieras have had their ups and downs, and the degree to which they were supplanted by credit cooperatives and private investment banks may have varied from industry to industry. The extent to which the National Development Bank has, in fact, been developmentally oriented appears to have fluctuated from one time period to another. These are all important points to take into account if one is really to understand how Argentine industry has financed itself, but such vital information does not emerge from balance sheets or financial ratios alone. Nor would a general survey of the evolution of each of the various sources of financing be sufficient. Those would have to be supplemented by analytical commentaries on certain financial data in the light of individual industry circumstances and opportunities. Nothing less would do and no studies of that type are available to date.

CONSEQUENCES OF INADEQUACIES IN THE AVAILABILITY OF INDUSTRIAL FINANCING

An inadequate level of industrial financing or inadequate terms for the financing obtained can lead to serious problems for industrialization. This section outlines some of the most important consequences of both, along with problems that are attributable to inadequacies in the allocation of industrial financing. New challenges already aggravating the financial arena and likely to worsen are discussed in the secion on that subject, and in the final section two proposals are advanced that deal with one of the fundamental problems: a lack of appreciation of what constitutes an adequate level or allocation of industrial financing.

The Basic Adverse Consequences

The most obvious adverse consequence of not providing an adequate level of industrial financing is a reduced and suboptimal level of industrial development. This may be partially alleviated, or it may actually be aggravated, if the availability of financing does at times reach adequate or more than adequate levels. In such cases, with patterns of industrial financing that are erratic relative to the demand, the uncertainty factor that enters into economic calculations increases, discriminating against long-run projects. In addition, a boom-and-bust character of industrial expansion (sometimes referred to as stop-and-go cycles) tends to develop, resembling—indeed often part of—the boom-and-bust expansion patterns that result from the gyrations in the availability of foreign exchange. The impact of boom-and-bust tendencies are sometimes softened by the ability to delay tax and social security payments and by the increases in tax evasion that often accompany periods of credit restriction. In effect, one arm of the government provides a disguised loan to partially compensate for the withdrawal of credit by another, and, while this may be a necessary kind of safety valve, particularly where the degree of cutback in credit exceeds what might be described as official intent, it is not without its disadvantages. *

Discrimination against Those with Weaker Financial Standards

A second adverse consequence of inadequacy in the level of industrial financing that results from a cutback in previously prevailing levels can arise when the cutback is implemented (as it often is) by use of more stringent financial criteria, eliminating from eligibility for credits firms with financial standards weaker than those of some of their competitors, though not so weak that they would be unable to make the necessary repayments. Even among industrial projects there are many cases in which the ranking of projects according to financial criteria differs from the ranking according to economic criteria. Thus, credit cutbacks unaccompanied by special economic guidelines are likely to lead to a worsening of the allocation of credit in economic terms.

Discrimination against New Undertakings and Small Enterprises

Limitations in the availability of financing can be serious for all stages of industrialization—initiation of an activity, expansion, or rationalization—but the greatest potential for adversity may be in the initiation stage for new activities. This is because of their lack of an established record (making it difficult for them to obtain financing from commercial banks, which have little basis on which to judge the financial soundness of the firms) and also to their lack of profits from past periods, profits that might compensate to a degree, either directly or because of special tax treatment, for the lack of current profits. Financial opportunities certainly seem to be denied to new enterprises in greater proportion than is the case for those firms that have been in existence longer but have no more than comparable merit.

Small- and medium-scale enterprises are faced with the same kind of financing problems as those confronting Latin American industry as a whole, but with the additional factor that such smaller ac-

---

*Credit cutbacks larger in real terms than those intended might occur, for example, as a consequence of an unexpected acceleration in the rate of inflation.

tivities tend to have poorer access to financing (and to the technical assistance necessary to assure that the financing is productive) than industry as a whole. In part the poorer access is because of the fact that the small- and medium-scale group includes a larger proportion of new enterprises and in part it is because of the fact that the group includes a larger proportion of enterprises with only marginal economic prospects. In addition, however, the poorer access to credit and other financing is a result of being in an inferior market position —of being small entities confronting relatively large ones, of not having as effective means to solicit credit in more distant markets as do large enterprises (many of which may not be any more efficient in their operations or any more financially sound), or of not having sufficient information to be able to uncover the most advantageous financial market. It is desirable for economic reasons to provide some means of assisting the latter two groups to gain added (more nearly equal) access to financing, and it is often decided for political reasons to offer special consideration to the entire small- and medium-scale group, irrespective of the economic merits.

Little has been done to quantify the extent to which small- and medium-scale enterprises are confronted with special financing problems because of their size.[14] (The exception: it has been shown that interest rate ceilings on loans—the so-called usury laws—most hurt small and medium-sized firms by encouraging banks that would be willing to lend to higher risk firms at higher interest rates to simply eliminate most such higher risk firms from their portfolio.)[15] Moreover, although a wide variety of measures have been proposed and undertaken to assist small- and medium-scale industry, little has been done to estimate the relative cost effectiveness of the various approaches. Further consideration of the special problems of small- and medium-scale industry should not continue without quantitative work along both of these lines.

Working Capital Bottlenecks and the Anti-Labor-
Using Bias of Use-Specific Industrial Financing

One of the problems confronting industrialists is that while medium- to long-term financing may be readily available for certain purposes (notably the purchase of equipment), it is much less available for others (notably working capital). Economists have given attention to the problem of country-tied aid, but the cost of imperfectly transferable, use-tied financing has never been estimated (independent of country-tied financing). Tying industrial financing to its use in the purchase of capital goods tends to create a working capital bottleneck (which sometimes leads to an underutilization of the capital goods financing potential). Also, use-tied industrial financing sometimes discourages the utilization of more labor-using processes in situations in which they might be more efficient and the development of more labor-using adaptations of the processes imported from the highest wage, most capital-intensive economies. To verify these possibilities would require studies more complex than those used to estimate the cost of country-tied financing.

Consequences for the Efficiency of Plant Operations

Economists at Carnegie-Mellon University have shown that U.S. enterprises tend to eliminate slack and use resources more efficiently when confronted with difficulties, including difficulties in obtaining financing. [16] There is doubtless an inclination to eliminate slack when confronted by difficulties in Latin America as well. Surely, efforts are made to improve operations so that available funds can cope with needs. It is possible, however, that insofar as financing difficulties lead to an inability to obtain certain machinery or critical raw material inputs from abroad, firms may be confronted with additions to their cost structure rather than the reductions that would result from the elimination of slack. This is a question with important policy implications and should be subjected to empirical analysis. Under what circumstances do additions to costs in situations of adversity tend to cancel out reductions in costs emanating from the elimination of some slack?

Problems Arising from Inadequacies in the Terms of Industrial Financing

It is not possible to respond to the question of the adequacy of industrial financing without considering the terms of that financing—the interest rates or other payment for use of funds, the time period for repayment, the grace period, if any, and a variety of other matters including the extent to which the financing is tied to use in particular countries or for particular purposes. The relative importance of some of these terms varies greatly from one activity to another and, to a degree, from one place to another.* Interest rates are a less important determinant of investment for manufacturing industry than

---

*Also, the range between the terms available to best risk and greater risk firms also appears to vary from industry to industry in a number of countries.

for sectors such as construction or gas, water, and electric power supply; they are less important for industries with prospect for rapid growth in demand than for more traditional activities with slower growth potential. In economies characterized by high rates of inflation, the time period allowed for repayment is ordinarily more important than the rate of interest. (The potential subsidy from a long-term loan may be greater than the potential subsidy from a shorter-term loan with a lower interest rate.) In industries highly dependent on recently developed technology nothing may be so important as the countries in which the funds can be expended (the state of technology in the countries in which tied funds must be expended). In a situation characterized by heavy unemployment or underemployment, the most significant factor may be the extent to which the use of the funds is unrestricted and can be used for working capital as well as capital goods.

In order to evaluate the significance of the terms of industrial financing it is necessary to examine much more than the average interest rates, time repayment periods, and the like. Data on the cost of all forms of domestic and international financing should be considered in comparison with both the terms of financing available to other sectors of the economy in question and the relative terms available to industry in the most industrially advanced countries. Inasmuch as there is an element of disguised subsidy resulting from the negative real rates of interest, ex ante and ex post estimations of the subsidy component should be prepared, along with estimates as to whether (or under what circumstances) a given value of subsidy is more effective in stimulating response from industrialists if it takes the form of a lower-than-market interest rate, special tax treatment, technical assistance services, evening vocational training programs, subsector studies identifying investment alternatives (or evaluating process options), or the like.

Consequences of Inadequacies in the
Subsectoral Allocation of Industrial Financing

In addition to the consequences implicit in several of the aforementioned points, it should be noted that a number of the developments in industrial financing during the past two decades or so have had still other consequences for the sectoral composition of industrial activity. Domestic as well as foreign funds have been made available first for the funding of newly favored import-substitution industries and recently for export-oriented activities. Some traditional, home goods industries have suffered in absolute as well as relative terms. * The limited evidence available seems to suggest that the industries with the highest rates of return on their investments have been among the most successful in obtaining financing, but there is little evidence concerning the extent to which the ranking of financial rates of return corresponds to the ranking of economic rates of return.

There is another matter, moreover. In several countries a major influx of foreign investment has been followed by relatively great foreign exchange demands in the period immediately thereafter. This has sometimes precipitated a foreign exchange crisis that in turn has fostered a restrictive monetary policy to help stave off import demands and equilibrate the balance of payments. Insofar as such a credit squeeze ordinarily is not worldwide, the effect has been that the industries that are most dependent on financing from sources in their own country are most adversely affected. Even with respect to local financing, the agreements with large-scale projects in the newer industries are often longer-term than those in the more traditional industries, so that the latter often find themselves with a smaller portion of local financing in such a situation.

Finally, there appear to be some instances in which a branch of industry that faced serious difficulties in obtaining financing on a few occasions has found itself worse off than other industrial groups with ongoing difficulties. The explanation is simply that the latter sought out and ultimately located alternative, regularly available sources of financing at higher costs. Those with less frequent need for special assistance sometimes found themselves seriously constrained in countries with a weak structure of financial intermediaries.

Problems Relating to the
Location of Industrial Activity

Some leaders often insist that there is a need to undertake special measures to decentralize industrial activity or at least to promote

---

*The traditional activities have suffered in relative terms, in part because a relatively smaller portion of investment in those areas has been large enough to be attractive to foreign investment. This problem has been alleviated somewhat through the loans of the IDB, the World Bank, and the bilateral agencies to national and regional development banks for relending to smaller enterprises. International financing still is not readily available to activities seeking financing of more than $1 million but less than $3 million or $4 million.

the industrial development of more of the secondary communities of Latin America. Political forces as much as economic factors usually underlie such efforts, but there is no denying that the secondary metropolitan areas ordinarily lack adequate access to finance and a wide range of socioeconomic infrastructure. This is beginning to change. Government development banks are establishing branches in more communities and sending out industrial specialists to canvass opportunities. Regional financieras and even a few regional stock markets have been established. There are, of course, external economies that favor clusters of industrial activity and that constitute a case against extensive decentralization. Granting that, however, it must be acknowledged that there still is substantially less access to financing and to the often vital project preparation assistance outside of the leading industrial centers than would seem warranted, and the result may well be a greater geographic concentration of industry than is justifiable in economic terms.

NEW CHALLENGES FOR INDUSTRIAL FINANCING

The Higher Price of Energy

The dramatic rise in the price of petroleum (and, as a consequence, all other sources of energy) since late 1973 has had a multitude of implications for the industrial sector. Already prevailing problems of finance have been aggravated, and those countries with minimal energy resources have found themselves particularly hard hit. In addition, the countries from outside the region that had been the traditional suppliers of foreign investment and other foreign funding have been weakened financially. Those who have benefited internationally have, in most cases, been nations less associated with Latin America and less knowledgeable of the region's industry. Nor can the majority of the Latin American countries expect much in the way of additional financing assistance from those nations in the region that have been among the gainers (although Venezuela did provide notable assistance in the initial years of the crisis). The Latin American energy exporters plan to use the added resources primarily for their own development, and in any event the gains of those Western Hemisphere nations that have come out ahead are much smaller than the losses of the other members of the region, not to mention the losses of the countries that have been the traditional suppliers of finance from abroad. Beyond that, with the emphasis now being placed on basic needs and on low-income groups, there are reasons to believe that in the 1980s neither multilateral development programs nor private financing flows will be as oriented to industry as in the 1970s. A mea-

sure of assistance to help cope with the increased demands for financing that have resulted from the higher price of energy can be attained
through greater use of sector and subsector studies. Such analyses
may be employed not only in helping to identify projects that are
among the most profitable but also in ascertaining their energy requirements, indirect as well as direct; this would enable countries
with limited domestic sources of energy and serious balance-of-payments problems to select less energy-intensive alternatives from
among the potentially most profitable group of projects.

The Financing of Manufacturing Exports

Manufactured goods have become a significant component of
overall exports from Latin America in the last decade, and many
countries of the region are assigning an increasing importance to this
area. Initially, the subsidiaries of foreign-owned multinational firms
accounted for a tremendous share of manufactured exports, but Latin
American owned enterprises are gaining the industrial maturity and
export experience to figure more and more in this trade, and this
latter trend is likely to continue in the future for political as well as
economic reasons.

But the emergence of manufactured exports on a major scale
points up a problem; there is probably no other area in which the competition from abroad is keener than in the financing of manufacturing
exports. This is a relatively new field for Latin America. It first
received special attention in 1963/64, when Argentina and Brazil were
evincing signs of their new capacity to export manufactures, Mexico
was establishing its agency to finance industrial exports, and the Inter-American Development Bank was setting up the Program for Financing Interregional Exports of Capital Goods. Such facilities and
preshipment financing are critical elements in the competition for
export markets with producers from the industrially most advanced
nations, which are often backed by the low-cost, long-term export
financing schemes of their countries. In the years since, export financing arrangements have been established by Argentina, Brazil,
Colombia, Jamaica, and several other countries in the region. As
of early 1979, the IDB program, which is intended to be small and
catalytic in nature, had disbursed over $375 million. It is no longer
limited to interregional financing, and since 1977 the coverage has
been extended to all nontraditional exports, though capital goods still
account for more than 90 percent of the program. Another addition
to the field of Latin American export financing took place in 1978 with
the creation of the Banco Latinoamericano de Exportaciones (BLADEX)
by a group of commercial banks. BLADEX will deal in foreign bankers' acceptances in the Panamanian market.

Only a fifth of the manufacturing exports of Argentina, Brazil, and Mexico benefited from special governmental financing arrangements in the period 1970-73, and the proportion does not appear to have increased much since that time. With the possible exceptions of Jamaica and Colombia, the proportion is even lower in other Latin American countries. But the export of manufactures from Latin America suffered so strong a setback in 1974/75 that the value of such exports in constant dollars still may not have exceeded the 1974 totals as late as 1977 (though there does appear to have been a substantial rise in 1978). The real test for the financing of Latin American manufacturing exports still lies ahead.

Financing the Transfer, Modification,
and Development of Industrial Technology

The third of the major new financing challenges arises from the activities involving the transfer of technology and the emerging demand for the modification and even indigenous development of industrial technology. There is much more concern about technological change in Latin America than there was a decade ago. It is not that the regional lag is greater than before nor that the rate of industrial growth is lower than in the more advanced nations. There is, however, a greater awareness of the lag, combined with a desire for still more rapid rates of growth. The problem of technological needs is aggravated, moreover, by the change in the structure of productive activity from an essentially resource-based model to one that is relatively more technology-based—a change brought on partly by difficulties in exporting primary products and partly by other factors, including political ones, that have led to a greater emphasis on industrialization. *

There are additional concerns—first, with respect to the appropriateness of foreign techniques to factor scarcities in Latin America and, second, with respect to equity objectives, both in relation to

---

*The former export of agricultural products and other raw materials embodied a degree of technology equivalent to that in other producer countries in some cases and, in others, did not require as sophisticated a technology to establish a position of comparative advantage. Products that were needed or desired and that contained advanced technology were obtained by imports and paid for by the exchange earnings of exports. The approach admittedly focused on short-run solutions, and it probably will never be possible to state whether it involved long-run costs.

payments to those abroad who have developed much of the technology and to the employment opportunities for those most threatened by labor-saving processes.

To date, the technology inputs have emanated overwhelmingly from the more advanced nations and have been transmitted by means of licensing agreements and technical assistance programs and incorporated into capital goods, especially by direct foreign investments embodying all of these elements.[17] There have been contributions from the region, a few innovations, and a number of notable adaptations,[18] but they have not yet accounted for a major proportion of the technological inputs employed in Latin America.

Payments to foreigners for know-how are high and growing rapidly. In the absence of a more rapid rise in foreign demand for Latin American exports than has been seen in recent years, the region may soon be unable to find the foreign exchange to pay for all the technological inputs it desires. There is yet another problem. Prior to 1930, virtually all of the direct foreign investments, as well as the import of technical assistance, were oriented toward activities in which the region enjoyed a comparative advantage. Since those investments were made to develop exports, there was every incentive to employ the most appropriate technology. If the choice of techniques was limited and the dominant know-how for an activity was one based on an intensive use of factors other than those relatively abundant in the country in question, it generally did not prove advantageous to produce the commodity. In the 1950s and early 1960s, however, many Latin American governments singled out activities for development without attention to their comparative advantage position or potential. This phenomenon is no longer as serious a problem as in the early days of enthusiasm for import-substituting industrialization, but it has not disappeared altogether. To keep such protected activities technologically up to date poses new difficulties and new balance-of-payments burdens.

For a long time Latin American industry was relatively inclined to accept the technology that was being developed elsewhere in the world, and thus the problem of financing technology was no different than the general problem of financing industry; the technology that was sought came embodied in the new equipment or was transmitted in the form of know-how, as in turn-key operations. There was some modification of foreign technology, though only in the most advanced of the Latin American nations. Efforts to develop new technology were few, indeed, so that there was never really an independent question of how to finance technological development. Now the technological objectives have changed, and the changes will entail major expenditures. Several countries have taken out sizable loans from the Inter-American Development Bank and the World Bank for tech-

nological development, and various others are considering loan or
technical assistance requests, but these reflect only a small portion
of what is likely to be required.

CONCLUSIONS

1. While there have not been any serious efforts to define what
constitutes an adequate level of industrial financing, there are reasons to doubt that the level of industrial financing has been adequate
in recent years in most countries of Latin America.

2. Studies, reports, and other materials available on industrial financing in Latin America have not been developed in terms of
an economically meaningful methodology and have done little to point
out which branches of industry have been confronted with relatively
major financing problems or what the nature of those problems has
been.

3. One of the leading problem areas affecting almost all
branches of industry has been the financing of working capital. Working capital requirements are much higher in Latin America than in
more advanced industrial nations. First, there is a much greater
reliance upon suppliers credits, implying that even if the overall level
of industrial financing is adequate, there may be serious problems in
the allocation of industrial financing. Second, there is proportionately
much more inventory financing, yet few efforts have been undertaken
to define what constitutes optimal inventory levels (or optimal inventory financing) under various conditions, either from an economic or
a financial point of view. [19]

4. Economically sound long-term financial intermediation can
originate from sources other than organized stock and bond exchanges.
Such financing can emanate from government development banks and
private financieras, and indeed it may be unwise, in the short run,
to place major hopes on thin public equity markets (which are unlikely
to attract many more investors because of the continuing importance
of family control of enterprises, high debt/equity ratios, and the high
probability that in any given decade, government regulations may constrain profit opportunities in organized financial markets).

5. It is possible to sustain rapid industrial growth with a financial system that relies a great deal on medium-term financing and,
not insignificantly, on short-term credits that are rolled over. How
much more this costs an economy than installing a full-fledged, well-
organized public securities market in a financially underdeveloped
nation (or whether it does, in fact, entail higher economic costs at
early stages of industrialization) is not clear.

6. The proportion of industrial financing that comes from the
resources of the enterprises themselves is lower than it would be if

legal depreciation allowances kept pace with replacement costs. At the same time, the proportions indicated may well be understated due to the widespread underreporting of profits.

7. The problems of Latin American industrial financing are likely to be greater in the period ahead than they have been in the recent past because of (1) the higher price of energy and the new emphasis on the energy sector, (2) the manifest interest in exporting manufactures, (3) the new technological objectives, and (4) the increasing emphasis on Latin American ownership of Latin American industry. The altered market for international financing and the reawakened interest in agriculture also may play a role in increasing difficulties in the short- to medium-term period.

8. The need for serious studies of industrial financing can be illustrated by the simplified, but plausible, example in Table 8.5 of

TABLE 8.5

Plausible Consequences of a Foreign Recession on the Allocation of Industrial Financing

Sub-sector	Ranking in Terms of Economic Profitability		Probable Access to Financing from All Sources
	Long-term	Short-term	
A	1	2	Much more difficult than previously
B	2	1	Much more difficult than previously
C	4	4	Somewhat more difficult than previously
D	2	3	More difficult than previously

Note: Subsector A represents small firms with external financing dominantly from local banks and suppliers with a small proportion from financieras and none from abroad, good export opportunities, and a high economic rate of return. Subsector B represents small firms with financing sources as in Subsector A, limited export opportunities, and a high economic rate of return. Subsector C represents large firms with external financing from a large group of domestic banks with a substantial proportion from domestic financieras and from foreigners, as well as some from local stock market, limited export opportunities, and a low-middle level economic rate of return. Subsector D represents large firms with financing sources as in Subsector C, good export opportunities, but mainly of intrafirm type, and a fair economic rate of return.

the allocational consequences following a serious foreign recession (combined with the failure of local financing to expand sufficiently to offset the reduced foreign financing inflows). Four subsectors of industrial production are considered, all of which are assumed to have comparably good financial prospects in normal times.

It would take a great deal of space to explain the assessments of these differential effects of altered financing opportunities on the various subsectors. However, if the assessments can be assumed to be plausible in a reasonable number of such situations, then there may easily be a negative correlation between the economic potential of particular industries and the relative access to financing. Government policies might attempt to offset such tendencies, but if there is little idea as to where the economic damage is likely to occur, then public policy measures might even aggravate matters. All this is of particular import because Latin America's years of relatively easy access to industrial financing may be ending, and the cost of continuing to ignore the economic analysis of industrial financing in the years ahead may be even higher than in the last two decades.

PROPOSALS FOR A NEW APPROACH

Proposal A

The kind of data that are required to seriously analyze the current status of industrial financing in Latin America and that will be increasingly necessary in the future are more complicated than what is currently available. Such data are referred to in the second proposal. However, a good deal more can be done even with the limited data currently available. It is possible to provide a rough notion of industrial financing realities by turning first to the country-by-country data on industrial credits outstanding (available for most nations in the region) and to the data on industrial investment (available for only a few countries, unfortunately). In addition, data on the sources and uses of funds for manufacturing enterprises should be examined. The data on sources and uses of funds are now available for a number of countries, although only in a few cases, with separate breakdowns for the various branches of industry.

The industrial credit and investment data might be employed in the following manner: first, ratios might be prepared relating the overall level of industrial investment and industrial credit to such variables as GDP and industrial value added in each of two or three time periods (preferably with two or three years used for each time period calculation). Second, similar ratios might be prepared for the other major sectors of the economy and for each of the major branches of industry. Reference to these ratios and particularly to the differences in the trends of the various ratios would contribute to providing some first approximation gauge of the adequacy of industrial financing, relative to the current and past financing of other sectors and relative to recent financing of the industrial sector as well. The ratios also would provide a first approximation gauge of the relative adequacy of the financing for the major branches within the industrial sector. This rough gauge could then be fleshed out by reference to the shifts in the proportions of financing from different sources in recent years, which would be revealed by the sources and uses of funds data. Both the financing ratios and the sources and uses of funds proportions should be supplemented with discussions of the conditions in each of the major sectors of the economy and in each of the major branches of industry. The branch-by-branch breakdown would be important for understanding the consequences of major changes that might affect the various subsectors differently and limitations of market mechanisms or government credit allocations, which also might vary in effect according to the branch under consideration. The branch-by-branch data breakdowns and follow-up discussions are particularly important for drawing meaningful conclusions from the trends in the sources and uses of funds proportions because of the wide range in the proportions that different sources of financing have for the various industries and because of the tendency for some of those proportions to fluctuate significantly from year to year.

To help analyze foreign financing, ratios might be developed between total inflows of foreign funds and the industrial proportion of GDP or possibly between foreign financing and certain balance-of-payments variables. The analyses might consider not only the recent trend of various financing ratios but likely shifts in the ratios as well (with respect to the proportions of financing emanating from different sources). In addition, indication might be given of the levels of financing that would be necessary in order to maintain certain ratios of industrial finance to industrial value added or to attain different ratios that would represent what might be deemed to be more adequate levels of industrial financing. The analysis should give as much consideration to the various sources of the supply of financing as to the sources of the demand for financing. Finally, note might be taken of the situations of industries that tend to be especially affected by changes in the rates of inflation and of industries whose direct and indirect consumption of fuel is especially high and that thus might be expected to have been subjected to unusually large demands for financing during the period since 1974.

Proposal B

It must be recognized that the use of ratios of the type outlined above can serve only rather limited purposes. It would be desirable to develop new data that not only indicate the actual amounts of industrial financing granted to industry in a recent year (or expected to be granted in the year ahead) but that relate to the underlying supply and demand considerations determining the financing flows that are realized and recorded. Only by focusing on such factors can we do much to make the past work for us in helping to resolve future problems. What is needed, then, is to know something about the demand for industrial financing at various prices (that is, interest rates or other terms of financing) and something about the supply of financing that can be expected at various rates of return (real and nominal, as well, since some sources of financing may be subject to an appreciable measure of money illusion or at least an appreciable lag in fully adjusting to the rate of inflation).

Estimates of such supply and demand curves for industrial finance or, indeed, even good information on the shape of the demand curve for each major industry grouping and the shape of the supply curve for each major source of industrial finance would greatly facilitate the recognition of problem areas in advance. Having these data available would encourage the formulation of alternative strategies for dealing with many problems prior to their actual occurrence. In some cases this information might lead to solutions based primarily on measures that influence the supply of financing available or the supply available from particular sources; in other cases, analysis of the data might encourage measures intended primarily to influence the demand for industrial financing or the demand for financing from certain industries. Supply curves for some sources of financing might be constructed relatively easily. The task undoubtedly would be more difficult for other sources of financing, however, and for most demand estimates. But the need to have such data and to have them on a relatively disaggregated basis is clear. This need is underscored by the extraordinary range in the proportion that different sources of financing have for the various branches of industry and by the amount that these proportions fluctuate from year to year for some groups of industry.

Summary

The main point of these proposals is that the situation confronting Latin American industry has changed, and changed in such a way that it is imperative to analyze the question of industrial financing more thoroughly than has been done heretofore. To some extent this can be done by referring to certain data already available. Beyond that, however, new data relating to the underlying supply and demand factors should be generated. This should be done to assure that industry receives the level and type of financing that can be judged adequate in overall terms according to some clear standards and criteria. Equally as important, data revealing the underlying supply and demand factors should be developed so as to promote an awareness of the relative adequacy or efficiency of financing between the various branches of industry, thus facilitating any improvement that might be called for in the allocation of that financing within the industrial sector.

NOTES

1. The only broadly focused inquiry into the topic remains the report prepared for the Inter-American Development Bank in late 1969 and early 1970: Inter-American Development Bank, Analysis of the Possible Formation of a Regional Finance Corporation for the Expansion of Latin American Industry (Washington, D.C., 1970). Other references of note are United Nations, Economic Commission for Latin America, "The Financing of Industrial Expansion," in The Process of Industrial Development in Latin America (66/11/G/4), 1966, pp. 186-216; and the Inter-American Development Bank studies on capital markets in six countries, which were summarized in Antonín Basch and Milic Kybal, Capital Markets in Latin America: A General Survey and Six Country Studies (New York: Praeger, 1970).

2. In a review article on savings in developing countries, Mikesell and Zinser concluded merely that "aggregate saving is a function of a number of interdependent variables which together with saving propensities, determine the course of economic development." Raymond F. Mikesell and James E. Zinser, "The Nature of the Savings Function in Developing Countries: A Survey of the Theoretical and Empirical Literature," Journal of Economic Literature 11 (March 1973): 1-26. In other words, we are a long way from really understanding savings behavior in developing countries. An expanded version of this report is available in Spanish: Mikesell and Zinser, La naturaleza de la función ahorro en los países en desarrollo, (Mexico City: Centro de Estudios Monetarios Latinoamericanos, 1974).

3. United Nations, Economic Commission for Latin America, "The Financing of Industrial Expansion."

4. This summary draws heavily on Mario S. Brodersohn, "Financiamiento de empresas privadas y mercados de capital" (Paper presented to the Buenos Aires Symposium of the Organization of Amer

ican States (OAS) Program for the Development of Latin American Capital Markets, May 2-5, 1972); and Fundación de Investigaciones Económicas Latinoamericanas (FIEL), La financiación de las empresas industriales en la Argentina, 1961-69 (Buenos Aires, 1971). In addition, reference has been made to Banco Central de la República, Inversiones y fuentes de recursos, balances agregados y resultados de un conjunto de sociedades anónimas nacionales, 1955-1959, Suplemento del Boletín Estadístico, No. II, año IV, noviembre 1961; and David Eiteman, Financing Argentine Industrial Corporate Development (Buenos Aires, October 1969), which are among the principal other sources used by Brodersohn.

    5. See especially Amalio H. Petrei, "Rates of Return to Physical Capital in Manufacturing Industries in Argentina," Oxford Economic Papers 25 (November 1973): 378-404.

    6. See, for example, Hugh T. Patrick, "Finance, Capital Markets, and Economic Growth in Japan," in Financial Development and Economic Growth, ed. Arnold W. Sametz (New York: New York University Press, 1972). As Sametz has observed, "If there is one great lesson to be learned from Hugh Patrick's paper it is that weak capital market development does not inhibit very rapid economic development." Ibid., p. 2. (Perhaps the phrase "does not" ought to be replaced with "need not.")

    7. Brodersohn observes that in the period 1956-60, self-financing was one of the most important sources of funding, varying from 35 percent to as high as 57 percent in the years in which the law permitted asset revaluations. He maintains that the degree of reliance of Argentine enterprises on internal financing was not much greater than in the United States, England, and West Germany. "Financiamiento de empresas privadas," pp. 68-69. Later he adds that inasmuch as the savings effort of Argentine industrial enterprises is comparable to that of countries considered to be developed, it is to be hoped that some of the key financial indexes also would be similar, and he concludes that this is true. Ibid., p. 84.

    8. Consejo Federal de Inversiones and Instituto de Investigaciones Económicas Financieras de la Confederación General Económica, Programa conjunto para el desarrollo agropecuario e industrial (Buenos Aires, 1963), 1: 271.

    9. Banco Central de la República Argentina, "Inversiones y fuentes de recursos balances, años 1955-1959," reprint of Boletín estadístico, vol. 4, no. 2 (November 1961).

    10. Estimates by the Central Bank indicate that evasion of income taxes increased from 31 percent of the potential collection in 1952 to 43 percent in 1957. Banco Central de la República Argentina, "Estimaciones de la evasión fiscal en el impuesto a los réditos," Boletín estadístico, vol. 5, no. 1 (January 1962), appendix 2, pp. 53-

57. Although the rate of tax evasion was considerably lower among corporations (which were relatively more important for industry than for the economy as a whole), the rate of increase in corporate tax evasion exceeded that for the economy as a whole.

11. Fernando Tow concluded that tax evasion of personal income taxes rose from 50 percent in 1952-57 to 75 percent in 1959 and still further by 1967. Tow, "Una contribución al estudio de la evasión al impuesto a los réditos personales en la Argentina," Jornadas de finanzas públicas, vol. 3 (Córdoba, 1970).

12. This data, based on FIEL, La financiación de las empresas industriales en la Argentina, deals with sources of funds net of depreciation.

13. Other comparisons of this type for 1961-66 can be found in ibid., 4: 1-29. It is noted, for example, that while bank credits during this period averaged 30 percent of the external financing sources of the industrial corporations sampled, the proportions varied from less than 1 percent in petroleum derivatives and 3 percent in nonelectric machinery to 88 percent in basic metals and 80 percent in rubber. Suppliers credits ranged from 1 to 3 percent in tobacco and basic metals to 55 to 74 percent in petroleum derivates, nonelectric machinery, foodstuffs, textiles, and transport equipment. (A scatter diagram of the information referred to indicates that the data points are not normally distributed.)

14. For a discussion of financing small industry in Peru that contains some data on the sources of initial investment and of subsequent financing, see Máximo Vega Centeno, "El financiamiento de la pequeña industria" (Paper presented to the Organization of American States Symposium on Capital Markets in Lima, Peru, December 1972), pp. 23-25, 30.

15. Ernesto V. Feldman and Samuel Itzcovich, "Estructura financiera y concentración bancaria: el caso argentino," Económica, University of La Plata, Argentina, 17 (January-April 1971): 43-73.

16. See especially R. M. Cyert and J. R. March, A Behavioral Theory of the Firm (Englewood Cliffs, N.J.: Prentice-Hall, 1963).

17. For a stimulating review with respect to Brazil, see Nuno F. de Figueiredo, A transferência de tecnologia no desenvolvimento industrial do Brasil (Rio de Janeiro: IPEA/INPES, 1972).

18. See Jorge Katz, Importación de tecnología, aprendizaje local e industrialización dependiente (Mexico: Fondo de Cultura Económica, 1976), especially the three dozen documents in the IDB/ECLA Program of Research in Science and Technology, summarized in Katz, "Cambio tecnológico, desarrollo económico y las relaciones intra- y extraregionales de la América Latina" (Buenos Aires, August 1978).

19. For an initial effort, see Francisco Thoumi, "La utilización del capital fijo en la industria manufacturera colombiana," Revista de planeación y desarrollo, vol. 10, no. 3 (September-December 1978).

9
THE DEVELOPMENT AND FINANCING OF SMALL-SCALE INDUSTRY IN BRAZIL

William G. Tyler

INTRODUCTION: ECONOMIC SETTING

The key to Brazilian economic growth in the past 20 years has been rapid industrial expansion. During that period industrial output has increased by an annual average of about 9 percent. This industrial growth has been fostered by the Brazilian government through a myriad of commercial, credit, and fiscal policies, along with direct governmental productive activity in a few key sectors such as electric energy, chemicals, and steel. Although not explicit, the emphasis in policy has been on large industrial operations. Substantial resources have been marshaled in the formation of public industrial firms, and the operations of these firms, without exception, have been large scale once established. Another dimension of the Brazilian industrialization strategy has been to create a hospitable environment for transnational firms to encourage their establishment and increased output in Brazil. Like the public firms, transnational firms tend to be large. In addition to an implicit emphasis on public and transnational firm activities, the effect of industrial policy, operating through various government programs, has been to promote large-scale enterprises. Those firms best organized and equipped to take advantage of the incentive programs have tended to be large enterprises.

The author expresses his gratitude to the World Bank for its support for the study on which this chapter is based. He is particularly grateful to Xavier Simon, whose comments and counsel proved invaluable. In addition, the author benefited from the suggestions and assistance of Frederico Robalinho de Barros, Henrique Rattner, Marina Carvalho, and Roberto Fernandes Goncalves. Thanks go to all of the above. The normal caveats apply.

141

The economic effects of Brazilian industrial policies have been well documented.[1] Besides promoting impressive industrial growth, numerous distortions have resulted. Relatively little labor absorption has occurred in manufacturing, and the industrial sector that has emerged after a period of continuing intense industrial growth is relatively capital intensive. The much debated, observed increased inequality in relative income shares in part must be seen as a reflection of the type of industrialization pursued. Clearly the emphasis on large capital-intensive industrial projects and enterprises has exacerbated the situation.

That small and medium-sized enterprises (SME) have been largely bypassed by Brazilian industrialization policy has gradually come to be recognized in many governmental quarters. To offset the bias in favor of large-scale enterprise a number of specific programs for SME have been initiated in recent years. Aside from some special credit programs, to be discussed later in this chapter, the main expression of governmental concern for the problems and role of SME has been the establishment of the Brazilian Center for Assistance to Small and Medium-Sized Enterprise (Centro de Brasileiro de Apoio à Pequena e Média Empresa, or CEBRAE).

This chapter will discuss the role of SME in the Brazilian economy, examining SME participation in total industrial value added and employment. Sectoral, as well as regional, differences between SME and large enterprises will be analyzed along with differences in productivity and capital intensity. In the section on growth of SME, attention will be devoted to the performance of SME over time. The reasons for success and failure are treated separately in the section examining the problems evident with SME in Brazil. The following section will concentrate on the existing institutional arrangements for providing financing to Brazilian SME. The final section contains a summary and concluding remarks.

The definition of SME is necessarily an arbitrary one. In Brazil various definitions exist. While a <u>micro</u> enterprise is commonly thought of as one having less than ten employees, exactly what constitutes a <u>small</u> or <u>medium</u>-sized enterprise is subject to a wide range of operational and other interpretations, employing different types of criteria. For example, for the Central Bank an SME is one having annual sales up to 85,000 times a standard reference value (MVR) equal to Cr$1,150.70 in 1978; in June 1978 this meant a firm with annual sales up to U.S.$5.5 million qualified as an SME.* The National Development Bank (BNDE) considers an SME as any establishment hav-

---

*In December 1977 the cruzeiro-dollar exchange rate was Cr$16.05 = U.S.$1.00; by June 1978 it was Cr$17.60 = U.S.$1.00.

ing fixed assets plus the projected investment up to 500,000 times the value of the readjustable treasure bond (ORTN), the latter being equal to Cr$263 in June 1978. Thus to qualify for BNDE as an SME, the firm's fixed assets plus intended investments could total up to U.S.$7.5 million. CEBRAE, while employing both criteria involving sales and employment totals, has maintained a more operationally flexible definition by stressing qualitative criteria such as the organization of the firm, market conditions, and the relationship between owner and employees. Recognizing the importance of sectoral differences, CEBRAE has sought to be pragmatic in its provision of assistance to SME. It should be noted, however, that, in general, what constitutes an SME for CEBRAE is much smaller than for either the Central Bank or BNDE.

For the purpose of our analysis we will employ a definitional criterion widely used by Brazilian observers analyzing official census data. An enterprise is considered small if it employs less than 100 persons, medium-sized if it employs between 100 and 249 individuals, and large if it employs more than 250 persons. An alternative definition could just as easily have been chosen; the results of the analysis, however, could not differ appreciably in their import.

PARTICIPATION OF SME IN
BRAZILIAN MANUFACTURING

The primary statistical sources for analyzing the participation of SME in the Brazilian industrial sector are the industrial censuses undertaken by the Brazilian Geographic and Statistical Institute (IBGE). The most recent available census information is for 1970.* Table 9.1 summarizes the participation of small, medium-sized, and large enterprises in total Brazilian manufacturing.[2] As to be expected, small firms account for the lion's share of the total number of manufacturing enterprises. In 1970 nearly 98 percent of all such enterprises employed less than 100 individuals.

---

*A later industrial census was conducted for 1975. As of July 1978, the results were not yet available. It is doubtful, however, that there has been observed much change in the relative importance of SME. Using the 1970 IBGE industrial census data provides another important advantage. The published census data, because of some omissions and incomparabilities, are not particularly suitable for the type of analysis depicted in Table 9.1. CEBRAE, however, has had IBGE undertake some special computations from the census tapes. CEBRAE has been kind enough to make these special tabulations available, and it is these data that have been employed in our analysis.

TABLE 9.1

Participation of Small, Medium-Sized, and Large Enterprises in Brazilian Manufacturing, 1970

Firm Size^c	Number of Establishments (N)		Value of Production (X)		Employment^a (L)		Salaries and Wages (W)		Taxes,^b Percent of Total	Value Added (VA)		Value Added per Employee (VA/L) (thousands of cruzeiros)	Average Salary per Employee (W/L) (thousands of cruzeiros)
	Number	Percent	Millions of Cruzeiros	Percent	Number	Percent	Millions of Cruzeiros	Percent		Millions of Cruzeiros	Percent		
Small													
1-4	87,555	61.7	4,114.0	4.6	199,624	9.6	271.8	2.9	1.9	1,574.4	3.9	7.89	1.36
5-19	38,364	27.4	9,875.1	11.0	343,916	16.6	1,045.3	11.3	6.9	4,146.7	10.3	12.06	3.04
20-99	12,245	8.6	19,584.7	21.9	499,670	24.1	2,118.0	22.8	16.6	8,705.2	21.5	17.42	4.24
Total	138,164	97.7	33,573.8	37.5	1,043,210	50.3	3,435.1	37.0	25.3	14,426.3	35.7	13.83	3.14
Medium	2,035	1.4	15,079.3	16.8	313,168	15.1	1,501.8	16.2	15.2	6,777.2	16.8	21.64	4.80
Large	1,213	0.9	40,961.6	45.7	718,533	34.6	4,339.1	46.8	59.5	19,210.1	47.5	26.74	6.04
Total^d	142,110	100.0	89,621.9	100.0	2,074,911	100.0	9,276.0	100.0	100.0	40,486.5	100.0	19.48	4.47

^a Includes all economically active personnel.
^b These taxes are the ICM and IPI.
^c Measured by number of workers.
^d The totals may differ slightly from the sums of the listed components because of rounding and some data omission.

Source: Special IBGE tabulations from the 1970 economic census made for CEBRAE.

144

In terms of either total output or value added small firms were also seen to be significant. In 1970, 36 percent of all manufacturing value added was provided by small enterprises. It is clear, however, that large enterprises were the most important in contributing to total output, tax collections, and manufacturing value added.

Small enterprises occupy a special importance when it comes to employment generation. Table 9.1 indicates that 50 percent of all Brazilian manufacturing employment was in small enterprises in 1970. Of that amount—equal to over 1 million workers—approximately one-half was in very small enterprises, those with less than 20 employees. The conclusion of this analysis is inescapable. Small manufacturing enterprises are extremely important in providing employment in Brazil.

As seen in Table 9.1, small enterprises accounted for 37 percent of the total 1970 salaries and wages paid in Brazilian manufacturing. Comparing this figure with the 50 percent share of small enterprises in manufacturing employment, it is evident that salaries and wages per worker are lower in small enterprises than in larger enterprises. Average salaries and wages have been computed for different-sized establishments and are listed in the last column of Table 9.1. It is apparent that as establishment size increases, average salaries and wages increase. In the very smallest category, that is, establishments with one to four workers, there is a tendency to understate actual labor remuneration because frequently the owner and his immediate family, while counted as workers if so engaged, do not actually receive wage payments. Even discounting these establishments, there is nevertheless a clear increase in average labor remuneration with increases in establishment size. This can be interpreted as an increase in skilled labor requirements accompanying an increase in establishment size. Small enterprises employ more in the way of unskilled labor than do larger enterprises. Not only do small firms employ more labor than larger establishments, but they also contribute more to absorbing Brazil's excess supply of unskilled labor.

Disaggregating the manufacturing sector by industry, there are evident some important differences. Small enterprises are much more important in some industries than others. Table 9.2 presents information on the participation of small, medium-sized, and large establishments in the total employment and value added of 21 manufacturing industries. In terms of providing a large share of total industry employment, small establishments are especially important in the following industries: lumber and wood (84 percent of industry employment), furniture (81 percent), miscellaneous (70 percent), nonmetallic mineral manufacturing (60 percent), food products (61 percent), printing and publishing (60 percent), plastics (59 percent), and leather (57 percent). A similar picture emerges when the small es-

TABLE 9.2

Participation of Small, Medium-Sized, and Large Enterprises in Total Industry Employment and Value Added, by Industry, 1970
(in percent)

Industry	Establishments			Employment			Value Added		
	Small	Medium	Large	Small	Medium	Large	Small	Medium	Large
Mining	97.2	1.3	0.8	43.0	12.6	44.4	22.1	10.2	57.6
Total manufacturing	97.2	1.4	0.9	50.3	15.1	34.6	35.7	16.8	47.5
Nonmetallic minerals	99.2	0.5	0.3	69.0	8.5	12.5	39.4	13.3	27.3
Metallurgy	95.2	3.0	1.8	40.5	17.6	41.9	26.5	14.8	58.7
Machinery	94.0	3.7	2.3	39.0	19.1	39.1	39.9	19.7	40.4
Electric and communication equipment	90.4	5.7	3.9	28.9	18.8	52.3	21.7	18.7	59.6
Transportation equipment	94.2	3.0	2.8	25.3	10.2	64.5	13.1	6.4	70.5
Lumber and wood	99.3	0.6	0.1	84.2	10.6	5.2	81.1	12.6	6.3
Furniture	99.3	0.6	0.1	81.9	11.0	7.1	72.5	15.9	10.6
Paper	89.0	7.8	3.2	37.6	25.1	37.3	30.3	25.0	45.0
Rubber	95.8	2.5	1.7	43.3	13.2	43.5	24.0	7.3	68.7
Leather	97.5	1.8	0.6	57.2	18.6	24.2	46.0	22.0	32.0
Chemicals	93.3	4.3	2.3	36.0	17.6	46.4	26.1	17.9	56.0
Drugs	86.9	6.9	5.3	31.2	21.2	47.6	21.7	27.3	50.9
Perfumery and soaps	97.0	1.9	1.0	50.8	21.5	37.7	32.2	18.8	49.0
Plastics	95.7	3.3	1.0	58.7	19.4	21.9	40.6	23.5	35.9
Textiles	88.6	5.5	5.9	23.6	15.1	61.3	28.1	14.4	57.5
Apparel and shoes	97.1	2.1	0.8	56.4	18.8	24.8	44.2	19.7	31.3
Food	98.8	0.7	0.4	61.3	15.6	23.1	52.2	21.6	26.2
Beverages	98.1	1.2	0.6	53.9	17.3	28.8	34.3	26.6	39.1
Tobacco	77.0	7.2	15.8	8.2	12.0	79.8	1.9	3.1	95.0
Printing and publishing	98.0	1.4	0.6	59.8	15.0	25.2	49.8	14.5	35.7
Miscellaneous	98.2	1.2	0.6	69.7	13.4	16.9	66.4	15.7	17.9

Note: Percentages may not add up to 100 because of rounding and the omission of undeclared data.

Source: Special IBGE tabulations from 1970 economic census made for CEBRAE.

tablishment share of industry value added is examined; the same industries possess high shares for small enterprises.

While some industries are important for having a large participation by small establishments, there are other industries, generally far more concentrated in market structure, where large firms predominate, accounting for very large shares of either total industry employment or value added. The most striking example of this is the highly concentrated tobacco industry, with 95 percent of industry value added being produced in large establishments. Although less dramatic, other industries such as transportation equipment, rubber, chemicals, and electrical machinery are dominated by large establishments.

With some exceptions, the regional distribution of small, medium-sized, and large establishments roughly parallels that for the country as a whole. It should be noted, however, that the regional distribution of manufacturing as a whole is highly concentrated geographically, with three Center-South states (São Paulo, Rio de Janeiro, and Minas Gerais) accounting for 79 percent of total Brazilian manufacturing value added in 1970. The problematic and low-income Northeast, today an area with an estimated 34 million inhabitants, accounted for only 6 percent of Brazilian manufacturing output in 1970 (see Table 9C.2). At the same time, however, since the Northeast's share of total manufacturing establishments is larger than its share of manufacturing output or employment, the establishments in the Northeast tend to be smaller on the average.

Table 9.3, a counterpart of Table 9.1, has been prepared for analysis of the participation of small, medium-sized, and large manufacturing establishments in the Northeast. Three northeastern states have been selected: Pernambuco, Bahia, and Ceará. Together these three most industrialized northeastern states accounted for 76 percent of total northeastern manufacturing value added in 1972, but for only 4 percent of the national total. In the three selected northeastern states, small establishments demonstrated similar shares of employment and value added to the national totals. As shown, small establishments accounted for 98 percent of total establishments, 50 percent of employment, 39 percent of total production value, 24 percent of taxes collected, and 37 percent of value added. See also Tables 9C.3, 9C.4, and 9C.5.

Comparing Tables 9.1 and 9.3, it is evident that average manufacturing salaries are lower in the Northeast than for the country as a whole. In addition to indicating some differences in labor market conditions between regions, the average wage disparity suggests a product composition favoring less skilled labor usage in the Northeast. Table 9.4 examines the extent to which the regional wage differences reflect a product mix phenomenon. Focusing on the three most important manufacturing industries in the Northeast—food products, textiles,

TABLE 9.3

Participation of Small, Medium-Sized, and Large Enterprises in Manufacturing for Three Northeastern States, 1970

Firm Size[d]	Number of Establishments (N)		Value of Production (X)		Employment[a] (L)		Salaries and Wages (W)			Taxes,[b] Percent of Total	Value Added (VA)		Value Added per Employee (VA/L) (thousands of cruzeiros)	Average Salary per Employee[c] (W/L) (thousands of cruzeiros)
	Number	Percent	Millions of Cruzeiros	Percent	Number	Percent	Millions of Cruzeiros	Percent	N_w		Millions of Cruzeiros	Percent		
Small														
1-4	10,448	66.9	278.6	4.9	25,817	14.1	19.2	3.5	7,054	1.3	117.2	4.9	4.54	1.10
5-19	4,032	25.8	746.1	13.1	35,592	17.9	59.7	10.8	3,876	6.2	296.0	12.4	9.08	1.91
20-99	814	5.2	1,202.6	21.2	33,315	18.3	106.7	19.2	823	16.3	471.7	19.8	14.16	3.17
Total	15,294	98.0	2,227.3	39.2	94,724	50.3	185.6	33.5	11,753	23.8	884.3	37.1	9.64	2.63
Medium	195	1.2	1,151.8	20.3	26,873	14.8	109.3	19.7	170	16.5	446.9	18.7	16.63	4.66
Large	99	0.6	2,305.0	40.5	63,695	34.9	259.6	46.8	99	59.7	1,052.2	44.1	16.52	4.08
Total[e]	15,609	100.0	5,684.1	100.0	182,292	100.0	554.7	100.0	12,022	100.0	2,384.4	100.0	13.08	3.95

[a] Includes all economically active personnel.

[b] These taxes are the ICM and the IPI.

[c] Since the sample size for employment and salaries differed, an adjustment was made to reflect the average for the size group. The resultant average salary was computed as $W/L \cdot N/N_w$.

[d] Measured by number of workers.

[e] The totals may differ slightly from the sums of the listed components because of rounding and some data omission.

Note: The three northeastern states are Pernambuco, Bahia, and Ceará. These are the largest and most economically important states.

Source: Special IBGE tabulations from the 1970 economic census made for CEBRAE.

TABLE 9.4

Comparison of Value Added per Employee and Average Wages
between Brazil and Three Northeastern States for the Food
Products, Textiles, and Apparel Industries, 1970
(thousands of cruzeiros)

| Industry and Size* | Value Added per Employee | | Average Wages | |
	Brazil	Three North-east-ern States	Brazil	Three North-east-ern States
Food products				
Small	15.15	9.16	2.39	1.88
1-4	10.79	5.51	1.39	1.20
5-19	14.24	9.84	2.38	1.77
20-99	21.39	15.16	3.63	2.46
Medium	24.62	15.64	3.79	3.40
Large	20.34	12.16	3.73	2.60
Textiles				
Small	16.97	18.38	3.65	2.37
1-4	10.73	4.75	1.85	1.35
5-19	15.91	24.44	3.25	2.38
20-99	17.79	18.01	3.94	2.43
Medium	13.60	8.27	3.92	2.07
Large	13.36	9.45	3.66	3.06
Apparel				
Small	9.62	5.98	2.92	2.18
1-4	7.56	3.65	1.57	1.59
5-19	8.91	5.15	2.81	1.59
20-99	10.49	8.95	3.28	2.29
Medium	11.62	8.70	3.49	2.71
Large	13.97	13.59	3.34	2.57

*Measured by number of employees.

Note: The three northeastern states are Pernambuco, Bahia, and Ceará. These are the largest and most economically important states.

Source: Special IBGE tabulations from the 1970 economic census made for CEBRAE.

and apparel—it can be seen that the average wages for Brazil are still considerably higher than for the Northeast. Even in the Northeast, however, small establishments pay lower average wages than larger establishments, indicating that also in the Northeast small enterprises employ proportionally more unskilled labor.

The question of capital intensity for small versus large enterprises is one of direct relevance to any lending program designed to promote SME. The normal contention is that small firms are less capital intensive than larger firms and that therefore the capital cost per job created via an investment program for SME is lower than it would be in the case of larger enterprise investments.[3] Such is the case for Brazil. The analysis is rendered somewhat precarious because of the absence of reliable fixed assets data in the industrial census. First, to analyze the factor intensity of small, medium-sized, and large establishments a proxy for fixed capital assets has necessarily been employed. It can be noted in both Tables 9.1 and 9.3 that the ratio of value added to employees increases with the size of establishments. This ratio, indicative of labor productivity, reflects the use of capital on the part of individual establishments. The greater the use of capital, on a per worker basis, the greater the value added per employee.* Thus, the differences in value added per employee between small and large establishments, for both Brazil and the three northeastern states, indicate that small establishments are less capital intensive than larger establishments. In both cases—Brazil and the Northeast—the ratio VA/L for large establishments is nearly twice as high as for small establishments. Nothing definite about total factoral productivity or technical efficiency can be concluded from the measure of value added per employee. A firm employing much in the way of capital, as expressed by a high VA/L ratio, may nevertheless display a low productivity in the use of its capital. In the very small establishments, that is, those with one to four workers, the value

---

*The use of value added per employee as a proxy for capital intensity (that is, the K/L ratio) necessarily implies that there are no systematic differences in the average productivity of capital over firms. This can be seen in the tautology:

$$VA/L = VA/K \cdot K/L$$

If more capital-intensive firms systematically exhibited lower average capital productivity (that is, lower VA/K), it is possible that there is no difference in the VA/L ratio. In our case we have no reason to believe that small establishments demonstrated appreciably lower average productivities for capital.

added per employee was even lower. It should be further noted that in the Northeast, manufacturing in general is less capital intensive than for the entire country.

Second, to arrive at some current estimates as to the investment cost per job created, two different approaches were followed. The first procedure involved the fitting of values to an assumed production function possessing a Cobb-Douglas functional form. This procedure requires (1) the specification of the Cobb-Douglas functional form for the production function,* (2) profit-maximizing behavioral assumptions on the part of firms, (3) observations concerning the parameter values of the production function for small manufacturing enterprises, and (4) observations concerning factor prices. This procedure is outlined, along with the necessary assumptions, in Appendix A. Although a range of estimates of the fixed capital cost per job created in small enterprises was generated, our best estimate using this procedure is around U.S.$4,000 per job created. This should be considered an average, as there are likely to be sectoral differences.

The second approach in estimating the fixed capital cost of each job created is to examine the observed results of existing SME lending programs in Brazil. In this regard, two separate strands of evidence were examined. First, the Bank of the Northeast's (BNB) Program of Financing for Small and Medium Industry has been in operation since 1967, during which time it has extended loans involving investments of Cr$1,745 million (in 1977 prices) in some 958 lending operations. An estimated 13,982 new jobs were created by these loans. Accordingly, it has been estimated that the average cost of a new job created through this program has been Cr$125,000 (in December 1977 prices) or approximately U.S.$7,800.[4] There are two difficulties apparent with this estimate. The investment cost is overstated since the numerator includes working capital as well as fixed capital. On the other hand, the estimate of employment generated (in the denominator) is probably overstated. This information was pro forma data supplied by the borrower at the time a loan application was made. The tendency in such cases is to exaggerate the expected increase in employment for the borrowing firm.

A second strand of evidence from lending programs relating to the capital cost of job creation in small-scale enterprise (SSE) is from CEBRAE-affiliated financing programs for micro enterprises. An analysis of two such programs in the very disparate states of Rio

---

*A more general functional form could be employed at the cost of some simplicity and additional necessary assumptions. The Cobb-Douglas functional form, however, does not appear to be unduly unreasonable, given a growing body of supporting empirical evidence.

Grande de Sul and Piauí revealed average lending costs per job created in 1977 of Cr$40,000 and Cr$39,000, respectively. This amounted to approximately U.S.$2,500 per job. This amount considers only the investment made by the borrowing firm and not the administrative costs of lending to the firm incurred by the lending agency or technical assistance affiliates. Moreover, since the U.S.$2,500 figure is for micro enterprises, it can reasonably be expected that the fixed capital costs per job created for small enterprises in general will be somewhat higher. Looking at these programs and the BNB program estimates in conjunction with our estimates from the production function analysis, the latter best estimate (U.S.$4,000) appears to be both consistent and reasonable.

THE GROWTH OF SME IN BRAZIL

The past 25 years in Brazil has been a period of substantial economic growth. As noted, the industrial sector has spurred such growth. Accordingly, it is logical to expect that manufacturing firms have expanded, their numbers have increased, and their productivity has grown. Whether or not different-sized firms experience similar growth performances, however, is another question. To examine the performance of small, medium-sized, and large establishments over time in Brazil a comparison has been made between the 1950 and 1970 industrial censuses. The basic results of this comparison are presented in Table 9.5. The total number of industrial enterprises increased by 74 percent during the period. Since the number of small enterprises increased by about the same percentage (73 percent), their share of the total number of industrial enterprises remained roughly the same. Medium-sized enterprises grew the most rapidly over the 1950-70 period, suggesting, in part, that some of the small enterprises grew into medium-sized establishments.*
The growth of industrial employment in Brazil between 1950 and 1970 was 74 percent, as seen in Table 9.5. For small enterprises the proportional growth was the same, indicating no change in their share of total industrial employment. The greatest observed absolute employment growth occurred in medium-sized establishments.
Examining value-added growth, the disparities are more uneven. As in the case of employment and the number of establishments, medium-sized establishments enjoyed the greatest absolute increase

---

*It should be noted that medium-sized establishments have been defined in Table 9.5 to encompass larger firms than before, that is, those establishments having between 100 and 499 persons employed.

TABLE 9.5

Percentage Growth of Small, Medium-Sized, and Large Industrial Enterprises, 1950-70

Size	Number of Establishments	Employment	Value Added	Value Added per Establishment	Value Added per Employee
Small	73.2	72.5	85.4	7.0	7.5
Medium	95.3	94.2	172.7	39.6	40.3
Large	67.3	53.2	144.4	46.1	59.6
Total	73.7	73.0	127.6	31.1	31.6

Notes: Small, medium-sized, and large establishments were classified as follows: small, 1-99 persons employed; medium, 100-499 persons employed; large, more than 500 persons employed.

Current price value-added data were deflated by the wholesale industrial price index. Although this procedure has somewhat understated the growth of real value added, the understatement has affected the small, medium-sized, and large categories in the same way. Therefore, the observed relative changes among categories are unaffected by an understatement of real income growth.

Source: Computations based upon IBGE data as published in the industrial censuses.

in value added—172.7 percent between 1950 and 1970, while that for large establishments was slightly lower at 144.4 percent. On the other hand, growth in value added per establishment for small establishments was quite modest during the period—only 7 percent.

In great part the slow growth in value added per establishment for small enterprises reflects their slow growth in labor productivity. Value added per employee for small establishments grew by only 7.5 percent for the entire 1950-70 period. This suggests that little in the way of capital deepening took place for small firms. These firms have remained labor intensive. On the other hand, labor productivity grew significantly in medium-sized and large establishments. In the latter, the 20-year growth in value added per employee was 59.6 percent, equal to a simple annual average growth rate of 3 percent. This suggests an increase in capital intensity, especially in large establishments.

In examining the different performance of small and large establishments over time, the question arises as to what can explain the observed disparities in growth. In great part, the answer lies in the economic policies pursued by the Brazilian government over the past 25 years. Economic policy has favored the growth and establishment of large firms and has essentially, although to a great degree inadvertently, discriminated against SSEs. This inherent discrimination can be seen in several ways.

First, the industries promoted by Brazilian economic policy, along import substitution lines, have been those that tend to be universally the most concentrated and, in general, the least suitable for SSE. Responding to differential incentives and resource pulls introduced by economic policy, the composition of Brazilian industrial output has changed in favor of those industries where SSEs tend to be least important. The highest rates of industrial growth during the last 25 years have occurred in metallurgy, electrical machinery and communications equipment, transportation equipment, chemicals, rubber, drugs, and machinery.[5] In other countries, as well as in Brazil, these industries appear to be the least conducive to SSE activities.[6] Industrial strategy has promoted the rapid growth of these industries over the last 25 years. These rapid growth industries are also those where public firms and transnational corporations have exercised their greatest role and where such firms tend to account for large shares of output and output growth. As noted previously, these firms tend to be large.

Industries that possess a higher participation of small enterprises with respect to value added and employment have tended to grow more slowly. These industries include food products, apparel and footwear, furniture, lumber, printing and publishing, and nonmetallic mineral manufacturing. By and large, import substitution in these industries had been complete by 1950, implying that further increases in demand had come either from domestic market expansion or exports. The domestic market did not grow dramatically for the products of these industries, and manufactured exports were discriminated against rather substantially until the late 1960s. Had the constellation of economic policy been more open, that is, export oriented, in the 1950s and early 1960s, the composition of industrial output would have most certainly undergone a change more conducive to SSE activities. Brazil possesses a natural comparative advantage in lumber and wood products, leather goods, furniture, apparel and footwear, and many food products, and these industries display a large participation on the part of SSE.

Second, in addition to looking at the overall industrialization strategy and the resultant change in Brazil's industrial output composition, individual policies can also be examined and shown to be discriminatory against SSE. One commonly used policy instrument to spur industrial development has been fiscal incentives. A firm's tax liability is reduced if the firm engages in designated practices such as investment in certain indicated activities or geographical regions. By and large, SSEs do not have the administrative ability to take advantage of such programs nor do they possess sufficient size to render the tax breaks in fact attractive.

Aside from commercial and exchange policies, a la protection, affecting the relative profitability in different sectors and therefore the distribution of investable resources, the main policy instrument by which industrial investment has itself been promoted has been credit incentives and subsidies. Investment has been heavily subsidized through the availability of credit at low, or negative, real rates of interest. This has particularly been the case in those sectors favored by policy makers such as the so-called dynamic manufacturing industries. The result of the credit incentives has been twofold: (1) the more capital-intensive manufacturing sectors have grown the fastest, and (2) more capital-intensive technology has been selected in all sectors for the firms (projects) able to avail themselves of the subsidized credits. While promoting substantial industrial investment and growth, this policy has greatly exacerbated Brazil's labor absorption problem. It is interesting to speculate as to what type of industrial profile would have emerged in Brazil had labor use been subsidized instead of the use of capital.

The credit incentive schemes, financed through a multitude of different programs and institutions, have in large part bypassed SSE. This, in fact, can be considered a redeeming feature. Consequently, SSE has remained labor intensive, as was seen in Table 9.5. The distortions visited upon the Brazilian industrial sector as a result of distortions imposed in factor markets through economic policy have left

SSE largely untouched. Small enterprises have simply not been able to obtain large amounts of subsidized credits. Their partial exclusion from the official credit and banking system has made it impossible to reach SSE with subsidized credits in the absence of special programs designed to do so, and such programs have not existed in a meaningful way. Moreover, small firms have not been in a position to take advantage of exchange rate incentives to import capital equipment at overvalued exchange rates with tariff exemptions. Again, the effect has been largely beneficial in that it has prevented the growth and emergence of a capital-intensive SSE sector.

Despite the discriminatory dimensions in Brazilian economic policy designed to promote industrial development and the absence, at least until recently, of any special programs attendant to the needs of SSE, the small enterprise sector in Brazil is remarkably resilient and healthy. In fact, the failure of SSEs to become more capital intensive like the rest of the industrial sector can be at least in part attributed to the fact that they have remained relatively untouched by government programs. The resilience of Brazilian SSE was demonstrated in Table 9.5; the number of small enterprises grew substantially between 1950 and 1970, as did their employment and their value added. SSE is in no danger of disappearing in Brazil. This is not to say, however, that SSEs do not have serious problems or that special programs, designed to accentuate the special features of SSE, are not desirable.

The comparison of two industrial censuses for two different years, as presented in Table 9.5, although shedding light on the development of SSEs as a whole, does not permit the identification of what has happened to individual establishments over the period in question. For example, Table 9.5 does not indicate whether the individual small establishments existing in 1950 continued to grow or disappeared. One can only surmise. The small establishments in 1970 might be different establishments altogether. Knowing something about the growth, survival, and mortality of individual SSEs, along with their causes, will permit the identification of problems facing SSE.

A recent study coordinated by Henrique Rattner at the Getulio Vargas Foundation's School of Business Administration in São Paulo has, for the first time in Brazil, addressed the problem of mortality and failure of small and medium-sized industrial firms in Brazil through a longitudinal analysis. [7] Building upon a study done earlier that interviewed randomly selected small and medium-sized firms in 1963/64, Rattner's team returned to the same firms in 1977 for a follow-up interview. These firms were spread across a number of manufacturing industries and located in São Paulo, Salvador, or Porto Alegre. Out of the original 165 firms only 99 (60 percent) had survived until 1976. The mortality rate of 40 percent seems even higher in view of the sale of majority control of 16 of the surviving 99 firms to other individuals or firms. If this mortality experience for SME is representative, and there is no reason to believe that it is not, the relevant question concerns the factors associated with success or failure of individual firms.

PROBLEMS OF SMEs

The experience of growth, survival, and mortality for individual firms over time provides lessons as to the dfficulties that small and medium-sized enterprises confront. In conjunction with information gained from other interviewing sources, the Rattner study provides a unique basis for drawing some conclusions as to the factors contributing to success or failure of SMEs.

After having eliminated those (19) of the surviving firms that refused to be interviewed, Rattner et al. undertook an analysis of the characteristics associated with survival. First, it was found that firm age is positively correlated with survival. Surviving firms tended to be relatively older than the group average. Mortality was particularly high for those firms that, at the time of the 1963 interview, had not yet attained three years of operation. Second, the individual firm's manufacturing sector was seen to be important. A firm had a greater probability of surviving if it was in an expanding industry, such as metalworking or automobile parts. The highest rate of mortality was observed in the slow growing textile industry. Thus, a growing market demand, perhaps consisting of an export market, as most notable in the case of shoes, tends to be important as a factor contributing to the survival of small firms.

A third factor found to contribute to a firm's chances of survival is regional location. Of the three regions studied by Rattner, Salvador was found to have the highest SME mortality rate and Porto Alegre the lowest. These regional differences have been attributed to regional differences in sectoral composition. Salvador, for example, had many textile firms, while São Paulo and Porto Alegre had more firms producing automobile parts, agricultural implements, and shoes. Another factor reflected in the observed regional firm mortality differences is what Rattner has termed a difference in "cultural background." The business ethics and determination of entrepreneurs descended from German and Italian immigrants, along with greater community stability in Porto Alegre and, to a lesser extent, São Paulo, were considered by Rattner to be important.

Summarizing the features found to be associated with survival in the Rattner study and examining their opposites to identify problems small firms face, a few implications are apparent. Small firms appear to have a reduced probability of surviving if they are (1) young, especially less than three years old; (2) producing in an industry with a slowly growing demand; and (3) located in a region that is growing slowly.

Looking solely at the surviving firms in the Rattner study, a number of characteristics of the firms are noteworthy. First, many of the surviving firms have evidently been quite successful, as evidenced by their growth in size. A full 83 percent of the responding firms indicated that they expanded their work force during the 1963-76 period; over half of the firms had at least doubled their work force. A good number of firms grew to the extent that they no longer could be considered small firms. As seen in Table 9.6, significant differences are seen in the comparison of the original 1963 sample with that of the reporting survivors. By 1976, 17 firms (27 percent of the reporting survivors) employed more than 200 employees. Small firms, if they can survive, frequently grow substantially.

A second noteworthy characteristic of the surviving firms in the Rattner study is the degree to which these firms have had export experience. A full 41 percent have exported, and 31 percent continue to export and view the export market as essential. This not only suggests that small firms are capable of exporting and successfully competing in export markets but that export activity may be a key to success.

TABLE 9.6

Distribution by Firm Size of Firms Observed in 1963 and 1977
(in percent of total)

Number of Employees	1963	1977
1-19	31.2	9.7
20-49	40.3	21.0
50-99	22.7	14.5
100-49	3.2	14.5
150-200	2.6	12.9
201 and above	*	27.4
Total	100.0	100.0

*Insignificantly small.

Source: Rattner et al., "Pequena e média empresa no Brasil: 1963-1976" (Book manuscript, São Paulo, May 1978), p. 76.

A third feature of the surviving firms concerns education. Although the stereotype of small industrial entrepreneurs generally involves an individual without much formal education, this picture was not apparent in the case of the surviving firms in the Rattner study. A full 76 percent of the present entrepreneurs (managers) in the surviving firms had received some university-level instruction, and all had at least some exposure to secondary school. [8] Moreover, there is an emphasis placed by the entrepreneurs on the education of their own offspring. The dramatic expansion and democratization of the Brazilian university system in the past 15 years has meant that successful small businessmen almost always send their own sons to the university. The entrepreneurs themselves obviously consider education important, and part of their success as the managers of successful, that is, surviving, SSEs may stem from their own educational backgrounds.

Although analyzing the performance and characteristics of successful small firms illustrates some of the difficulties facing SSEs, a more direct approach to analyzing such problems is to examine the characteristics of failing firms and the apparent reasons for their failure. The Rattner study showed that of the original 165 firms, the 40 percent that failed tended to be distinct from the total sample of SSEs in several ways. First, the failing firms tended to be quite small, with 50 percent having less than 20 employees. Second, unlike the surviving firms, failing firms tended to be young, as noted. Over one-half of the failing firms were less than three years old in 1963. Finally, failing firms tend to be partnerships. Only 11 percent of the failed firms were single proprietorships.

The reasons given by the former entrepreneurs for the failure of their firms vary, but certain similarities are apparent. The most common reason given for the failure of the firm was competition. While this explanation can cover a large range of situations and more basic reasons, 39 percent of the failed firms indicated competition as the primary reason for their demise. In general, when the firm did not require more complex equipment and was using a relatively simple technology, the competition that was felt came from other small firms. Only in the case of sectors requiring sophisticated technology and equipment was the competition coming from large enterprises.

Financing is an important problem for SSEs. In the Rattner study the unavailability of credit, particularly for working capital, was cited by 25 percent of the failing firms as the principal reason for their failure. It is difficult for SSEs to obtain credit either for the private banking system or from official government sources. While the public banking system now accounts for about 80 percent of all credit extended in Brazil, less than 40 percent of all the firms interviewed in the Rattner study had experience with government credit.

For small firms in general, this proportion is bound to be less given the nature of the firms included in the Rattner study. There are definite problems of accessibility, and entrepreneurs complain bitterly about paper work and bureaucratic requirements necessary in obtaining official credit. While only one-half of all the firms interviewed in the Rattner study admitted that they encountered problems in actually obtaining credit, entrepreneurs thought that the lack of sufficient credit constituted a problem for SSEs in general. Frequently, the complaint involved the magnitude of interest rates. Two-thirds of the failed firms thought that insufficient credit was the primary reason for small firm failure, although this explanation was not necessarily applicable in their cases.

It has already been noted that a large proportion of the failed firms in the Rattner study were partnerships. It is not surprising to find that disagreements between partners over the period 1963-76 constituted the third single most important reason for SSE failure given by the failing firms. Also related to this were other difficulties in providing continuity to the firms' operations over time. Since small firms are generally associated with a small number of key individuals, sickness and death were also contributing causes for failure. In the case of a small family firm, there is frequently no one available to take over for the principal owner and entrepreneur. Additional problems that SSEs encounter in Brazil, as seen in the Rattner study and elsewhere, include difficulties in obtaining skilled labor and in acquiring access to raw materials, particularly when the raw material supply is controlled by a large competitor.

Bearing in mind the varied problems of SSE, the question is, What can be done in terms of policy to assist SSE? It is clear that little can be done about disagreements between partners and that the problem of competition complained about by firms is frequently a disguise for a firm's management, production, or marketing difficulties. The major area where public policy can play an important role in ameliorating the problems facing SSE in Brazil is in the area of financing. The provision of credit is indeed the conventional policy handle on the problem, and the next section will examine the existing financing arrangements and programs available to small-scale enterprices.

FINANCING SMALL AND MEDIUM-SIZED INDUSTRIES

There are a number of credit programs in Brazil available to small and medium-sized industries. In examining these assorted programs individually, it will be argued that the total impact of these programs, although beneficial, is not sufficient to adequately attend to the varied credit needs and requirements of small enterprises in Brazil. The major credit programs to be discussed are the Special Agency for Industrial Financing (FINAME) of the National Development Bank (BNDE), the Program for Working Capital (PROGIRO), the Joint Operations Program (POC) of the BNDE, the small and medium-sized industry financing program of the Bank of the Northeast (BNB), CEBRAE-assisted lending programs to micro enterprises through the state development banks, the Central Bank Resolution 388 program, Banco do Brasil programs, and regular commercial bank financing activities relevant to SSEs.*

A distinction should be made between those credit programs open to all firms and those especially designed for and restricted to small and medium-sized firms. The FINAME program belongs to the first category. It includes, but is not limited to, financing for small and medium-scale industries (SMI). The FINAME is an affiliate of the BNDE and finances the purchase of machinery and equipment for industrial firms under very favorable, that is, subsidized, terms. In 1977, FINAME approved loans totaling Cr$27.2 billion (or U.S.$1.8 billion) of which Cr$2.6 billion, or 9.6 percent, was approved for small and medium-sized firms.[9] This proportion of FINAME lending, of course, is considerably lower than the share of SMI in total industrial value added. Moreover, it is likely that even this amount is concentrated among the larger firms within the BNDE classification for SMI.

The PROGIRO program is designed to attend to the working capital needs of SMI through a fund of approximately Cr$7 billion on the part of the Caixa Econômica Federal with on-lending through the state development and investment banks. Like other official credit programs, PROGIRO's interest rates are heavily subsidized. The nominal interest rates for small and medium-sized firms are 22 and 27 percent annually. Inflation in 1977 was about 45 percent. The PROGIRO operational definitions for small and medium-sized industrial firms were annual sales of up to 35,000 standard reference values (MVRs) for small firms and up to 85,000 MVRs for medium-sized firms. In June 1978 these cutoff points were equal to CR$40.8 million (U.S.$2.3 million) and CR$97.8 million (U.S.$5.5 million), respectively. Both of these limits are substantial. A small firm under this definition, conservatively assuming an average fixed capital-output ratio of 1 and a capital-labor ratio of U.S.$10,000 per employee, could easily employ over 200 individuals. Thus, while ostensibly a program directed toward SMI, the PROGIRO program has the mak-

---

*Please see Appendix B for a more detailed list of abbreviations and acronyms used in this chapter.

ings of a program that can conceivably leave truly small enterprises untouched. PROGIRO is still too new for an assessment of its performance, but previous experience with other programs suggests that upper limits on sales may very well define the composition of the firms making the greatest use of the funds in favor of larger firms.

While the BNDE has, in general, concentrated its efforts and resources on large industrial projects, there have been some concessions to the need to provide long-term financing to SMI. In 1965 the Fund for Financing Small and Medium-Sized Enterprise (FIPEME) was established within the BNDE to finance fixed investment for the initiation or expansion of small and medium-sized industrial enterprises. Until the time of its replacement in 1974 by the POC, it had financed about 2,000 credit operations for SMI throughout Brazil, with the projects totaling U.S.$555 million (in 1973 prices and exchange rates).[10] This indicates that only about 1.4 percent of the SMI in the country were reached by the FIPEME program. Moreover, the average loan was much higher than would be supposed for an SSE lending program; the average FIPEME loan amounted to U.S.$277,000. One study analyzing the FIPEME loans granted between January 1972 and July 1973 calculated that only 14 percent of the value of all FIPEME loans were made to firms employing less than 100 workers.[11] In view of the limited impact and the large size of loans FIPEME cannot be thought of as having adequately attended to the credit needs of small-scale enterprises.

The establishment of the POC by the BNDE, replacing the FIPEME, can be viewed in many ways as a continuation of the FIPEME under another guise. To be sure, there were administrative changes and the use of POC resources was broadened to include working capital financing as well as that for fixed assets. Yet the guarantee requirements remained the same (real assets of 1.3 times the amount of the loan) and the firm size cutoff limits to qualify for credit have remained high. Under the POC operational definition a firm can be considered small or medium in size, and thus qualify for a loan, if its fixed assets plus the projected investment total less than 500,000 readjustable National Treasury bonds (ORTNs). In June 1978 prices and exchange rates this amounts to U.S.$7.5 million. Only the largest firms in the country cannot qualify for POC's subsidized credits.

The performance of the POC and affiliated programs also suggests that small firms are not being reached. In 1977, BNDE programs, including the POC and involving financing through the Projects with Agents Program (APA), approved loans to 950 small and medium-sized firms, according to the BNDE definition based upon ORTNs. These loans totaled Cr$3.6 billion.[12] Accordingly, the average loan was Cr$3.8 million, or about U.S.$252,000—hardly a small loan. Of the total amount only about 17 percent went to firms whose fixed assets plus loan were equal to less than 50,000 ORTNs (about U.S.$750,000). Looking solely at the POC operations in national currency, 27 percent of the SMI loan total (Cr$1.9 billion) went to firms with fixed assets plus loans of less than 50,000 ORTNs. Even here, however, the average loan size was still rather high—about U.S.$100,000.

The oldest continuous official credit program exclusively for SMI is administered under the auspices of the Bank of the Northeast (BNB) with the cooperation of the Superintendency for the Development of the Northeast (SUDENE). Loans for both fixed investment and working capital are provided. Established in 1967, the small and medium-sized industry financing program of the BNB through 1977 had financed 958 loans totaling Cr$1,248 million (in December 1977 prices).[13] The average loan thus amounted to Cr$1.3 million or roughly U.S.$81,000. While the average loan is rather high for a program purporting to deal with SSEs, it is nevertheless much lower than the comparable figures for BNDE-related programs.

Because of its lending at negative real rates of interest and the resultant decapitalization, the BNB's resources for its SMI program have dwindled. Recent years have seen less activity than previously.* Furthermore, the average size of loan has increased. In the first two years the average loan size, in 1977 prices, was about one-half the average over the entire 11-year period. This suggests that the program has been partially drawn away from its original purpose of extending loans to SSEs.

One of the problems apparent in the BNB program, as is also the case in other official SSE lending programs, is a high degree of bureaucratization and, as a result, high administrative costs for the program. The loan application process is formidable and seems to restrict the access of smaller firms to credit. One participating development bank is reputed to require no less than 42 documents and forms in support of a loan application. In the case of small firms possessing only rudimentary accounting practices, the requirements appear to be overly exacting. The accompanying delays are also substantial. Rarely is a loan actually dispersed within three months after application is undertaken. All of this, of course, results in substantial administrative costs. Streamlining the loan application process, perhaps with the use of credit scoring techniques, would serve both to reduce administrative costs and increase the accessibility of small firms to credit.

The size of the BNB SMI program must be considered quite small. As noted, only 958 loans have been approved in a period of

---

*The program's real lending total for 1977 was smaller than that for either of the first full two years of the program.

11 years. This represents only about 6 percent of the total eligible establishments in just Pernambuco, Bahia, and Ceará. If the BNB is to have a significant impact on SSEs in the Northeast, its annual operations to SSEs will have to be expanded substantially.

The SMI program of the BNB extends credit at negative real rates of interest. While it has been argued that such subsidies are politically—if not economically—necessary, the BNB, to its credit, has recently initiated a program with full monetary correction, that is, with theoretically positive real interest rates. This program, called the Program for Supplementary Industrial Credit (PCIS), has grown and enjoyed some success. Although not limited to SMI lending, some small and medium-sized firms have taken advantage of this line of credit.[14]

CEBRAE and its regional affiliates are often involved in the development of projects for financing by the BNB. Technical assistance is frequently provided to obtain financing for SSEs through credit institutions. In addition to the BNB program, CEBRAE affiliates are involved in a program to assist micro enterprises in obtaining credit through the state development banks. Although the impact of this program has been positive, it appears rather modest in scope.

An attempt of the federal government to deal with the scarcity of working capital for SSEs is indicated in Resolution 388 of the Central Bank in 1976. According to this regulation, all commercial banks in Brazil are required to set aside an amount equal to 12 percent of their total demand deposits for lending to small and medium-sized enterprises. Accounts receivable are provided as guarantees for these loans for a period of 12 months. For the purposes of the program SMEs are defined as those firms with annual sales less than 85,000 times the standard reference value (that is, the MVR, which in June 1978 was equal to Cr$1,150.70). This means firms can qualify if they have sales less than U.S.$5.5 million. As in the case of other programs designed to benefit SSEs, the cutoff limits for qualifying for the program are drawn very high so that firms that are indeed not small enterprises also qualify.

The interest rate for Resolution 388 borrowing is heavily subsidized, a mandated cost imposed by the Central Bank upon the commercial banks. Resolution 388 funds are currently (July 1978) lent at a nominal interest rate of 16 percent. Naturally, at such an interest rate, given Brazilian conditions, there is a scramble for the available funds. The result is that very little of the mandated Resolution 388 resources ends up being lent to SSEs. The original intention of Resolution 388 has been subverted. The commercial banks frequently use Resolution 388 lending as a bargaining instrument in their dealings with larger clients. Subsidized Resolution 388 funds are provided to the firm—or frequently to the economic group of which the firm is a

TABLE 9.7

The Annual Nominal Cost of Short-Term Borrowing from
Brazilian Commercial Banks, May 1978
(in percent)

	Monthly Interest and Charges	Required Compensating Balance	Effective Annual Cost of Borrowing
Cheap	2.1	10.0	33.21
Average	2.4	30.0	53.14
Expensive	2.5	35.0	61.65
Very expensive	4.2	33.3	124.35

Source: "Quem lucra com o dineiro caro," Visão, May 1, 1978, p. 51. The information was compiled from an interviewing survey of 11 commercial banks.

part—in return for the purchase of other types of banking services at nonsubsidized prices. In the words of the president of one of the state development banks: "The resources of Resolution 388 are always lent to the SME which are the largest and/or are the best clients, and as such are capable of offering reciprocity to the banks."[15] The smallest firms, which are those generally most in need of credit, are left out. Especially if they are located in the developing areas of the country or outside the state capitals, they never even learn of the existence of the subsidized Resolution 388 or PROGIRO working capital credits.

The largest commercial bank in Brazil is the government-owned Banco do Brasil. In addition to its own Resolution 388 program, it also possesses, unlike most private banks, a number of special credit programs and lines. Except for one relatively modest program involving fixed asset financing for SMEs, the Banco do Brasil's programs do not deal specifically with SMEs. As a whole, the Banco do Brasil has not directed large amounts of resources into SSEs.

For their part, the commercial banks have also neglected the SSEs and their special credit problems and needs. The transaction costs of lending to SSEs or in making small loans in general are higher than for other types of lending. To the extent that commercial banks do lend to SSEs these higher transaction costs, as well as a premium for perceived higher risk, are recouped in higher interest rates. A problem is that commercial banks frequently do not want to be bothered with SSE, and they simply are not equipped to deal with SSE. The lending to SSE that does take place by commercial banks is short term in nature and commonly involves the discounting of accounts receivable.

As indicated in Table 9.7, private interest rate charges in Brazil are high, even discounting the inflation. Compensating balances are required by commercial banks, rendering the effective interest charges high in nominal terms and, in some cases, even high in real terms. Small firms, to the extent that they can obtain credit at all, are generally forced to pay the highest effective interest rates. There is a demand, however, for credit at positive real interest rates, and SSEs are frequently willing and able to pay these rates.

SUMMARY AND CONCLUDING REMARKS

The small-scale industrial sector has been largely bypassed in the process of Brazilian industrialization. Economic policies to promote industrial development have, in effect, concentrated on bigness. Government enterprises and transnational corporations, both of which are relatively large in scale, have played important roles in Brazil's substantial industrial growth during the past 25 years. Despite the impressive gains made by large-scale firms, SSEs continue to be important in the economy. They are significant in providing employment, making the economy more responsive to change, and serving as a training ground for entrepreneurs.

Our analysis of the participation of SSE in the Brazilian manufacturing sector is undertaken with data from the 1970 industrial census. Previous analysis has frequently been based upon less comprehensive IBGE annual industrial survey information. The data employed in the study are the best available in Brazil to date for analyzing SSE. Importantly, unlike the incomparable annual IBGE surveys, the 1970 census information lends itself to comparison with previous censuses.

When comparing SSEs with larger enterprises in Brazil, two characteristics stand out. First, average wages are less in small enterprises, indicating a less extensive use of skilled labor. Second, the capital intensity of SSEs is lower than that for larger manufacturing establishments. Value added per worker generally increases with the size of the establishment. On the basis of some production function analysis for SSEs and the examination of some existing SME lending programs in Brazil, some estimates of the capital cost per job were developed. Our best aggregative estimate is that it costs about U.S. $4,000 to create a job in Brazilian SSE.

To analyze the aggregate performance of SSE over time a comparison of the 1950 and 1970 industrial censuses was made. The results demonstrate that SSE in Brazil has grown. Despite severe problems and discrimination, SSE shows a certain amount of resilience and vitality. In relative terms between 1950 and 1970 its share in the total number of establishments and total manufacturing employment has remained virtually unchanged. The SSE share of manufacturing value added, however, has fallen. While medium- and large-scale establishments recorded significant increases in value added per worker, SSEs witnessed little in the way of increases in labor productivity. Small-scale industry in Brazil has remained relatively labor intensive. In great part the reasons for this differing performance between SSEs and larger establishments relate to the impact of economic policy. Through a myriad of programs and incentives, industrial policy has had an effect of increasing the capital intensity of the Brazilian industrial economy, while leaving SSEs largely untouched.

If the results of the only longitudinal study of Brazilian SME are at all representative, the mortality rate for SME in Brazil is rather high. Over a 13-year period a mortality rate for established firms of 40 percent was observed. The reasons for failure underline the problems that small and medium-sized firms confront in Brazil. A major difficulty that can be meaningfully addressed by government policy is the perceived scarcity of credit available to SSE.

The existing financing programs and institutional arrangements in Brazil largely bypass SSE. The private banking sector, accounting for only about 20 percent of all loans extended in the country, has generally, and with some reason, been unresponsive to the credit needs and requirements of SSE. The official programs, of which there are several, also are not sufficient to adequately attend to the special and varied credit problems of small enterprises in Brazil. The resources of these programs are not particularly large, but, more important, there is a tendency to concentrate banking efforts on the larger firms within the range of those that qualify. These firms are almost never small-scale enterprises.

To the extent that subsidized credit in Brazil has contributed to the growth in the capital intensity of the larger manufacturing enterprises, the failure to reach SSE with subsidized credit can be thought of in more positive terms. Clearly, efforts to provide financing to SSEs should involve lending at positive real rates of interest. Otherwise, the increase in SSE financing will result in an erosion of the attraction of the small-scale industrial sector as a provider of employment in a surplus labor economy.

APPENDIX A

Estimations for Fixed-Capital Costs per
Job for Brazilian Small-Scale Industry

Begin by assuming the constant returns to scale form of the
Cobb-Douglas production function for all small-scale industrial firms
in Brazil:

$$X_i = A K_i^{\alpha} L_i^{\beta}, \quad \alpha + \beta = 1 \tag{1}$$

where

X_i = firm i's output, or value added, measured in money terms
K_i = firm i's fixed capital assets, measured in money terms
L_i = the labor employed in firm i, measured in man years
A = a technological constant
α, β = the output elasticities with respect to capital and labor.

Differentiating (1) to obtain the marginal products of capital (K) and
labor (L) and assuming that the price-taking small firms are successful in maximizing profits so as to equate the marginal productivities
with factor prices, a well-known property of the Cobb-Douglas production function is obtained:

$$\frac{rK}{wL} = \frac{\alpha}{\beta} \tag{2}$$

where r and W are the costs of capital and labor, respectively. Thus,
the ratio of the factor income shares is equal to the ratio of their output elasticities. Manipulating (2) we have:

$$K/L = \frac{\alpha/\beta}{r/w} = \alpha/\beta \cdot w/r \tag{3}$$

Therefore, knowing, or assuming, factor prices and the values of the
parameters α and β, the capital cost per job is determinate.

Values of $\alpha = 0.20$ and $\beta = 0.80$ have been assumed. That these
are reasonable values is suggested by a study undertaking such estimates for SSE in Colombia.*

---

*See William G. Tyler and Lung-Fei Lee, "On Estimating Sto-
chastic Frontier Production Functions and Average Efficiency: An
Empirical Analysis with Colombian Micro Data," Review of Economics and Statistics, in press.

Two estimates of the wage rate were utilized, as seen in Table
9A.1. The first, Cr$20,180, is an annualized current minimum wage.
The second wage estimate, Cr$26,705, is equal to the ratio of the ob-
served average wages for small establishments in 1970 to the prevailing annualized minimum wage in 1970 multiplied by the 1978 annualized
minimum wage. Various assumptions concerning the real cost of capital are given in Table 9A.1.

TABLE 9A.1

Estimates of Fixed Investment per Worker Using a Cobb-Douglas
Production Function for Small Enterprises
(in U.S. dollars)

Annual Average Wage (W) in Cruzeiros (1978 prices)	Interest Rate (r)				
	0.06	0.08	0.10	0.12	0.15
20,280	4,592	3,444	2,755	2,296	1,837
26,205	5,934	4,451	3,560	2,967	2,374

APPENDIX B

Commonly Used Abbreviations and Acronyms

APA   Projects with Agents Program of the BNDE (Área de
               Projetos com Agentes)

BNB   Bank of the Northeast (Banco do Nordeste do Brasil)

BNDE   National Development Bank (Banco Nacional de De-
               senvolvimento Econômico)

CEAG   Center for Managerial Assistance (Centro de Apoio
               Gerencial)

CEBRAE   Brazilian Center for Assistance to Small and Medium-
               Sized Enterprises (Centro Brasileiro de Apoio á
               Pequena e Média Empresa)

FINAME   Special Agency for Industrial Financing of the BNDE
               (Agência Especial de Financiamento Industrial)

FINE   Studies and Projects Financing Agency (Financiadora de Estudos e Projetos)

FIPEME   Fund for Financing Small and Medium-Sized Enterprises (Fundo de Financiamento à Pequena e Média Empresa)

IBGE   Brazilian Geographic and Statistical Institute (Instituto Brasileira de Geografia e Estatística)

ICM   Imposto sobre a Circulação de Mercadorias

IPI   Imposto sobre Produtos Industrializados

MVR   standard reference value (maior valor de referência)

ORTN   readjustable National Treasury bonds (obrigações do Tesouro Nacional)

PCIS   Program for Supplementary Industrial Credit of the BNB (Programa de Crédito Industrial Supplementario)

POC   Joint Operations Program of the BNDE (Programa de Operacões Conjuntas)

PROGIRO   Program for Working Capital (Programa de Capital de Giro)

SME   small and medium-sized enterprises

SMI   small- and medium-scale industries

SSE   small-scale enterprise

SUDENE   Superintendency for the Development of the Northeast (Superintendência do Desenvolvimento do Nordeste)

APPENDIX C

Tables 9C.1-9C.5.

TABLE 9C.1

Participation of Small, Medium-Sized, and Large Manufacturing Establishments in Brazil

Size Class[c]	Number of Establishments (N)		Value of Production (X)		Employment[a] (L)		Salaries (W)		Taxes,[b]	Value Added (VA)	
	Number	Percent of Total	Millions of Cruzeiros	Percent of Total	Number	Percent of Total	Millions of Cruzeiros	Percent of Total	Percent of Total	Millions of Cruzeiros	Percent of Total
Small											
1-640	98,361	69.3	2,915	3.3	321,331	15.5	450	4.9	1.7	1,439	3.6
641-1,000	10,279	7.2	1,545	1.7	75,498	3.6	220	2.4	1.0	720	1.8
1,001-3,000	17,649	12.4	5,675	6.3	231,655	11.2	814	8.8	4.5	2,717	6.7
3,001-10,000	8,719	6.1	8,877	9.9	286,794	13.8	1,163	12.5	7.8	4,187	10.4
Total	135,008	95.0	19,012	21.2	915,278	44.1	2,647	28.5	15.0	9,063	22.4
Medium (10,000-70,000)	5,362	3.8	24,634	27.5	604,652	29.1	2,794	30.1	23.9	11,183	27.7
Large (above 70,000)	1,043	0.7	45,976	51.3	553,741	26.7	3,835	41.3	61.1	20,171	49.8
Total[d]	142,110	100.0	89,622	100.0	2,074,911	100.0	9,276	100.0	100.0	40,417	100.0

[a]Includes all economically active personnel.

[b]Includes the payment of IPI and ICM taxes, as recorded in the census.

[c]Ranked according to the value of the establishment's production and measured in multiples of the minimum wage.

[d]The totals may differ slightly from the sums of the listed components because of rounding and some data omission.

Source: Special IBGE tabulations from the 1970 economic census made for CEBRAE.

TABLE 9C.2

Regional Distribution of Brazilian Manufacturing Establishments: Employment and Output, 1970
(percentage share of total)

Region	Number of Establishments	Total Employees	Total Salaries and Wages	Value of Output	Value Added
North	1.9	1.5	0.8	0.9	1.0
Northeast	18.8	10.2	5.6	6.4	5.8
Center–South	51.8	69.7	80.3	78.3	79.5
South	23.0	16.9	11.8	12.8	11.9
Center–West	4.4	1.4	0.7	1.1	0.8
Total	100.0	100.0	100.0	100.0	100.0

Note: Because of rounding, totals may not add up to 100 percent.

Source: Brazilian Geographic and Statistical Institute, Censo industrial: Brasil, 1970.

TABLE 9C.3

Participation of Small, Medium-Sized, and Large Establishments in Manufacturing for Bahia, 1970

Firm Size	Number of Establishments (N)		Value of Production (X)		Employment[a] (L)		Salaries (W)			Taxes,[b]	Value Added (VA)	
	Number	Per-cent of Total	Millions of Cruzeiros	Per-cent of Total	Number	Per-cent of Total	Millions of Cruzeiros	Per-cent of Total	N_W	Per-cent of Total	Millions of Cruzeiros	Per-cent of Total
Small												
1–4	5,258	75.0	114	5.8	12,768	22.4	9.0	4.3	3,517	1.4	55.7	6.6
5–19	1,415	20.2	206	10.5	10,820	19.0	21.1	9.9	1,342	4.6	92.9	11.1
20–99	260	3.7	364	18.6	11,027	19.3	41.2	19.4	259	15.7	167.8	20.0
Medium	72	1.0	405	20.7	7,629	13.4	35.0	16.5	47	13.2	140.0	16.7
Large	6	0.1	869	44.4	14,828	25.9	105.6	49.8	31	65.0	382.1	45.6
Total[c]	7,011	100.0	1,957	100.0	57,072	100.0	212.0	100.0	5,196	100.0	838.5	100.0

a Includes all economically active personnel.
b Includes the payment of IPI and ICM taxes, as recorded in the census.
c The totals may differ slightly from the sums of the listed components because of rounding and some data omission.

Source: Special IBGE tabulations from the 1970 economic census made for CEBRAE.

TABLE 9C.4

Participation of Small, Medium-Sized, and Large Establishments in Manufacturing for Ceará, 1970

Firm Size	Number of Establishments (N)		Value of Production (X)		Employment[a] (L)		Salaries (W)			Taxes,[b]	Value Added (VA)	
	Number	Per cent of Total	Millions of Cruzeiros	Per cent of Total	Number	Per cent of Total	Millions of Cruzeiros	Per cent of Total	Nw	Per cent of Total	Millions of Cruzeiros	Per cent of Total
Small												
1-4	1,975	58.4	57.6	5.3	5,036	12.8	3.4	4.3	1,517	4.4	20.8	5.3
5-19	1,131	33.5	249.0	23.0	9,667	24.6	13.6	17.1	1,113	20.2	83.4	21.2
20-99	212	6.3	376.5	34.8	8,239	20.9	21.2	26.6	212	31.3	116.0	29.5
Medium	37	1.1	243.2	22.5	5,686	14.4	19.4	24.4	37	17.5	95.4	24.3
Large	22	0.6	155.2	14.3	10,743	27.3	22.1	27.7	22	27.5	77.2	19.6
Total[c]	3,380	100.0	1,081.6	100.0	39,371	100.0	79.7	100.0	2,901	100.0	393.0	100.0

[a]Includes all economically active personnel.

[b]Includes the payment of IPI and ICM taxes, as recorded in the census.

[c]The totals may differ slightly from the sums of the listed components because of rounding and some data omission.

Source: Special IBGE tabulations from the 1970 economic census made for CEBRAE.

174

TABLE 9C.5

Participation of Small, Medium-Sized, and Large Establishments in Manufacturing for Pernambuco, 1970

Firm Size	Number of Establishments (N)		Value of Production (X)		Employment[a] (L)		Salaries (W)			Taxes,[b]	Value Added (VA)	
	Number	Percent of Total	Millions of Cruzeiros	Percent of Total	Number	Percent of Total	Millions of Cruzeiros	Percent of Total	N_W	Percent of Total	Millions of Cruzeiros	Percent of Total
Small												
1–4	3,215	61.6	107.0	4.0	8,013	9.3	6.8	2.6	2,020	0.6	40.7	3.5
5–19	1,486	28.5	291.1	11.0	12,105	14.1	25.0	9.5	1,421	5.1	119.7	10.4
20–99	352	6.7	462.1	17.5	14,049	15.4	44.3	16.9	352	14.1	187.9	16.3
Medium	86	1.6	503.6	19.0	13,558	15.8	54.9	20.9	86	19.0	211.5	18.3
Large	71	1.3	1,280.8	48.4	38,124	44.4	131.9	50.2	71	61.2	593.0	51.4
Total[c]	5,218	100.0	2,644.8	100.0	85,849	100.0	263.0	100.0	3,950	100.0	1,159.0	100.0

[a]Includes all economically active personnel.
[b]Includes the payment of IPI and ICM taxes, as recorded in the census.
[c]The totals may differ slightly from the sums of the listed components because of rounding and some data omission.

Source: Special IBGE tabulations from the 1970 economic census made for CEBRAE.

NOTES

1. See, for example, Joel Bergsman, Brazil: Industrialization and Trade Policies (London: Oxford University Press, 1970); and William G. Tyler, "Brazilian Industrialization and Industrial Policies: A Survey," World Development 4 (November 1976): 863-82.

2. An alternative definitional treatment, involving the use of sales information as the discriminating criterion, has been used to develop Table 9C.1. The most comprehensive and best analysis available of SME in Brazil is Frederico Robalinho de Barros and Rui Lyrio Modenesi, Pequenas e médias indústrias: Análise dos problemas, incentivos a sua contribuição ao desenvolvimento, Relatório de Pesquisa no. 17 (Rio de Janeiro: IPEA/INPES, 1973). Unfortunately, Robalinho and Modenesi did not have the results of the 1970 industrial census available at the time of writing. Instead, they relied upon a less complete IBGE industrial survey for 1969. Because of sampling procedure changes, intertemporal comparisons of the IBGE annual industrial surveys are highly misleading.

3. See World Bank, "Employment and Development of Small Enterprises: A Sector Policy Paper," Prepared by the Industrial Development and Finance Department, Washington, D.C., World Bank, February 1978.

4. NAE/CE, "Programa de financiamento da pequena e média indústria," Report of the Banco de Nordeste do Brasil e Centro de Apoio à Pequena e Média Empresa de Estado de Ceará, May 1978, p. 11.

5. See Regis Bonelli, Tecnologia e crescimento industrial: A experiência brasileira nos anos 60, IPEA/INPES Monograph no. 25 (Rio de Janeiro: IPEA/INPES, 1976). See also William G. Tyler, Manufactured Export Expansion and Industrialization in Brazil (Tübingen: J. C. R. Mohr, 1976).

6. See Eugene Staley and Richard Morse, Modern Small Industry for Developing Countries (New York: McGraw Hill, 1965).

7. Henrique Rattner et al., "Pequena e média empresa no Brasil: 1963-1976" (Book manuscript, São Paulo, May 1978).

8. Ibid., p. 149. The unusually high educational attainment reported in the surviving firms is not representative of SSE management in general. The selected firms were all located in capital cities where educational levels and opportunities have always been higher, especially in Porto Alegre and São Paulo. Furthermore, it has been noted that the firms in question are the surviving firms, frequently operating in industries in which some technical knowledge is essential. Also, a selectivity bias may be evident in the exclusion of those successful firms that refused to be interviewed. Since by their refusal the managers of these firms have shown themselves less interested

in research and university contacts, they are probably less likely to have been exposed to a university environment.

9. National Development Bank, Relatório das atividades, 1977, p. 32.

10. Frederico Robalinho de Barros, "O problema do financiamento à pequena e média indústria no país" (Unpublished IPEA/INPES report, December 1974). Robalinho concludes that "the truly small and medium sized industrial firms in the country were not benefitted by FIPEME, but were instead marginalized from the financing process," p. 6.

11. Francisco E. Thoumi, "A Report on the Size Structure of Industry in Brazil with Special Reference to Small-Scale Industry," Unpublished paper, World Bank, November 3, 1973.

12. National Development Bank, Relatório anual de atividades, 1977, Área de Projetos com Agentes, ASCOA/APA.

13. Bank of the Northeast, "Programa de financiamento da pequena e média indústria," Unpublished report, May 1978.

14. In 1977 loans authorized under PCIS totaled CR$205 million, of which less than 10 percent went to SME. Bank of the Northeast, Relatório, 1977, p. 44.

15. Quoted from a speech manuscript in preparation.

10
BRAZILIAN PULP AND PAPER SITUATION AND OUTLOOK

Robert S. Reitzes

INTRODUCTION

U.S. multinational companies have become increasingly aware of other parts of the world as possible investment sites. Since the Organization of Petroleum Exporting Countries' (OPEC) first major price rise (1973/74), some Latin American countries have become more important as sites for U.S. investment. This chapter is a preliminary study of the macro- and microeconomic factors affecting the Brazilian paper industry. The study assesses the investment opportunities in Brazil for foreign paper companies and the competitiveness of the Brazilian paper and pulp industries in the world marketplace.

Before a multinational company selects a foreign country as an investment site, it must analyze the economic, political (including business environment), and infrastructure considerations. A country or region with a strong economic base, large population, and a high level of per capita income (for example, Europe in the 1950s and 1960s) is extremely attractive to multinational enterprises. However, a country with a strong economy must also have a stable political situation and laws favorable to foreign investment to attract a foreign investor. In addition, a good system of transportation, communications, banking and commercial services, and distribution will further support foreign investment.

Prior to the 1973 oil crisis, U.S. companies earmarked most of their investment for Europe and Canada, areas that showed strong economic growth and that had favorable political and business climates and developed infrastructures. Between 1968 and 1973, U.S. direct private foreign investment totaled $45.6 billion, of which $29.5 billion was invested in Europe and Canada. U.S. investment in Europe was also stimulated by the formation of the Common Market, which eliminated tariff barriers among member nations.

During the same period, U.S. private direct investment in the Far East averaged less than $1 billion per year. The low amount of investment in the Far East by the United States reflected in general a weak economic and political situation and an inadequate (except for Japan, Taiwan, Korea, and Singapore) infrastructure. For example, despite the large populations in India and Pakistan, per capita income is not much above the subsistence level and the infrastructures, especially the distribution system, are inadequate.

Prior to the oil crisis, Latin America was not a large recipient of U.S. corporate investment because of the relative weakness of these economies and the perception by U.S. corporations of political problems in this region. However, since the mid-1970s U.S. investors have invested more heavily in Latin America, reflecting stronger economic growth compared with Europe; political stability in Mexico, Brazil, Colombia, and Venezuela; and a cutback of investment by U.S. companies in Europe. Between 1973 and 1978, U.S. private direct investment in Latin America totaled $11.6 billion (which accounted for 25 percent of total foreign investment), compared with $6.5 billion between 1968 and 1973 (which accounted for 14 percent of total foreign investment).

The fast-growing Brazilian economy has attracted a large amount of foreign investment. The major factors that have influenced the growth of foreign investment in Brazil are (1) a large internal market projected to continue to grow rapidly, (2) political and economic stability, and (3) a favorable attitude toward foreign investment.

Foreign paper companies have also been interested in Brazil as a source of wood fiber and as a possible competitor in the world marketplace (especially Europe). Since the mid-1960s Brazil has encouraged forestation projects and has built four large world-scale pulp mills, while internal demand for paper and paperboard has risen at an annual rate of 10 percent. All of the pulp mills have been financed either partially or solely by foreign firms.

BRAZILIAN ECONOMIC SITUATION AND OUTLOOK

Real gross national product (GNP) in Brazil is forecast to rise at an average annual rate of 6.5 percent between 1977 and 1990, compared with an 8.4 percent annual rate between 1965 and 1977. The rapid growth of the economy during the earlier period was due to growth in the manufacturing sector, low-cost food and fuel, extensive foreign borrowing, and foreign and domestic investment.

The quintupling of oil prices in the mid-1970s coupled with the rapid growth of internal demand contributed to the acceleration of the inflation rate and the severe balance-of-payments problems. To reduce the rate of inflation and improve the trade situation, the government imposed austerity measures in 1976. These measures led to a slowdown in the growth of real GNP to 4.7 percent in 1977, compared with 9.2 percent in 1976. The government is expected to continue these policies through 1980, and real GNP is forecast to rise 5.0 percent per year for the rest of the decade.

During the 1980s, the government plans to emphasize the industrial sector, especially for those products presently imported, and the development of the agricultural, mineral, and petroleum sectors. In the early 1980s, real GNP is forecast to accelerate to an average annual growth of 7.5 percent per year because of improvement in the balance of payments, productivity increases, and the removal of the government's austerity measures. Between 1986 and 1990, real GNP is projected to rise at an average rate of 6.5 percent as economic development matures.

The government plans to continue the restrictive economic policies, at least until the new administration takes office in March 1979. Inflation is expected to moderate between 1977 and 1980 to 30 to 35 percent and slow to 20 to 25 percent in the 1980s.

BRAZILIAN PAPER INDUSTRY

Historically, the Brazilian consumption of paper and paperboard has grown more rapidly than real GNP. Between 1965 and 1977, paper and paperboard consumption rose at an average annual rate of approximately 10 percent compared with an 8.4 percent rise in real GNP. From 1977 to 1990, real economic growth is forecast to rise 6.5 percent per year, and paper and paperboard consumption is projected to increase at an average annual rate of 7.3 percent.

Despite the rapid growth of total consumption, Brazil's present level of per capita consumption is only 48 pounds, compared with a level of approximately 600 pounds in the United States, 300 pounds in Germany, and 95 pounds in Argentina. The relatively low level of consumption also indicates that the market potential for the Brazilian paper industry remains high. (See Figure 10.1 for the growth trends of paper and paperboard consumption compared with GNP.)

The rapid but erratic rate of growth of the paper industry in Brazil conforms to the general pattern of paper and paperboard consumption for developing countries. Consumption of paper and paperboard in a developing country correlates closely with four factors: (1) rate of growth of income, (2) literacy, (3) population growth, and (4) real prices.

As Figure 10.2 indicates, paper and paperboard consumption per unit of real GNP increased steadily between 1965 and 1974. This

FIGURE 10.1

Real GNP and Paper and Paperboard Consumption

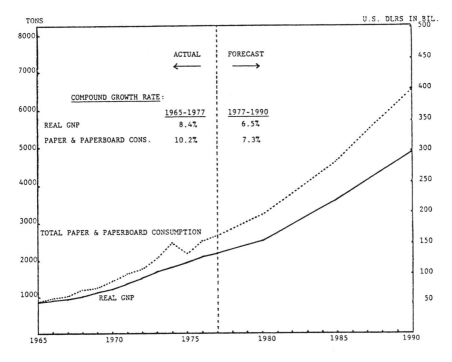

increase corresponded to the rapid advances in economic and population growth, relative paper price stability, and improvements in literacy. In this period, the average annual growth rates were 9.0 percent for real GNP, 6.2 percent for per capita income, and 2.8 percent for population. Literacy levels rose from 65 percent to 75 percent of the population and university enrollment rose from 130,000 to 1.2 million.

However, in the mid-1970s the Brazilian economy experienced a sharp slowdown and inflation accelerated. The imported price of paper and pulp exceeded the general rate of inflation. (Brazil imported between 10 percent and 17 percent of its paper and pulp requirements during the 1973 and 1977 period.) These factors contributed to the downturn in apparent consumption in 1975. The pickup in demand for paper and paperboard in 1976 and 1977 reflected, in part, the recovery in economic activity and the decline in the imported price of paper and pulp products.

In the forecast period 1977 to 1990, the economic and demographic factors that influence paper and paperboard consumption are

FIGURE 10.2

Ratio of Total Paper Consumption to Real GNP
(in billions of dollars)

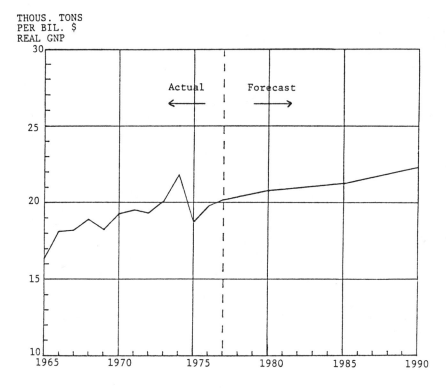

expected to continue to support strong growth in this sector. The literacy level is forecast to rise from 75 percent to 85 percent and college enrollment to grow rapidly. However, real GNP, per capita income, and population growth rates (see Table 10.1) are forecast to slow down from the prior period, leading to a decline in the rate of growth of paper and paperboard consumption.

Consumption of printing and writing papers, which correlates closely to literacy rates, population growth, and income, is forecast to rise 8.0 percent per year, compared with 11.6 percent per year in the preceding years. Packaging is forecast to rise 7.5 percent, compared with 9.9 percent in the prior period, reflecting increased substitution and continued economic growth. Newsprint historically has correlated more closely to population growth and is forecast to rise 3.5 percent per year compared with 4.6 percent from 1965 to 1977. Total per capita consumption of paper and paperboard is fore-

TABLE 10.1

Brazilian Selected Economic and Demographic Indicators

	Real GNP (in billions of 1977 dollars)	Per Capita Income (in 1977 dollars)	Consumer Price Index (1970 = 100)	Population (in millions)	Cruzeiro Value (Cruzeiros per dollars)
1965	50.92	628	29.83	81.01	2.200
1970	73.24	792	100.00	92.52	4.920
1974	111.07	1,075	201.26	103.35	7.395
1975	115.51	1,087	259.66	106.23	9.020
1976	126.14	1,155	379.62	109.18	12.275
1977e	132.07	1,180	526.92	111.91	15.957
1980f	152.89	1,269	1,211.89	120.51	31.920
1985f	219.49	1,610	3,698.40	136.35	76.170
1990f	298.00	1,922	9,202.80	154.27	153.210
Compound Growth Rates (in percent)					
1965–77	8.4	5.4	27.0	2.8	18.0
1977–90f	6.5	3.8	25.0	2.5	19.0

Note: e = estimate; f = forecast.

TABLE 10.2

Apparent Consumption of Paper and Paperboard
(in thousands of short tons)

Year	Newsprint	Printing and Writing	Packaging	Industry and Other	Total	Per Capita Consumption (in pounds)
1965	186	170	354	124	834	20.6
1966	191	199	432	147	969	23.4
1967	206	225	414	177	1,022	24.0
1968	258	263	440	202	1,163	26.5
1969	255	285	461	218	1,219	27.1
1970	277	305	563	267	1,412	30.5
1971	297	379	620	296	1,592	33.4
1972	333	436	671	313	1,753	35.8
1973	334	461	844	394	2,033	40.4
1974	313	561	1,028	522	2,424	46.9
1975	317	543	859	441	2,160	40.7
1976	322	540	1,068	573	2,503	45.8
1977e	319	634	1,100	613	2,666	47.6
1980f	355	770	1,320	740	3,185	52.8
1985f	420	1,200	1,950	1,100	4,670	68.5
1990f	495	1,750	2,790	1,590	6,625	85.9
Average Annual Compound Rate of Growth (in percent)						
1965-77	4.6	11.6	9.9	14.2	10.2	7.2
1977-90f	3.5	8.0	7.5	7.5	7.3	4.6

Note: e = estimate; f = forecast.

Sources: Brazilian Pulp and Paper Association; Brazilian Development Bank.

184

cast to rise from 48 pounds in 1977 to 86 pounds in 1990. (See Table 10.2 for growth rates of apparent consumption.)

To ensure that domestic production will satisfy demand, the government is actively encouraging local and foreign paper manufacturers through tax incentives, low-cost financing, and tariff protection either to enter or to increase their position in the market. Government forecasts indicate that possible shortages may occur in the printing and writing, newsprint, and specialty paper sectors during the 1980s but that capacity expansions in the packaging sector will be sufficient to meet new demand. Incentives for the packaging sector will be more difficult to obtain than for the other paper sectors. Between now and the mid-1980s, there are plans to either expand or add new capacity for approximately 40 paper, paperboard, or pulp mills. The capacity additions in paper and paperboard are scheduled to be between 1.6 million and 1.7 million tons. One million tons of capacity expansions, planned for the packaging sector, are sufficient to meet projected new demand. But printing and writing, newsprint, and specialty paper expansions (approximately 600,000 to 700,000 tons) are somewhat below the projected increase in demand.

Most of the new or expanded mills will be relatively small (by U.S. standards), integrated facilities except for several hardwood pulp mills, one softwood pulp mill, and one linerboard mill. The production of the smaller mills is earmarked for domestic consumption while the output of the larger facilities is directed toward the export market. Some of the larger nonintegrated hardwood mills (Aracruz, Jari, and Riocell) are also considering the possibility of establishing a white papers facility at their site. The Jari management is also considering the possibility of manufacturing newsprint for the domestic and Latin American markets.

At present, the Brazilian pulp and paper industry is an amalgam of old, inefficient, and small facilities interspersed with newer, more modern mills. This fact explains the relatively low operating rates of 80 percent achieved during the last several years even when demand was relatively strong. An investor must be careful not to add capacity too quickly because the market is still relatively small and may not be able to absorb immediately the output of a new facility. The construction of Braskraft, a 220,000-ton linerboard facility, has been delayed, officially because of pollution problems. However, the government may also be concerned that the 60,000 to 70,000 tons production earmarked for the domestic market will cause some short-term oversupply problems.

The government's tight import restrictions and price supports have led to substantially higher paper and paperboard prices in Brazil than in the United States. The pretax profit margins for the major efficient producers are in the range of 15 to 25 percent on net sales.

After-tax returns on equity can run 15 to 20 percent under normal conditions. U.S. companies operating in Brazil have become acclimated to high inflation and interest rates and constant monetary corrections, and the effect of these factors on local operating results appears to be small. The profitability outlook of the paper industry still appears to be strong, given the continued growth of demand and the government's elaborate protectionist and incentive measures.

NEW HARDWOOD AND SOFTWOOD PULP EXPANSIONS

During the mid-1970s the Brazilian government, in partnership with domestic and foreign investors, initiated an ambitious program to develop Brazil's hardwood market pulp export potential. The government and investors alike wanted to capitalize on Brazil's comparative economic advantage relating to wood and labor costs. The

TABLE 10.3

Brazilian Hardwood: Capacity, Demand, and Exports, 1976-88
(in thousands of short tons)

Year	Capacity	Domestic Demand[a]	Excess Availability	Export Potential[b]
1976	1,250[c]	775	475[d]	110[d]
1980	2,200	1,000	1,200	900-1,000
1983	2,550	1,250	1,300	1,000-1,100
1985	2,575	1,500	1,075	800- 900
1988	2,675[e]	1,875	800	500- 600

[a]Assumes an average annual growth in GNP of 6.5 percent and in printing and writing paper of 8.0 percent.

[b]Several of the old facilities, which account for approximately 150,000 to 250,000 tons of capacity, are unlikely to be operating at full capacity, and some new facilities are earmarked for the domestic market.

[c]Riocell's 230,000-ton capacity is included.

[d]Actual.

[e]If Flonibra and Torras do Brasil are bought on stream by the late 1980s, Brazilian hardwood capacity will be increased by 375,000 tons.

TABLE 10.4

Major Brazilian Hardwood Pulp Projects
(in thousands of short tons)

	Estimated Capacity			
	1980	1983	1985	1988
New facilities				
Aracruz[a]	330	440	440	500
Cenibra	275	275	275	275
Embrasca[b]	n. a.	n. a.	n. a.	60
Guatapara[c]	20	190	190	190
Jari[d]	175	200	200	175
Klabin[e]	75	75	75	75
Riocell[f]	200	230	230	230
Other	75	100	125	150
Total	1,150	1,510	1,535	1,650

Possible new facilities

Flonibra: 275,000-ton capacity; Japanese and Brazilian partners presently doing market research evaluation of proposed project; earliest start-up date in late 1980s.

Torras do Brasil: 192,000-ton capacity, 50/50 hard- and softwood; planting but having difficulty getting financing; if built, start-up not till late 1980s.

Canceled or doubtful projects

Bracel: 300,000-ton capacity
Cetrisa: 275,000-ton capacity
Mobasa: 360,000-ton capacity
Itapeva: 192,000-ton capacity

n. a. = not available

[a]The project's planned capacity is 550,000 tons.

[b]The facility's capacity is 280,000 tons, of which 55,000 tons are scheduled for short fiber production and 225,000 tons are scheduled for long fiber production.

[c]Production from this facility is earmarked for domestic consumption.

[d]The facility's capacity is 275,000 tons, of which approximately 75,000 tons are scheduled for long fiber production in the early 1980s and 100,000 tons for long fiber production by the late 1980s.

[e]Production from this facility is planned to be integrated with a packaging mill.

[f]A bleachery is planned to be added to Riocell during the early 1980s, but the mill has been producing unbleached hardwood pulp for several years.

plan was based on the assumption that the pulp shortage that then existed would continue. The foreign exchange revenues earned from the exports of the market pulp would also help to offset the sharp increase in the cost of imported petroleum and capital. The prolonged pulp surplus, however, has caused the government and private investors to reevaluate their positions, resulting in the delay, postponement, or cancellation of several projects.

Approximately 1,425,000 short tons of hardwood pulp capacity is expected to be added to Brazil between 1976 and 1988, but internal demand for hardwood pulp is forecast to rise by 1.1 million short tons. The export potential for hardwood pulp is expected to peak in the mid-1980s at approximately 1 million tons and gradually fall off as internal demand increases. (Some of the current mills are old and inefficient and are unlikely to be operating at full capacity, thus reducing Brazil's export potential. See Tables 10.3 and 10.4 for details of the forecast.)

Most of the new softwood pulp facilities are small or fully integrated or both, with the exception of four mills: Jari, Embrasca, Celulose da Bahia, and Braskraft. Braskraft will have the capability of producing over 200,000 tons of softwood pulp, but the pulp mill is designed to be integrated with a linerboard facility. According to Abecel (a Brazilian pulp exporting association), most of the excess capacity in the Brazilian softwood pulp sector in the early 1980s will not be exported. The pulp is unbleached long fiber, inefficiently pro-

TABLE 10.5

Brazilian Bleached and Unbleached Sortwood Capacity: Demand and
Exports, 1976-88
(in thousands of short tons)

Year	Capacity	Domestic Demand	Excess Availability	Export Potential
1976	715	510	205	*
1980	1,150	660	490	150
1983	1,550	850	700	300
1985	1,575	1,000	575	300-350
1988	1,800	1,250	550	300-350

*Insignificantly small.

duced. By the late 1980s, with the completion of Embrasca, softwood pulp exports are expected to range between 300,000 to 350,000 short tons. (See Table 10.5.)

Brazil's emergence as a leading world exporter of market hardwood pulp in the 1980s could significantly affect the international hardwood pulp markets. At present, world hardwood market pulp demand is approximately 2.7 million short tons. World hardwood capacity is currently 3.4 million short tons. The addition of approximately one million short tons of market pulp from Brazil may force the less profitable producers (for example, Scandinavia) to forward integrate or leave the business. Brazilian softwood pulp and linerboard exports over the next ten years will not be a serious factor in the international markets.

Cost Structure

The cost structure of new Brazilian mills has been the subject of much discussion and study. A Goldman Sachs study places total manufacturing costs of the new mills at $266 per short ton while White Weld (now owned by Merrill Lynch) estimates Aracruz costs at $153 per short ton.[1] But estimates based partially on discussions with Brazilian business and government officials and partially on other published sources place costs somewhere in between at $225.[2] However, these estimates should be regarded as an order of magnitude rather than a precise estimate of Brazil's cost position.

While estimated total manufacturing costs of Brazilian hardwood facilities appear to be comparable to the United States's costs, Brazil enjoys a substantial variable cost advantage, especially in wood. Furthermore, the Aracruz and Riocell mills and, to a lesser extent, Cenibra have received significant low-cost government financing. A large portion of the loans are payable in cruzeiros. The principal and interest are indexed to a special formula that will increase over the next five to ten years at a slower rate than the devaluation of the cruzeiro. Therefore, in dollar terms, the cost of part of the principal and interest payments will be reduced.

The government has also supported these projects by removing the income tax and the value-added taxes on exports. Because most of the production of these new hardwood pulp mills will be exported, these firms will pay virtually no income taxes. Therefore, their pretax profits can be between 36 percent and 48 percent below their U.S. counterparts and they can make a comparable return on sales.

Because of the relatively high fixed-cost position of these facilities and the export incentives, it is likely in the short run that these companies will aggressively try to capture a portion of the world hardwood pulp markets in the 1980s. The government can also guarantee the viability of these projects by renegotiating loan or payback agreements. (See Appendix B for the government's financing for the Aracruz project.)

The depressed world market pulp situation in 1977 and 1978 led to the formation of the Brazilian trade association, Abecel, made up of three of the new export mills (Aracruz, Riocell, and Cenibra). Two of the mills have been experiencing difficulties in selling their output. (Aracruz recently started up.) In 1977, Cenibra lost approximately $13 million and sold its output significantly below cost. Riocell has been running at less than 50 percent of capacity, and it must add a $100-million bleaching facility to become competitive. Its current owners, a consortium of state and local banks, purchased the mill from a military pension fund that lacked the expertise to run the plant. In addition, the facility has been severely criticized for polluting the local environment.

The output of the four large hardwood facilities (1.2 million tons) is aimed primarily at the European market (50 percent), followed by the domestic market (18 percent) and the Japanese market (17 percent). The remainder of the output is planned to be sold to the United States and to other Latin American countries. Most of the exports, except for Jari's output, will be marketed through agents. (Of Cenibra's output, 50 percent is sold to the Japan Brazil Paper and Pulp Resources Company, which owns a 49 percent share of the mill.) Export sales from these facilities could run over $300 million per year during the 1980s and could contribute significantly to the improvement of Brazil's balance of payments.

In the short run, Brazilian hardwood producers (especially Jari) are likely to offer their product at a discount to gain customers. Even though the existing cost structures are comparable, the government's generous incentive package (including subsidies, negative interest rates, and no taxes on exports) provides the Brazilian producers with a competitive advantage relative to U.S. producers. Over time, as depreciation and interest charges decline, Brazilian hardwood producers will tend to achieve an improved cost position relative to the United States. Brazil's entry into the marketplace will probably have a more detrimental effect on the high-cost Scandinavian producers.

The nonintegrated European printing and writing manufacturers, who are the largest consumers of market pulp, are likely to benefit significantly if Brazilian pulp exporters pursue an aggressive pricing strategy. This pricing strategy would adversely affect the Scandinavian integrated white paper producers who export to Europe. In addition, the nonintegrated producers would have more flexibility regarding their suppliers.

CONCLUSION

As stated in the introduction, this chapter represents a preliminary analysis of the micro- and macroeconomic situation affecting the Brazilian paper industry. Given the growth of the economy
and strong profits of the paper producers, investment opportunities
for U.S. companies would appear favorable. However, the domestic
market is relatively small, and industrywide capacity utilization
levels are about 80 percent. On the basis of the expected size of the
market, the early to mid-1980s would appear to be a more favorable
time to establish a new facility in Brazil.

Brazil will be able to compete in the international hardwood
pulp market because of large-capacity expansion to be completed by
1980. By the mid-1980s Brazil is expected to export over 1 million
tons of hardwood pulp. However, Brazilian softwood pulp and linerboard exports over the next ten years will not be a significant factor
in international markets because domestic demand will consume most
of the production.

APPENDIX A

Selected Fiscal Incentives

Category A: Investment in Export Industries

Income tax exemption on profits from exports,
Customs duty exemption,
Fiscal credit on industrial products tax (IPI) for domestic op-
erations corresponding to the total of exports, and
Domestic and customs duty exemption for equipment not avail-
able in Brazil.

Category B: For Government-Approved Domestic Investments

Import tax exemption or reduction on the acquisition of machinery and equipment not available in Brazil.

For Categories A and B

Regional incentives for investment in the North, Northeast,
and the State of Espirito Santo;
Sectional incentives for investments in fishing, forestry, and
tourism;
Accelerated depreciation of installations and equipment; and
Extension of payment periods for government loans.

Repatriation of Funds

Under existing regulations, remittances of profits and dividends, up to a limit of a net annual return on investment of 12 percent, are subject to a withholding tax of 25 percent. When profit and dividend remittances exceed the net average of 12 percent over a three-year period, the following additional withholding taxes are imposed:

Return on Investment (in percent)	Rate of Tax (in percent)
12 to 15	40
15 to 25	50
Over 25	60

The 25 percent rate is applied to total distributions, and the additional levies are applied to the excess portion.

APPENDIX B

Aracruz Capitalization at Project Completion

	U.S. dollars
Long-term debt:	
Payable in cruzeiros to Brazilian government agencies	205,833
Payable in other currencies and guaranteed by Brazilian government agencies	108,943
Total	314,776
Equity capital	
Brazilian government agencies	67,000
Private investors	125,320
New equity	40,000
Total	232,320
Total capitalization	547,096

Note: Almost 70 percent of the total capitalization for the Aracruz project has been financed or guaranteed by the Brazilian government. The government can renegotiate its Aracruz loan agreements if difficulty is encountered in meeting the scheduled payments. Owing to its large commitment to the project's success, it seems likely that the government would renegotiate the agreement if the need arose.

NOTES

1. Thomas Clephane, "Brazil: The Growth of the Internal Paper Market and Its Developing Role as a Pulp Exporter," Goldman Sachs Investment Research, November 15, 1977.

2. White Weld and Co., "$40 Million AEROCRUZ-CELULOSA S.A. Equity Capital," August 1977.

11
THE ROLE OF FINANCIERAS IN DEVELOPMENT

Stewart E. Sutin

What is a financiera? No single or simplistic definition is applicable for all of Latin America, for each country defines its own rules of the game. In its most basic form, a financiera is a commercial bank in miniature, with similar lending and deposit-taking functions. Local regulations usually prohibit certain activities, such as accepting demand deposits, while encouraging others, such as medium-term lending. For the purpose of this study, attention will be restricted to financieras in Colombia, Ecuador, and Venezuela and to those operations that qualify as development finance companies. This will permit desirable depth of coverage, yet it is imperative to recognize that significant differences may exist between financieras in any one country as to the style and scope of operations, not to mention cross-border differences. The regulatory climate, the talents of management, and the residual benefit to development are variables to be studied closely.

This chapter is segregated into three basic sections, one for each country mentioned above. Within each section, there is a review of the business environment, the contributions to development, and comments on how these companies are perceived as investment opportunities and credit risks by foreign banks. A final commentary is devoted to the long-range potential of finance development companies as models in the development process in both developing and industrial countries. Before proceeding, a word of caution is advisable: this chapter is intended as an introduction to a subject that is highly complex and not as a definitive appraisal of the industry in general or in any particular country.

COLOMBIA

The financieras in Colombia are perhaps the most closely regulated and, as a group, are probably the most illustrative of private sector financial entities that promote, by design, subregional development. As the primary local source of medium- and long-term loans, it is difficult to overestimate their importance to industrial development in particular. There are nearly 20 finance companies in the country, and the government has carefully approved their charters with the objective of encouraging operations in as many different geographical zones as possible. Most of the major companies were founded in the 1960s as a cooperative effort of Colombian businessmen and bankers, with varying amounts of capital supplied by international public and private sector banks. The largest companies, on which this study is primarily focused, generally received capital from the International Finance Corporation of the World Bank. Other foreign shareholders have included Manufacturers Hanover Trust, Bankers Trust, Bank of London and South America, Bank of Tokyo, Industrial Bank of Japan, Continental Illinois, Marine Midland, Wells Fargo, Philadelphia National, Citibank, Citizens and Southern, and Algemene Bank Nederland N.V. Local banks, companies, and businessmen are majority shareholders, although the National Coffee Federation has recently made significant infusions of fresh capital to foster the growth of operations. Even though the boards of directors reflect the diverse ownership, management has been notably independent and positions are held by full-time professionals.

Decree 2369 of 1960 created the legal foundations for the establishment and operation of financieras. Among the more significant provisions are those reflective of the development role assigned to financieras through mandating them to help create, reorganize, and transform companies by means of direct lending and investments. Time deposits can be received for periods of not less than 90 days. Loans under one year in maturity can be made only in support of international trade transactions. Investments are permitted as so-called seed money only to foster the growth of new companies and not for portfolio or return-on-investment purposes. Emphasis is to be given to medium- and long-term lending. In brief, the financieras were assigned a role quite different from that already delegated to private sector commercial banks, which remained the primary vehicles for full-service banking and short-term lending. They are intended to complement, rather than compete with, existing commercial banking operations. As a matter of practice, a number of private sector banks are minority shareholders, are active on the boards of directors, and do not view financieras as competitors.

The emphasis of the loan portfolio has been to promote manufacturing activities, although other areas such as fishing, agriculture, and mining have been given varying amounts of support. Conventional credit criteria are maintained in evaluating potential loans, acceptance of a quasi public sector role in promoting subregional development notwithstanding. Borrowers are compelled to provide full financial statements, bank references, full historical data on their operations, and a specific plan as to how the proceeds of the loan would be used. Medium- and long-term borrowers are commonly asked to provide adequate collateral in the form of liens on property and equipment. Internal credit committees on each company meet to evaluate and decide upon the loan proposals, with larger loans requiring additional approval from the boards of directors.

Lending priorities tend to conform both with the needs of the regions in which the financieras are situated and with overriding government priorities such as the promotion of export diversification. In addition to conventional lending, financieras often undertake roles that private commercial banks are not involved in, such as providing financial counseling to new operations, supplying venture capital, and underwriting capital issues for emerging operations. Feasibility studies and other forms of technical assistance are also given to new operations, but the priority is helping companies to overcome start-up difficulties and to become self-sustaining. Since the financieras rarely receive outside guarantees, they are compelled to remain sensitive to profitability and cannot offer services and loans to entities that do not exhibit the immediate or eventual promise of repayment.

A review of funding sources suggests that a close relationship exists between the major financieras and the national government, as well as with international private and public sector banks. Short-term operations are funded by an amalgamation of time deposits (only banks can accept demand deposits for checking accounts), internally generated resources derived from common stock and reinvested profits, and lines of credit granted by overseas correspondent banks. Medium-term operations may qualify for a variety of government funding programs or for access to the facilities granted by the World Bank and, more recently, the Inter-American Development Bank.

The financieras, especially the larger ones that have qualified for access to the World Bank facility, have something of a special status in the country. The Colombian Central Bank, Banco de la Republica, closely monitors their operations and is empowered either to provide direct loans to them or to act as guarantor on loans provided by third parties. Government funding for specific types of loans may be available, within preestablished guidelines, from the Fund for the Promotion of Exports (PROEXPO), Industrial Finance Fund (FFI), Private Investment Fund (FIP), Urban Development Finance Fund

(FFDU), Agricultural Finance Fund (FFA), and National Development Fund (FONADE).

The Industrial Finance Fund, perhaps the major source of government funding, provides resources to assist primarily small and medium-sized industries. Through the use of these funds, the financieras can provide loans for working capital and for the acquisition of capital goods for terms up to five years. FIP resources are intended to assist fledgling companies that offer the potential either to diversify the nation's export base or to assist balance of payments through import substitution. The overall objective is to provide funding for companies that may eventually contribute to the nation's balance-of-payments position, and financing is available for terms up to ten years. FFA, PROEXPO, and FFDU are, effectively, rediscount facilities for loans directed to the agricultural sector, export promotion, and urban development, respectively. In all cases, the financieras sustain the credit evaluation and risk functions, which is appropriate since they are the lenders of record. The funds, however, are provided by the government. FONADE, on the other hand, has a special purpose. Its resources are used to finance feasibility studies on a variety of themes concerned with development.

The triangular relationship between the financieras, the Banco de la Republica, and the World Bank merits special attention. Beginning in 1966, the World Bank has granted, on a renewable basis, substantial credit facilities to the Central Bank for the specific purpose of funding certain long-term lending operations of specifically qualified development finance companies. This has enabled the financieras to lend on terms up to 18 years. The primary intention of this program is to stimulate growth in the manufacturing sector, although the idea of establishing a separate facility for the promotion of agricultural development is being explored. Accessibility to the World Bank facility is limited to those financieras that have demonstrated a capacity to involve themselves in development projects. To date only seven financieras have been awarded full or partial access to the World Bank facility. Qualification is largely based upon adequacy of staff equipped to undertake feasibility studies and upon experience in medium-term lending.

In accordance with the terms of the formal loan agreements between Banco de la Republica and the World Bank, the Central Bank has accepted several specific responsibilities. While certain sections of the agreements have been modified somewhat, such as those designating the maximum debt-to-worth ratio permitted, the general nature of the agreements has undergone little change. In the first instance, although the financieras are the actual lenders, the responsibility for repayment to the World Bank for drawdowns under this facility belongs to the Central Bank. Indeed, the Central Bank is designated as the borrower in the World Bank loan agreement. Should a loan go into a default situation, the Central Bank repays the World Bank and must then resolve the matter directly with the financiera. In addition, the Central Bank has the continuing responsibility of monitoring the financieras and ensuring that both their management and financial condition remain sound. The Central Bank must also make certain that the financieras do not exceed the maximum allowable leverage position under the terms of the World Bank agreement, which up to recently was held to a seven to one ratio. Credit decisions are reviewed as are interest rate charges. All financieras are required to use an acceptable external auditor. As a matter of practice, most financieras have used a highly regarded Big Eight firm.

From a procedural point of view, the financieras pinpoint projects that are qualified for drawdowns under the agreement. A feasibility study is then made of the project. If the results are positive, the study and recommendation are then submitted to the Central Bank for review. Drawdowns are made only after the Central Bank has reviewed and endorsed the proposal. Since there is a ceiling on the amount of money any one financiera can borrow, the larger projects are usually syndicated among a number of financieras.

The Colombian government has recognized the contributions made to development, especially on a subregional level, by the nation's financieras. Government support has been direct and indirect in nature. The government funding facilities have been most helpful. The pivotal role of the Central Bank in gaining continued access to World Bank resources is another illustration of the importance attributed to development financieras. Furthermore, the National Coffee Federation has stepped forward with major capital contributions to the larger and more important financieras in recognition of the government's need to sustain their capital adequacy. Along with the capital contributions, a more active and expanded role can be expected by the designated representative of the Coffee Federation, usually someone from its associated entity, Banco Cafetero, on the respective boards of the financieras.

Notwithstanding government support, one should recognize that these financieras are fundamentally a vehicle of private sector initiative in the regions in which they operate. The modus operandi and objectives of management are characteristic of the private sector. The development role is taken seriously, but with full recognition that the interests of the shareholders must be served through sustaining efficient and profitable operations.

Brief mention has already been made of the support given to Colombian financieras by foreign banks through both investments and the extension of credit facilities. The lines of credit have helped in the promotion of short-term trade operations. Each financiera is re-

viewed as to its creditworthiness on a case-by-case basis. Even
though these companies have certain like traits, it would be poor
judgment to assume that mangement capabilities, lending criteria, and
attention to sound practice and policy are homogeneous. In general,
the size of credit facilities extended by overseas lenders has grown
in proportion to the level of capital growth of the finance companies.

During the past few years, many international private sector
banks have been going through a process of reexamination of overseas
investments in general. The reasons are many, with some being
purely internal and others brought about by such external considerations as increasing needs to demonstrate profitability to shareholders
and bank analysts in both the private and public sectors. There is an
increasing need to ascertain whether overseas investments fulfill
what might be called strategic objectives. Foreign banks are somewhat less able to play the role of amiable "big brothers" who invest
money and provide additional financial and managerial support as
needed, yet remain essentially passive with regard to overseeing management and insisting upon a fair return on their investments. Apart
from return on investment considerations, there is a need to examine
such other factors as whether adequate collateral benefits are derived
by means of gaining access to business not otherwise obtainable.

Colombian foreign investment codes pertaining to financial institutions are especially restrictive, particularly Decree 55. That
law, which constitutes the local implementation of Andean Pact fade-
out guidelines, prohibits the reinvestment of dividends or any form
of additional investment by foreign banks in Colombian institutions.
Since the financieras have had to expand their capital bases in order
to do additional business yet remain within the leverage limitations
assigned under the World Bank agreements, foreign shareholders
have had no choice but to witness the erosion of their equity positions.
In practical terms, it has become increasingly difficult for foreign
shareholders to justify their positions on boards of directors.

Perhaps even more important is the accounting treatment of
these investments, for this has longer-range implications for the
bottom-line profitability of foreign banks. As long as U.S. banks are
able to sustain a 20 percent ownership position in a foreign entity, the
equity method of accounting is the customary treatment afforded to
such items as income and devaluation. Once the investment erodes
appreciably beneath a 20 percent level, it is common practice under
generally accepted accounting principles (GAAP) to revert to the cost
method of accounting. Perhaps the key issue is the treatment of devaluation, for under the equity method devaluation losses are recorded
as they occur. On the cost basis, devaluation losses are reflected
only at the time of divestiture. Since the Colombian peso has devalued
steadily against the dollar and in all probability will continue to do so,

foreign shareholders have recognized that an eventual divestiture would precipitate a potentially large foreign loss on quarterly and annual financial statements. A modification of Colombian Law 55 pertaining to foreign investors is not considered as probable at this juncture. The result has been that several foreign banks have reluctantly either already divested themselves of their shareholdings or are considering the possibility. A discussion of the intent of that law and the full implications pertaining to the private banking sector as a whole are beyond the scope of this chapter. Suffice it to say that the law was probably designed more to bring about the "Colombianization" of the commercial banking sector and that its impact with regard to financieras was something of a by-product, perhaps unintentional, of that effort.

VENEZUELA

If the Colombian financieras are characterized by strong similarities in their objectives and scope of operations, the Venezuelan financieras are noteworthy for the varieties of activities in which they engage. Each financiera merits attention as a separate entity. Some undertake medium-term lending and have developed rather sophisticated corporate finance and money desk capabilities (see Chapter 12). Others are straightforward household and consumer finance operations. Several companies are majority owned by prominent financial groups, such as those associated with Banco Union and Banco de Venezuela. For the purpose of this study, attention will be given to those entities that most closely resemble development finance companies.

In a broad sense, Venezuelan financieras sustain less of a quasi-official function than do their Colombian counterparts, if only because there is far more investment capital available in this petroleum-exporting nation. Consequently, the World Bank does not extend a credit facility for use by development finance companies. The Central Bank does not serve as an intermediary with external lenders. The finance companies are, however, closely and professionally regulated by the superintendent of banks.

More than any other single causal factor, the development finance companies have emerged in the context of a boom economy that has the capacity to sustain large-scale private and public sector development needs. Indeed, the so-called development financieras, which combine certain traits of commercial and investment banks, were first mandated by local law in the early 1970s. New financieras are still being founded. In brief, these years may be thought of as the formative period in which objectives, functions, and operational styles are still being pieced together. These companies are just approaching maturity and a feeling for their respective positions in the marketplace.

Five basic types of activities have been undertaken. These include lending, corporate finance, money desk, leasing, and investments. As a group, the first three activities customarily consume the bulk of management time and are the source of most profits. Most lending is medium term on a fixed interest rate basis and has thus far been primarily used to finance plant expansion and modernization as well as the importation of capital goods. Corporate finance has been fundamentally done by only the largest and most sophisticated finance companies. Corporate shares and bonds have been placed on both underwritten or best-efforts bases. Occasional work has been done in consulting and arranging for mergers and and acquisitions. With regard to the money desk, the instruments retained in the investment portfolio and those traded tend to include certificates of deposit, mortgage bonds, corporate bonds, commercial paper, government bonds, and financiera bonds. Trading is often done on a repurchase and reverse repurchase agreement basis. Buying and selling of foreign currencies have generally not been done. The money desk assists the internal funding operations of the finance companies, although trading for profit and acting as a broker for third parties on a fee basis is not uncommon. Leasing and investment operations differ markedly from one financiera to another. Each has a set policy as to the types of activities that are considered acceptable. The tendency has been for each financiera to constitute a separate subsidiary to conduct these activities. Since the annual statements of these operations are not usually consolidated with those of the parent, it can be somewhat difficult to measure the success or lack of it for operations overall.

Even though the Venezuelan financieras do not have quite the well-defined role in development that their Colombian counterparts have, one should not underemphasize their importance. The marketplace in which they operate is complex, yet the functional tools at their disposal enable them to provide a wider assortment of services to local industry. There has been, however, a pronounced tendency for most financieras to establish their operations in Caracas rather than to spread out on a geographical basis. Most lending and other services are provided to entities in the greater Caracas area.

Since these financieras are involved in numerous activities not commonly seen in Colombia, the foreign lender faces a greater challenge in analyzing the creditworthiness of these entities. In the first instance, relative to Colombia, there is a diminished degree of visible or implied government assistance by means of the relationship between these private sector companies and the Central Bank. Medium-term lending is usually done at fixed interest rates, implying that profitability will fluctuate proportionate to changes in the cost of funds. Since substantial funding has been derived from short-term overseas correspondent bank lines, with rates readjusted quarterly or semiannually, profit margins are vulnerable to cyclical pressures. Another consideration is the effect of bond issues. While these bonds give access to a certain amount of medium-term funding, it is not uncommon to have specific portions of the loan portfolio consigned as security to the bond holders. There is also a tendency to run an unmatched book, which means that most loans are medium term and are often funded on the basis of short-term lines of credit. Finally, it is essential to evaluate management of the money desk and corporate finance activities. Underwriting activities, for example, can yield high profits but carry elements of risk that one must consider. In summation, credit features of overseas lending to Venezuelan financieras may be somewhat complicated, but can certainly be undertaken successfully by lenders who expend the necessary time and effort needed to evaluate each company.

The Venezuelan regulations governing foreign investment are somewhat less restrictive than in Colombia, particularly with respect to the percentage of ownership permitted. Venezuelan codes allow foreign shareholders a maximum of 20 percent ownership in any single financiera. The basic difference with Colombia is that foreign shareholders are not preempted from reinvesting profits or investing new capital in order to sustain their percentage of ownership as the aggregate capital base expands. Applications to invest these monies must be approved beforehand by the superintendent of banks, but as a matter of practice the government has not, thus far, been disposed to force divestiture beneath the 20 percent level. Accounting for these investments on an equity basis has not proved to be an issue of concern to foreign shareholders. Instead, the questions of collateral benefits, return on investments, and the relationships with fellow shareholders have attracted most attention. More than one foreign bank has concluded that insufficient benefits are derived relative to management time expended to justify a continued investment position.

As in the case of Colombia, the Venezuelan financieras are a basic source of medium-term funds to local industry. The lending and corporate finance activities are a major factor in fostering industrial growth in a rapidly expanding economy. These are activities that local commercial banks do not engage in owing to law and custom. Most major financieras are somehow linked, usually through common ownership, to substantial commercial banks. They tend to complement rather than compete with one another. It is altogether probable that financieras in this country will have an even more expanded and important role in development in the years ahead.

ECUADOR

The rapid emergence and growth of financieras in Ecuador is attributable to the need brought about by an economy spurred on by petroleum exports and to the fact that Ecuadorian private commercial banks were relatively small and oriented toward a traditional and basically agricultural economy. Existing commercial banks tended to have small capital bases that were adequate to meet the needs of the country until the early 1970s, when Ecuador became a large-scale petroleum exporter. Ever since that time, the nation has undergone a significant metamorphosis and consumer needs have grown proportionately, with proportionate increases in loan demand. It is not, therefore, surprising that only one financiera existed in the country prior to the so-called petroleum boom—namely, Corporacion Financiera Ecuatoriana de Desarrollo (COFIEC). Three additional financieras were founded between 1976 and 1977, and several additional entities have been constituted of late.

The notion of rivalry between the banks and financieras is thus far more theoretical than actual. In the first instance, growth of loan demand has been so strong that there is ample room for banks and financieras alike. Additionally, only commercial banks can accept sight or demand deposits, and they remain the basic short-term lenders in the marketplace. International trade is financed by both entities. The newer financieras will eventually embark upon medium-term lending and may seek access to the World Bank funding facility. At this point, only COFIEC, which was founded in 1969 and has the depth of staff and experience that is required by the World Bank, has accessibility to that credit facility. Perhaps most indicative of the close relationship between banks and financieras is the fact that the shareholders of virtually all financieras show the presence of a number of commercial banks. For example, Financiera de Guayaquil is partially owned by Banco de Guayaquil, and the general manager of the bank is also titular president of the financiera.

Both financieras and banks are regulated by the superintendent of banks, who functions under the overall supervision of the Monetary Board (Junta Monetaria). According to the governing codes, financieras are specifically mandated to promote new enterprises or assist the expansion of existing ones, especially in the industrial sector. New financieras are given a three-year exemption on income taxes on undistributed earnings in an effort to encourage augmentation of the capital footings. A minimum of 10 percent of annual profits must be added to legal reserves until those reserves constitute at least 50 percent of total capital.

A review of funding underscores similarities with financieras in both Colombia and Venezuela. As mentioned previously, the World

Bank has extended a line of credit to the Ecuadorian Central Bank to which COFIEC has access. The terms of that facility and the type of operations to be promoted are similar to the arrangement existing in Colombia. In promoting the growth of new and existing industries through medium-term lending, COFIEC has also utilized funding from the Agency for International Development and Ecuador's Social Security Institute. To varying degrees, all financieras have made use of certain Central Bank rediscount facilities and funding operations designed to encourage agricultural and industrial development. Short-term loans are funded by a combination of lines of credit from foreign correspondent banks, time deposits, and internally generated funds.

The loan portfolios reflect a combination of national priorities, local loan demands, and management preferences. As is the case in Venezuela and Colombia, there is a decided concentration in loans to manufacturing companies (usually 60 percent or above of the loan portfolio). Construction loans are a distant second and generally do not consume more than 20 percent of total loans of any single financiera. The remaining loans are usually a varying mix between transportation, agriculture, services, tourism, and a number of less emphasized areas.

Ecuadorian financieras tend to have their head offices in either Quito or Guayaquil. Suboffices are being opened in other locations such as Cuenca and Manta. This pattern is at variance with Colombia, where the tradition of regional rather than national financieras is firmly implanted. At the same time, one does not find the tendency toward centralization that exists in Venezuela. These patterns tend to reflect concentrations of existing loan demand as well as the traditional growth and cultural biases of each country.

With only one exception, these financieras have only token capital contributions from foreign banks. That exception is Ecuatoriana de Financiamiento (ECUFINSA) where Wells Fargo holds an equity position. Government foreign investment statutes are more similar to Venezuela than to Colombia in that foreign shareholders are not expressly prohibited from either reinvesting profits or investing new monies as the capital bases expand. Nevertheless, foreign banks seem increasingly reluctant to embark upon joint ventures in those countries where there is a firm limitation on the percentage of ownership and control that is permitted.

Evaluation of most Ecuadorian financieras as to creditworthiness may appropriately proceed along lines similar to the manner in which one evaluates the nation's private commercial banks. Primary attention should be given to ownership and management. Thus far, only COFIEC resembles the operational style and closeness to government exhibited in certain cases in Colombia, and most Ecuadorian financieras do not as yet engage in the type of broad-ranging activities—

such as corporate finance, money desk, and leasing—in evidence in Venezuela. Standard analysis of management, capital adequacy, and analysis of the loan portfolio are routine. One should additionally ascertain whether the tenor of loans and funds are relatively matched.

AN OVERVIEW

There have been two broad objectives of this study. The first has been to highlight the existing and potential contributions to development that financieras can render and their ties with foreign banks. The second, and perhaps more important, has been to underscore the fact that financieras have different functions in different countries and sometimes within the same country. Generalizations can be made, but only after a review of the realities of each country.

Usually these entities are intended by the government to promote industry and other forms of development. Unlike private commercial banks, financieras cannot accept demand deposits and are designed to focus attention upon medium- and long-term lending. Supervision and regulation are commonly sustained by the same government authorities who oversee commercial banks. The perception of these entities as acceptable credit risks or investment opportunities to foreign banks will logically vary. During the past few years one can detect an increasing tendency toward divestiture by foreign banks of equity positions in financieras, especially in Colombia and to a reduced degree in Venezuela, owing to the restrictive nature of foreign investment codes and increasing needs to appraise both direct and collateral benefits accruing from such investments.

Measurement of the influence of development finance companies on a nation's growth is difficult to quantify, in part because these are relatively new operations and in part because of paucity of data. But the types of services and lending operations that are performed complement commercial banking activities, especially the medium- and long-term lending functions. Where government funding and other forms of support are provided, it is largely due to recognition of the important contributions that financieras render to the nation's industrial advancement.

One can hypothesize that the approach being followed in Colombia offers an interesting model for other countries to study. The government has made a special effort to foster a subregional approach, thus avoiding concentration of activities in one or two cities. Rather than opt for the establishment of government-owned development banks and finance companies, much initiative has been left to the private sector. The shareholders are fundamentally businessmen, corporate entities, and banks from the private sector. Minority ownership by the government is held through the investments of the National Coffee Fund. A degree of public sector funding is available for those loans that quality. But in all cases the initiative is with financiera management to chart their own courses. As one might expect with private operations, these development finance companies started as relatively small operations and evolved gradually. The shareholders and management have consistently understood and supported the important tasks their organizations have in promoting subregional development. Yet these financieras have the basic responsibility to remain profitable and to evaluate each credit and investment opportunity closely and on its own merits. The regions in which they operate benefit from the presence of these financieras, yet are conspicuously aware that these companies are not in business to dole out money or to serve as a source of so-called soft window financing. The result is that each region, and the nation as a whole, benefits in the developmental sense from the presence of these development finance companies. New or expanding companies that are responsibly managed have access to needed funds. This approach toward development is an interesting model of public and private sector cooperation that might well be applied in a number of countries, even in economically distressed subregions of industrialized countries. It is a method of encouraging growth of areas in a gradual, but efficient and cost-sensitive, manner.

12
THE DEVELOPMENT OF THE
MONEY MARKET IN VENEZUELA

Juan Rada

INTRODUCTION

The money market in Venezuela is young. It started, by coincidence, during a time when the given conditions were ideal for its development. Yet it did not become widely recognized until its effect on the financial markets was such that its existence was a necessary factor for their further development. The capital markets, on the other hand, have evolved by design but at a much slower pace and as a separate segment of the financial system. At this time, the participants have finally become aware of the similarity of their common goals. For these reasons the following analysis will review the development of the money market with a general look at the capital markets, hoping that it will leave food for thought about the future of the money market in terms of the economy as a whole.

HISTORICAL BACKGROUND
OF THE STOCK EXCHANGE

Access to the Venezuelan financial markets has generally been reserved for those institutions with a long tradition of conservative activities. This market, despite its apparent youth, dates back to December 1805, when the first commercial exchange was conceived with the explicit intention of creating a common place where well-known merchants would be able to barter, share information, entertain their clients, and negotiate the debt instruments of the time. The exchange was founded in November 1807 with the participation of six brokers, and in 1946, after several suspensions and minor changes in philosophy, a project was signed enacting a specialized mechanism that was to aid the public negotiation of stocks and bonds.

The stock exchange opened officially on April 21, 1947, under the name of Bolsa de Comercio de Caracas, as a limited company boasting one of the most exclusive stockholder structures of any institution in the country.

In 1958 a second exchange, the Bolsa de Comercio del Estado Miranda, was established, with its headquarters only a few miles away from the original exchange, but it was unable to generate enough interest and finally closed down in 1974, leaving behind a strengthened Bolsa de Valores de Caracas.

PERFORMANCE OF THE CAPITAL MARKETS

The financial market transactions were negotiated until 1973 on a relatively informal basis with no set special regulations and were done either through the stock exchange, through the existing financial institutions, or, much more often, privately, with no records except in the accounting books of the corporations or individuals themselves. The most important consideration for the ownership of stock at the time, and to a lesser extent during the following five years, was the ability to hold large segments, if not the majority, of the equity, with a secondary consideration given to amount of dividends generated by the stock.

In January 1973 the Capital Markets Law was enacted and was reformed in April 1975. This document, partly original and partly borrowed from other regulatory mechanisms from Mexico, Argentina, and the United States, created an equivalent of the Securities and Exchange Commission, the Comision Nacional de Valores. This body, which had ample powers, was to regulate all new issues, watch over existing transactions, and design and implement any new regulations. The law also took into consideration such nonexistent features and mechanisms as transfer agents, preferential treatment for corporations with a wide shareholder base Sociedad Anónima Inscrita de Capital Abierto (SAICA), mutual funds, protection for minority shareholders, rules of conduct, definitions of publicly offered instruments, and minimum requirements for the issue of these.

Parallel to the enacting of the capital markets law, the banking law was revised, defining a base for the establishment of a propitious environment for the creation of a money market. This law was able to define clearly the role of the financial institutions without hindering their traditional scope of activities, a necessary condition recognized by the legislators.

As a result of the efforts on the part of the government as well as the financial intermediaries to channel the newfound oil wealth, the stock market experienced a marked growth in the years 1974 through 1977 (see Table 12.1).

TABLE 12.1

Growth of Venezuelan Stock Exchange
(in millions of U.S. dollars)

| Year | Stock Exchange | | M_2 Money Supply* | Subscribed Corporate Capital in the Metropolitan Area |
	Volumes Negotiated	Total Amount of New Issues		
1974	239.8	n.a.	6,522.6	1,040.9
1975	248.8	158.2	9,629.3	1,726.0
1976	338.1	154.7	11,903.9	3,552.8
1977	262.3	407.3	14,775.6	3,477.2
1978	248.7	251.2	n.a.	n.a.

n.a. = not available
*Includes currency in circulation as well as demand and time deposits in the banking system.
Note: Approximate figures exclude all private transactions. One dollar equals Bs.4.30.

Yet the growth of the structured capital market remains quite limited. The growth in the stock exchange volumes since 1947 has been on the average slightly over 11 percent interannually, and has experienced a decline both in prices and in volumes during the 1977/78 period. The stock price index has fallen from 176.4 (November 1973 = 100) in July 1978 to 151.8 in May 1979 and is expected to remain at those levels at least until the end of 1979, particularly in view of the continued increase in interest rates experienced during the past two and one-half years. Even though the money supply, as well as the corporate capital base, has been growing quite rapidly, the capital markets have as yet been unable to keep the same pace. Significant amounts of money have been raised as of late either from foreign sources, through financial institutions in the form of short- and medium-term loans, through the money markets, or through the reinvestment of profits. The propensity to invest or even save through stocks and bonds has remained low, probably because of traditionally greater returns on other investments, the preference for consumer product acquisitions, a general lack of understanding on the part of the public of the trading mechanisms, and the resistance of the larger investors to search diversified investment portfolios as opposed to large blocks of stock or venture capital investments.

It was evident already in the early 1970s that the investment and debt mechanisms of the time were not sufficient for aiding development of the private-sector projects.

DEVELOPMENT OF THE MONEY MARKET

The first indication of an organized effort to develop a money market in Venezuela is found in a World Bank feasibility study in 1973 giving rise to the creation of Valinvenca, a financial institution with attributes similar to those of the merchant banking institutions in London or New York. It was not until April 2, 1975, when Sociedad Financiera Union, working independently in collaboration with a Marine Midland Bank affiliate, orchestrated the first money market operation, giving rise to a new era in the Venezuelan financial markets. Thus the traditional financieras would slowly become sufficiently flexible to offer most merchant banking services and acquire the ability to compensate for temporary declines in the long-term markets with short-term mechanisms.

The basic elements necessary for the development of a money market were apparent already:

1. There were relatively large numbers of transactions carried out utilizing existing financial instruments. The 1974 to 1977 increase both in stock exchange and in private placement negotiations generated sufficient paper for use in money desk transactions, while the 1977 to 1979 decline provided a test for its ability to deal in the secondary markets.

2. A constant flow of considerable volumes of resources for investment purposes capable of satisfying demand was apparent. With the mass influx of oil moneys, the first money desks were able to operate in a very liquid market, their success hinging on the availability of enough short-term investment alternatives.

3. The market was sufficiently stable in terms of the price structures of the various available negotiable debt instruments. As a matter of fact, in 1975 the great majority of debt instruments were being negotiated at a premium, thus allowing sufficient initial leeway in the sale of those instruments bought in the primary market to minimize capital loss risks.

4. A large volume of transactions were of a short-term nature, assuring the necessary stability and potential continuity to this rising market. The Venezuelan consolidated corporate liability structure, because of the relative unavailability of long-term funds earmarked

for expansion of manufacturing activities, has been funded by short-term moneys for many years. This fact guaranteed a welcome to the money market alternative in terms of the treasury function.

5. Finally, the domestic resource base was large enough for the money market to be able to function independently of external factors that might have caused undesirable fluctuations within the system.

The main problem remaining was the lack of sufficient short-term investment alternatives available to the institutional client. The solution came in the form of the creation of two new financial mechanisms, the commercial paper figure and the establishment of the repurchase agreement on existing long-term vehicles.

These two alternatives, added to the wider use of the certificate of deposit, became the base for those first deals, looked upon originally as an isolated but interesting mechanism with a limited potential for success. It was not long before the financial groups through their financieras realized at first the mechanism's profit potential and later its importance as a form of channeling their participation in the capital markets and as a complement to their own treasury function. Within one and one-half years the number of money market dealers numbered six, including such entities as Banco Mercantil y Agricola, Sociedad Financiera Metro América, Sociedad Financiera de Occidente, Sociedad Financiera Union, Sociedad Financiera Valinvenca, and Sociedad Financiera de Venezuela.

It was the result of a three-year soft-sell promotion campaign that helped this mechanism become an integral part of the economy.

MECHANISMS OF THE MONEY DESK

The money desk in the Venezuelan case performs functions almost identical to those of most other financial systems that enjoy institutionalized money market mechanisms. It is a financial intermediary, generally dependent on a bank or financiera, that channels excess funds of a short-term nature from cash-poor prime quality corporations to institutional cash-rich investors. The great majority of the operations are denominated in the local currency, and the trading profits are reflected in interest differentials, straight commissions, and, to a lesser extent, discount or premium differentials.

The Venezuelan money desks act in four basic areas. One of these is dealership or portfolio operations. The financial institutions acquire a portfolio of fixed-rate negotiable instruments of a medium- or long-term nature. They then proceed to place these for shorter tenors via repurchase agreements (REPOs) until the instruments' maturity or final sale.

The risks involved in shortfunding these long positions and the possibilities of price fluctuations aided in the creation of the REPO counterpart, the reverse repurchase agreement (REV REPO). As a result, many desks, despite a lower yield of the REV REPO portion of their portfolios, have opted to decrease REPOs on long positions in favor of placing paper with repurchase agreements in their favor. In other words, money desk A would purchase paper from institution B with a repurchase agreement to be executed by B within a specific period. Then A would proceed to place this paper with institution C for a period equal to or less than the repurchase agreement issued by B, thus minimizing its price fluctuation as well as funding risks.

These combined operations have decreased credit risks via the aval implicit in the repurchase agreement, as well as providing an important mechanism for the future institutionalization of debt instrument arbitrage operations.

Another area of money desk operations is in commercial paper. When there is no paper available in the portfolio of the money desk clientele, the market conditions are such that the money desks find it difficult or not in their interest to place their own portfolios, or, simply as an alternate source of operations, the money desks will act as brokers on behalf of a select group of corporate clients. These operations are instrumented with short-term paper in varied market conditions and with little notification. Because the Venezuelan code of commerce does not contemplate bearer notes, a new figure that would adjust to these conditions has had to be developed. The solution in this case is a note, issued and endorsed in blank by the same issuer, to be traded in a similar manner as commercial paper is traded in the international markets. The advantages of the aceptacion have been immediately apparent, offering higher than average yields to the investor, tenors in accordance to specific needs, almost immediate availability, flexibility of denominations and a wide choice of issuers, often unavailable in the open market.

While not fully developed yet, the amount of outstandings in April 1979 was already approaching the B1 billion mark. The regulation of this market is still handled almost entirely by the money desks themselves, and the responsibility for investors' protection rests largely in the hands of the sponsoring financial institutions.

A third area of money desk activity is in brokerage operations. With access to large numbers of investors, the money desks have been able to develop a reliable placing power. This capacity has been utilized particularly during the past two and one-half years since financieras have become involved in acting as placement agents for primary market issues under deteriorating market conditions. The money desks have been able not only to place large blocks of bonds and to a lesser extent stocks but also to absorb portions of the issues for their

TABLE 12.2

Indicative Conditions for Venezuelan Money Market Instruments as of April 1979

Instrument	Issuers	Tax Status of Interest	Tenors	Coupon (in percent)	Effective Yield (in percent)	Secondary Market	
						Volume	Trading Conditions
Certificates of deposit[a]	Banks, financieras	Tax free for non-financial institutions	180 days to 5 years	9.50-14.00	9.50-14.25	Average	Small
Public sector bonds	Government and autonomous institutes	Tax free	10 to 12 years	7.00-7.50	7.15-8.00	Average	Excellent
Corporate bonds	Private corporations	Tax free 50 percent taxable Taxable	7 to 10 years	8.00-10.50 10.00-11.00 10.75-12.00	11.10-14.25 11.20-20.00 11.75-14.00	High	Good
Financiera bonds, mortgage guaranteed	Financieras	Tax free	5 to 12 years	8.50	8.50-12.00	Average	Small
Mortgage bank obligations	Mortgage banks	Tax free	10 to 15 years	8.50	8.50	High	Excellent
Financiera bonds, commercial effects guarantee	Financieras	Taxable	3 to 7 years	9.00	9.00-14.50	Low	b
Financiera and mortgage bank bonds, no specific guarantee	Financieras, mortgage banks	Tax free	2 to 5 years	9.00-9.50	9.00-15.50	High	Average
Aceptaciones	Mostly corporations, to a lesser degree financieras and banks	Taxable	7 to 180 days	9.75-12.00	9.75-15.50	High	Small

[a]Applicable to Venezuelan buyers only.
[b]Almost nonexistent.

own account when the institutions with which they are affiliated act as placement guarantors.

In addition to the activities specifically assigned to the money desks, they have fulfilled in many cases liability management functions not only for the institutions under which they operate but also often for other affiliated group companies. This they have been able to do advantageously by placing and maintaining a secondary market for their own paper and by placing their excess funds internally, thus providing considerable savings that otherwise would have been paid in the form of commissions or yield differentials.

INSTRUMENTS USED

At the time when the first few money market operations were instrumented, the available instruments were limited to mortgage bank and financiera mortgage guaranteed obligations (cedulas hipote-carias and bonos financieros), certificates of deposit, aceptaciones, and public sector bonds. This remained the situation for two years, after which time new instruments entered the market (see Table 12.2). As a matter of fact, the market continues to evolve, and a new set of mortgage-guaranteed mortgage bank high-yield obligations as well as short-term government-issued treasury bills are expected to be issued. The secondary market conditions are expected to be excellent for both since the Central Bank will probably participate as a discounting agent.

NATURE OF THE MARKET

Though precise orders of magnitude are extremely hard to determine for any portion of the internal money market, the nominal amount of outstanding fixed-rate obligations can be expected to be in the area of B2.1 billion (approximately U.S.$488 million), reflecting a total approximate market size of close to B3 billion, including commercial paper transactions.

There are presently nine major money desks and seven newer ones handling a total monthly volume of approximately B4.75 billion, with an average place tenor of 14 days in the case of portfolio operations and 30 days in the case of commercial paper. These statistics, as in any developing relatively small market, are substantially affected by a limited number of large longer-term operations of a seasonal and industrial cycle nature.

The participants comprise financial, industrial, and, on a smaller scale, large construction and commercially oriented entities

TABLE 12.3

Approximate Participation Structure of Money Desk Clientele as of April 1979
(in percent)

Type of Participant	Volume of Transactions	Volume in Cash
Nonfinancial entities	30.0	23.0
Banks (commercial and mortgage)	14.0	18.0
Financieras (except money desks)	5.0	7.0
Money desks	25.0	25.0
Individuals	3.0	0.5
Own group of companies	5.0	7.0
Public and semipublic sectors	3.5	4.5
Insurance companies	3.5	4.0
Trust funds	9.0	9.0
Brokers	2.0	2.0

(see Table 12.3) numbering already about 330. Only approximately 120 of these may be considered as active, operating both as net placers of money and net borrowers, depending on their own economic cycle.

It is interesting to note that there are a number of brokers who are presently participating in the money market, either as intermediaries or in some rare cases for their own account. This phenomenon has been a product of the slowdown in their own traditional activities and the increase in the number of their corporate clients participating in the money market, particularly those who enjoy a relatively sophisticated treasury function.

The average operation, as of April 1979, has been steadily increasing in size to the present B2.5 million (approximately U.S. $581,000) mark, leaving an approximate average spread of 1.00 percent on repurchase agreement operations on long-term portfolios, 0.70 percent on repurchase agreements on short-term portfolios, and 0.60 percent in commercial paper transactions.

The average portfolio of the money desk varies between B70 million and B90 million, with the largest portfolio having probably reached at one time the B300 million mark; it has the ability to handle up to 75 operations per day but has an average volume of approximately 12 per day for the average-sized money desk.

The number of active intermediaries has almost tripled in the past three years. These are made up almost entirely of those larger financial institutions directing their services toward the better-known low-risk corporations in the Caracas and Maracaibo regions, a logical situation in this young market because of the relative ease of access and communications and because of geographic location.

The market is by no means saturated. The potential size of the market may be placed at B10 to 18 billion, a figure based on such factors as the flow-of-funds models reported by the Central Bank of Venezuela, partial private and public cash holdings, net foreign fund inflows, and possible disinvestment in some low-yield liquid assets and excluding such factors as contingency funds, savings, and corporate near-liquid investments.

The rates in the money market have been steadily climbing (see Table 12.4). Because of the increase in interdesk competition and general increases in rates throughout the system, the desks were often left with comparatively low-yield portfolios while rates were increased to attract the existing clientele.

At present there exist no specific regulations as far as money market activities are concerned. The desks are generally structured as brokerage departments within commercial and merchant banks (bancos comerciales y sociedades financieras) and are therefore subject to the Venezuelan Banking Laws (Ley de Bancos y Otros Institutes de Crédito) and Capital Market Laws (Ley de Mercade de Capitales)

TABLE 12.4

Comparative Money Market Rates for June 1976 and 1979
(in percent)

Rate (days)	Tax-Free REPOs		Taxable REPOs		Commercial Paper	
	June 1976	June 1979	June 1976	June 1979	June 1976	June 1979
7	5.50	7.50	7.00	8.10	7.20	10.0
30	6.00	8.60	8.00	9.25	8.25	12.2
60	6.75	9.50	8.50	10.00	n.a.	12.8
90	7.25	10.00	8.75	10.50	9.00	13.4
180	8.00	10.25	9.25	10.70	9.75	15.0
Call	6.00	8.50	8.00	9.00	n.a.	n.a.

n.a. = not available

regulated by the Superintendency of Banks and the Securities and Exchange Commission (Comision Nacional de Valores).

BENEFITS OF THE MONEY MARKET

Possibly one of the most important additions of this decade to the financial market structure was the introduction of the money desk. For the corporations it represented the most viable means of investing their short-term cash surpluses and an alternate means of covering short-term needs. It meant the possibility of fine tuning the treasury department in the Venezuela-based institution into a relatively sophisticated function, requiring some knowledge of market alternatives well beyond the traditional short- and medium-term debt instruments.

This modality offered an incentive for implementing self-financing improvements such as reductions in opportunity costs of idle resources, establishment of guarantees for further relatively low-cost short-term funds, and the increase of the bank float for the purpose of investment in very liquid short-term instruments.

Additionally, as a result of the money supply growth rate decrease and the increase in the local cost of money, particularly in the case of multinationals, the wider use of the money market was encouraged as an often lower-cost or more available source of funds.

In the case of those brokers and institutions active in the capital markets sector, the money market meant a source of significant net buyers of securities. The money market, through the repurchase agreement mechanism, had the ability to place instruments of a long-term nature in large blocks for short tenors without having an immediate effect on secondary market prices. This characteristic tended to impart stability to the investment vehicles negotiated by the money desks. It also meant that large blocks of instruments with yields unnatural to given market conditions were able to remain placed until the market, through its self-regulating mechanisms, was able to absorb them.

Presently one of the more debated issues on the part of the authorities is the effect the desks are having on the economy. Despite the relative potential increase in the velocity of money imparted by the money desk, it has brought about a number of specific, and often very tangible, benefits to the system as a whole:

1. Channeling of idle funds toward the productive sectors of the economy: By efficiently matching cash surplus and deficit participants in a competitive market, the resource allocation mechanism has noticeably improved, locating sources of medium- and long-term

funds for the purpose of investment in the productive sectors of the economy. Not only has the market been able to transfer short-term funds from the cash-rich to the cash-poor sectors of the system but it has also had the ability to transfer short-term excess funds by way of the repurchase agreement, a necessary condition for productivity improvement within the system. Previously the industry has had to base most of its expansion plans on a short-term funding base, but it has now found an alternative—to fund itself more rationally through long-term debt instruments marketed indirectly through money markets and directly through the stock exchange structure.

2. Reduction in operating costs and increase in efficiency: Because of the large volumes negotiated by means of the money desks, economies of scale have been incorporated into the financial system, decreasing the transaction costs. While the traditional financial intermediaries have incurred larger costs because of the need to transfer small blocks of savings toward final investment or, as in the case of stockbrokers, because of negotiation of lesser volumes, the money desk has been able to develop simple low-cost systems, basing its profits on the size of the transactions alone. It has been a welcome instrument because of its ability to transact large volumes efficiently and safely, saving both time and money by means of the capacity to locate funds or investment opportunities in time spans unheard of previously.

3. Stabilization of financial markets: The money desks have the tendency to negotiate on a par value or stable price basis, buying and selling paper within the particular transaction at one given price, maintaining their own dealership portfolios for terms longer than the average of the market. Because of this fact they have the ability to negotiate instruments without being affected by the general market forces, absorbing in many instances those instruments that are not absorbed by other means.

4. Increase in the size of financial markets: Without the existence of the money market, the ownership of investment instruments would be limited to those entities with a propensity to hold these for relatively short periods of time, based on the conditions of the market. The money desk offers the option to invest without regard to temporary market condition changes and to maintain a position, if necessary, until such time as the market is able to buy.

5. Establishment of a true rate structure: Before the establishment of the money desk, there existed no rationalized risk or term rate structure. The interest rates were assigned arbitrarily, regardless of tenor, and in many cases, the risk involved in the ownership of the paper. Most taxable corporate long-term paper in 1975 carried a coupon of 10 percent, while tax-free paper carried a coupon of 8 percent, not taking into consideration the financial strength of the

corporation or the relative term structure of the issue. With the establishment of the desk, rates were immediately assigned on the basis of risk and tenor. In the case of dealership operations, the desks rationalized the risk factor by purchasing long-term instruments at a discount or premium and selling at par, thus availing implicitly the risk factor to the investor during the term of the negotiation while varying the rate of return, depending on the term of the investment. In the case of commercial paper intermediation, the desks would negotiate at equal investment—funding tenors and assigning the rates in accordance with both risk and term of the transactions, but at higher general rates than those offered by the dealership (REPO) operations under the same term and market conditions because of the fact that the risk factor was transferred to the investor. In fact, the desk not only was able to lengthen the funding tenors by purchasing an aggregate amount of long- and medium-term paper in the market but it also encouraged the use of very short-term tenors for bridge financing and investment purposes.

6. Maintenance of currency in the economy: In view of the increase in investment opportunities available in the country, the potential investor in foreign instruments would tend to reexamine his reasons for exporting capitals for the purpose of investing locally in the money markets. The money desk offers the possibility of adjusting conditions to specific needs rapidly with a wide scale of risk alternatives.

7. Finally, the money desk could become an agent for the monetary authorities in the implementation of monetary policy. It would be perfectly feasible for the authorities, through the central bank, to channel funds or public and private debt instruments through the money market, keeping the source confidential in order to regulate the money supply without affecting substantially the prices of the instruments. By channeling public debt instruments such as treasury bills and some new medium-term issues, the government would be able to fulfill a double purpose. The central government could offset the lag in oil revenues with respect to expenditures while improving the overall quality of paper in the system. It is possible to envisage a money desk trading in the new treasury bill issues as well as in an eventual federal funds market, adding the necessary dimension for the maturity of this particular market.

THE FUTURE

The growth of the Venezuelan money market has been impressive, with relatively few major problems. The prospects for the future seem bright, particularly in view of the possibilities of government participation, potential size, and the needs of the industrial sector. The corporations are already aware of the usefulness of a mature money market. The authorities, through the Fondo de Inversiones de Venezuela, are dealing successfully on the international markets, generating substantial volumes in numerous sophisticated transactions. Yet all future growth will require a much greater degree of self-regulation. The prime factors to be considered are as follows:

1. The unification of operational criteria as well as legal framework.

2. The widening of the client base, making the market more accessible both geographically as well as in terms of investor size.

3. The improvement of back office and information systems, including the simplification of documentation and transportation of documents and the mechanization of operative aspects.

4. A greater participation of the high-level executive strata in the decision-making process.

5. The establishment of a rational risk rating system.

6. The acceptance and adjustment to rapid changes in shifting market conditions.

7. An increase in availability of qualified personnel by means of the education process.

If these conditions are met, the market will be able to enter another phase of growth, possibly more slowly, but certainly more rationally. The market exists and has room to expand but will necessarily have to follow an established pattern in order to reach maturity.

13
LATIN AMERICA AND AFRICA: THEIR RAPIDLY EXPANDING ECONOMIC TIES

Sheldon J. Gitelman

INTRODUCTION

If Latin America is to continue to obtain the external financing it requires it will, of course, have to exhibit its ability to earn the foreign exchange needed to service its external debt. As discussed elsewhere in greater detail, agricultural and mineral products have traditionally been—and continue to be—the primary source of such foreign exchange earnings. But given the frequent fluctuations in commodity demand and prices, as well as the need to broaden its base of foreign exchange earnings, Latin America is searching for ways to increase its nontraditional exports. Such exports consist of consumer and capital goods, both manufactured and semimanufactured, as well as services and technology.

Although a market for some nontraditional exports such as certain manufactured consumer goods can be found in developed countries, that market is highly competitive and likely to run into local protectionist sentiment whenever it threatens to become substantial. Thus, the most likely markets for all forms of Latin American nontraditional exports would appear to exist in the developing world. In fact, that is what businessmen and governments in a number of Latin American countries have recently discovered with respect to Africa—a continent of developing countries with a great need for many of the nontraditional goods and services that Latin America can supply and with a growing ability, in many countries, to pay for them.

For many years it was usually assumed that since developing countries were essentially raw material producers, they were more likely to be competitors for world markets than economic collaborators or trading partners. Furthermore, until very recently, economic reality supported that view, especially as it applied to the countries of Latin America and Africa. Where collaboration did exist, it was in the form of commodity cartels, such as the Intergovernmental Council of Copper-Exporting Countries (CIPEC) or the Organization of Petroleum Exporting Countries (OPEC), or as signatories to international commodity agreements. Even in those cases, with the exception of OPEC, the basic tension between these developing countries as competitive raw material producers most often resulted in a breakdown of the attempted collaboration.

But with increasing momentum, economic collaboration and trade between the countries of Latin America and Africa is becoming more frequent in a variety of ways. Sometimes that collaboration takes the form of renewed attempts to coordinate pricing of commodities, such as coffee, that are produced on both continents. But it has even taken the form of assistance to a competitor in difficulty, such as the offer of technical assistance made to Zaire by Chile for the purpose of helping Zaire to reopen copper mines closed by rebel action.

It has also taken the form of outright economic assistance, as evidenced by the fact that both Brazil and Argentina have contributed to the African Development Fund, the soft loan window of the African Development Bank.

THE RECENT GROWTH OF TRADE

However, what has been of greatest importance and possibly the foundation for most other forms of recent economic collaboration between Latin America and Africa is rapidly growing trade in goods and services between the two continents. In such cases, African countries have usually provided commodities to Latin American buyers while the Latin American sellers have usually (but not always) provided finished or semifinished manufactured goods or services. A new chapter in Latin American-African relations is being written as a result of this trade. Furthermore, it is in this growing volume of trade that there exist even greater markets for Latin American sellers and, at the same time, an even greater need for expanding the means for financing this trade.

It is seldom possible to point with certainty to any specific date or event that marks the beginning of an era or trend. But if any single event marked the beginning of the present era of expanding Latin American-African trade, it was the 1972 visit to nine African countries by the Brazilian foreign minister, Mario Gibson Barbosa. From that point on, one can see a growing volume of trade between Brazil and Africa and the more recent interest of other Latin American countries in African trade. One can also see a growing interest by public

officials and private citizens of countries from both continents in each
other. For example, recently the former Nigerian commissioner of
external affairs, Brigadier Joseph Garba, visited Brazil (1977);
Leopold Senghor, president of Senegal, visited Venezuela (1978); and
the Nigerian vice-president, Brigadier Shehu yar' Adua, visited Brazil (1979). These high-level visits were augmented by visits of official and unofficial groups of Latin Americans and Africans to each
other's countries for the specific purpose of developing concrete economic ties. These included Brazil's presence at the First Lagos International Trade Fair in 1977 and the presence of several African
delegations at the 1978 São Paulo Export Fair. In addition, there
have been numerous visits by ad hoc delegations to and from Africa
and Latin America, among the most recent of which was a series of
two visits to Africa by a delegation of Argentine businessmen and
bankers, one to Francophone and the other to Anglophone Africa.

As buyers, Latin American countries have need of many of Africa's raw materials. The most important is the oil of Nigeria, Algeria, and Gabon, which is needed by many countries, as are the
phosphates of North Africa. While production exists in Latin America, the copper and zinc of Zaire and Zambia are sold to Latin America, as is the cocoa of Ghana and the Ivory Coast. The woods of
Gabon and Ghana also find their way to Latin American users. Brazil has even purchased West African coffee to support its price, to
substitute for its own exports, and to freeze-dry. Finally, some
tropical fruits are sold by West African countries, although local production of some exists in some Latin American countries.

However, it is as sellers that Latin American countries are
making the greatest strides. It is primarily these rapidly growing
sales that are stimulating Latin American interest in Africa, and it
is these sales that are creating more important trade links between
the continents. In addition, these sales are creating a need to finance
Latin American exporters and their African buyers, although, as yet,
export finance is not as available to most Latin American sellers as
it is to the sellers and buyers from the developed world, which has a
longer history of export sales of manufactured goods.

The largest and most rapidly growing trade links exist between
Brazil and Nigeria. This is not surprising since each is the most
populous and most politically and economically powerful country in its
own continent. Although, as will be seen, the Latin American-African
trade story is more than simply the story of Brazilian-Nigerian trade
(which alone has multiplied by 50 times in the last five years), a brief
review of the recent trade experiences between these two countries is
useful because it has set a pattern for Brazilian activity elsewhere in
Africa. Furthermore, it is a pattern other Latin American countries
are likely to follow in Africa if they can.

Brazilian literature of the mid-1970s on the subject of Brazilian-
African, and primarily Brazilian-Nigerian, trade is a recitation of
problems faced by every country trying to do business for the first
time in Nigeria or elsewhere in Africa. In most cases, early Brazilian exporters faced a language problem, since all of their instruction materials were written in Portuguese. Packing was often inadequate and exporters were not familiar with necessary customs regulations and documents. Of greater significance—and more difficult
to surmount—was the unfamiliarity of local buyers with strange Brazilian brands. Nigerians and other Africans typically hesitate to
stray from familiar brands with reputations created by companies of
the former colonial powers. Furthermore, there was no established
distribution system for Brazilian products, no direct transportation
system, and no system for financing Brazilian exports in competition
with well-established systems of finance available to traditional exporters.

None of these problems were unique to Brazilian-Nigerian trade.
They were, are, and will be problems for every new exporter to every
African country whether the exporter is from a Latin American country, from North America, or, indeed, from anywhere other than a
former colonial power. But Brazil is overcoming these hurdles in
Nigeria and elsewhere in Africa, and other Latin American countries
are slowly doing the same.

Brazilian sales to Nigeria are many and varied. In amount they
now exceed $500 million, while total trade approaches $1 billion. Indeed, a recent Brazilian-Nigerian trade agreement provides for $5
billion in trade (including oil sales) in five years, and this is considered conservative given the level of trade that can be expected.
These sales began primarily with automobiles and beef, both frozen
and canned, which represented the largest volume of sales in the beginning of this new era of increased trade. But sales now include a
growing volume of household appliances, industrial tools, agricultural
implements, motors, generators, iron and steel rods, and cotton and
polyester threads. In addition, road construction and telecommunica-
tions systems are representative of a growing volume of sales of services. Sales of services also include agricultural and technical training programs supplied by Brazilian agricultural cooperatives and private firms under contract to Nigerian government agencies. Over 100
Brazilian or Brazil-based companies or groups now engage in trade
with Nigeria.

There are a number of reasons for these growing sales in a
wide variety of fields. Primary credit must be given to the aggres-
siveness and inventiveness of the Brazilians themselves. In order to
better market a wide variety of unknown items, many sellers utilized
Petrobrás Comércio Internacional (Interbrás), a subsidiary of

Petróleo Brasileiro (Petrobrás), which was organized in 1976 to market Brazilian manufactured products, commodities, and services overseas. While Interbrás does not limit its sales to Petrobrás products, the fact that Petrobrás, as its parent, is a large purchaser of oil products gives it a certain leverage in countries such as oil-producing Nigeria. Thus, Interbrás was available as the marketing arm of any Brazilian exporter who chose to use its services, whether because of Interbrás's knowledge of the Nigerian market, because of the cost and difficulty of setting up a separate sales office, or for any other reason.

Then, in order to meet the problem of introducing a variety of trademarks into a trademark-conscious market, Interbrás created its own trademark, TAMA, with which to market products no matter what their Brazilian source.

Finally, in addition to the financial infrastructure that is being put at the disposal of Brazilian exporters and that is described later, direct transportation facilities were created. At first, direct transportation was limited to special cargo flights to Nigeria for the purpose of carrying frozen meat. Later Varig instituted direct passenger flights. In addition, a joint venture shipping line between Brazil and West Africa, with emphasis on Nigeria, was established. In fact, as evidence of its importance, Brazil West African line was awarded a portion of the scarce berthing facilities of the new Tin Can Island Island Port at Lagos.

There is also a built-in factor that served to help Brazilian exports and that could help exports of other Latin American countries as well. As an advanced developing country, Brazil only recently began to manufacture and export capital goods, agricultural equipment, transportation and communications equipment, and household appliances. As a result, many of its products, although technologically sound, are less sophisticated than those of advanced industrialized countries and therefore often suitable to the African environment.

In addition, the presence of multinationals with a manufacturing base in Brazil has served to increase exports. The most dramatic example of this has been one of Brazil's leading exporters to Africa, Volkswagen, whose Brazilian-made automobiles have been shipped to Nigeria for assembly in a Volkswagen plant outside of Lagos.

Brazilian exports to Nigeria are beginning to reach the point where manufacturing joint ventures are being created between Nigerians and Interbrás (representing over 20 different Brasilian companies) or Brazilian companies independently. In the future, it can be expected that some products will be produced by Nigerians alone under royalty agreements. This trend has become necessary as nationalist feelings and trade barriers for balance-of-payments reasons have threatened Brazil's Nigerian markets. But these are conditions with which Brazilians should be familiar and with which they should be able to deal effectively. Indeed, a joint Brazilian-Nigerian commission has recently been created to coordinate joint ventures and technology transfers.

While the Brazil-Nigeria experience has been described because of its lessons for the future of Latin American-African trade, Brazil's African experience is not limited to Nigeria, nor is Brazil the only Latin American country with an interest in African trade.

Brazilian-made bus parts are being used in bus assemblies in Ghana, while Brazilian Volkswagens (Brasilia) are being sold in Sierra Leone. Brazilian contractors have built roads in Mauritania (as well as in Nigeria), and a Brazilian cooperative is assisting Ivory Coast in the cultivation of soybeans. In addition, Brazilian aircraft are being sold to Cameroon and elsewhere in Africa, and Brazilian fishing boats have been sold to Togo.

As might be expected, Brazil is seeking to increase its trade with the newly independent Portuguese-speaking African countries of Mozambique and Angola. A new shipping line to Angola is contemplated to meet the needs of a rising volume of trade with Angola, trade that now exceeds $50 million.

Finally, foreign multinationals located in Brazil are taking advantage of the opening of trade throughout Africa. Participants include Massey-Ferguson, Ford, General Motors, J. I. Case, and Caterpillar.

The foregoing evidence of increasing Brazilian trade with Africa is not intended to be all-inclusive. It is intended to reflect the growing and varied nature of this trade, which is all the more remarkable because almost none of it existed less than five years ago.

Although Brazil is the Latin American leader in trade with Africa, it is not the only participant in such trade. Argentine meat is flown to Gabon on special Air Gabon cargo flights, and Argentina purchases oil, wood, and cocoa from Gabon. In addition, Gabon and Argentina have signed a general economic and technical cooperation agreement and a trade agreement. These agreements are designed to increase Argentine purchases of Gabonese products, including those already purchased plus others such as manganese and iron, of which Gabon has a substantial supply. Gabon will, for its part, acquire not only more meat and other agricultural products presently being acquired but also Argentine manufactured goods and Argentine technology, especially agricultural technology.

In addition to the trade with Gabon, Argentina has purchased raw materials from a number of West African countries and negotiated for the sale of some finished products such as its aircraft. The trade missions to Francophone and Anglophone Africa referred to earlier are part of an attempt to increase the level of Argentine trade. Argentina's recent contribution to the African Development Fund must also reflect an increase in economic relations with Africa.

Whenever one finds a Latin American government seeking to diversify its exports into nontraditional goods, one finds a substantial interest in seeking markets in Africa. For example, a Colombian development minister recently speaking on this subject noted that an attempt to revitalize Colombia's exports of nontraditional exports would be directed toward Africa as well as Asia. Chile, which seeks to diversify its nontraditional exports, is also actively seeking sales in Africa, and its offer to assist Zaire must be viewed in that context.

Since Latin American-African trade has been substantially ignored by researchers, the exact volume of this trade is unknown. Furthermore, to the extent statistics are kept they are often difficult to find. However, it is not uncommon to find manufacturers exporting to Africa from unexpected places. Thus, for example, there is the Ecuadorian manufacturer of stoves, one of whose models can operate on either electricity or kerosene. He inadvertently discovered that such a model was very useful to Africans residing just beyond existing electric transmission lines but who expect them soon or to those who reside in areas with electric power but with frequent power failures. The West African market for his stoves has grown to the point where he is planning a distributorship in West Africa with the capability of servicing his equipment and storing parts. It has also grown to the point where he is developing other products for the same market. This is a story that is beginning to be repeated in much of Latin America.

Although for a variety of reasons the Brazilian experience is not likely to be repeated exactly by other Latin American sellers, that experience has shown not only that a growing market for Latin American exports exists in Africa but also how to go about taking advantage of that market on a systematic basis. It is not likely to be ignored by governments craving nontraditional exports. However, whether or not government assistance on the Brazilian model is provided by other Latin American governments, sales to Africa by Latin American sellers will increase as entrepreneurs like the Ecuadorian stove manufacturer discover that a market for their products exists. They will be encouraged in this view as they discover that many of their products are well suited for the developing countries of Africa and that the African market, while not yet large by American or European standards, is large enough to make a substantial impact on sales and earnings of smaller Latin American companies.

CULTURAL AND POLITICAL FACTORS
IN LATIN AMERICAN-AFRICAN TRADE

In trading with African countries, especially in selling to African markets, Latin Americans will have to be sensitive to African cultures as well as to African political concerns.

Brazil is particularly well suited to respond to Africa's cultures. Over almost 300 years, millions of African slaves were brought to Brazil, primarily through Salvador. These Africans brought with them their customs and culture, which spread south from Northeast Brazil with the result that some evidence of African culture can be found in most of the country. It is now estimated that about 20 percent of Brazil's population is of pure, or nearly pure, African descent and a far greater number are partially of African descent. This exchange has worked both ways as some Brazilians of African descent have returned to Nigeria to live in Lagos.

The cultural ties between Brazil and Africa have been of use in strengthening Brazil's trade relationships through reminders of those ties and the employment of some Brazilians of African descent in Brazilian-African trade.

Other Latin American countries do not have the advantage of strong ties to Africa and its cultures, but sensitivity to African cultures will be a necessity if they wish their trade with Africa to increase. This sensitivity to African cultures will be especially important to those countries that have long prided themselves on being of primarily European background and that therefore do not have a recent history of living with, and understanding, other cultures.

As important as it is for Latin American traders to understand African culture, it is even more important for them to understand African political interests. Certainly an understanding of the politics of each African country with which trade is carried on is important. Each country has a political system that is capable of being broadly categorized, whether as a one-party state, a multiparty democracy, a military government, or some other form. But each has different nuances in its political system of which a trader must be aware, whether caused by tribal considerations, economic orientation, or substantial influence retained by the former colonial power, especially in some Francophone countries. Although each case is different, Latin Americans who are accustomed to orienting themselves to a variety of political systems that change from time to time should be sufficiently sensitive to the local political climate of each country with which they trade to be able to deal with each as circumstances require. This will be especially true if the culture of the African country is also well understood.

However, there is one overriding African political concern that Latin Americans are not, by background, prepared to deal with but that they must understand and be sensitive to. It is a concern that may ultimately require Latin Americans to make choices of the markets with which they choose to deal. It is the problem of southern Africa.

For the moment, it is possible to trade with both black Africa and South Africa (Rhodesia is the subject of a UN embargo) despite protests against such trade by some black African countries. The only possible exception relates to trade in arms with South Africa. This type of trade, or some form of military cooperation, might very well prompt strong negative reactions from many African trading partners, especially Nigeria. Military cooperation is conceivable because Latin American countries in the Southern Cone do have a common interest with South Africa in protecting South Atlantic sea-lanes. Such countries should be aware of the possible trade consequences of military cooperation with South Africa.

It is also true that even today black African countries differ in their reactions to trade with South Africa. Certain countries still believe in the possibilities for a constructive dialogue with South Africa, some still carry on substantial trade themselves with South Africa, and many, including Nigeria, believe in a full embargo on South African trade. Thus, a distinction can be made between those to whom trade with South Africa could have a negative impact and those to whom it would make no difference at all. Over time, however, assuming present trends continue, it is possible that trade with South Africa could disturb trade relations—at least for Latin America as a seller—with much of black Africa.

The choice, if it has to be made, will not be easy, especially for those Latin American governments whose political orientation makes them more sympathetic to the aspirations of the white minority than the black majority. Indeed, given the current size of the South African market, it is possible that some may simply choose to trade with South Africa no matter what the price.

But the growing ability of black Africa not only to sell needed raw materials but also to buy the world's manufactured goods makes it a potential buyer that is not easily ignored. For example, Nigeria has now become a more important trading partner to the United States and the United Kingdom than has South Africa. Neither of these two countries, nor any others, have had to choose between trade with black Africa and trade with South Africa. But Latin Americans will have to be sensitive to this issue and to the fact that their actions concerning South Africa, whether in trade, in military cooperation, or in positions taken at the United Nations, could eventually affect trade with their new and growing trading partner. Furthermore, since not only South Africa but also Rhodesia (Zimbabwe) and South-West Africa (Namibia) are part of the total southern African problem, Latin American countries will also have to be sensitive to the impact their UN votes on these issues could have on relations with black Africa.

To the extent that Africa becomes an arena for East-West confrontations, Latin Americans would be well advised, and are likely, to remain aloof from such problems and to pursue their own interests. The need for such an attitude was best illustrated by Brazil's speed in recognizing the Marxist Popular Movement for the Liberation of Angola (MPLA) government in Angola despite the hesitancy of others to do so.

THE FINANCING OF AFRICAN TRADE

As buyers, Latin Americans have well-established means of financing their own imports. However, as sellers, particularly of manufactured or semimanufactured goods, Latin Americans are relative newcomers and therefore have to establish means of competing with the financing provided by the more developed countries to finance their own sales of such goods. The evidence indicates that Latin Americans are beginning to do just that.

The developed world finances its exports through such well-known institutions as the Export-Import Bank of the United States (Eximbank), Cofass (France), Hermes (Germany, and Export Credits Guarantee Department (ECGD) (Great Britain). In order to meet this competition, Brazil provides export financing to its sellers through Banco do Brasil's Carteira de Comercio Exterior (Cacex), and Argentina through special discount facilities of its Central Bank. In both cases existing programs are subject to constant change as experience indicates that new forms of export assistance are needed.

At present, Cacex financing[1] takes the form of both preexport financing and financing of the ultimate sale. Preexport financing provides subsidized rate financing in the form of working capital for manufacturers of exports. It is also available to Brazilian trading companies seeking to finance accounts receivable and inventory acquisition. Both exporters and trading companies also qualify for financing of export merchandise stored in customs warehouses. In all cases, loans are made to qualified borrowers by commercial banks to whom rediscounting facilities are available through Cacex.

In addition, Cacex will provide subsidized fixed-rate financing of Brazilian exports of capital goods and consumer durables. This is done through the discounting by Cacex of accepted U.S. dollar denominated drafts on the foreign importer. The drafts, in order to qualify, must have received export credit insurance from the Institute de Reseguros do Brasil (IRB), which provides insurance on up to 85 percent of the face value of the drafts for both principal and interest. Since a 100 percent down payment is usually required, the export credit insurance covers only the financed portion. The tenor of the financing will depend on the item exported and the amount of the sale. In this case, as in the case of preexport financing, a commercial bank acts as intermediary. Cacex also provides special programs for financing studies that could result in increasing the export of manufactured products as well as the sale of technical services related to projects, including large-scale public works carried out by Brazilian civil engineering companies.

It is important to note that major changes in these subsidized export credit facilities can be expected as Brazil prepares to comply with U.S. Treasury and General Agreement on Tariffs and Trade (GATT) guidelines on trade policy.

While differing in details, programs for prefinancing of certain priority exports as well as financing of priority exports are available to Argentine exporters. These programs are provided through rediscount facilities made available to Argentine banks by the Central Bank of Argentina.[2]

The foregoing Latin American export finance facilities are, of course, a response to export finance agencies existing in the developed world and are not limited to sales to Africa. In addition, however, it would be possible for Latin American countries to finance their exports through loans to African governments that are tied to exports. It is a device used by developed countries and used by Brazil when, shortly after Angola's independence, Banco do Brasil offered it a loan to finance imports of Brazilian motor vehicles.

Finally, financing of Latin American exports could be expedited by the presence of Latin American banks in Africa. As long as Latin American banks do not know Africa, they will not feel comfortable taking African risks for their own account, and Latin American exporters will have to rely primarily on existing facilities provided by their own governments.

In this area, as in others, Brazil is leading the way by example. Banco do Brasil has acquired a 20 percent interest in the International Bank for West Africa (Banque Internationale pour l'Afrique Occidental) which has a long history in Africa and a presence in 13 African countries. Banco do Brasil has also opened a representative office of its own in Lagos. In addition, Banco Real has created a full service subsidiary in Abidjan (Banque Real de Côte d'Ivoire). Although no other Latin American banks have established themselves in Africa, as trade with Africa increases, Latin American banks can be expected to follow

In the meantime, some Latin American exporters have begun to recognize that foreign banks now operating in Africa could finance their exports to Africa. It is, for example, not unusual for a bank from one developed country that is active in Africa to help finance an export of another developed country destined for Africa. Obviously, such banks prefer to finance their own customers who are customarily their own nationals, but third-country financing does occur. As long as it does, it could be a source of financing for Latin American exporters. But this will never be as satisfactory a source of private financing for Latin American exporters as having the banks that do business with them at home—and that therefore feel a greater obligation to them as exporters—actually located in Africa and available to provide financing to African buyers. Competition for exports to African markets requires Latin American exporters to be able to compete on financing terms as well as on price and quality. Although government banks will always be one source of such financing, competitive private banking sources will also be needed to provide the required flexibility and variety of financing sources available to other exporters.

CONCLUSION

Without a great deal of fanfare, Latin America has discovered the possibility of increased trade with Africa. These two continents, each of which has historically looked north, have suddenly found that direct trade links across the Atlantic are possible and beneficial. Although the most economically powerful countries of each continent, Brazil and Nigeria, are leading the way, others are following. There are hurdles to be overcome, but they are being overcome by the ingenuity of some Latin American businessmen and are capable of being overcome by others. This is a development worth watching. It is in its infancy and its full potential, both economic and political, is yet to be felt or understood.

NOTES

1. Banco do Brasil, Carteria de Comercio Exterior, Bulletin no. 78/3.
2. Banco Central de la Republica Argentina, Circulars R.F. 20 and 21, and R.C. 693.

III

THE BASICS OF LENDING

Private commercial banks engaged in lending operations in Latin America have a multitude of factors to consider, ranging from analysis of individual credit opportunities to the manner in which legal documentation is structured in support of those operations. This section begins with comments by Robert Hampton III on the types of accounting practices one may see in various Latin American countries and some advice as to how lenders might interpret that information. Joseph Martin offers practical suggestions for analysis of credit risk associated with major types of facilities, ranging from loans to government entities to correspondent banking and corporate lending. Whitman Knapp offers a basic level description of the Eurocurrency lending process and describes how syndications are negotiated and brought to the market. Andrew Quale, Jr., draws attention to significant legal issues associated with lending money in Latin America. This section concludes with a listing of sources, compiled by Leila Jenkins, of published materials available to those embarking on country studies.

14
ACCOUNTING AND REPORTING: PERSPECTIVE FOR THE LENDER

Robert Hampton, III

INTRODUCTION

That financial accounting and reporting standards differ among
nations is, of itself, probably not surprising to members of the U.S.
business and financial community familiar with the difficulties of resolving accounting issues within our own country. Even the most
knowledgeable of those members, however, including persons involved
directly in foreign commerce, may be wholly unaware of the breadth
and the depth of the differences in point.

During 1978, the author's firm, Price Waterhouse and Company,
surveyed current accounting principles and reporting practices in 83
countries with respect to 267 propositions covering fundamental concepts, broad principles, and specifics of application. Except for a
few emerging nations that have chosen to follow in all respects the
principles and practices of another country, no two countries had
identical standards of financial accounting and reporting; moreover,
all 267 propositions show differences—usually wide differences—in
application among the nations surveyed.

The Price Waterhouse survey included all the independent nations that make up Latin America. There, as elsewhere, the patterns are numerous, and widespread differences exist among the nations in point. Even to catalogue those differences, let alone to evaluate their significance, would be a monumental exercise in massive
detail, beyond the scope of this book and any reasonable needs of its
readers; moreover, it would constitute information that inevitably
starts to obsolesce as soon as it is gathered and inexorably loses reliability as practice evolves and as new standards appear.

This chapter focuses on Latin American financial accounting
and reporting in order to furnish a useful perspective for the lending

official familiar with U.S. financial statements prepared in conformity
with U.S. generally accepted accounting principles (GAAP). To be
meaningful and relevant, that perspective must encompass the differences between U.S. and Latin American accounting and reporting, but
the result must be a broad overview of such differences and their significance to the lending official, rather than a vade mecum of specifics.

The several purposes of this chapter are:

1. to review sources of international differences and reasons
for their persistence,
2. to illustrate the specific differences that the lender in Latin
America will encounter in financial statements prepared under local
standards, and
3. to offer some useful dos and don'ts for coping with differences.

THE CAUSES AND NATURE
OF INTERNATIONAL DIFFERENCES

Accounting has traditionally been called the language of business. This descriptive characterization has a normative dimension
as well: if accounting is to be useful for business decision making in
the real world, it must track business as actually conducted.

To the extent that commercial tradition, custom, practices,
laws, and taxation differ from country to country, so too does the conduct of business, with direct consequences for accounting as its local
language. All nations have business-oriented laws, codifying local
commercial custom, tradition, and practice or amending them in response to changes in the political, social, and economic climate. All
these laws influence local accounting; some of them virtually determine it. Variations in national commercial law are a prolific source
of international accounting and reporting differences, and clearly
these differences are particularly stubborn.

A second important source of international differences in accounting is taxation of business entities. The direct influence of tax
law on accounting can be seen in the United States, where the last-in
first-out (LIOF) method of accounting for inventories must be used
for all external financial reporting if claimed for taxes. Apart from
that rather dramatic example, however, financial accounting in this
country is largely unconstrained by tax rules, a situation that does
not prevail in many areas of the world. In some countries, the accounting provisions of the tax law tend to fill a vacuum created by an
absence of enunciated financial reporting standards. In other coun-

tries, reporting entities regard minimization of taxes as a more important objective than fair presentation or a true and fair view of financial results, and they account for a variety of transactions accordingly. The resulting international differences in financial reporting are hardy perennials.

A third key source of international differences is the extent to which local accounting is formalized. Formalization is a natural phenomenon in countries, such as our own, with vibrant commercial activity, a widely shared stake in that activity, and a general expectation of reliable public reporting on the success or failure of the activity. General interest in and concern with financial reporting produce a consensus for ongoing improvement. The private sector, through its designated professional bodies, is encouraged to promulgate authoritative pronouncements intended to improve the financial statements issued by business and used by a spectrum of persons at interest.

The result is a structured private sector system coexistent with, but separate from, legal requirements that strongly influences or even governs the reports of business entities. No national system at present is more highly structured than our own, but many other countries, including some in Latin America, have moved and continue to move in that direction. As desirable as formalization may be from a local standpoint, it is unfortunately true that private-sector national accounting pronouncements differ widely, producing firmly embedded international differences.

Formalization of reporting has another significant dimension as well: the extent to which independent attestation of business financial reports is required, by law or custom, and effectively carried out by qualified professional auditors. The greater this aspect of formalization within a given country, the greater the general credibility that attaches to business financial statements issued in that country. Variations in the quality of business financial reports as such may be even more significant to the international lender than specific differences in accounting treatment, display, and disclosure. (The author stresses the importance of that emphasized phraseology. Requirements for statutory audits may be illusory. The mere existence of requirements does not assure compliance or enforcement; statutory audits vary greatly in objectives and scope, and those who perform them may or may not have substantive qualifications.)

Finally, international variations in accounting and reporting arise simply from differences of national ethos—the differences in culture, history, and temperament that distinguish one nation from another. To the German accountant, reporting is a matter of law, and financial reports that comply with the detailed prescriptions of German law are, ipso facto, full and correct; to the British accountant, the essence of accounting-oriented law is the "true and fair view," and it is achieved not by mechanical compliance with rules but by applying sound judgment in particular circumstances. In Germany, it would be unthinkable to restate any prior year's figures duly filed as prescribed by law. In the United Kingdom, by contrast, it would be unthinkable not to restate prior years' figures if, in the accountant's judgment, restatement is necessary for meaningful comparisons.

The long delay that preceded adoption in 1978 of uniform basic reporting standards for the European Economic Community stemmed largely from this fundamental cleavage between the judgmental (British) and legalistic (German) approaches to financial reporting. The matter was finally resolved by pragmatic compromise; the two approaches do not admit of conceptual harmonization.

FOCUS ON LATIN AMERICA

The geographical expanse called Latin America extends from the Rio Grande River to Cape Horn—well over half the Western Hemisphere. Millions of Latin Americans inhabit a score of independent, strongly nationalistic countries characterized by extremes of wealth and poverty among and within nations, varying degrees of political stability and of commercial activity, and strong crosscurrents of foreign influence.

It is thus to be expected, and is in fact the case, that all of the previously described forces that create and perpetuate differences in accounting and reporting among countries are at work in Latin America. Those differences are as variegated as Latin America's climate and, if not as numerous as its inhabitants, literally as widespread as its constituent nations.

To grapple with this amalgam the author has found it useful to divide it into three discrete types: differences that relate to broad fundamental concepts, differences in specific accounting principles applied and in their details of application, and differences in the extent and quality of disclosure.

Certain obvious, and in the author's view trivial, points of difference can simply be eliminated from consideration. These are the use of Spanish (in several variants) and Portuguese rather than English and the presentation in financial statements of familiar items in unfamiliar format. For purposes of this chapter it is assumed that the lender has in hand financial statements adequately translated into appropriate technical English and that, for example, listings of assets and liabilities in ascending rather than descending order of currentness or the display of operating results in profit-and-loss account form rather than in single-statement form will present no difficulties when and if encountered.

Differences in Basis of Preparation

Differences in broad fundamental concepts run to the very basis of preparing financial reports, and five areas merit particular attention: measurement, the reporting entity, the basic reporting package, consistency, and conservatism.

Measurement

For perspective on Latin American reporting, by far the most significant of the five areas is measurement. The concept of measurement has two aspects: the attribute to be measured and the unit to be used as the common denominator for expressing the spectrum of resources, obligations, and business transactions in additive financial terms.

For nearly 500 years, the figures in financial reports have been based on measuring the attribute of historical cost in completed transactions and expressing the measurement in historical units of money. Inflation impairs the integrity of the unit of money as a measure; the more severe the inflation, the more rapid and complete the impairment. This is so because money of different worth at different dates is commingled in financial reports, a result directly analogous to commingling lire, pounds, dollars, and cruzeiros in the same balance sheet or earnings statement.

For 50 years accountants have been well aware of this problem, have studied it with intensity and concern directly proportional to the rate of inflation, and, in the United States at least, have reached no consensus on a solution. The present conditions of chronic and severe inflation, now global in scope, have made it a problem of crisis proportions. It is now widely and properly recognized as the single most serious unsolved problem confronting accountants of all nationalities.

At this writing, a worldwide debate centers on the most effective accounting riposte to inflation, with nothing approaching consensus and little prospect of achieving it soon. At the heart of the debate are two basic schools of thought. The first school focuses on changing prices of specific items and advocates accounting measurements of some attribute other than historical cost—typically, current cost of replacement or current value.

The second school focuses on general inflation and advocates retaining historical cost as the attribute for accounting measurements but using a measuring unit other than historical money—specifically, units of general purchasing power, determined with reference to any of several possible indexes.

(The respective approaches to measurement address separate questions, and their conceptual bases are very different. They are not mutually exclusive, and some accountants advocate combining the approaches to measure the attribute of current value and express the results in units of constant general purchasing power.)

Inflation has long been endemic in Latin America and in some countries has reached levels beyond the practical comprehension of people in areas with relatively low rates of inflation. No Norte Americano can readily envision the conduct of business or personal affairs amid Brazil's 40 percent inflation, let alone Argentina's triple-digit level. In Latin America, responsive accounting has long since become a problem for practical action rather than a topic for scholarly debate. The actions taken range from government decree of radically new systems of measurement and reporting to voluntary experimentation with restatement of selected assets, liabilities, and transactions. This gamut of actions is sometimes lumped under the label indexing, an imprecise term that needs definition in the specific circumstances.

For instance, the Brazilian government has required indexing since 1964, with ensuing periodic refinements in the prescribed system. At present, fixed assets are revalued annually by applying a government wholesale price index, and depreciation is based on the revalued amount. In addition, annual income is charged with an amount intended to maintain the purchasing power of working capital. These adjustments for inflation, based strictly on practical necessity rather than on conceptual purity, apply to both tax and financial reporting.

Chile requires the presentation of complete financial statements expressed in units of purchasing power, side by side with the traditional statements based on historical units of money; similar practice prevails in Argentina as a result of private-sector initiatives. These adjusted supplementary financials address the effects of general inflation, and in both Argentina and Chile the primary statements must also address changing prices via the annual indexing of fixed assets to amounts that approximate current replacement levels; depreciation is based on revalued amounts.

Elsewhere in Latin America, pervasive restatements in units of general purchasing power are rarely found, but periodic (or sporadic) revaluation of fixed assets to approximate current replacement levels is not uncommon; again, depreciation is based on revalued amounts.

Assuming continued, severe inflation in Latin America, it seems highly probable that decisive action by local governments and local accounting professions will produce more inflation-oriented reporting in more Latin American countries, in the form of general price-level accounting, of selective or broad-based current value accounting, or of both. The measurement area thus promises to remain an important source of differences between accounting in Latin America and in the United States for the immediate future and, in addition, a continuing source of differences, major and minor, among Latin American countries.

The Reporting Entity

Universal U.S. practice is to issue consolidated financial statements that include the accounts of the parent entity and all of its significant operating (nonfinancial) subsidiaries owned over 50 percent; the reporting entity is thus the consolidated enterprise. In Latin America, the reporting entity is far more commonly the parent company only; the most notable exceptions are Mexico and Venezuela, which require consolidated statements accompanied by those of the parent company. The concept of consolidation has no applicability in most South American countries and only limited applicability in Central America.

In the United States unconsolidated subsidiaries and investee companies owned 50 percent or less are reported in consolidated financial statements on the equity method—that is, the investor's proportionate share of subsidiary or investee earnings is included each year in consolidated results, contra to increases in the investment account in the consolidated balance sheet. By contrast, equity-method accounting is not prevalent in Latin America, with investments carried mainly at cost and income reported only as dividends are received.

The Basic Reporting Package

U.S. GAAP require a statement of changes in financial position (the so-called funds statement) as a basic financial statement. Latin American practice in presenting this most useful (especially for the lender) financial statement varies widely. It is required in a few countries, and its presentation ranges from rare to prevalent in others.

Consistency

The concept that accounting policies should be consistently followed and applied is a cornerstone of U.S. financial reporting. U.S. GAAP impose certain constraints on changes and rigid requirements for disclosing the fact and effect of any such changes.

That is, happily, an area of basics in which Latin American reporting as a whole exhibits few differences either with the United States or among the constituent nations. Nevertheless, practice is not uniform, and the consistency concept is not always honored, nor is the all-important disclosure of departures from it always furnished in Latin America. In short, the problem of working with inconsistently prepared statements is not widespread in Latin America, but neither can it be dismissed. Its existence, and its importance, depend on the particular situation.

Conservatism

The concept of conservatism (or prudence, as it is often called outside the United States) is a centuries-old fundamental of financial reporting, with different applications in different countries. The continental European tradition, with its deep concern for the protection of creditors, tends to view with equanimity understatements of assets, creation of hidden reserves, and overstatement of liabilities. By contrast, the English-speaking countries, in the British tradition, tend to view overconservatism—however lofty its purposes—with the same distaste as underconservatism, because neither is compatible with fair presentation ("true and fair view") in financial reports.

Both traditions have substantial influence in Latin America, and no broad-brush characterization of Latin American reporting as conservative (or otherwise) would be meaningful. Suffice it to note that the practices of providing general reserves by charges to income and of using those reserves to absorb current charges in subsequent periods are encountered in certain Latin American countries and that today's overconservatism is tomorrow's underconservatism, with the results of at least two accounting periods distorted.

A corollary aspect of the concept of conservatism is the influence of taxation on financial reporting in a given country. In Chile, it is the predominant practice to conform financial reporting strictly with tax requirements; it is the minority practice in several Latin American countries. Although tax accounting does not necessarily result in unfair presentation of financial results, it creates a presumption that financial accounts adhering strictly to tax requirements will reflect charges based on what the tax collector will allow and credits based on what the tax collector requires, rather than on the objective best estimates that underlie sound accrual accounting. The results could be either overconservative or underconservative; the crux is to introduce a dimension of difference and perhaps an important one.

Differences in Accounting Principles

In this category of difference, only the patience of the reader and the energy of the author impose ultimate limits. The impracticability and the futility of preparing an exhaustive list of differences in specific accounting principles and details of their application in Latin America have already been noted. A selected few examples of particularly significant differences between U.S. and Latin American reporting should give a useful overall feel for approaching particular lending situations.

Tax Allocation

U.S. principles require comprehensive accounting for the tax effect of timing differences, that is, items of revenue and expense that are reported in one period for tax purposes and in another period for financial accounting purposes. In no Latin American country is comprehensive tax allocation required; with the sole exceptions of Venezuela and the Dominican Republic, it is a minority practice or is not practiced.

Research and Development Costs

In the United States, both research and development costs must be charged to expense as incurred. Generally speaking, this is the prevailing (but not uniform) Latin American practice as regards research costs; development costs, on the other hand, are usually deferred and amortized over some future period.

Leases

U.S. GAAP requiring that certain leases be accounted for as assets and obligations of the lessor or as sales or financing arrangements by the lessor or as both have little currency in Latin America. Leases are commonly accounted for as operating leases, regardless of their provisions.

Termination Indemnities

Requirements to pay a predetermined amount, usually based on rate of pay and length of service, to employees discharged with (or without) just cause arise in the United States mainly from specific union agreements. Under normal operating circumstances in this country, such payments usually constitute relatively remote contingencies.

Throughout Latin America, however, social legislation commonly provides for some such payment by all employers in specified (and widely varying) circumstances. In some countries, termination indemnities are "hell-or-high-water" liabilities; in other countries, they become liabilities only upon the occurrence of some future event, probable or improbable. And in virtually all Latin American countries, substantive sums of money are at least potentially involved.

Termination indemnities are accounted for variously in Latin America, most commonly on a pay-as-you-go basis, with expense recorded when actual payment is made. Other accounting practices are, however, followed, including current accrual based on an average yearly requirement or on assuming a complete shutdown of operations.

Because of the variety of termination indemnity arrangements in Latin America, the divergences in the related accounting, and the potential materiality of related payments, this is clearly an area that deserves careful attention in working with Latin American financial reports. This is all the more true for the relative unimportance of termination payments in the experience of most lenders with a U.S. orientation.

Receivables and Payables

The U.S. practice of recording at an imputed present value all receivables and payables not subject to normal trade terms and subsequently recording imputed interest income and expense is required in Venezuela, prohibited in Colombia, and virtually unknown elsewhere in Latin America.

Scores of other such differences could be adduced, but stated objectives of this section would appear to be adequately attained without doing so.

Differences in Disclosure

The user of external, general purpose financial reports issued by business entities in the United States routinely receives disclosure unexcelled anywhere else in the world in either scope or quality. Many in the U.S. business and financial community consider this disclosure to be too good—to have reached the point of ever-diminishing returns from a cost benefit standpoint.

Be that as it may, there are a variety of disclosures widely accepted in this country as necessary and useful that would certainly survive any pruning of disclosure deadwood, and many of these disclosures are rare, sketchy, or absent in foreign financial statements.

Some of the most important of these disclosures that are usually missing or sketchy in Latin American financial reports are listed below (Latin American disclosure practice is, unfortunately, deficient by U.S. standards, with only isolated exceptions):

Accounting policies followed,
Hypothecation of assets,

Terms and interest rates of separate issues of long-term debt,
Contingent liabilities and assets,
Commitments for future capital expenditure,
Terms of lease agreements,
Relative rights and preferences of classes of capital stock,
Restrictions on retained earnings,
Significant events after balance-sheet date,
Transactions with related parties,
Segment information.

A key point is that absence of a particular disclosure in a Latin American report (with rare exceptions) does not necessarily imply that the pertinent circumstances do not apply in the case of the reporting entity, as it would invariably in a U.S. report conforming with U.S. GAAP.

The matter of divergent disclosure is extremely important for the perspective of the U.S. lender, and it has further implications noted in the next section.

CONCLUSION: SOME SUGGESTED DO's AND DON'T's

As stated at its outset, this chapter is intended to provide a useful perspective on Latin American financial accounting and reporting for the lending official familiar with U.S. standards.

Although country-by-country guidance in specifics is necessarily beyond its scope, it nevertheless seeks to serve practical rather than merely philosophical ends. It is aimed toward the real-life lender in the arena of lending operations. Forearmed with awareness of—and, it is hoped, a healthy respect for—the myriad potential differences between financial reports issued in the United States and those issued in Latin America, that lender faces a consummately practical question: What do I do about it?

Some suggestions follow:

Do get help. To work effectively with general purpose financial reports issued by prospective borrowers in any Latin American nation, the lending official needs on-the-scene professional help. International firms practicing (or having affiliates) in Latin America are particularly qualified to advise on significant differences between local and U.S. reporting standards, but not uniquely so: there are reputable local firms with the necessary international orientation.

Do the necessary homework. The need for competent professional help does not imply unquestioning reliance by the lender. Far from it. Before sitting down with the professional adviser, the lending official should be ready to ask questions and to evaluate answers critically. For example:

Does local financial reporting have real stature in government and business circles, or is it largely the end product of perfunctory compliance with regulations unrelated to an objective of fair presentation?

Do tax considerations affect local financial reporting to any important extent? If so, do the effects introduce either over- or under-conservatism into financial reporting?

Are there local audit requirements? Is so, are they such that the required examinations of financial reports add real credibility to those reports? How do local auditing standards compare with those of the U.S. profession?

To what extent are local reporting and disclosure standards formalized? Are the principal initiatives for formalization governmental or professional? Are the initiatives ongoing? Are the results a continuing improvement in financial reporting?

Depending upon the actual lending situation, there might be specifics of local accounting and disclosure practice in which the lender is particularly interested and about which the professional adviser should be queried. The Appendix to this chapter suggests some sources that might prove useful in marshaling such queries.

And finally, having obtained the help and done the homework, don't try to go it alone. No matter how conversant he may be with U.S. accounting and reporting standards, no matter how extensively he has reviewed local practice with his professional adviser, the lender should not take on a hopeless do-it-yourself project to convert a set of local financial statements to a set of U.S. financial statements to use for decision making.

The bar to doing so is lack of disclosure. As to matters both of accounting policy and of substantive financial information, data absolutely prerequisite to a meaningful conversion from local GAAP to U.S. GAAP may simply be missing from the local statements. Do make informed use of those statements for what they are; don't try to use them for what they are not—and cannot be.

APPENDIX

Sources of Specific Information about Financial
Accounting and Reporting in Latin America

The references cited below are those best known to the author, most of them published by his firm; other firms also publish a variety of reference material on international and local taxation and business. Cited references not available through direct access are obtainable from the library of the American Institute of Certified Public Accountants.

All materials that deal with specifics of accounting, reporting, taxation, and business regulation are inherently subject to obsolescence, sometimes rapid obsolescence, depending on the particular country. Accordingly, all such materials—those listed below and any others of a similar nature—should be reviewed for current applicability and accuracy by an adviser familiar with local conditions.

American Institute of CPAs. Professional Accounting in 30 Countries. New York, 1975.

> Included among the 30 countries are 8 in Latin America. A chapter on each country includes a discussion of reporting requirements, professional standards, and accounting principles and practices.

Price Waterhouse. Guide for the Reader of Foreign Financial Statements. New York, 1975.

> Summarizes major differences in accounting principles and reporting practices between the United States and each of 24 foreign countries, including 7 in Latin America. A superseding updated edition is scheduled for publication late in 1980.

_____. Information Guides for Doing Business. New York, various dates.

> A series of guides on business conditions, regulation, and taxation in 70 individual countries, including for each a section on accounting practices and audit requirements.

Price Waterhouse International. Survey of Accounting Principles and Reporting Practices. 3rd ed. New York, 1979.

> The third updating of this unique international survey, showing current practice as of January 1, 1979, in 83 countries, including all of Latin America, with respect to 267 specific points of accounting and disclosure.

15
CREDIT CONSIDERATIONS

Joseph M. Martin

The essence of the credit decision must be an assessment of the likelihood of contractually punctual return of the goods provided by the lender, most commonly cash or guarantees. Unfortunately, this is a probabilistic assessment not always easily summarized into the simpler, binary yes-or-no outcome. The credit decision is but one element in the broader lending decision, which encompasses other portfolio considerations of yield, maturity, geographical and industry concentration, and the like; it nonetheless requires the greatest sensitivity to the subjective concepts especially relevant to international lending. The number and complexity of such concepts in international lending are notably greater than in the domestic context, but as they relate to the credit decision itself these concepts are evaluated for their effect upon the likelihood of timely repayment, which at least is a straightforward goal. The outcome is not always so clear. The intent of this chapter is thus to briefly identify the major elements of the credit decision to be evaluated within the principal types of lending markets in Latin America, here limited to governmental units, commercial banks, and commercial and industrial corporations. Whereas the concepts covered do not exhaust the subject, they should at least provide a basic framework for systematic analysis of representative decisions confronting the offshore lender.

The concept of contractually punctual return, stated above as the object of credit evaluation, must be defined to include consideration of the contracted amount of principal, interest, and other charges, as well as timeliness in the payment of each. Once the borrower has been found unable to pay on schedule, a restructuring must be considered. Restructuring can often lead to lower negotiated interest rates, substantially longer terms, local currency substitution, or other potentially unfavorable considerations. Hence the breach of timeliness can be the leading indicator of future or opportunity loss.

FOREIGN GOVERNMENTAL ENTITIES

The credit decision toward the financing of foreign governmental entities is paradoxically one requiring the most comprehensive and profound analysis and evaluation, with the least precise results. As the essential evaluation is that of the likelihood of timely repayment, the ability of the borrower to meet a debt-payment schedule and willingness to do so are the primary objects of analysis.

As all foreign governmental borrowings represent an underlying need for foreign exchange, the ability to deliver foreign exchange at specified future dates can be estimated through the study of economic performance and liquidity measures as described in greater detail in Part I. The "need for foreign exchange" qualification is fundamental here, of course, as clearly from the credit (that is, timely repayment) viewpoint, sovereign government debt in its domestic currency can be inherently risk free in that through the role of money creation governments can always generate the currency as needed. Repayment of money alone is not usually an adequate alternative in that no currency (Latin American or any other) would be acceptable to foreign lenders when the governmental borrower itself has been unable to convert its own currency into hard foreign exchange. Evaluation of a foreign government's ability to provide proper exchange need not be an entirely passive credit exercise, as occasionally in negotiation the conditions of lending can be specified that can influence the borrower's actions as they affect the future availability of exchange; in practice the implementation of such conditions by foreign commercial lenders has been quite limited, however.

Evaluation of the willingness of a government to repay foreign indebtedness perhaps seems facile at first glance, yet it is the more comprehensive analysis. The inability to deliver fixed amounts of foreign exchange at fixed dates (default) is a dilemma of timeliness that often lends itself to a compromise modification of dates and amounts through restructuring. Whereas such a resolution has its attendant costs, they are usually not ultimate. A unilaterally declared moratorium on debt payments, or a repudiation of existing debts, obviously is a more grave outcome. This has not been a frequent occurrence in Latin America since the 1930s. Nevertheless, the potential effect on foreign lenders is so great as to require ongoing consideration, and the immediate actions of recourse for lenders can be quite limited after such an occurrence. Symptomatic of this, in the United States most commercial banks are subject to (and regularly examined by regulatory authorities for compliance with) specific exposure limits to foreign governments. These limits are related directly to the capitalization of the bank and are thus clearly intended as a measure of prudence in the event of loss, not of accommodative renegotiation of outstanding obligations. The best indicators of a foreign government's willingness to honor its debts would be its historical record of debt service and its projected future need for additional capital from presumably similar sources. Obviously during the life of the transactions underlying the specific credit decision at hand the borrowing government may change, and today's evaluation might not be accurate with regard to future policies. Although a few Latin American nations have had more governments than there have been years over much of this century, a change in government alone has not been a cause to suggest an unwillingness to honor debts of prior administrations. A change in the form of government and economic system would seem more indicative of ensuing risk. Predicting governmental changes and consequent effects remains a profoundly subjective element in overall country risk analysis. Analyzing existing statistical economic data can be mere sublimation when a change in willingness to honor commitments is impending. The most recent Latin American experience of comprehensive commercial debt repudiation has been with Cuba (where through nationalization of major industries even private sector debts became governmental and were not paid) and clearly was not directly caused by such economic data as the price of sugar.

Financing foreign governments is a generic concept, requiring further scrutiny on a transactional basis as each credit decision is identified. Different types of government borrowings can mean different categories of risk, to be analyzed accordingly.

In the broadest sense financing foreign governments might be separated into either seasonal and consumption loans or development financing. Seasonality is meant to imply that during the normal course of existing activities foreign exchange will be obtained or created to repay borrowings covering immediate shortages. Examples might include the following, distinguished as to the likely repayment sources:

Commercial activities: Export and preexport financing might be required to purchase and handle raw materials immediately, pending final collection of export proceeds. Import payments in foreign exchange might be financed in anticipation of future seasonal net exports or other government borrowings.

Tax and royalty anticipations: Frequently fiscal payments related to ongoing exports are received by Treasury authorities on fixed dates, and financing might be sought in advance of these receipts for immediate usage.

Reserve disbursements: Existing exchange reserves may be targeted for or committed toward specific activities or investments, and in anticipation of final governmental approval of disbursements, financing might be sought for immediate preliminary payments. Each of the above examples are normally short-term in nature, where the timing differences are readily identifiable, and represent the most traditional forms of foreign government financing.

Development financing is imprecise terminology, keyed to longer-term capital (foreign exchange) shortages than the examples cited above, to include:

Specific functions and industries: Industrialization programs may require foreign technology and goods; broadening of internal financing markets might be aided by making foreign exchange available through government financial intermediaries.

Economic infrastructure: Energy, communications, transportation systems, and other support functions in promoting economic investment activity might require foreign exchange outlays to permit eventual production of final goods and services. Such projects do not necessarily provide a source of repayment themselves.

General welfare: Components of local social and economic welfare projects, such as schools, housing, and health-care facilities, frequently also require foreign source goods. As these expenditures are not normally expected to generate related sources of repayment for foreign exchange borrowed, additional government borrowing at a later date is the most common source of liquidation.

Additional types of more specialized financing exist, of course, and the above merely distinguish between the broadest conceptual categories. No specific mention is made regarding the actual governmental borrowing entity, as therein the credit evaluation comes to the fore.

It is presumed that any foreign government would wish to be perceived as an identifiable entity composed of various subunits, and as such with regard to ultimate repayment all government debt should bear an equal risk premium. The evident reality that different governmental borrowers are able to borrow at very different risk premiums (for example, lending spreads) is a function of probable timeliness. Central banks are expected to be more prompt in meeting obligations than subsidized social welfare ventures in many cases. The government or nongovernment clarification is not always a simple distinction, unfortunately; determining whether a borrower with only partial government ownership is a part of that identifiable government body of equivalent ultimate risk must be based upon the percentage of ownership, whether or not effective control is exercised, the extent to which the borrower is managed by public officials, and the relative national priority of its underlying function.

Differentiating among borrowers identified as governmental for credit purposes then can be evaluated on the basis of the following:

Country risk: The initial analysis must, of course, be an assessment of the likely ability and willingness to repay at maturity at the national level. No financing is attractive unless this assessment can be made. It is worth noting that the ensuing factors are best evaluated on an intranational basis and are not readily compared with other nations. Comparisons across country borders are difficult because an incremental exposure in a country where the lender has a large existing exposure might be less acceptable than a riskier loan in a country where little exposure exists; this, of course, is part of an overall lending strategy, as distinct from strict transactional credit analysis.

Purpose: The national interest and benefit related to the specific borrower and underlying transaction are inherently important. Importation of basic foodstuffs is likely to be a high-priority governmental concern. Debts contracted for government-sponsored hotel construction is a priority more difficult to assess, presumably based upon the importance of tourist receipts to the individual nation. The assumption herein is, of course, that higher priorities of an ongoing nature are more likely to be repaid promptly than lower priorities.

Authority to borrow (guarantee): Unauthorized borrowings (guarantees) present a clear risk to lenders. Contracting obligations without full and proper authorization violates the premise of equivalent government risk and becomes a target for eventual repudiation. Documentation of the authority underlying each transaction cannot be overlooked.

Manner of borrowing: If a fully authorized borrowing is not contracted properly it can subsequently provide unpleasant surprises to the lender. At the extreme, transactions that do not result from honest, arm's-length negotiation are obvious candidates for repudiation. Less dramatically, financing steel mills with short-term debt (improper structuring) can lead to timeliness difficulties should credit availability contract.

Source of repayment: With lenders seeking repayment in foreign exchange, in some cases a borrowing entity that generates foreign exchange through collection of export proceeds can be a more prompt payer than purely domestic obligors. This is not often the case among governmental entities, and that it should ever be so is as a result of ineffective controls of the whole (the central government) over its parts.

Documentation: Proper documentation is valuable in establishing and identifying conditions of borrowing, and it can influence the timeliness of repayment through specification of procedures or penalties or both. It is unlikely that any documentation could ever allow the imposition of another Maximilian and Carlota on the throne (the 1860s product of an ostensible effort of debt collection),[1] but by at least providing definitions and procedures it can facilitate structured discussions should eventual difficulties arise.

Financial statements: Governmental entity financial statements are not usually independently audited, but they at least provide a perspective of the type and magnitude of government support to the underlying function of the potential borrower, of the likely source of repayment (internal operations or government subsidy), and of changes over time in these areas that could signal possible policy changes.

FINANCIAL INSTITUTIONS

To the offshore lender local financial institutions are a fundamental element in developing a business presence and awareness in the local market. They are usually the best sources of complementary services, information, and business contacts. Commercial banks are particularly valuable in this comprehensive role, hence this discussion focuses upon them, given that they invariably constitute a part of the offshore lender's portfolio in a given country. Credit decisions of the lender toward his exposure to local financial institutions of course depend to some extent upon the specific nature of the operations being considered, given different periods of exposure and documentation.

Whatever the transaction, analysis of the risk inherent in the credit decision lends itself readily to the collection of data; unfortunately, in the case of most financial institutions the data are usually not specific or precise enough to permit the lender to obtain a meaningful understanding of the current financial trends of the institution. The reporting discretion exercised in the timing of recognition of interest and other income and expense items alone is ample to assure that commercial bank statements remain primarily management's tools, not the analyst's, a phenomenon not exclusive in Latin America: "All over the world, it seems banks have accumulated special privileges for themselves in the area of accounting. . . . The inevitable result is that the bank accounts . . . are subject to great limitation—so great indeed that even the banks themselves now accept the need for improvements."[2] Quantitative financial data therefore are useful as preliminary screening criteria in identifying relative differences of banks' basic financial structures and as sources of leads for further questioning but are determinative in the credit decisions only in the most obviously negative circumstances; that is, if the statements are awful, the credit decision is easy. Most often, however, a checking with other interested parties (local and foreign) regarding appropriate aspects of reputation and quality of management and operations is the more meaningful approach.

The focus of the credit decision, whatever the transaction or sources of information, should encompass at least the following categories of importance, with more specific emphasis as appropriate:[3]

Management/ownership: Clearly this is the most vital longer-term factor in any institution and perhaps the most difficult to evaluate. An evaluation should consider leadership, planning, and responsiveness; technical and administrative competence and compliance with policies and regulations; ability to direct additional resources into the institution in the event of need; and depth and provision for succession. Historical measures of performances are symptomatic of the relative quality of past management but do not always accurately reveal much of the future under changing circumstances. Opinions of other knowledgeable sources and direct personal contact and evaluation are the most reliable sources.

Capital adequacy: The dichotomous roles of leverage (leading, it is hoped, to a higher return on capital) and solvency (protection against losses) must be properly in balance. Balance, of course, is imprecise here, but capital in relation to past performance and other comparable institutions can be fairly analyzed. The relative proportion of capital to deposits and other liabilities is a conventional gauge; similarly, capital in relation to the asset portfolio is meaningful. In this latter measure capital is most often related to risk assets (total assets less primary and secondary reserves) as more consistently indicative of adequate capital. The term capital is not a precise one, and the decision to include capital notes, reserves, or other items must be based upon an investigation of the terms, accounting, and applicability of each.

Liquidity: Awareness of the composition of liquid assets and the relative need for them (that is, reserve requirements, structure of liabilities, and asset expansion rate) should include an evaluation of availability of assets readily convertible into cash, volatility, and interest; sensitivity of deposits; volume and frequency of borrowing from the central bank and other banks; and access to alternate money market sources. Commonly primary (cash, deposits with the central bank and other banks, and certain collection items) and secondary (government securities of shorter maturity) reserves are measured against deposits, particularly the more volatile deposits of a demand nature, for historical changes and in relation to other comparable institutions.

Asset portfolio: The objective here is to determine management' policies of investing excess reserves in earning assets. Of interest are the compositions of the investment and loan portfolios and how they relate to deposit levels and the trends of local business activity. During periods of increasing economic activity, loans particularly might be expected to demonstrate proportionate growth; during periods of recession or declining growth, if a relative decline in loan activity is not apparent it can be indicative of accommodative credit policies related to an inability to liquidate (collect) loans at maturity. Other factors such as volume of nonperforming assets and diversification of assets are valuable but usually not readily determined. An understanding of the exposure to other companies controlled by the shareholders of the bank being reviewed can be an important indicator of asset integrity, as banking laws in most countries address this issue.

Earnings: The income statement of the financial institution should provide information indicative of the relative efficiency of operations by relating earning assets to operating income, net after tax income, and losses and reserves. Earnings as related to capital is important both as a standard of performance and as a primary source of new capital generation (retained earnings) to support future growth.

Given that quantitative data are not often accurate or complete, an intuitive analysis should focus upon these same concepts. A current intuitive approach is often more valid because of the rapidity with which a bank's financial condition can deteriorate once a problem trigger mechanism is set off.

As previously mentioned, relative emphasis upon each of the categories above may vary in accordance with the nature of the transactions proposed. Most commonly offshore and local banks join together in facilitating international trade, serving as intermediaries between buyers and sellers of goods, with financing revolving around the particular documentary considerations of each transaction. These are normally self-liquidating cases, in which an identifiable short-term source of cash repayment for financing granted is foreseeable; the foreign exchange necessary for repayment is often not a part of this foreseen liquidation, however. The foreign exchange implication leads to variations in such financing, in that government restrictions intended to preserve exchange reserves may require minimum terms of financing beyond the date of anticipated liquidation or may entail financing of import deposits with governmental agencies prior to true initiation of the transaction being considered. Also common as lending opportunities between local and foreign banks are repass operations, in which funding is provided to the local bank for on-lending to its customers for domestic transactions; similarly, the offshore lender might directly fund the local borrower, accepting notes guaranteed by the local bank. The latter concept of accepting a guarantee requires special caution in that the lender can in some cases be legally bound to exercise substantial collection efforts prior to drawing under the guarantee. These transactions normally are short term also, and the credit decision toward undertaking these is not heavily based upon historical data. Analysis of historical data trends certainly becomes more meaningful as the maturities of transactions are extended and as the purposes of financing become less specific, as in the current Euromarket term note issues and standby funding facilities. Clearing agreements and maintenance of cash balances with local institutions each require a monitoring of data trends also because of their ongoing nature.

Notwithstanding the credit considerations above relating to judgments of the particular local commercial bank being analyzed, an equally necessary evaluation is that of the relative strength of the financial sector as a whole in each country, as well as the implied or evident support of the national government to the banking system. The regulatory framework within which the local financial sector operates is a crucial element in this evaluation. Where local banks are closely and competently monitored by regulatory authorities for compliance with criteria of function and financial condition, this can be expected to be indicative of government support of the system; where regulation is lax and the functions of local incorporated institutions are not strongly tied to the local economy, there of course is not likely to exist a strong motivation for ultimate government support of individual banks. The record of government intervention in Latin America to maintain financial stability in the local economy when an important repository of local financial resources (for example, commercial bank) is under duress is an encouraging one of support for local and foreign creditors in most countries. An assessment of the importance of the local bank in its market is therefore also a most important effort.

COMMERCIAL AND INDUSTRIAL CORPORATIONS

Credit considerations in lending to foreign corporate borrowers are usually more evident in financial statement analysis than in the areas discussed above. Essentially, this results from the more precise nature of financial reporting categories, allowing greater ability to trace the flow of cash in the operations of the borrower, presumably therefore improving the ability to assess the likelihood of timely repayment. Of course, such analyses are only as valid as the data presented, but, increasingly in Latin American financial reporting, standards are improving. This is at least partially a consequence of greater capital inflows from external sources that have accordingly required more ample and standardized information. Certainly wide variations remain in the quantity and quality of such information from one country to another, but offshore lending institutions must, as a practical necessity for their own needs, establish consistent analytical formats in reviewing regional portfolios, and it is hoped that this will abet the trend toward improved reporting. As always the credit procedure requires addressing the basic relevant concepts, accounting or intuitive, with resulting value judgments varying according to circumstances of collateral, extent of parent support, the effect of the local inflation rate upon return on capital requirements, breadth of local capital markets as alternative sources of funds, and other factors. To narrow the focus somewhat, the ensuing concepts are primarily directed toward the offshore lender's consideration of credit extension to a locally owned entity, excluding those in which implicit support from overseas parent or affiliated companies substantially influences the decision process.

Structure

Obtaining a perspective of the potential borrower within its national context should be the initial step. Understanding the nature of the business, its ownership, history, position within the industry and national economy, financial and management strength, and related corporate structures and ownership support are necessary in determining the relative depth of analysis needed in reaching a credit judgment. Certainly, established and substantial industry leaders should not require extensive research for borrowings related to ongoing business, as local checkings and performance summaries should be readily available; lesser entities should require a more profound analysis, focusing upon the topics herein discussed. Most of these topics eventually become reflected in financial statements if they are sufficiently detailed and accurate, and a general framework for review can be based upon customary statement formats.

Balance Sheet

Describing the financial position of a company at a given date, the balance sheet statement of financial condition is the best tool for determining its ability to achieve or withstand certain goals and effects. The dates must be carefully selected and compared to assure true representation and not seasonal imbalances. These stock balances can be utilized to measure such traditional concepts as liquidity (relating all or part of current assets and liabilities) and leverage (liabilities and capital), which are symptomatic of a company's relative strength or vulnerability. The most important preliminary step to understanding the balance sheet, however, is a determination of the true underlying value of the accounts listed, as they relate to the off-shore lender's needs. As in any region the reliability and quality of the auditors and the opinion given provide the context for evaluation.

Cash itself has a limited value to the offshore lender if it is exclusively local currency in a country where foreign exchange is not freely obtainable. The currency denomination of receivables presages this same cash effect. Receivables also require judgment as to whether they are all truly short term or truly represent arm's-length sales. This is difficult to determine, of course, but is frequently best addressed through an investigation of transactions with related companies or other companies with similar shareholders. Not uncommonly, such companies should be, but are not, consolidated into the borrower's financial statements, and sales to these related entities may thus not be any more than mere consignment of inventory, transferred only to "improve" financial reporting. Discounting of receivables with financial institutions is also an activity requiring attention, in that usually these are sold with recourse back to the seller, and it is most accurate, therefore, to add back to assets and liabilities the discounted receivables. Analysis of the volume and proportion of receivables discounted is often reflective of local monetary conditions (bank liquidity and interest rates).

Inventory accounts must of course be understood as to the valuation technique, which also has a strong effect on the income statement. In consistently inflationary economies a last-in/first-out (LIFO) technique will normally leave inventory stocks undervalued to the same extent that expensing cost of goods sold penalizes (compared with average costing, for instance) the income statement. The most important element here is to be able to identify the effects of whatever technique is used; cases such as trading companies, in which the acquisition prices of inventory may vary widely higher and lower during a reporting period, clearly require special scrutiny in determining true inventory and income data. The inventory mix of raw, in-process, and finished goods is also valuable information, as a change in the mix over time could be symptomatic of production difficulties; most obviously, unusual accumulation of finished goods could indicate product obsolescence or marketing and distribution problems. Relating existing stocks to prior periods' cost of goods sold is a convenient gauge of proper inventory levels. The effects of inventory accumulation upon future earnings can be difficult to judge without a precise knowledge of cost accounting treatments used in determining sales and production costs. If only a small percentage of a production run can readily be sold at current prices, the company may choose to expense only an equivalent portion of direct operating expenses; that is, the remainder of these direct expenses are effectively capitalized in inventory in anticipation of future sales. Whereas a reconciliation of cash flows could conceivably detect this, the eventual effect upon future earnings might not be easily discerned.

Investments and fixed assets each represent particular valuation problems. Investments are normally carried at cost, as no market value can be determined in most cases, and this can seriously overstate the true value of subsidiaries or affiliates in difficulty, masking their potential effect on a company.

In some Latin American nations unconsolidated affiliates have different year-end closing dates, permitting transfer of ownership between companies during the year as convenient, and carrying the investments on the balance sheet at cost is not always a reflection of true value. Fixed assets can be difficult to evaluate because of the common practice of revaluation, either as a result of local inflation or the appreciation of the local currency value of an asset purchased with foreign exchange. In most cases local accounting firms identify these revaluations as exceptions to normal accounting procedures (except for revalued real estate in some cases) and issue qualified opinions; nevertheless, the practice is widespread. Understandably, revaluations can be valid concepts, particularly in highly inflationary economies, but accurately assessing the true appreciation in value of assets is uncertain at best. The decision to request a qualified audit or assessment for revaluation will, of course, only be made when convenient, not under adversity; as the circumstances surrounding such convenience wane, what value then? Indirect effects, such as tightening of local credit, can also diminish the price a buyer could reasonably finance and pay for an asset, regardless of current audit value. The ability to depreciate the incremental value of revalued assets for reporting or tax purposes should also be determined where revaluations have been made, as there is not always uniform treatment even within one country under differing circumstances. The offsetting account (credit entry) for revaluation of assets should be identified, as it is not uncommon to first establish a revaluation reserve, then issue a stock dividend for the value of this reserve and reclassify it as capital. If the true realizable value is in fact different from the revaluation figure, distortion of the relationship of capital to the remainder of the balance sheet can thus result.

Intangible assets can include a wide array of capitalized expenditures or miscellaneous payments and, as in any region, should normally be separated from valuations of net worth.

Liability accounts are usually more clear than asset accounts insofar as valuation. Foreign exchange liabilities must be identified to assess current or potential value, and long-term liabilities must be investigated to identify those that are, in fact, short term but in which only an implicit or best-efforts understanding exists to renew such obligations at maturity. An area of increasing concern currently is the accounting for pension and severance reserves. Reserve funding requirements for different companies within one country can vary, and a determination of the appropriateness of the actual funding or the extent of the likely liability is not often possible by the offshore lender. As local legislation and labor agreements increasingly focus on such labor protection in Latin America today, this is one area where much more is likely to be heard in the future.

Capital and reserve accounts should be closely investigated to determine to what extent required allocations or payments exist. Local legislation may require the distribution of earnings to certain reserves up to certain limits or the payment of cash dividends to shareholders each year; the effects upon financial conditions or cash available for debt service can be distorted accordingly. Also, as national savings rates are not so high nor capital markets so deep in most Latin American economies, it is helpful to try to determine where possible if what is apparently equity has a fixed repayment schedule, that is, how much of the equity represents the proceeds of a loan to the shareholder, who must repay the loan in installments over a period of time that may exceed a reasonable dividend stream from the company.

Income Statement

The income statement of transactions between two dates should demonstrate how efficiently management converts its assets into sales, how effectively liabilities are used to support operations, and what degree of operations and administrative control exists.

In most instances, the offshore lender looks to the operating cash flow of the borrower for the ultimate source of repayment, as opposed to the asset-based (collateralized) or interim financing frequently provided by local lenders. Therefore, sales trends of the borrower are often the leading indicator of the likelihood of timely repayment, and sales value trends are thus important. It is also helpful where possible to consider physical volume trends in order to segregate the effects of price inflation. Understanding the derivation of sales data is an integral part of a thorough analysis, identifying the validity of the point in transactions when income is recognized (which is eventually reflected in the loss experience) as well as the economic authenticity of the sales (for example, excluding sales to related companies that serve merely as intermediaries to end users). Similarly, trends in reported cost of goods sold, once underlying cost accounting assumptions are identified, are reflective of operations efficiency, given a known or comparable product mix of sales.

Administration, selling, and financial costs, of course, are measures of effectiveness and control in each area; financial costs are also symptomatic of the capitalization evident on the balance sheet. Taxes are perhaps most meaningful to the extent that they change in accordance with legislation and investment incentives or otherwise affect normal financing planning. For instance, in a year of high reported profitability it may be deemed beneficial to expense certain outlays that might normally be capitalized and amortized over the medium term, in order to conserve cash by reducing taxes payable; the balance sheet effect may seem quite damaging here, although the economic effect is salutary.

Analyzing gross, operating, and net income margins is the most succinct approach to summarizing the effects of the factors above, as they change over time, as they compare to industry competitors, and in relation to minimum rates of return necessary for long-term economic viability in proportion to prevailing inflation and the cost of capital.

Cash Flow Statement

The cash flow statement is merely a consolidation and format change of the balance sheet and income statement data; however, it can be quite a valuable tool in identifying the true sources and uses of cash that must ultimately liquidate the financing. Frequently, this statement is set in a format first specifying the cash impact of the income statement, then the working account flows (short-term asset and liability operating accounts), outlays for longer-term assets and investments, and finally, financial (debt and equity) flows. Segregating the various phases of the cash movements in this manner is usually helpful in pinpointing the symptoms of potential problems, as evidenced in the strength of cash flow from ongoing operations, the quality of sales as reflected in receivables trends, funding of short- or long-term assets with the proper term of financing, and other concepts. Again, this is merely a useful format change, as the data are drawn from other existing sources.

Sensitivity Analyses

All of the foregoing is based upon historical, reported information, which need not always be a valid basis for extrapolation toward judging the likelihood of future events. If existing trends could be extrapolated the credit components of the lending decision could easily be generated. History would indicate that trends do change, however, and the true worth in credit analysis is to project the ability of the borrower to withstand foreseeable changes. It is in the consideration of the sensitivity of the borrower to these potential changes that the dynamism of credit evaluation rests. Detecting a particular vulnerability to one event can lead the lender to request additional security or other support in direct anticipation of the problem area identified, for example. This transcends the somewhat passive exercise of dissecting past occurrences. An infinity of possible changes exists, of course, but a few of the more commonly encountered concepts warrant comment.

Price controls are a common phenomenon in Latin America, and whereas it is not the intent of any government to limit prices such that the producers are driven out of business, not infrequently the producers' ability to comply with obligations on a timely basis is impaired. An awareness of vulnerability of a borrower subject to price controls and to increasing raw material costs becomes imperative. The accessibility of raw materials is, of course, equally important.

Competitive pressures and product life-cycle stages are difficult to define but clearly are most important as a longer-term consideration in the context of a borrower's position within an industry and an economy.

Financial vulnerability is a concept that can be directly analyzed for sensitivity, particularly the foreign exchange implications. Whereas it is always most reliable to analyze a borrower's performance in terms of his principal transaction (presumably local) currency to avoid translation distortions, potential exchange rate movements and their immediate consequences can be readily projected. The accounting treatments of exchange gains and losses are not uniform in all countries, however. Susceptibility to local monetary policy tightening could be seriously damaging to a growing firm needing additional debt, and this can be addressed by determining the borrowing reserve of the borrower. Specifically, what unused credit facilities remain available, and is the borrower periodically able to liquidate short-term borrowings? Of course, facilities available under ample liquidity scenarios can become unavailable quickly as monetary policies are tightened, but borrowing reserve must therefore include the diversity of sources of credit also.

Fixed and variable cost components of production and operating break-even analyses are helpful in determining an ability to withstand production interruptions owing to technical, labor, transportation, or other problems. Obviously, high fixed-cost or break-even levels engender greater concern about the potential causes for interruption of normal activities.

All of the comments regarding commercial and industrial corporations are nonspecific as regards individual transactions that the lender may be considering. Maturity and documentation factors would influence the respective value of any combination of the preceding concepts in the evaluation process.

Whereas the preceding discussion should at least be indicative of a means of evaluating credit decisions in lending, there is a tradition of skepticism as to the underlying premise of such analysis itself. As Adam Smith expressed it, in 1776, in his Wealth of Nations, "A bank which lends money, perhaps to 500 different people, the greater part of whom the directors can know very little about, is not likely to be more judicious in the choice of its debtors than a private person who lends out money among a few persons whom he knows, and in whose sober and frugal conduct he thinks he has good reason to confide."[4]

NOTES

1. For one account of this episode, including a description of the underlying debt, see T. R. Fehrenback, Fire and Blood (New York: Macmillan, 1973), pp. 424-32.

2. "World of Banking Supplement," Financial Times, May 29, 1979, p. xx.

3. A comprehensive analytical framework is discussed in F. L. Garcia, How to Analyze a Bank Statement, 6th ed. (Boston: Bankers Publishing, 1978).

4. As cited in Harry E. Miller, Banking Theories in the United States before 1860 (Cambridge, Mass.: Harvard University Press, 1927), p. 96.

16
SYNDICATED EUROCURRENCY LENDING IN LATIN AMERICA

Whitman E. Knapp

In order to provide clarity and perspective, any discussion of syndicated Eurocurrency lending in Latin America must begin with a definition of the term and some general background discussion of the various types of financing available to Latin American borrowers from the Eurocurrency market.

DEFINITION

Exactly what is meant by syndicated Eurocurrency lending? In this chapter we will be referring to commercial bank loans that are funded in the Eurocurrency markets (principally in Eurodollars) and that are provided by a group of commercial banks, normally five to six or more (a syndicate). The Eurocurrency market is principally made up of dollars, deutsche marks, and Swiss francs on deposit with financial institutions that lie outside the boundaries of the respective currency's home country. As of December 31, 1978, this market in terms of net international bank lending was estimated by the Bank for International Settlements (BIS) to be approximately U.S. $540 billion in size. It is from this pool of Eurocurrencies that borrowers world-wide raise funds via various methods and financial intermediaries. The syndicated loan is but one vehicle.

BACKGROUND

If the syndicated Eurocurrency loan is one of the many vehicles for tapping the market, what are the other vehicles and how do they apply to Latin American borrowers? Using Organization for Economic

268

TABLE 16.1

Types of Loans Raised: 1977 and 1978
(in millions of U.S. dollars)

	1978	1977
Syndicated credits		
Latin America	18,746	10,047
Europe	24,179	15,306
Middle East	6,949	3,556
Africa	3,044	598
Asia	11,999	7,400
North America	12,613	3,067
Bonds		
Latin America	2,158	2,266
Europe	10,802	11,175
Middle East	683	243
Africa	40	17
Asia	3,785	3,202
North America	3,869	3,014

Note: Quick addition and a comparison of the totals for figures from Eurostudy will reveal a disparity between them and the figures from the OECD presented. It should be noted that the different sources of statistics on the Eurocurrency markets vary somewhat in terms of both numbers and format of presentation.

Source: William F. Low, ed., Eurostudy (Brussels: International Insider, 1979).

Cooperation and Development (OECD) figures, in 1978 loans totaling $98.1 billion were raised in the Eurocurrency markets. These were made up of both commercial bank loans (syndicated and direct) of $66.0 billion and bond issues of $32.1 billion. Table 16.1 gives a breakdown of both the type of loans raised in 1977 and 1978 and the geographic distribution by borrower.

As Table 16.1 indicates, the principal source of financing for Latin American countries tapping the Eurocurrency markets has been the syndicated loan. This reflects the fact that bond investors, both institutions and individuals, are by definition conservative in their lending. Purchasers of bonds normally are either unable to evaluate or unwilling to assume the risk associated with lending to Latin American names. Argentina, Brazil, and Mexico have for years placed some bonds with institutional investors; however, the amounts involved have always been negligible compared with the funds obtainable from commercial bank loans. Although a greater variety of countries in Latin America can tap the bond markets today, over the past two years only the following names have raised money via the international bond market: Argentina, Bolivia, Brazil, Mexico, Panama, Trinidad and Tobago, and Venezuela. Additionally, Costa Rica and El Salvador have tapped the floating rate note (FRN) market, which, while technically a public market like the bond market, tends to be a market where most of the issues are placed with commercial banks and hence is somewhat of a halfway house between the true public bond market and the syndicated loan market.

Who are the borrowers and what have been the purposes for which the borrowings have been undertaken? In Latin America, virtually all borrowing has been either directly by or has been guaranteed by the central governments and central government agencies (that is, central banks). In the case of Brazil, state and occasionally municipal borrowers have appeared in the market. Mexico has produced some private-sector borrowers. However, as a general rule, the majority of lending has been for direct or indirect sovereign risks.

Over the past five to six years, the bulk of the financing raised in the Euromarkets has been for either balance-of-payment purposes or project financing. With the sharp increase in the price of oil in 1974, many countries worldwide were forced to turn to the Eurocurrency markets to finance the deficits in their balance of payments caused by the increase in oil prices. Many Latin American countries faced a double flow, as at the same time prices dropped significantly for commodities, such as copper, tin, and cocoa, on which they depend to finance their needs for the import of manufactured and other finished goods. However, as the effects of the increase in oil prices have worked their way through the system, more and more Latin American borrowers have moved to general development and project financing. While it has often been difficult to differentiate between balance-of-payment financing and general development financing, a number of significant projects, such as the major Yacyreta electrification program in Argentina and the massive Itaipu dam project in Brazil, have raised funds via the syndicated loan market. Another notable use of this market has been the refinancing of foreign debt. The best example of this phenomenon was the refinancing of the Argentine debt in 1977. In conjunction with the International Monetary

Fund (IMF), a $500-million syndicated loan was raised in the Euro-currency market to restructure the Argentine foreign debt maturity profile at a time when the country was experiencing severe liquidity problems. Finally, during the latter part of 1978 and into 1979, a number of Latin American borrowers have taken advantage of the significant liquidity in the Eurocurrency markets and the corresponding lower spreads and longer maturities to refinance some of their existing debt on more favorable terms.

The question of refinancing debt at more favorable terms and conditions brings us to the question of exactly what terms and conditions Latin American borrowers have faced in the Eurocurrency syndicated loan market over the past years. Taking an eight-to-ten-year time frame, changes in the terms and conditions faced by Latin American borrowers have closely paralleled changes in the market as a whole. Latin American borrowers, led by Brazil and Mexico, became active borrowers in the market in the early 1970s. At that time rates in the 2 percent over London Interbank Offered Rate (LIBOR) range with maturities of 5 years were the norm. Latin American borrowers then benefited from the gradual easing of terms and conditions that took place in the market during the 1973/74 period leading up to the Herstatt crisis and the temporary close of the market in June 1974. While the first cycle started off with prime Latin American borrowers paying 2 percent over LIBOR for 5 years, just before the Herstatt crisis borrowers such as Brazil were attracting terms of 0.75 percent over LIBOR for 15 years. The second cycle of the market now in its final stage has moved from prime borrowers paying 2 percent over LIBOR for 5 years at the end of 1974 and in early 1975 to paying as little as .88 percent over LIBOR for 15 years. The slightly higher rates of the present cycle can be explained by two factors: first, we are not yet at the end of the present cycle, and it

TABLE 16.2

Syndicated Loan Volume
(in millions of U.S. dollars)

Country	1973	1978
Argentina	80	1,249
Brazil	800	5,648
Mexico	1,200	7,259

Source: William F. Low, ed., Eurostudy (Brussels: International Insider, 1979).

is very possible that rates, if not terms, may improve further for borrowers, and second, the amounts being borrowed have increased significantly. Table 16.2 gives a clear indication of the vast increase in syndicated loan volume that has taken place over the past five to six years.

The increase in the amounts lent to Latin American borrowers not unexpectedly has been accompanied by a significant increase in the number of lenders. While the providers of funds for syndicated Euro-currency loans to Latin America in the early 1970s were dominated by the major North American banks and the leading banks in Europe and Japan, today the range of banks has increased markedly with the full spectrum of banks in the United States and each European country now lending to Latin American names as well as banks representing the Middle and Far East and some Latin American banks themselves.

Given the level of pricing indicated above and the prevailing availability of funds, a number of Latin American countries have taken the opportunity to build foreign exchange reserves in anticipation of a period when borrowing may be either more difficult or on less favorable terms. The understanding of the market and the sophistication with which the market is approached by Latin American borrowers has grown over the years to the point that a number of the Latin American central bankers and finance ministers have become well-known personalities in the market and are considered among the most astute users of the Eurocurrency loan market. These bankers have developed aggressive strategies in dealing with the commercial banks in the market, strategies that have resulted in much more favorable terms and conditions for their countries. It will be instructive, however, to watch whether these same practitioners enjoy equal success in a market that is moving against them.

THE SYNDICATION OF A EUROCURRENCY LOAN

With the above general background we must now look at the process involved in bringing a syndicated Eurocurrency loan to the market. This process can be broken down into the following stages: identification of a borrower, assembling a management group, developing documentation, syndication and negotiation, and closing. We will look at this process from the vantage point of a syndication officer in a commercial bank or a syndication manager of a merchant bank that has made the conscious decision to extend medium-term Eurocurrency loans to Latin American borrowers and is willing to commit both the financial and human resources to the market on a continuous basis. A successful syndication capability can be developed only over a period of time. Infrequent participation in the market or one-off transactions will, at best, only lead to a high level of frustration and at worst total failure.

Identification of a Borrower

The first step in developing a syndicated lending program is the most obvious; that is, one must review what various borrowers have done in the past. (At the same time one must keep track for use later in actual syndication of which banks have been providers of funds for these borrowers.) Three of the most complete sources of information on past borrowings can be found in The Times Euromarkets and Foreign Bond Quarterly, published by the Financial Times of London; Eurostudy, published by International Insider in Brussels; and Euromarkets Annually, published by Euromarkets Monthly Inc. in conjunction with the International Herald Tribune in Paris. After a comprehensive review of which countries have borrowed in the past, with specific reference to precisely which entities have represented these borrowers, two key decisions must then be made: (1) what kind of financing does one want to introduce to the market, that is, project financing, general balance-of-payment financing, or to the extent available, private-sector financing; and (2) in which countries are there established contacts or in which countries can contacts be developed most easily to pursue a syndication?

Once the country and general syndication target have been identified, some useful preparation can be undertaken prior to a visit to the target country itself. For bankers located in the United States, discussions with World Bank, IMF, Inter-American Development Bank (IDB), and U.S. State Department country economic officers often provide useful background information as to the existence and status of current projects in the target country. However, the essential step in developing a syndication must be a comprehensive visit to the target country. Only from such an on-the-spot visit and from discussions with local bankers, businessmen, and government officials can a specific syndication opportunity be identified and developed.

The question of selecting a borrower and then setting the appropriate terms and conditions to bring that borrower to the market presents a lead manager with one of the most crucial elements of loan syndication. In bringing a loan to the market one must find the fine balance between borrower's and lender's interests, that is, acceptability of name and correctness of terms. Although the task of finding an acceptable name, particularly in a highly liquid market such as that prevailing today, may not be too difficult, setting the right terms and conditions is always difficult. If terms are too generous to the lenders, one runs the distinct risk of losing the loan to a bank that has more accurately read the market. If one sets terms and conditions that are too favorable to the borrower, the risk of either not being able to find other banks to underwrite the loan or subsequently being unable to place the loan becomes a reality. Success in setting the appropriate terms and conditions comes from a careful following of the market over a period of time coupled with close and frequent contact with those institutions that are active in the market.

In addition to determining appropriate terms and conditions, the question of the exact type of transaction must also be answered before presenting an offer to the prospective borrower. The decision must be made whether a fully underwritten transaction or a best-efforts bid is the most appropriate approach and what kind of subsequent marketing of the transaction is required. The two elements most relevant to this decision will be, first, the amount of assets a bank wishes to take on its own books as a result of the operation in question and, second, the competitive state of the market. If a bank is prepared to underwrite and subsequently keep a significant portion of the total loan, then only two or three underwriters are necessary and a club deal, that is, a loan placed with only a small group of banks well-known to the lead bank would be the most appropriate structure. If the bank is willing or able to underwrite up to 20 percent and wishes to see its commitment reduced via the syndication process, then a slightly larger underwriting group would be necessary and a full selling (syndication) effort to reduce all the underwriters' positions would be called for. Finally, if a bank is unwilling or unable to take the risk of having an underwriting position reduced during syndication, then a best-efforts transaction where the borrower is offered services in putting together a group of banks to lend but is given no assurances as to the final amount of a loan is the appropriate approach. Once again the correct approach must be determined by the evaluation of not only the bank's own position vis-à-vis the size of the transaction contemplated but also the competitive pressures of the market. Clearly under most circumstances borrowers prefer a fully underwritten bid. However, a borrower who is a highly sought-after name and who feels assured of getting the required funds from the market may not feel the necessity of paying the higher fees associated with an underwritten bid and therefore may opt for a best-efforts-basis transaction. (A detailed review of fees follows below.)

Assembling a Management Group

Assuming that the decision has been reached to present the prospective borrower with a fully underwritten bid, the next step in the syndication process is to assemble the management or underwriting group. Before proceeding with a discussion of forming the underwriting group, it is important to review the management fee and its various elements so as to have an appreciation of what can be offered to other banks to induce them to join the management or underwriting group. For the sake of simplicity let us say that the market indicates that a 1 percent front end management fee is appropriate for the borrower in question. Under these circumstances the lead bank might retain from this amount a 0.25 percent praecipium as its compensation for finding and negotiating the loan. This would be 0.25 percent off the top on the entire amount of the loan, that is, $125,000 on a $50 million loan. Of the remaining 0.75 percent one would normally offer that full amount to the underwriters who commit for equal amounts as the lead manager. This fee would normally be offered on the amount of their underwriting that they retained for their book after the syndication selldown is completed; that is, if they underwrote U.S.$10 million and retained $6 million at the end of the syndication, their fee would be 0.75 percent on $6 million or $45,000. Those underwriters committing for less than an equal share would receive, for example, 0.63 percent on a similar basis. In addition to the underwriting fee it is normal practice to divide the pool (that is, those fees left over after paying out the underwriting fees and participation fees, which are always at a lower level than underwriting fees) based on a percentage of each bank's underwriting commitment to the total transaction (as opposed to a percentage of loan retained to the total transaction). It goes without saying that the management or underwriting fee is a function of the competitive pressure of the market. (The above figures are only for purposes of a demonstration; indeed, in today's competitive market, management fees are normally one-half of the amounts cited above.) Each transaction must be priced in accordance with the market at the time of the transaction.

In forming the management group, an important factor that must be taken into account is the ultimate selldown objective of the managers and the borrower. If a wide selldown is envisioned either because the managers wish to reduce their underwriting or because the borrower wishes a wide distribution of the loan in order to establish new banking contacts, it is essential to put together a management or underwriting group that is broadly diversified geographically and that contains banks known to have good contacts in their respective markets and willing to use their contacts to assist in the placement of the loan within their market. The makeup of the management group is also an important factor in attempting to win a mandate. A broad geographic distribution of banks in the management group can be a definite competitive advantage when a borrower reviews various offers.

Once the management group for the loan has been assembled and the terms and conditions that will be offered to the prospective borrower have been agreed on by the management group, the lead manager will present to the borrower on behalf of the management group a formal bid, usually in the form of a bid letter or telex. (An example of a bid letter is found in Appendix A.) This document spells out in detail the various terms and conditions of the loan including rate, maturity, and fees, as well as any appropriate covenants or special features. The bid letter will also normally request the borrower's agreement not to allow any competing financing in the Eurocurrency market during the period of time allotted for the syndication of the loan under offer. While suitable change-of-circumstances language is always included in any bid letter, once the bid is presented to the prospective borrower the management group is morally, if not legally, committed to bring the loan to market on the terms and conditions offered. Once the bid is accepted, the borrower is equally morally obligated to allow the banks to proceed on the terms agreed. Actual experience has revealed very few situations in which either a borrower or a group of lenders has tried to break a commitment once agreed upon.

While the competitive nature of the market may vary somewhat over a period of time, one can always assume that there will be stiff competition to bring any good borrower to the market. The financial incentives for the lead manager, indeed all managers, in a syndication in terms of increased yields resulting from the management fee can be significant. The opportunity to play an active and direct role in a borrower's banking picture is also of importance to many banks. Given these factors, the maximum effort possible must be mounted in bringing the borrower to accept a proposal.

Documentation

Once the mandate is finally awarded, the documentation stage of the syndication is reached and the lead manager must produce an information memorandum and draft loan agreement. The contents of the information memorandum that is normally provided to the prospective lenders should, to the extent possible, be provided in its entirety by the borrower. The whole purpose of the information memorandum is fraught with legal issues that must be examined by the lead manager and the manager's counsel. However, the practice that has evolved over the past several years has been for the lead manager to act simply as an intermediary between the borrower, who supplies the information, and the prospective lenders, who use the information as but one factor in arriving at their decision whether or not to extend credit to the particular borrower. Clearly some degree of arranging and presenting the information received from the borrower will be necessary, perhaps including narrative to pull together the financial and statistical information. But in order to minimize potential liability for misrepresentation, the lead manager should make every effort to keep narrative to a minimum and include only a recitation of facts provided by the borrower. Although there is some divergence of practice over the extent to which the draft information memorandum should be presented to the other managers for review, unless one is dealing with a particularly large number of managers or under extreme time pressure, it is strongly recommended that each manager be given the opportunity to review the information memorandum in draft and to offer comments. This process will help to minimize errors of fact or presentation that inevitably creep into even the most carefully prepared document.

The preparation of the loan agreement is technically the most difficult and exacting step in the whole syndication process. Although there is frequent reference to boiler plate and the repetitive similarity of Eurocurrency loan agreements, to maintain the professional standards of the market each transaction must have a loan agreement that has been thought out virtually word by word. The business terms of the transaction will have been worked out and discussed with the borrower during the course of seeking the mandate and will have been finalized in the awarding of the mandate. One useful technique that saves time and misunderstanding is to incorporate the terms and conditions that will form the basis of the loan agreement into the bid letter originally presented to the borrower. With the basic business terms thus agreed upon, the lead bank will outline these to its counsel for preparation of the loan agreement. Here again one useful technique to employ is a term sheet (see example in Appendix B), which, while providing for the broad outlines of a Eurocurrency loan, nevertheless requires the lead manager to provide the specifics of the transaction.

Again, while market practice is not consistent, once the draft loan agreement has been completed by counsel, it should be submitted to the other banks in the management group for their comment. As with the information memorandum this provides an opportunity to catch any mistakes, but more important it ensures that any problems among the managers are ironed out before starting negotiations with the borrower. Complete agreement among the managers on the loan document will place the lead manager in the strongest possible position in the negotiations with the borrower.

Syndication and Negotiation

Timing and order at this point in the syndication become largely a matter of individual preference. To recapitulate: The management group has been assembled; the mandate has been awarded; the information memorandum and draft loan agreement have been prepared. Now the remaining steps are negotiation of the final agreement and syndication of the loan. In planning the sequence of steps to complete these final tasks one must carefully weigh two factors: first, negotiating position with a borrower is strengthened by the presence of a significant number of lenders who have expressed interest in the loan and are simply awaiting loan documentation before finalizing their commitment. However, on the other hand, if one syndicates the loan and then is unable to finalize the loan agreement with the borrower within a reasonably short period of time, one at best runs the risk of tarnishing one's professional reputation or at worst losing a number of potential lenders who have made commitments subject to receipt of documentation but wander off to pursue other lending opportunities.

Assuming that the syndication of the loan is undertaken first, the lead manager will draw up a list of banks that are to receive offering telexes. The number of banks on the list will be a reflection of the selldown interest of the management group; that is, the greater the selldown objectives, the greater the number of banks. However, this phase of a syndication provides a true reflection of the lead bank's understanding of the market and skill in knowing the interest of the banks participating in it. It does not take any participating genius to determine the telex number of the top 200 to 300 international banks in the market (some transactions have actually seen banks sending out 200 telexes in search of 20 or so lenders).

The skill of knowing the market well enough to come up with a comparatively short list of banks will be of importance, particularly when, as often happens with borrowers who are frequently in the market, a restriction is placed by the borrower on the total number of banks that can be approached. In developing the list of banks to be approached, it is important to request names from the other managers. Their assistance in the selling process will be far greater if they are involved in the formulation of the list of banks to be approached. Indeed, it is a frequent practice as well as a useful tactic to assign to the other managers follow-up responsibility for those banks that they have suggested for the syndication as well as any other banks in their geographic location. Banks are offered participation in a loan by means of the offering telex, the format of which has evolved over the years and has become fairly standard. The telex, which is sent by the lead manager on behalf of the management group, outlines the terms and conditions of the loan and the participation fees being offered and ends by giving the name of an individual to be contacted in response and the date by which responses must be given. (See Appendix C for an example.) Affirmative responses to the offering telex are always subject to satisfaction with final documentation. In reality, few banks ever back away from a transaction once they have given a positive response to the offering telex. One important element in ensuring that an offering telex does get proper attention at the bank to which it is sent is to address it to the officer responsible for syndicated lending. Again, this requires a detailed knowledge of the market and its participants but will reduce the chances of an offering telex simply getting lost in the paper mill.

Little useful comment can be made on the actual process of negotiating the loan agreement with the borrower. Each negotiation is different and depends significantly on the expenses, personalities, and so on, of the parties involved. One must, however, always remember that as lead manager one is negotiating not only on behalf of the other managers but of the entire group of prospective lenders as well. Careful attention to detail and skillful negotiation with the borrower is of the greatest importance. If a lead manager gives away too many points to the borrower, a great many requests for additions or changes to the agreement will be made by the prospective lenders when the negotiated loan agreement is sent out to the participants for their approval. Having to go back to the borrower with fundamental changes at this point of the syndication will certainly be embarrassing and may not produce the alteration required by the prospective lenders. However, with a skillfully drawn up and negotiated loan agreement, the inevitable few comments that come from the syndicate can be dealt with easily and quickly.

Closing

The location of the signing of the loan agreement is usually dictated by the governing law, that is, London for United Kingdom law transactions, New York for New York law transactions, and so on. Whatever the location, the signing ceremony and the customary post-signing lunch or dinner provide the opportunity to further relationships with not only the borrower but other members of the lending syndicate. Although the lead manager role ends with the signing of the agreement, this normally marks the beginning of a role as agent bank. While in large transactions the agent's role may go to a bank other than the lead manager's (this position may be used to entice another bank to join a management group or to drop a competing bid), normally on signing the lead manager assumes agent's role during the life of the loan. The duties and responsibilities of the agent are significant, but that is the subject of another discussion.

APPENDIX A

Name of Borrower

Dear Sirs,

We are pleased to confirm that we have formed a management group (the managers), which, as you requested, will provide a loan to _____ in the aggregate amount of U.S.$_____ on terms and conditions including, but not limited to, those outlined below and subject to the preparation of loan documentation satisfactory to all parties.

Borrower:	_____.
Amount:	U.S.$_____.
Purpose:	To finance _____.
Commitment:	The undersigned managers, either directly or through their parent banks or wholly-owned subsidiaries, have committed in aggregate to lend up to U.S.$_____.
Lenders:	A syndicate of international financial institutions.
Agent:	_____.
Availability period:	From signature of the loan agreement to and including _____.
Borrowings:	Each borrowing shall be in a maximum principal amount of U.S.$_____ and a minimum amount of U.S.$_____ or an integral multiple of U.S.$_____ (or such lesser amount as remains available) on five business days prior notice to the agent. Each borrowing shall not be made within five business days of the immediately preceding borrowing.
Repayment:	_____approximately equal consecutive semiannual installments, commencing _____ months from signature of the loan agreement.
Voluntary prepayment:	Permitted upon at least _____ days prior notice to the agent on the relevant interest payment date or dates in minimum amounts of U.S.$_____ and integral multiples of U.S.$_____ without

penalty or premium. The amounts so prepaid
will be applied to the repayment schedule in in-
verse order of maturity and cannot thereafter be
reborrowed.

Final maturity: _____ years from signature of the loan agreement.

Interest rate: An interest rate that shall be computed on the
basis of a margin of _____ percent per annum
over the six month London Interbank Offered
Rate (LIBOR) for dollar deposits quoted to the
reference banks to be specified in the loan agreement. Interest shall be payable on the last day
of each interest period.

Commitment fee: There shall be a commitment fee of _____ of
_____ percent per annum, payable upon the daily
average undrawn amount of the commitment on
the earlier of the expiry of the commitment or
full drawdown.

Computation of
interest: Interest will be calculated on the basis of a 360-
day year for the actual number of days elapsed.

Cancellation of
commitment: Permitted upon at least _____ days prior notice
to the agent during the availability period in
minimum amounts of U.S.$_____ and integral
multiples of U.S.$_____ .

Management fee: _____ percent on the total principal amount of
the loan, payable to the agent for the account of
the managers upon signature of the loan agreement.

Agent's fee: U.S.$_____ per annum payable to the agent on the
signature of the loan agreement and in advance
annually on such date in each year thereafter.

Taxation: All payments of principal, interest, and other
amounts payable by _____ to the lenders, the
managers, or the agent in connection with this
financing shall be exempt from, and made free
and clear of, and without deduction for, any and
all present and future taxes, withholdings, duties,
charges, and other levies of whatsoever nature
imposed thereon by any nation or political or
taxing authority (other than, with respect to the

	applicable payee, income and franchise taxes of the jurisdiction of organization of said payee).
Documentation:	This offer is subject to the execution and delivery of a mutually satisfactory loan agreement.
Governing law:	Laws of _____ .
Miscellaneous:	_____ will reimburse the managers and the agent for all out-of-pocket expenses incurred in connection with the development, negotiation, and completion of the financing, including for all printing costs in connection with the preparation and execution of the loan agreement and information memorandum and for all legal fees charged by counsel to the agent in connection with the preparation and execution of such agreements.
Expiration:	This offer shall expire on _____ unless accepted on or prior to such date.

It is a condition of this offer that there be no other syndicated bank loan for _____ either directly or indirectly (including by way of guarantee) from the date of acceptance of this offer until _____ . In addition, neither _____ nor any public-sector entity will solicit such financing or grant other mandates until signature of the loan agreement for this transaction.

If the terms of this offer are satisfactory to you, kindly notify the agent bank in writing or telex of your approval thereof on or prior to _____ .

Yours very truly,

The Managers:

APPENDIX B

Eurocurrency Loan Term Sheet

1. Lending Entity:
2. Borrower:
    Name
    Address
    Form of organization
      (Corporation, limited partnership, and so on)
    Jurisdiction of incorporation

3. If multibank financing:
    Agent
    Comanager(s)
    Member of syndicate and amounts
    Agency fee
4. Amount and currency of Loan:
    Mutlicurrency option
    Which currencies
    Whose option
5. Type of loan (that is, term, revolving, and so forth):
6. Term of loan:
7. Repayment schedule:
8. Commitment period:
    Take-down schedule
9. Minimum amount of each take-down:
10. Where funds will be made available:
11. Purpose of loan, that is, use of proceeds:
12. Where payments are to be made:
    Boston
    Bank of Boston International, New York
    Other
13. Interest rate:
    Reference banks, if syndicated loan
14. Interest rate on overdue amounts:
15. Interest payment dates:
16. Funding periods:
    Three months
    Six months
    Other
17. Closing fee, management fee, and so on:
    Amounts and date(s) payable
18. Commitment fee:
    Amount or rate and date(s) payable
19. Prepayment option:
    Notice required
    Dates on which permitted
    Minimum amounts
    Premium
20. Evidence of indebtedness:
    Note(s)
    Loan account(s)
21. Payments to be free of deductions:
    (that is, net of any withholding tax, and so on)
22. Change of law:
    Option only to terminate commitment
    Option to require prepayment

23. Additional costs (reserve requirements, and so on) to be borne by borrower:
    Option to prepay if additional cost imposed
24. Any required representations and warranties in addition to minimal customary warranties:

APPENDIX C

Example of Offering Telex

Re: U.S.$_____ million medium-term loan for _____.

The undersigned have been authorized by the borrower to arrange the following medium-term credit. We are pleased to invite you to join the lending group for this credit on the terms and conditions outlined below:

Borrower:

Guarantor
 (if necessary):

Purpose:

Amount: U.S.$ _____ million.

Availability: Not to exceed _____ months from the date of the
                       loan agreement.

Term: _____ years from the date of the loan agreement.

Repayment: _____ equal semiannual installments commencing
                       _____ months from signature of the loan agree-
                       ment.

Interest rate: _____ per annum over the six month London In-
                       terbank Offered Rate (LIBOR) for U.S. dollar
                       deposits.

Commitment fee: _____ per annum payable on the daily average
                       undrawn amount of the commitments to accrue
                       from _____ after signature of the loan agreement
                       and to be payable on the earlier of the expiry of
                       the commitments or the date the loan is fully
                       drawn.

Participation fees: _____ percent on participations of U.S.$_____
                       million, _____ percent on participations of U.S.
                       $ _____ million, _____ percent on participations

of U.S.$_____ million and over. Allocation will be at the sole discretion of the managers, and participants will receive fees on their amount in accordance with the above schedule.

Taxes: All payments of principal, interest, fees, and other amounts due under the loan agreement will be made free and clear of, and without reduction by reason of, any present or future _____ taxes.

Documentation: Completion of this transaction is subject to the execution of mutually satisfactory legal documentation including a credit agreement and promissory notes governed by the laws of _____, containing clauses customary for Eurodollar loans for _____.

Legal counsel to
  the lenders:

Agent bank:

An information memorandum containing information on the borrower has been prepared and will be forwarded to you upon receipt of your indication of interest.

We would be pleased to receive indication of interest in principle in taking part in this transaction at your earliest convenience but no later than close of business on _____. Copies of draft legal documentation will be forwarded upon receipt of such indication of interest.

Please address all responses and requests for information memoranda and loan documentation to _____.

We look forward to working with you.

Lead Manager

Managers

17
LEGAL ASPECTS OF LENDING IN LATIN AMERICA

Andrew C. Quale, Jr.

The legal complexities of international lending have caused sleepless nights for many commercial and official bankers and their counsel. This is not surprising since such transactions bridge two or more nations having legal systems, political structures, and business and social cultures that may be quite different. Lending to Latin American borrowers is certainly no exception. Indeed, because of the nationalistic attitudes taken by some Latin American countries toward questions of governing law, submission to jurisdiction, and waiver of sovereign immunity, the legal issues currently confronting lenders to governmental borrowers in Latin America may well be more complicated and demanding of careful analysis and innovation than those arising in any other region.

The legal systems of Latin American countries were founded on a civil law system that may be unfamiliar to those reared under the common law. Even European-trained civil lawyers will encounter many alien features in Latin American civil law systems because of the noncivil law elements, especially originating from the United States, that have been grafted onto the civil law foundations to deal with new economic and social pressures.

Among Latin American countries there is, of course, an extraordinary diversity in forms of government and attitudes toward foreign

The author would like to express his appreciation to the following persons for their assistance in the preparation of this chapter: his colleagues at Coudert Brothers, Timothy J. McCarthy, Vicki Marmorstein, Peter J. Reichard, and David Wolf; Drs. Hector Mairal and Javier Negri of Buenos Aires; Drs. Tarcisio Neviani and Condorcet Rezende of Rio de Janeiro; Drs. Dario Cardenas and Felipe Vallejo of Bogotá; Dr. Roberto Danino of Lima; and Drs. Eloy Anzola and Jose Rafael Bermudez of Caracas.

borrowing that inevitably results in a comparable diversity in the
legal regulation by these countries of foreign loans. For example,
the establishment of a governmental borrower's power and authority
to undertake a foreign loan may involve a process in countries under
a military regime, such as Argentina, Chile, and Peru, which have
no legislature to enact empowering laws, very different from that under popularly elected governments, such as Colombia and Venezuela.
In order to attract foreign capital, some countries, such as Chile,
have adopted measures designed specifically to eliminate or reduce
legal barriers to foreign lenders.[1] Other countries, such as Colombia, while still active borrowers, have enacted laws and regulations
that make the lender's task more difficult.*

This chapter highlights the principal legal issues that arise in
lending to Latin American borrowers and is intended to serve as a
guide to lenders and their counsel in the negotiation and documentation of loans. Examples will be given of how these issues are treated
under the laws of various Latin American countries. The objective
is not to provide a survey of the relevant laws of each country but to
illustrate the variety of ways these issues are treated and to alert
lenders and their counsel to the key problems more quickly so that
they may develop creative solutions for them.† The chapter will focus
on commercial bank term lending to public sector borrowers, although
much of the discussion will also be relevant to lending to nongovern-
mental borrowers.

SOME PRELIMINARY CONSIDERATIONS

It is important to consider at the outset the ultimate legal objectives in the structuring, negotiation, and documentation of a loan.
First and most important, the loan and related documentation should
constitute legal and binding obligations of the borrower that the lender
can enforce on the terms as originally agreed. (If this sounds suspi-
ciously like the boiler-plate language found in legal opinions—"legal,
valid and binding obligation of the borrower enforceable in accordance

---

*Colombia requires that certain loans to the government and gov-
ernmental agencies must be governed by Colombian law, as distinguished from the law of the lender's country. See sections on governing law and procedural issues.

†Since the references to laws and regulations of Latin American
countries are intended primarily as illustrations, they should not be
relied on in an actual lending transaction without prior confirmation
by counsel.

with its terms"—it should, and for good reason, since this is the ultimate legal objective of loan documentation.) Second, if the lender eventually has to resort to judicial remedies to collect the loan, the loan should be judicially enforceable and collectible through the most expeditious legal processes available.* Third, in the event the borrower's financial plight is such as to necessitate a workout or standby arrangement or, worse yet, trigger a flurry of attachments by creditors or a filing in bankruptcy, the lender should be in as good a position as possible vis-à-vis the borrower's other creditors so that it can negotiate with leverage, act quickly if necessary, and be assured that its loan will benefit from whatever priority in ranking is possible under the circumstances.

As a practical matter, most sovereign borrowers will fulfill their loan obligations on a timely basis and the legality or enforceability of the loan and the loan documentation will never come into question, irrespective of whether or not it might be legally defective. Problems tend to arise primarily when there has been abrupt political change or upheaval, such as has recently occurred in Nicaragua, El Salvador, and Bolivia; not too long ago in Chile and Peru; and, before that, in Argentina, or when there has been substantial economic disruption or severe balance-of-payments deficits (which may or may not be linked with internal political problems), such as has occurred in the last five years in Argentina, Chile, Nicaragua, and Peru. Problems may also arise when the integrity of a government or of particular individuals is impugned because such government or individuals may have received bribes or the proceeds of the loan were improperly distributed. In fact, this is one of the grounds on which the revolutionary junta of Nicaragua has threatened not to repay the loans entered into by the Somoza regime.

Although these various problems, fortunately, are not common occurrences, when they do occur one can be sure that someone will take a long, hard look at the outstanding loans and their documentation in order to find technical legal insufficiencies or other defects that might be used as a justification, however insubstantial and frivolous, not to repay the loans. For this reason, in order to have a chance of withstanding such scrutiny, of preventing the nonpayment of a loan for legal insufficiencies, and, ultimately, of enforcing the loan, it is essential that bankers and their counsel insist that the loan and all related authorizations, approvals, and documentation are legally and ethically correct, even if the process to ensure this may seem time consuming and picky and even if the borrower itself is prepared to

---

*See the discussion of the expedited proceeding called "executive action" in the section on procedural issues.

represent that all aspects of the loan are legal and valid, although in fact they are not.

Before embarking on a discussion of the legal aspects of lending in Latin America, three practical bits of advice are offered here. First, in negotiating with our Latin American colleagues, one must be flexible and imaginative, especially since the region's nationalistic attitudes are increasingly being expressed in loan documentation. Second, the boiler plate that has evolved over the years in Eurodollar loan documentation may not seem so sacred and obvious to a Latin American borrower, and if a provision is not acceptable or workable in the context of a particular country, one should be willing to find a solution that is. Finally, la vida tropical can be frustrating, but it is also enchanting—even more so if you bring along a sense of humor.

The discussion that follows focuses on a variety of issues, all of which relate ultimately to the enforceability of external loans against governmental borrowers. First, the threshold question of whose law shall govern is examined. In the second section, procedural issues relating to judicial enforcement are considered—in particular, submission to the jurisdiction of the lender's courts, waiver of sovereign immunity, the availability of executive action, and the satisfaction of judgments rendered against a foreign sovereign. The third and fourth sections analyze the legal status of the borrower and alternative possibilities for structuring a loan. The fifth section examines the borrower's power and authority to borrow. The sixth section considers usury questions, and the final section reviews certain controversial loan agreement covenants.

GOVERNING LAW: WHOSE LAW SHALL GOVERN, THE BORROWER'S OR LENDER'S?

The so-called governing law provision, which for many years quietly invoked the laws of the lender's country in a clause buried at the end of loan agreements, has in recent years given rise to heated negotiations, the expression of nationalistic pride, and the boycotting of borrowers by certain lenders. The attitudes of governmental borrowers vary greatly on this question: some consider the issue of governing law to be a matter of negotiations like many other provisions, some are indifferent or anxious to encourage lenders, and, as a result, the lender's law is invariably selected; and some insist that their country's law govern because of existing legal or policy requirements. To the extent that some countries require that their own laws govern, such attitude may reflect the tradition of the Calvo clause, which requires foreign investors in Latin American countries to submit to local laws.

Notwithstanding the borrower's position on governing law, it is important to recognize that, irrespective of which law is to govern, the transaction should comply with the laws of both the lender's and borrower's jurisdictions to the extent they are compatible. In addition, the documentation should be drafted so that the borrower's obligations are enforceable under the laws of both such jurisdictions as well as any other jurisdiction where enforcement is likely to be sought.

The Borrower's Law as Governing: Does This Create Unacceptable Legal Risks for the Lender?

Colombia has taken perhaps the most nationalistic position on the issue of governing law. Decree 150 of 1976, which regulates the contractual relations between the national government and certain of its instrumentalities and third parties, requires that all loan agreements with the government must provide that the parties submit to Colombian law as the governing law of the agreement.[2] Nevertheless, subsequently enacted Law 63 of 1978, which empowered the government to increase the aggregate amount of its foreign indebtedness, granted the parties to loan agreements "to be performed abroad" the freedom to designate whatever governing law they wanted.[3] The purpose of this provision was apparently to give the government the flexibility of accepting foreign law as the governing law in respect to Colombian bonds issued publicly abroad because bond markets normally accept only the law where the bonds are issued and sold as the governing law. Although Law 63 supersedes Decree 150 and permits the government to accept foreign governing law provisions in both law and public bond agreements, the government continues as a matter of policy to insist on a Colombian governing law in loan agreements.*

The requirement that loan agreements be governed by Colombian law caused some initial resistance to Colombian credits among international lenders, but this has subsided except for a few banks that still refuse to lend to Colombia for this reason. How troublesome is it to lenders to have their loan agreements governed by the borrower's law (in this case, Colombian law) rather than that of the lender, for example, New York or England? The law of Colombia may not be as developed in matters of international banking and financial law and practice as that of New York or England. But is this a problem? The key legal

---

*The Colombian minister of finance reportedly assured the Colombian Congress prior to the enactment of Law 63 that this would continue to be the government's policy in respect to commercial law agreements.

issues relating to the validity and enforceability of a loan obligation involve such questions as the power and due authorization of the borrower to contract the obligations, the legality of the loan agreement (does it contain those provisions required by law in order to be legal and enforceable?) and whether the interest rate is usurious. Irrespective of which law governs the agreement, if enforcement is sought in Colombia (and perhaps even elsewhere) these issues would probably be determined by Colombian law. Similarly, if enforcement is sought in Colombia, procedural questions such as sovereign immunity as a defense to jurisdiction, the applicable statutes of limitations, and the availability of executive action would also be determined by Colombian law. If enforcement is sought outside Colombia, such as in New York, even if Colombian law is the governing law under the agreement, these same procedural questions (to the extent relevant) would probably be determined by the law of New York or other jurisdiction where the proceeding was brought.

What issues or controversies, then, are likely to be affected when the governing law is that of Colombia rather than of New York? Such issues would appear to relate primarily to whether the borrower is in default under the loan agreement (have certain representations been breached or covenants violated?) or the calculation of interest based upon the London Interbank Offered Rate (LIBOR). The law of New York or England will no doubt shed greater light and accumulated experience than Colombian law on these matters. However, the Colombian Commercial Code recognizes that international custom shall have the authority of law in Colombia provided that it is not contrary to Colombian law and such custom is publicly and uniformly recognized.[4] Thus, it might be possible to prove certain international financial laws and practices that are accepted in the world's financial capitals as constituting international custom and, therefore, part of the law of Colombia. Issues such as these, moreover, often do not go to the heart of enforceability of the loan and usually will be resolved without resorting to litigation. Nevertheless, it must be recognized that if the parties seek to resolve such a dispute out of court, they will probably find more guidance in the laws and precedents of New York than those of Colombia. Also, if suit is brought in New York or before another non-Colombian court, to the extent Colombian law governs, such law will have to be proved to the court, a task that is time consuming and expensive. On balance, however, although it would be easier for the lender to have its own law govern, having Colombian law govern would not seem to give rise to unacceptable legal risks.

Laws and Policies of Several Countries

Chile, in contrast, enacted in late 1978 specific provisions designed to facilitate and encourage foreign lending to Chile and its agencies and instrumentalities. Decree Law 2349 of 1978 expressly declared to be valid international contracts of an economic or financial nature between foreign or international entities and the Chilean state, its "organisms, institutions, and companies" that are subject to foreign law.[5] Guaranty agreements entered by the state and such entities may also be subject to foreign governing law. The state entities to which these provisions are applicable are defined broadly to include all public service institutions (centralized or decentralized), state companies, and any autonomous organization established by law of which the state or any of its entities owns more than 50 percent of its capital.[6] For a governing law provision to be effective it must be authorized by the president of Chile and a general authorization to this effect was granted by the president to a list of state entities, including Corporación Nacional del Cobre de Chile and Corporación de Fomento de la Producción pursuant to Decree 1009 for a period of one year from December 13, 1978. (It presumably will be renewed annually.)[7]

In Argentina and Brazil there appears to be no impediment, legal or political, to having a loan agreement governed by the laws of the lender's country.[8] However, in Brazil this does not necessarily mean a local court will give effect to such a provision. The Brazilian Civil Code provides that a contract will be governed by the law of the country where it was executed. Thus, if a guaranty is executed in Brazil, a Brazilian court would probably apply Brazilian law. For this reason, it is common for lenders to arrange for the federal government of Brazil to execute a guaranty outside of Brazil pursuant to a special authorization given to a Brazilian ambassador or other official.

In Peru, in spite of a provision of the Political Constitution that would seem to preclude them from doing so, certain of the principal governmental borrowers are permitted by the government to include foreign governing law provisions in their loan agreements.* Decree Law 20050 authorizes Banco de la Nación and Corporación Financiera de Desarrollo, both of which serve as financial agents of the Peruvian government, to act on behalf of the state in the international financial markets in accordance with the rules and practices thereof. In re-

---

*Article 17 of the Political Constitution of Peru provides that contracts between the Peruvian government and foreigners must contain an express submission by the foreigner to the laws and courts of Peru.

liance on such provision, foreign governing law provisions are accepted by the Peruvian government. In order for such a provision to be effective, the loan agreement must be executed abroad. If so, it is argued that the contract is an extraterritorial act and therefore not subject to the constitution.* Some observers have doubts about this argument. It should be noted, however, that the Peruvian military government had the power, pursuant to Article 5 of its empowering statute—the Revolutionary Statute, Law 17063 of 1968—to have enacted a statute modifying the Peruvian Political Constitution. Thus, the government had the power, as an alternative to Decree Law 20050, specifically to permit foreign governing law and submission to foreign jurisdictions clauses. It apparently chose not to do so for political reasons. However, the government is willing in practice to include such provisions and therefore has adopted the foregoing argument in support of its position.

The proposed Political Constitution of Peru, which was promulgated by a constitutional assembly on July 12, 1979 and will become effective in July 1980, will clarify the issue of governing law. Article 136(2) requires, in general, that contracts between foreign companies and the state or public entities must contain provisions for the submission by the foreign parties to the laws and tribunals of Peru. However, Article 136(3) specifically exempts from such requirement contracts of a financial character.

In Mexico, there is a difference of opinion among lawyers as to the effectiveness of foreign governing law provisions. Some consider such provisions invalid by reason of Article 13 of the Civil Code of the federal district, which provides that the legal effects of acts and agreements executed abroad that must be performed in Mexico shall be governed by Mexican law. Other lawyers consider that this provision is not applicable to loan agreements that are executed abroad and that provide for disbursement and repayment abroad.

In Venezuela, the policy of the government toward governing law provisions and other issues of loan documentation has changed considerably recently, becoming increasingly more nationalistic. If the loan is to a private (as distinguished from governmental) borrower, the parties are free under general principles of Venezuelan law and the Bustamante Code (a treaty to which Venezuela and a number of other Latin American governments are signatories) to select which party's law will be the governing law of the contract. If the approval of the Superintendencia de Inversiones Extranjeras (SIEX) is required

---

*This argument is apparently based on the Peruvian Civil Code (Preliminary Title), which provides that contracts shall be governed by the law of the place of execution.

for the loan, as is the case for private borrowers and certain corporations owned by the government, the issue as to governing law becomes more one of policy than of law. Recently, the position of SIEX has been to require that loan agreements contain a provision to the effect that the governing law will be either Venezuelan or the lender's depending upon the jurisdiction in which the legal action is brought, but SIEX does accept upon occasion foreign law as the sole governing law.

The governing law of loans to the nation has become the subject of considerable controversy since President Herrera Campins' speech of September 1979 in which he denounced the borrowing policies and legal documentation of the prior administration and stated that the Venezuelan constitution was being violated by agreements containing foreign governing law provisions.[9] Article 127 of the constitution provides that "in contracts of public interest, if not inappropriate by reason of the nature of such contracts," a clause will be considered included to the effect that controversies will be decided by the competent Venezuelan law. Since 1974, except in the case of the first jumbo loan undertaken by Venezuela that was expressly subject to Venezuelan law as a result of an opinion issued by the attorney general (procurador general), it has been the position of the government that loan agreements with the nation could be governed by foreign law because such agreements were not public or sovereign in nature but, rather, private and commercial. Article 127 of the constitution was considered not to be controlling and, therefore, Venezuela could submit to foreign governing law as well as foreign jurisdiction.[10] President Herrera Campins' speech signals a change in this interpretation and Venezuela is now insisting that loan agreements with the nation be subject to Venezuelan law, with no provision for the submission to the jurisdiction of foreign courts. It is unclear whether this position implies that agreements entered before this change in position that have foreign governing law and foreign jurisdiction clauses are still valid or will be considered illegal. To the extent this new position is deemed to be one of policy rather than dictated by the constitution and other laws, presumably prior agreements would still be considered valid. It is understood that, as of January 1, 1980, the president's position is being scrutinized by both financial and legal officers of the government because it has made borrowing by the Venezuelan nation more difficult.*

---

*A large syndicated loan to the nation that was in the process of being negotiated was restructured so that the nation was replaced as borrower by autonomous institutions and wholly owned government corporations in order to avoid certain requirements, including that the loan be subject solely to Venezuelan law.

Making a Borrower's Governing Law
Provision More Acceptable to the Lender

Assuming that the loan agreement is to be governed by the laws
of the borrower, it may be possible to include in the governing law
clause several provisions that will enhance the predictability and usefulness of the borrower's governing law, thereby making it more
palatable to lenders. One of the concerns of lenders is that the borrower's laws and precedents may not have the depth and experience
of New York or English laws in international financial matters. To
alleviate this problem, lenders might seek to include in the governing
law clause a reference to international financial customs and practices
as a supplemental aid in interpreting the agreement. For example,
the governing law clause could state that the agreement will be governed by the laws of the borrower and the customs, uses, and practices of the international financial markets.

Another concern of lenders with a borrower's governing law
provision is that the borrower is usually in the position to change
such law, and thus the very legal foundation, the so-called rules of
the game, on which the loan was originally made could theoretically
be changed to the detriment of the lender. The laws of some Latin
American countries contain a fundamental legal principle against de-
priving a person of rights in this fashion. For example, some Colombian lawyers are of the opinion that there is an established Colombian
juridical principle that the rights of private parties under valid contracts with the nation may not be amended or nullified by subsequent
laws or decrees. Moreover, under general international law principles
of state succession, successor regimes are responsible for the obligations incurred by prior regimes. Nevertheless, some new governments have repudiated obligations of former governments claiming
inter alia that the new government in fact constituted a distinct new
state. Thus, subsequent governments, in Russia and Cuba, have repudiated or altered the agreements and obligations of prior governments. In 1918 the new Soviet government repudiated the debt obligations of the preceding Czarist government. In 1959 and 1960, Cuba
adopted regulations that in effect prevented foreign creditors of Cuba
from obtaining repayment in hard currencies of their loans. In Argentina, the administration of President Arturo Illia of the People's
Radical party in 1963 nullified, pursuant to Decrees 744/63 and 745/63,
a number of oil concessions and other agreements that had been entered
into by the previous government with foreign oil companies. Just recently, the Islamic Provisionary Revolutionary Government of Iran
has expressed its intention not to honor various loan and other contractual obligations incurred by the previous Iranian government.

The political risk of repudiation cannot be eliminated but perhaps it might be lessened, albeit slightly if at all, by including in the governing law clause a provision to the effect that the law governing the agreement shall be that of the borrower as in effect on the date of the agreement. Under the laws of certain countries, such as Colombia, this provision might well be considered superfluous; nevertheless, it still might serve as a useful confirmation of the intent of the parties. Of course, such a clause may not be effective in respect to all subsequent changes in the law and will not deter a government that is intent on repudiating obligations irrespective of their legal validity.

Some Compromise Positions

Assuming it is impossible to reach agreement on which particular law is governing, what options are available to the lender? One solution is to have no governing law provision. A court before which such an agreement is brought will then apply its general choice of law principles to determine what law applies to which issues. Since these questions tend to be resolved on the basis of certain traditionally recognized contacts, such as place of execution of the agreement, and in some countries by a weighing of contacts generally with the jurisdictions involved, it is helpful if the most significant contacts that are subject to being controlled occur in the desired jurisdiction—for example, negotiation and execution of the agreement, delivery of the notes, disbursement, payment of principal and interest, and submission to jurisdiction.

Some parties—including SIEX, as noted above—have attempted to reach a compromise on the governing law question by having the governing law be that of the jurisdiction of either party depending on where legal action is brought. Thus, if the action is brought in the lender's courts, the lender's law governs, and if brought in the borrower's courts, the borrower's law governs. This solution has a simplistic sense of equity. It can, however, lead to problems. The laws of the two jurisdictions may differ on a key point, leading to different results depending upon where suit is brought. This places a great premium on intelligent forum shopping and encourages each party to race to file an action in the jurisdiction most favorable to it, rather than trying to settle their dispute out of court. It also leaves in limbo which law is to govern a dispute under the agreement if the parties desire to settle their differences without resorting to litigation.

PROCEDURAL ISSUES AND
PROBLEMS RELATING TO ENFORCEMENT

The ultimate objective of good legal documentation is, of course, to ensure that the loan is enforceable. If and when the lender is forced to seek the judicial enforcement of its loan, several issues may arise, including whether the court will exercise jurisdiction over the borrower and whether the borrower can assert the defense of sovereign immunity. In addition, lenders and their counsel should be alert to the possible availability of the executory action as a more expeditious enforcement proceeding and to the problems that may arise in trying to obtain satisfaction of a judgment against a governmental borrower.

Submission to Jurisdiction

Just as loan agreements automatically used to designate the lender's law as governing, they also provided that the borrower expressly submit to the jurisdiction of the lender's courts in the event of a dispute. This is now no longer the case, and practices differ widely among Latin American governmental borrowers; some requiring that their own courts have exclusive jurisdiction of disputes and others submitting to the jurisdiction of the lender's courts.

The basic issue is not whether disputes under the loan agreement may be brought for resolution to the courts of either the borrower or the lender, because, as a general rule, the borrower's courts will have jurisdiction over suits brought against the borrower by a lender. The issue is, rather, whether the borrower's courts will be the only forum available to the lender or whether the lender will also be able to bring an action before the courts of another jurisdiction, preferably the lender's, before which the lender may feel more comfortable and which may have experience in international financial matters.

Although the issues of governing law and jurisdiction are related and are often discussed in the same breath, they are separate matters and should not be confused. Jurisdiction is concerned with which or whether <u>courts</u> will resolve disputes between the parties. Governing law provisions dictate which <u>law</u> such courts are to apply in resolving the disputes. The two concepts are closely interrelated because the courts are predisposed to apply their own law (even when the parties have agreed otherwise), since they are, of course, more familiar with it and there may be public policy reasons for not applying another country's laws.

In the absence of an express submission by the borrower to the lender's courts, such courts will nevertheless entertain an action against a foreign borrower if the jurisdictional requirements of such courts have been met. Assuming, for example, that a New York bank brings an action against a foreign borrower in the New York State courts or U.S. federal courts situated in New York, such courts will first have to decide whether they have personal jurisdiction over the borrower. The jurisdictional requirements of New York law, which are rooted in constitutional standards of due process, require that the defendant borrower be "present" or "transacting business" in New York before New York courts will exercise jurisdiction over the borrower.[11] Assuming that the borrower does not have a branch, agency, or other presence in New York sufficient to cause it to be present in New York, then the New York contacts of the borrower must be sufficient to constitute "transacting business" within the meaning of New York Civil Practices Law and Rules § 302(a)(1). Because such determination is dependent on the facts of each case (the quantity and quality of the contacts of the transaction and the defendant borrower with New York), it is not surprising that lenders prefer to avoid the resultant uncertainty by obtaining the borrower's written submission to the courts of New York.

Laws and Policies of Several Countries

As in the case of governing law, Colombia has adopted one of the most nationalistic positions among Latin American governmental borrowers on the issue of submission to jurisdiction of non-Colombian courts. Article 115 of Decree 150 of 1976 provides that loan agreements involving the nation and certain governmental agencies and instrumentalities shall be submitted to "national judges and tribunals."* Specifically excluded from this provision are loan agreements with foreign governmental or public international credit and financial institutions. Although the language of Article 115 is not particularly clear, it could be interpreted as requiring that disputes under loan agreements with foreign private financial institutions must be resolved exclusively in Colombian courts. However, a subsequently enacted law provides that loan agreements to be performed abroad shall be submitted to the jurisdiction of the courts (as well as to the governing law as noted earlier) of whatever country the parties may agree.[12] Nevertheless, as a matter of policy, the Colombian government and its agencies and

---

*The Spanish text is: "Los contratos de emprestito se someteran a la ley colombiana y a la jurisdicción de los jueces y tribunales nacionales."

instrumentalities have been unwilling recently to include a clause in commercial loan agreements providing for the submission of disputes to the jurisdiction of the courts of a foreign country. As a result, such agreements are usually silent on the question of jurisdiction. *

Brazil has adopted a position somewhat similar to that of Colombia, at least in respect to guaranties issued by the federal government. As a matter of policy, Brazil refuses to accept, in guaranty agreements executed by the federal government, a clause submitting the nation to the jurisdiction of foreign courts. As an alternative, the federal government of Brazil has, however, been willing to provide for the submission of disputes to arbitration outside of Brazil. In late 1977, several large New York banks withdrew from a syndicated loan because the guaranty agreement to be executed by the nation provided that the only tribunals for the resolution of disputes were the Brazilian courts or arbitration in England. These banks requested without success that jurisdiction of these tribunals be made nonexclusive or, alternatively, that the documentation remain silent on the question of jurisdiction, thereby hoping to preserve the right to seek to obtain jurisdiction over the guarantor in courts outside of Brazil, such as in New York, and to obtain the benefits of the U.S. Foreign Sovereign Immunities Act of 1976. Brazilian governmental and quasi-governmental borrowers other than the federal government itself are, nevertheless, permitted to accept submission to foreign jurisdiction clauses, even in a loan guaranteed by the federal government.

Chile, again, presents a striking contrast to Colombia and Brazil on the issue of jurisdiction. Article 1 of Decree Law 2349 of 1978 specifically confirms the validity of clauses providing that disputes arising under loan agreements may be submitted to the jurisdiction of foreign courts, as well as clauses designating agents abroad for purposes of service of process.

The Republic of Argentina has the power to submit to the jurisdiction of foreign courts and, as a matter of policy, does so in practice. The Argentina Constitution has been construed to permit the republic to submit to foreign jurisdiction when authorized by law, except in respect to matters directly governed by the constitution or by federal laws or treaties. [13] The necessary legal authorization is contained in Section 7 of Law 20548 of 1973.† If a guaranty issued by the

---

*Assuming the governing law is Colombian and the agreement is silent as to jurisdiction, query to what extent, if any, Article 115 of Decree 150 continues to have applicability.

†The first paragraph of Section 7 refers only to loans granted by foreign public institutions or international financial organizations (such as the World Bank). However, legal authorities both within and out-

republic entails a submission to the jurisdiction of U.S. or British courts, the government has taken the position that an executive decree authorizing such submission is required since, under the U.S. Foreign Sovereign Immunities Act of 1976 and the U.K. State Immunity Act of 1978, such a submission may give rise to a waiver of sovereign immunity that, in turn, may have an effect on Argentina's foreign relations, which, under the constitution, must be conducted by the executive (the president).

In Peru, Article 17 of the Political Constitution requires that all contracts between the government and foreigners contain an express submission by the latter to the courts of Peru. At the same time, as noted earlier, Decree Law 20050 authorizes the Banco de la Nación and Corporación Financiera de Desarrollo to enter into agreements that are in accord with the rules and practices of the international financial markets. The Peruvian government permits the inclusion in loan agreements of clauses submitting to the jurisdiction of foreign courts, provided that such loan agreements are executed abroad. The government reconciles this position with the apparently inconsistent Article 17 on the grounds that the constitution is not applicable to agreements executed abroad. As noted above, under Article 136 of the proposed Political Constitution, financial agreements are specifically exempted from the requirement of containing a submission to Peruvian courts clause.

The attitudes taken by Argentina, Brazil, Chile, Colombia, and Peru toward the issue of submission to the jurisdiction of foreign courts illustrate not only the broad range of positions that can be adopted but also the importance to the lender and its counsel of determining the basis of the government's position (constitution, law, decree, or administrative policy). Irrespective of the underpinnings of such position, the lender and its counsel should be alert to ways to accommodate the policy objectives of the borrower and the legal restrictions applicable to it, while obtaining the best means of resolving disputes with the borrower.

Does the Absence of a Submission of the Borrower to Lender's Courts Create Unacceptable Legal Risks for the Lender?

Assuming that the borrower will not submit to the jurisdiction of foreign courts, will this create intolerable legal risks for the lender? If the agreement does not specifically provide that the jurisdiction

---

side the government have taken the position that this provision also applies to loans made by private commercial banks.

of the borrower's courts is exclusive, then the lender may still be able to obtain jurisdiction over the borrower in the courts of its own country and the chances of doing so can be enhanced if certain steps are taken. For example, if the lender desires to have at least the possibility of obtaining jurisdiction over a borrower in New York in the event of a dispute or nonpayment, the lender should strive to maximize the contacts or nexus between New York and the loan transaction. The following steps, if taken in New York, will provide sufficient support for the exercise of jurisdiction by New York courts:

Conducting a meaningful part of the negotiations in New York,
Executing the loan agreement in New York,
Delivering the notes or other closing documents in New York,
Providing for disbursement of the loan in New York, and
Providing for payment of interest and principal in New York.

If all such steps take place in New York, a New York court would almost certainly find there were sufficient contacts with New York to exercise jurisdiction over the borrower.[14] Although a single such act in New York is usually not sufficient, if several of these steps take place in New York, such as significant negotiations or execution by the borrower of the agreement in New York coupled with the loan being repayable in New York, a New York court will probably grant jurisdiction.[15] Nevertheless, in the absence of an express submission by the borrower to the jurisdiction of the courts of New York, there is the possibility that New York courts will determine they have no jurisdiction or alternatively dismiss the action on the ground of forum non conveniens.* There is also the risk that the borrower will move to dismiss the action on the grounds of lack of jurisdiction, thereby necessitating a time-consuming and costly hearing to determine where jurisdiction lies.

In the absence of an express consent to jurisdiction, the borrower may also be subject to the jurisdiction of U.S. federal courts by reason of the Foreign Sovereign Immunities Act of 1976, which

---

*Assuming that the lender is successful in obtaining jurisdiction over the borrower, nevertheless, a U.S. court may refuse, as a matter of equitable discretion on the grounds of forum non conveniens, to hear an action that has insufficient nexus to the jurisdiction. Under New York law, a court ordinarily will not dismiss an action on grounds of forum non conveniens if the plaintiff is a New York resident and has a genuine interest in the outcome of the action and there is some other nexus with New York, for example, the loan is disbursed and payable in New York.

provides a statutory scheme for obtaining jurisdiction over and serving process on foreign governmental entities. Under 28 U.S.C. § 1330(a), which was added by the act, U.S. federal district courts are granted jurisdiction over a foreign state as to any claim with respect to which that state is not entitled to immunity under the act. Thus, if as a result of the foreign state's borrowing from a U.S. lender, the borrower is not entitled to immunity under the act, then the foreign state will be subject to the jurisdiction of U.S. federal district courts. Because of this provision of the Foreign Sovereign Immunities Act of 1976, it is possible that it is now easier to obtain jurisdiction over a foreign state in the federal courts than it is to obtain jurisdiction based on the New York "long arm" statute, CPLR § 302(a).

If the loan agreement provides for the exclusive jurisdiction of the borrower's courts, the lender still may have a chance to obtain jurisdiction over the borrower in another country. Traditionally, courts were reluctant to permit parties by agreement to oust them of their jurisdiction. Thus, they tended to interpret exclusive jurisdiction clauses narrowly and, under certain circumstances, would refuse to give them effect.[16] More recently, however, U.S. courts have tended to enforce an exclusive forum clause in an agreement unless to do so would be unfair and unreasonable.[17] To determine whether an exclusive jurisdiction clause is unfair or unreasonable, courts have examined such factors as serious inconvenience to the parties, whether the plaintiff, if forced to sue in the forum required by the contract clause, would thereby be deprived of an effective remedy or whether the clause was obtained by misrepresentation or the result of a contract of adhesion.[18]

Evaluating the Courts of the Borrower's Country

Assuming that the lender's only resort for enforcing its loan to a governmental borrower is the borrower's own court system, is this an unacceptable legal risk for the lender? Can a lender reasonably expect fair and objective treatment from the borrower's own courts?

These are not easy questions to answer. But, first, they should be put in perspective. Lenders have very rarely sued sovereign nations to enforce loan obligations. Some of such actions have arisen in the aftermath of political revolution, such as in Cuba or China, and, most recently, in Iran. In such instances, the lenders have tended to preserve a right of setoff or to attach assets of the borrower located within the lender's jurisdiction. In the cases of setoff, the borrower (or its successor-in-interest) has often initiated the suit against the lender in the lender's country or sought to remove its assets from the jurisdiction. Another factor to consider is that even if a lender is able to sue a sovereign borrower in the lender's country, unless the sovereign borrower has assets located within the jurisdiction that are

not immune from execution or the lender can execute against assets
in some other jurisdiction, the lender may be relegated to seeking
enforcement in the borrower's own country. This raises complicated
questions relating to the enforcement of foreign judgments under the
laws of the borrower's country. If the lender is faced with this necessity, some Latin American lawyers will advise it to bring its legal
action, in the first instance, in the borrower's country. Their reasoning is that if a Latin American country's courts are asked to enforce
a foreign judgment against the sovereign, although empowered to enforce such a judgment pursuant to a proceeding known as exequation,
the courts may, in effect, review the case de novo, particularly if it
is a matter of importance to the nation. Moreover, if such courts
would not decide in favor of the plaintiff lender a particular case
brought to it in the first instance, it is questionable whether the same
court would enforce a foreign judgment against the defendant sovereign
borrower in the same case.

Although, in certain circumstances, the foregoing factors may
lessen the benefits to the lender from being able to sue the borrower
in the lender's courts, nevertheless, there are good reasons why
lenders should seek, if at all possible, to maintain the right to bring
an action against the sovereign borrower in the lender's courts.
These include the lender's knowledge of, and familiarity with, its
country's courts; the greater likelihood that such courts will apply
the laws of the lender's country; the sense among litigants that there
exists a home court advantage; the greater knowledge of, and experience with, international finance and the intricacies of the Eurodollar
market that the lender's courts may possess; and the natural tendency
to believe that one's own courts are objective and free from influence
whereas the other's courts are biased and subject to manipulation.

But, returning to the earlier question, Are the legal risks to
the lender unacceptable if jurisdiction over disputes rests exclusively
in the borrower's courts? To answer this question, the lender and
its counsel should examine the following:

1. Two threshold questions: Is the sovereign subject to suit
in the courts of its own country?* Do foreigners have the right (also
known as "standing") to bring an action against a governmental borrower before the borrower's courts?†

---

*See the discussion on sovereign immunity.

†For example, access of foreigners to the courts of Colombia is
assured by the Colombian Constitution, which provides that foreigners
shall enjoy the same civil rights and guaranties that are accorded to
Colombians.

2. What courts in the borrower's country would have initial and appellate jurisdiction over a legal action involving a foreign lender and a governmental borrower?

3. What is the reputation of those courts, for integrity, objectivity, and independence?

4. What cases have such courts handled in recent years involving claims against governmental defendants? Have the courts been subject to governmental influence? Have they rendered judgment against the government when the situation warranted it?

5. What recent cases have there been involving foreign parties as either plaintiffs or defendants and have such parties been treated fairly, especially in cases where the other litigant is the government?

6. How are the judges who would hear the action named to the judiciary? Are they elected by popular vote, selected by the government, or selected by the other members of the court?*

7. How long do such judges serve? For life?† As a practical matter do they continue to serve even after the change of a governmental administration? Or, are they encouraged or forced to resign?‡

8. Is the general attitude within the borrower's country respectful of the rule of law?

9. Is the current political situation such that the country's recent experience in respect to the judiciary is likely to be an accurate portent for the future?

Although an examination of these questions is of particular importance where the borrower's courts have exclusive jurisdiction, such an examination should probably be undertaken by the lender as an integral part of its country-risk analysis, even if the loan documentation provides for submission to the jurisdiction of the lender's courts.

---

*In Colombia, for example, the constitution provides that members of the Supreme Court and the Council of State (which is the highest tribunal handling administrative cases) are elected by the other members of the court or council.

†The Colombia Constitution provides that judges shall serve until the age of compulsory retirement.

‡When Juan Perón came to power he adopted measures involving both pension and other financial incentives as well as intimidation to encourage members of the judiciary to resign so that he could replace them with persons more sympathetic to his policies.

Sovereign Immunity

The issue of sovereign immunity arises when a lender brings a legal action against a foreign state. Assuming that there is a sufficient nexus for the court to exercise personal jurisdiction, the borrower may nevertheless assert that it is immune from suit by reason of its sovereignty. Thus, sovereign immunity is not a defense to the merits or substance of a party's claim, but a bar to the jurisdiction of the court. Sovereign immunity may also be asserted by a foreign state in an effort to prevent a lender from attaching the state's property prior to the entry of a judgment by the court or from attaching and executing upon a state's property in satisfaction of a judgment rendered against the state.

The issue of sovereign immunity is usually governed by the law of the forum where the action is brought. Therefore, if a lender is interested in ensuring that it can bring legal action in the courts of both the borrower and the lender, it is important to understand the laws and policies on sovereign immunity of both these countries.

Is the Borrower Entitled to Immunity in Its Own Country?

In most Latin American countries, the general rule appears to be that the sovereign is not entitled to immunity from jurisdiction in respect to actions on loan obligations. Thus, the Argentine, Brazilian, Chilean, Colombian, Peruvian, and Venezuelan states are, in general, not entitled to immunity from suit within their own countries. However, an action against the nation may have to be brought before a particularly designated court or branch of the judiciary or a judgment against the nation may have to be confirmed by a particular court prior to such judgment's being collectible. Accordingly, the lender should ascertain to which court an action against the state must be brought in the first instance. The court's reputation for independence and integrity will be important, of course, to the lender's decision as to whether to sue the borrower in such court.

Although Latin American states are ordinarily subject to suit, their assets are generally immune from attachment and execution. This rule may or may not extend also to the state's political subdivisions, agencies, and instrumentalities. Therefore, the rights and immunities of each governmental borrower under its own law should be examined.* Even though a sovereign borrower may be immune

---

*In Peru, for example, the assets of the Central Bank are apparently not immune from attachment or execution. In Venezuela, on the other hand, the Central Bank's assets would not be subject to attachment or execution.

from execution of a judgment, there are usually procedures by which payment of a judgment can be obtained. These are discussed below.

If a governmental borrower's immunity from attachment and execution is established by law, the borrower may not have the power or authority to waive such immunity. It is important, therefore, to ascertain whether the lack of power to waive immunity from attachment and execution in the borrower's own country necessarily precludes the borrower from also waiving such immunity before the courts of a foreign jurisdiction.

Is the Borrower Entitled to Immunity in the Lender's Country?

If the lender wants the option to bring suit against a governmental borrower in the lender's own courts, it must take whatever steps it can to ensure that the borrower will not be immune from the jurisdiction of such courts and, it is hoped, will be subject to attachment and execution. Because of the recent enactment in the United States of the Foreign Sovereign Immunities Act of 1976, as well as the enactment of the U.K. State Immunity Act of 1978, the law in respect to sovereign immunity has been greatly clarified and the ability of lenders to obtain jurisdiction over sovereign borrowers substantially enhanced.

The U.S. Foreign Sovereign Immunities Act of 1976. Since the U.S. Foreign Sovereign Immunities Act has been the subject of many scholarly articles, it will be discussed only in passing. [19] Briefly, the act's principal provisions are as follows: The act provides that a foreign state (which is defined to include a political subdivision, agency, or instrumentality of such state) shall not be immune from jurisdiction of U.S. federal or state courts in any case in which (1) the foreign state has waived its immunity either explicitly or implicitly or (2) the action is based upon a commercial activity or act carried on or performed outside the United States that causes a direct effect in the United States. [20] The act also provides that the property in the United States of a foreign state that is used for a commercial activity in the United States shall not be immune from attachment in aid of execution or execution if (1) the foreign state has explicitly or implicitly waived its immunity from execution or (2) the property is or was used for the commercial activity upon which the claim is based. [21] Since a waiver of immunity by a sovereign state is irrevocable, the benefit to a lender of obtaining an express or even implicit waiver of immunity is substantial. Even if the borrower is unwilling or unable to give a waiver, the borrower and its assets may nevertheless be subject to jurisdiction and execution depending upon the nature of its activities and assets in the United States.

Illustrative Laws and Policies of Several Countries. The extent to
which Latin American governmental borrowers are empowered by
law or are willing as a matter of policy to give a waiver varies greatly
from country to country. In Argentina, for example, the republic has
the power to waive its immunity from the jurisdiction of foreign courts
and, prior to 1977, did so in numerous cases. Since October 1977,
however, the government has refused as a matter of policy to grant
express waivers of the republic's immunity, although it has accepted
language that has been construed by U.S. counsel as an implicit
waiver. Argentine governmental agencies and instrumentalities, on
the other hand, are still permitted to give express waivers. In Brazil, the federal government does permit the inclusion in loan agreements of provisions waiving its immunity to suit. Chile is perhaps
the most flexible country on the issue of sovereign immunity. Decree
Law 2349 of 1978 permits the state of Chile and its agencies and instrumentalities to waive their immunity from both suit and execution.
Moreover, a submission to the jurisdiction of a foreign court is expressly deemed to terminate the borrower's right to invoke immunity
from jurisdiction. The Colombian government, as a matter of policy,
will not expressly waive immunity nor permit its agencies or instrumentalities to do so.[22] The Peruvian government will permit the inclusion in loan agreements of waivers of immunity from jurisdiction
but has no power to do so in respect to execution.

If the borrower states that it is unwilling or unable to waive its
immunity even in respect to jurisdiction, lender's counsel should
probe carefully to ascertain the reason for such refusal. It may be
that a law unambiguously prohibits such a waiver. More likely, however, it may be a question of interpretation mixed with policy considerations involving nationalistic pride. In the latter case, it may be
helpful to make clear to the borrower that the waiver merely relates
to a foreign court's willingness to entertain a legal action against the
borrower and not to the relinquishment of the borrower's sovereignty.
Indeed, it may be helpful to avoid altogether the use of the word sovereignty (the use of which is not necessary to effect the waiver), which
in the abstract sounds quite sacred. For example, one Latin American republic refused to grant a waiver on the grounds it violated a
constitutional prohibition against "ceding the nation's sovereignty"
but was willing to do so once the word sovereignty was eliminated.

Does the Absence of an Express Waiver of Immunity by the Borrower
Create Unacceptable Legal Risks for the Lender? Assuming that the
borrower is not prepared to provide a waiver of sovereign immunity
even in respect to jurisdiction, what legal risks will result? To what
extent are the opportunities for legal enforcement of the loan diminished? If, pursuant to § 1605(a)(2) and § 1610(a)(2) of the Immunities

Act, the loan transaction constitutes "a commercial activity carried on in the United States by the foreign state" or "an act performed in the United States in connection with a commercial activity of the foreign state elsewhere" or "an act outside the territory of the United States in connection with a commercial activity of the foreign state elsewhere and that causes a direct effect in the United States," then the governmental borrower will not be immune from jurisdiction nor will its property be immune from attachment in aid of execution or from execution if such property is or was used for the commercial activity that is the subject of the action. Thus, the lender may still obtain jurisdiction over the borrower even in the absence of a waiver.

The definition of commercial activity in the Immunities Act was purposefully general and is not very helpful in determining whether governmental borrowing constitutes commercial activity. However, the House of Representatives report that accompanied the bill stated that such borrowing is a commercial act:

> Activities such as a foreign government's sale of a service or a product, its leasing of property, its borrowing of money . . . would be among those included within the definition [of commercial activity].[23] [Emphasis added]

In order to give added support to this interpretation it would be useful to include in the loan documentation a representation along the following lines:

> The Borrower represents and warrants that this Agreement and the Loans constitute commercial and private, and not governmental or public, acts of the Borrower and this Agreement constitutes a commercial and private transaction between the parties.

To provide further support for a U.S. court's determining that the borrower is not immune, the contacts or nexus of the borrower and the loan transaction with the United States should be as substantial as possible.

If the borrower has also been unwilling to consent to the jurisdiction of U.S. courts and the contacts or nexus of the transaction is minimal (for example, the only contacts are disbursement and repayment), the chances that a U.S. court would exercise jurisdiction over the borrower are slight. In this circumstance, the lender must determine whether the courts of the borrower present a sufficiently satisfactory alternative for the enforcement of the loan.

Enforcement of a Promissory Note by Executive Action

In most Latin American countries there exists a special summary or expedited judicial proceeding frequently referred to as an "executive action" (juicio ejecutivo) that is available for the enforcement of certain legal instruments if they qualify as executive instruments (títulos ejecutivos).* The advantages of the executive action over an ordinary proceeding are several. First, the executive action is usually substantially quicker and cheaper. The defendant must respond in a short period. (In Colombia, for example, an executive mandate is issued by the court requiring the defendant to pay the instrument within five days of the filing of the suit, although public entities have six months in which to pay.)[24] Ordinarily, there are no issues to be resolved that require prolonged hearings or proceedings. This is due, in part, to the fact that the plaintiff does not have to prove its right to payment because if the instrument on which the plaintiff is suing appears on its face to meet the requirements of an executive instrument, the plaintiff's right is deemed valid, undisputed, and due and payable unless proved otherwise by the defendant. Second, the plaintiff may commence the executive action by obtaining an attachment of sufficient assets of the defendant to pay the amount claimed. Such attachment not only serves to exert considerable pressure on the defendant but also provides assets against which the final judgment may be executed.

Although the advantages of executive action over an ordinary proceeding may be significant in terms of timing, the advantage of being able to attach the defendant's assets in advance of the proceeding will be meaningless if the defendant's assets are immune from attachment. This latter point is of particular relevance to loans to governmental borrowers whose assets are immune from attachment. For this reason, one should determine whether, in fact, executive action (which implies the "execution" against a defendant's assets) is available for use against a governmental borrower whose assets are immune from attachment.

---

*The following discussion of executive action will make reference to various provisions of Colombian law by way of illustration in order to highlight with some specificity the types of issues that arise. Colombian law in this area is, in general, reflective of the laws of most of the other Latin American countries. It should be noted, however, that other countries' laws will differ in specific respects and, therefore, a particular country's laws should be examined to resolve questions involving such country.

In order for a promissory note to be enforceable by executive action it must qualify as a título valor (this term is usually translated as "negotiable instrument"). The action available to enforce a negotiable instrument has a special name, acción cambiaría, which is derived from the Spanish term for bill of exchange or draft (letra de cambio). If a promissory note qualifies as a negotiable instrument and, therefore, for the acción cambiaría, the defenses that the defendant obligor may raise to its obligations on the note are limited.

The Colombian Commercial Code defines a negotiable instrument as a document incorporating a right that is "literal and autonomous" (literal y autonomo).[25] The code provides further that to qualify as a negotiable instrument, a promissory note (pagaré) must set forth the following:[26]

The signature of the obligor,
The obligor's unconditional promise to pay a determined (or certain) sum of money,
The name of the person to whom payment is to be made,
An indication of whether the note is payable to order or to the bearer, and
The date of maturity.

The maturity date may take a number of forms. Thus, a note may be payable at sight; on a day certain, whether determined or not; on successive maturity dates; or on a date certain after sight or a particular date.[27] If a note does not contain all of these elements, it will not qualify as a negotiable instrument.

Nevertheless, even if a note does not qualify as a negotiable instrument and for the acción cambiaría, it may still be enforceable by means of the executive action if it qualifies as an executive title. To qualify as such, the Colombian Code of Civil Procedure requires that the obligation contained in an executive title must be express, clear, and due and payable (expresa, clara, y exigible).[28]

The key question as to the enforceability by executive action of the normal form of promissory note used in Eurodollar loan transactions is whether it will qualify as a negotiable instrument under the laws of the particular Latin American country in question. Such notes are normally much more elaborate and complex than the simple promissory note or draft that was no doubt contemplated by the drafters of the provisions relating to executive action. Eurodollar notes have a number of characteristics that raise questions as to their qualification as negotiable instruments, but the following discussion will focus on only three of these: the floating interest rate based on the LIBOR, the payment of such notes in installments, and the acceleration of principal and interest in the event of a default.

The calculation of the interest payable on a Eurodollar note that is based upon a floating rate pegged to the LIBOR requires referring to information that is not contained in the note itself. For this reason, the note may not be considered literal and autonomous or for a determined or certain sum and, therefore, there is considerable risk that the amount of interest due and payable on a Eurodollar note cannot be enforced by executive action but only by an ordinary proceeding. This does not necessarily mean, however, that the principal amount of the note is not enforceable by executive action. Thus, under the Colombian Commercial Code, if certain parts of a note do not satisfy the requirements of a negotiable instrument, such parts will be ignored and if the other parts do satisfy such requirements, the principal will still be enforceable by executive action.[29]

Even though the interest rate on a promissory note is based upon a formula extrinsic to the note itself, such as that of the LIBOR, a reasonable argument can be made that it should be enforceable by executive action. Under the Colombian Commercial Code, a promissory note may bear interest either at a fixed rate or "the current rate," which is the bank rate fixed from time to time by the central bank.[30] Since this rate is a floating rate that is not expressed numerically on the face of the note but can be determined objectively and readily and since the LIBOR can also be determined objectively and readily (in fact, the Colombian Central Bank publishes LIBORs from time to time), a court could refer to such rates in calculating the interest due on a Eurodollar rate and, therefore, should be willing to enforce interest calculated on the basis of the LIBOR through an executive action.

The repayment of the principal amount of a promissory note in installments should not, at least under Colombian law, prevent its enforceability by executive action. The Colombian Commercial Code provides that the principal of a promissory note can be payable on successive fixed maturity dates.[31] Thus, successive principal installment payments can be enforced by executive action and, depending upon the existence of an acceleration clause, perhaps all remaining installments can be accelerated and enforced by executive action, as noted immediately below.

An acceleration clause in a promissory note providing that all principal and interest will be payable prior to the scheduled maturity of the loan if one or more "events of default" occur gives rise to the question whether the note matures on a date certain or is otherwise subject to a condition that cannot be determined on the literal face of the note. A strict reading of the requirements of a negotiable instrument would lead to the conclusion that amounts due by acceleration could not be enforced by executive action, but only by an ordinary proceeding. Nevertheless, if the condition or event of default giving rise to the right of acceleration can be objectively and readily ascertainable by a court, then executive action may be available. Article 490 of the Colombian Code of Civil Procedure contemplates the possibility of enforcing by executive action an obligation subject to such a condition and refers to means of proving the occurrence of such condition. The Colombian superintendent of banks, in a recent opinion, has given support to this view by determining that executive action is available to enforce future installments of principal that become due by acceleration in the event of a default in payment of any single installment.[32] Since the burden of proving payment of an installment of principal or interest when due is on the obligor and since such an event of default is ascertainable by a court without resorting to extrinsic evidence beyond the note itself, a nonpayment default should provide a sufficient basis for a court to enforce an accelerated promissory note by means of executive action. Other defaults, such as breach of a financial covenant, a misrepresentation or a cross-default, may be less easily determinable and, therefore, may not be permitted bases for enforcing an acceleration of payment by means of executive action.

One potentially simple means of avoiding the necessity of meeting the criteria for a negotiable instrument under local Latin American laws may be to provide for the creation or issuance of the promissory note in the lender's country so that the latter's laws will govern its status as a negotiable instrument. Thus, under Colombian law, an instrument "created" abroad will be treated as a negotiable instrument if it fulfills the minimum requirements established under the law governing its creation.[33] A negotiable instrument is considered created abroad if it is executed and delivered abroad. To be able to benefit from this provision, of course, the promissory note still must satisfy the requirements of a negotiable instrument under the laws where it was created.

Problems of Obtaining Satisfaction of a Judgment against a Governmental Borrower

Assuming that a lender has been forced to sue a governmental borrower and has been successful in obtaining a judgment in the borrower's own country, the lender nevertheless should not necessarily expect to collect promptly on such judgment. As noted above, the government's property is usually immune from execution in its own country, and accordingly, the lender will not be able to execute against the borrower's assets. The lender's recourse is to take its judgment to the paying agent of the nation, which may be the treasurer or comptroller, and demand payment of the judgment. If the amount of the judgment is small or the lender is lucky, the treasurer may pay the judgment immediately. More than likely, however, and particularly if the judgment is for a large amount, the treasurer may say that provision must be made in the budget for payment of the judgment, which may involve waiting until the following fiscal year.

This appears to be the case in respect to Colombia, particularly if the judgment involved an acceleration of the loan and, therefore, the national budget did not contain an item covering the repayment of the loan in the year in which the lender was seeking to collect on its judgment.[34] A similar result seems to obtain in Argentina where judgments against the republic are considered only declarative, which the Supreme Court has construed to mean that the republic must be allowed a reasonable time to pay a judgment in order not to affect the normal course of public administration.[35] In Venezuela, in order to collect on a judgment against the nation or certain autonomous institutions, the holder of the judgment must follow the procedures set forth in the Organic Law of Public Finance and arrange to include a provision in the national budget for payment of the debt.

NATURE AND LEGAL STATUS OF THE BORROWER: WHO REALLY IS THE BORROWER?

Understanding fully the nature and legal status or juridical character of the borrower is essential to answering such key questions as the following: What legal regime governs the borrower? Does the borrower have the power to contract the loan? Has the loan been authorized and approved by all authorities? Does the borrower benefit from sovereign immunity? Who really controls the borrower, particularly its sources of funds for repayment?

Because of the extensive participation by the government in most Latin American countries, there is a broad and complex range of governmental borrowers, which include the following:

The sovereign nation: The nation when borrowing usually acts through, or is represented by, the ministry of finance or its equivalent but may act through other ministries as well.

States, departments, or provinces: In certain countries, these political subdivisions are similar to states of the United States and may be subject to a state legal system as well as to federal or national laws. In other countries—such as Colombia, which has departments—these subdivisions may be subject to the legal and judicial system of the nation only, even though they may be administratively autonomous.

Municipalities: These are normally political subdivisions of the state, department, or province in which they are located and are subject to the laws and regulations of the municipal, state, and national governments.

Federal or special districts: These are often capital cities, such as Bogotá, Caracas, or Mexico City, which have a separate legal status somewhat analogous to that of Washington, D.C.

Central bank: The central bank is a key participant in all foreign lending in Latin America, whether serving as the borrower or guarantor or acting in its capacity as holder and administrator of the country's foreign exchange.

Decentralized or autonomous agencies or instrumentalities: The number and variety of such entities in Latin America is staggering, reflective of the important role that the state plays in the economy. They generally have a separate juridical personality, may be organized and incorporated as a corporation (sociedad anónima), have separate assets and budget, and may report directly to the president of the country or to a designated ministry. Their functions may range from performing public services, such as providing sewage or road systems, to fulfilling a traditionally private sector role, such as steel production.

Mixed enterprises: These are entities owned in part by the government and in part by the private sector.* They may perform services of a public or governmental nature or fulfill a traditionally private sector role.

Entities with no juridical personality: Some governmental borrowers, such as the armed forces, may have no juridical personality and, under certain circumstances, no enabling statute nor the equivalent of articles of incorporation or bylaws. In such cases, although their de facto power may be self-evident, their legal power and authority to contract loans may be obscure. A loan to a borrower under these circumstances may run greater risks of repudiation by a subsequent administration than one based on clearly established legal authority if such administration is looking for technical defects as a justification for repudiating the obligations of the preceding government.

The significance to bankers and their counsel of such a bewildering array of governmental borrowers is that one must make sure that all laws and regulations applicable to the borrower—whether national, state, or municipal—have been complied with and one must be sensitive to the fact that the legal requirements governing a loan to the na-

---

*This use of the term mixed enterprise is not to be confused with that of the Andean Pact, which applies such a term to entities in which foreign investors own between 20 and 49 percent of the equity.

tion may be quite different from those applicable to a decentralized
agency or other governmental instrumentality. Therefore, in structuring and documenting a loan to any of the foregoing kinds of borrowers, it is imperative to be familiar with the laws and regulations that
govern a particular borrower, give it its power to borrow, provide
it with its means of repayment, and set forth the authorizations and
approvals that are prerequisites to its incurring loans.

STRUCTURING THE LOAN

Because of the variety of governmental entities that can borrow
on behalf of a particular country, the lender and its counsel should be
alert to the fact that there may be several alternative ways to structure a proposed financing, some of which may be more advantageous
to the lender than others.

Loans to the Sovereign

If the proposed loan is a general purpose loan to finance balance-
of-payments deficits or economic development, it might be made directly to the sovereign nation itself or to the central bank, a national
development bank, or a decentralized agency, with or without the
guaranty of the sovereign. If it is to the sovereign itself or with the
guaranty of the sovereign, how should the sovereign be referred to?
Oftentimes the words "republic" (república), "state" (estado), "nation" (nación), or "government" (gobierno) are used interchangeably,
and the assumption usually is that they all refer to the sovereign with
the same legal effect. Such an assumption may or may not be correct
and should be examined in the context of each country. For example,
with respect to Argentina, the Argentine constitution provides the
following:

> The Argentine nation adopts for its government the repre-
> sentative, republican, federal system.[36]

From this it would follow that the term Argentine nation would super-
sede and take precedence over the Argentine republic and, therefore,
loans to the Argentine sovereign should be made to the nation as the
borrower. This conclusion is reinforced by the fact that a nation
such as Argentina theoretically could abandon the republican form of
government or, in the French style, establish a second republic. Ordinarily a political change of this sort would not cause a nation to disa-
vow obligations incurred by a prior government, nor would it be jus-

tified in doing so under principles of international law.[37] Fortunately, the Argentine constitution, in a subsequent article, specifically provides that the word republic may also be used to refer to the nation.[38] Thus, in the case of a loan to Argentina, the borrower can be referred to as the "nation" or the "republic" interchangeably. Nevertheless, it is important to bear in mind that if the political upheaval is great and a subsequent regime is looking for a pretext, however frivolous, to invalidate a prior regime's obligations, a distinction as seemingly insignificant as the one between nation and republic might be relied upon.

In Colombia, the constitution and laws speak of Colombia in terms of la Nación or la República.[39] Thus, it would seem either designation would be effective in contracting with Colombia. The constitution provides that the republic is responsible for the obligations, both domestic and external, of the country and refers to the territory of the country as belonging to the nation.[40] It describes the nation as consisting of the various departments and territories into which the country has been divided. The government, on the other hand, is defined as consisting of the president and the various ministers and directors of administrative departments.[41] In practice, sovereign loans made directly to Colombia are usually made to the Republic of Colombia.

Similarly, in Venezuela, reference is made to the sovereign nation in the constitution, civil code, and several other laws as the state (not to be confused with the states, which are political subdivisions), the nation, the republic, and the national treasury (fisco nacional). Each of these terms, if examined closely, has a different connotation or meaning. Fortunately, however, the Venezuelan Supreme Court has held, in effect, that the state, nation, republic, and national treasury are all one single legal entity.[42] Sovereign loans to Venezuela are usually made to the Venezuelan Nation.

Because of the variety of terms that may be used to refer to a sovereign borrower and the differences in meanings that can or might be ascribed to such terms, it is important to examine carefully whether the legal term used to refer to the borrower is the correct one. Because the term government may mean only the particular political administration in power at any one moment, it is usually preferable to contract with the nation or republic rather than the government in order to reduce the risk that the obligation of the government will be treated as binding only that government that contracted the loan and not subsequent administrations. This is especially true if the government in power is not constitutionally elected or popularly based and, therefore, the risks of repudiation by subsequent administrations are greater than normal. This problem is highlighted by the recent events in Nicaragua and Iran.

Loans to the Central Bank or a Decentralized
Agency with Guaranty of the Sovereign

Should the loan be structured as a direct loan to the sovereign
nation or as a loan to the central bank or a decentralized agency, with
the guaranty of the nation? The answer to this question will depend,
in part, on the powers and policies of the nation and the central bank
or other agency. Assuming such powers and policies will permit it,
there may be some benefits from structuring the loan as one to the
central bank, with the guaranty of the nation. Although the central
bank is usually involved to a certain extent in a Latin American nation's external borrowings, if the central bank is the borrower the
lender is assured of the direct participation in, and supervision of,
the loan by the central bank. Lenders often find it easier to deal
with a country's central bank than its ministry of finance, since central banks are usually more familiar with international financial practices. More important, perhaps, is the fact that the central bank is
the agency that manages the country's foreign exchange. Therefore,
when foreign exchange is in short supply it may be comforting to a
lender to know that its borrower has control over such foreign exchange.

For somewhat similar reasons, a loan to certain decentralized
agencies, guaranteed by the nation, may more likely be repaid on time
than a direct loan to the nation if the particular agency is of critical
importance to the nation's export earnings and generates its own foreign exchange. Thus, a nation may give priority to the repayment of
a loan to its principal export producer to ensure that the agency continues generating foreign exchange, and the nation's other international
creditors may even permit such preferential treatment since the foreign exchange may be critical to the repayment of their loans as well.
On the other hand, if an agency falls out of favor with the government
—for example, because of alleged bribes relating to loans or the improper use of loan proceeds—loans to the agency may be discriminated
against by the government (even though the loans bear a sovereign
guaranty) in favor of direct loans to the nation or loans to more favored
agencies.

For these reasons, lenders should be sensitive to the fact that
loans to different governmental agencies may give rise to different
credit and legal risks even though both carry the same guaranty and,
accordingly, in theory, the same degree of risk.

The Use of Guaranties

Assuming that a loan is to be guaranteed by the nation, the central bank, a governmental commercial or development bank, institute

or decentralized agency, there are many questions to consider, several of which will be highlighted briefly.

Affixing an Aval to the Promissory Note

Should the borrower's promissory note bear the aval ("guaranty") of the guarantor and is this sufficient? The aval is, generally speaking, a form of guaranty used for negotiable instruments. It is normally affixed to the instrument itself, but under the laws of certain countries may be set forth in a separate document. It is generally desirable to have the guarantor affix its aval on the borrower's promissory note. The extent of the obligations thereby incurred by the avalista ("guarantor") may vary somewhat from country to country. In Colombia, for example, the avalista is obligated to the same extent and on the same terms as the principal obligor.[43] The avalista is primarily liable with the principal obligor, not merely secondarily. Moreover, the avalista is still liable even if the obligation of the principal obligor may be unenforceable. Assuming the promissory note qualifies for enforcement through the more efficient judicial proceeding known as "executory action," the obligation of the avalista will be enforceable through the same proceeding. The avalista's defenses will be of the same type as those available to the maker of a promissory note, although not necessarily the same since the obligations of the principal obligor and the avalista are considered independent. Thus, even if the purported principal obligor is not liable on a note if its signature was forged, the avalista will still be liable (assuming, of course, that the signature was genuine).

Depending upon the extent to which the lender is actually looking to the guarantor for ultimate repayment of the loan, it may be desirable to have the guarantor execute a separate instrument or agreement of guaranty setting forth in full the guarantor's obligations. If the lender is primarily looking to the creditworthiness of the guarantor in making the loan, the guaranty agreement should contain as extensive representations, warranties, covenants, waivers of immunity, and other protections as would be included in a direct loan agreement with the guarantor. Even if a long-form guaranty such as this is used, it is still desirable to have the guarantor affix its aval to the promissory note because of benefits that may be accorded to the lender by law.*

----

*This may not be possible as a policy matter. In Colombia, for example, the president of the nation must execute guaranties undertaken by the nation, and Colombian officials who administer such transactions are unwilling to have the president burdened by signing every pagaré that may be issued in connection with a financing. Ac-

If the guaranty of the guarantor does not qualify as an <u>aval</u>, but is a <u>garantía</u> or <u>fianza</u>, the rights and remedies that the lender has against the guarantor may be less; for example, the guarantor may be only secondarily liable and may have more extensive defenses available to it in order to avoid liability under its guaranty. Accordingly, it may be preferable to obtain the obligation of a guarantor in the form of an <u>aval</u> and in the guarantor's capacity as <u>avalista</u>.

Statutory Guaranties

The obligations of certain governmental agencies of Latin American countries are guaranteed by statute by the sovereign nation. For example, the statutory Charter of the Argentine Central Bank specifies that the obligations of the bank are guaranteed by the nation. [44] The obligations of several other state-owned Argentine banks—for example, Banco de la Nación Argentina and Banco Nacional de Desarrollo, both active borrowers in the international financial markets— also by law carry the guaranty of the nation. [45]

In such a statutory guaranty as beneficial to the lender as an <u>aval</u> or a written guaranty? Probably not. Unfortunately, there are no statutory provisions defining the scope of the statutory guaranties referred to above, the preconditions that must be satisfied before they can be called upon, or the defenses that might be asserted by the nation. An <u>aval</u> in Argentina obligates the guarantor in the same manner and to the same extent as the principal obligor. [46] Under statutory guaranties, however, the nation is probably liable only secondarily (as contrasted with primarily). Thus, a lender cannot call on a statutory guaranty such as this as readily as on an express guaranty and would probably be required to exhaust its procedural remedies against the borrower before it could proceed against the nation as guarantor. The statutory guaranty would not provide the lender with the express waiver of certain defenses that is customarily included in a well-drafted guaranty. Moreover, it is doubtful that the expedited enforcement proceeding known as "executory action" would be available against the nation in respect to such a guaranty. For

---

cordingly, the president executes a single instrument or agreement of guaranty covering all obligations of the borrower. It may be possible, nevertheless, to obtain some of the benefits conferred by the Commercial Code on the beneficiary of such a guaranty by stating expressly in it that the guarantor is guaranteeing the obligations of the borrower in the capacity of <u>avalista</u>. For example, Article 634 of the Commercial Code provides that the <u>aval</u> does not have to be affixed to the note itself but may be set forth in a separate document.

these reasons, lenders should seek to obtain a written <u>aval</u> or guaranty agreement from the nation even though the loan purportedly already bears the statutory guaranty of the nation.

Powers, Approvals, and Authorizations

The lender and its counsel must ascertain whether the guarantor of its proposed loan has full power and authority to issue the guaranty and has obtained all necessary approvals for it. This process is similar to determining whether the borrower has full power and authority. (See the following section on powers and authorizations.) However, the fact that a particular agency has power to borrow does not necessarily mean it can guarantee the obligations of another.[47] Similarly, the authorization procedures necessary for an entity to guarantee the obligations of another may differ from those required for it to undertake a loan.

POWERS AND AUTHORIZATIONS

This section considers two important questions affecting the validity and enforceability of a loan: First, does the borrower have the legal power to undertake the loan? and, second, assuming the borrower has the legal power to do so, has it obtained all the necessary authorizations and approvals required by law or by the borrower's own charter or bylaws in order for it to incur the loan and to perform its obligations? Both these questions must be examined and answered affirmatively in order to be sure the loan is valid and enforceable. In lending to Latin American borrowers, ensuring that a borrower is duly empowered and authorized to borrow is complicated by several factors: (1) the legal power of de facto military governments and the validity of statutes or constitutions adopted by them may be called into question by subsequent administrations, (2) Latin American governments in recent years have tended to require an extensive series of authorizations prior to permitting a governmental agency to borrow abroad, and (3) many Latin American countries currently have in effect some form of exchange-control requirements that must be satisfied if the borrower is to be able to obtain the necessary foreign exchange to service the loan.

The impact on the lender of the borrower's not being duly empowered or authorized to undertake the loan may vary from the complete loss of the loan to merely a request to remedy the defect. The risk that the lender may be unable to recover its loan, however, is sufficiently severe that the lender and its counsel must exercise great care, no matter how tedious, to be sure that the borrower has acted with full power and authority.

Problems of de Facto Military
Governments and Repudiation of Loan
Obligations by Subsequent Governments

In lending to an agency or instrumentality of a nondemocratically
elected government, the lender is confronted with two questions: Can
the agency's or instrumentality's constitutional and legal power and
authority to borrow be clearly established? and Are the acts and obligations of such government likely to be honored or repudiated by a
subsequent government? The first question is susceptible of legal
analysis, while the second is primarily a matter for country-risk
analysis. Nevertheless, by ensuring that all laws have been complied
with, the risk of repudiation may be reduced.

An illustration of the questions that may arise in determining
the constitutional and legal power and authority of a borrower to undertake a loan may be found in the case of the revolutionary government
that assumed power in Peru in 1968. This new government enacted
a statute that provided that the revolutionary government would act
in accordance with the provisions of the Revolutionary Statute and the
constitution and other existing laws, provided that they were compatible with the objectives of the revolutionary government. [48] The government has subsequently adopted decree laws relating to foreign
borrowings by decentralized agencies that arguably may be inconsistent with previously existing constitutional and statutory provisions.
Assuming that the provisions of the subsequently enacted decree laws
have been satisfied, can a lender be sure that the loan is legally binding and enforceable?

Peru also provides a useful illustration of some of the questions
that may arise in analyzing the risk that a subsequent government
may repudiate a previous, nondemocratically elected government's
obligations. The proposed new Political Constitution of Peru, which
will not go into effect until July 1980, provides in Article 141 that the
state only guarantees the payment of public debt "which is contracted
by constitutional governments in accordance with the Constitution and
the law." Although it is believed that this provision was not necessarily intended to require Peru to abrogate obligations contracted by
the revolutionary government, it presumably gives the successor government the constitutional power to refuse to recognize the obligations
of the revolutionary government. Although there is no reason to believe the successor government will not recognize its predecessor's
debts, this does underscore the importance of trying to ensure that
loans are in full accord with applicable constitutional and statutory
provisions.

The announcement at the United Nations in October 1979 by a
member of the revolutionary junta of Nicaragua that Nicaragua does

not intend to honor the external debt contracted by the Somoza regime is a dramatic example of the risk that a subsequent government may repudiate the obligations of a predecessor. It is understood that the junta considered attempting to distinguish between those loans whose proceeds may have benefited Somoza's interests and those that truly benefited the country as a whole and to repudiate only the former. If this were the case, it highlights the value, in the structuring and documenting of a loan, of identifying clearly the purpose for which the loan will be used.

A less dramatic, yet still noteworthy, incident occurred in Venezuela in 1979 when the newly elected government denounced certain irregularities in the making of loans by foreign banks to several autonomous agencies and public sector companies. The officers of the borrowers in certain instances had apparently executed the agreements without fulfilling all the necessary legal formalities. In a speech to the nation in September 1979, Venezuela's President Herrera Campins announced that such officers would be prosecuted, but he did not talk of dishonoring the loans in question. It is not expected that Venezuela will do so since apparently the public sector received the loan proceeds and the circumstances surrounding the making of the loans were otherwise not questionable. This instance underscores the importance of obtaining all necessary authorizations and complying with all other legal requirements even when lending to countries where a democratically elected government is succeeded by another.

The political turmoil in Iran is further evidence of the risk that a sovereign nation may repudiate some or all of its loan obligations. Although the reported repudiation by Iran of its loan obligations to U.S. lenders was not apparently based upon technical legal deficiencies, in similar yet perhaps less emotional circumstances such deficiencies may be used as the excuse for repudiation.

Determining the Borrower's Power to Borrow

Determining a borrower's power to borrow is to be distinguished from its authority to borrow (which is discussed immediately below). Once it is determined that a borrower has been given the requisite power by the constitution, statutes, or regulations, then it is necessary to determine what authorizations, consents, or approvals are necessary before the borrower can exercise its power to borrow.

Usually a country's power to borrow is found initially in its constitution, which may delegate such power to the legislative or executive branch of the government. For example, in Colombia the constitution grants to the Congress the power to authorize the government to enter into loan agreements.[49] The constitution also provides that the Republic of Colombia shall be responsible for the foreign and domestic debt that it incurs.[50] The Congress, in turn, has enacted laws from time to time authorizing the government (executive branch) to incur foreign loans. The most recent of these laws, Law 63 of 1978, expands the maximum amount of external debt that the republic can incur and sets forth the various authorizations and approvals that are required in connection with an external loan. The president of Colombia has, in turn, promulgated Decree 150 of 1976, pursuant to authority delegated to him by the Congress, which establishes more detailed regulations governing foreign borrowings by the republic and various of its agencies and instrumentalities.

Determining the Borrower's Authority to Borrow

Assuming that the borrower has the power to borrow, what authorizations, approvals, and consents are necessary for it to undertake legally a loan obligation? Such authorizations and approvals may fall into two categories: internal authorizations, which are obtained within the borrowing entity's own organization, such as shareholder or board of directors approval, and external authorizations, which are obtained from other entities or organizations, such as the ministry of finance, the council of ministers, the central bank, and the like. Since internal authorizations are usually quite straightforward, only external authorizations will be discussed.

As Latin American countries have increased their external borrowing, they have become more careful in their organization and management of such borrowing. In the process, the number of authorizations that are required to undertake an external loan has grown considerably. This development, in general, is salutory, since it usually means there is more effective communication within the different parts of the government that should participate in, or at least be aware of, decisions to incur external loans. The result is better external debt management. However, this means that the lender must ensure that all such authorizations have been obtained, even those that are the direct responsibility and within the sole control of the borrower.

A brief description of the authorization process in Brazil and Colombia will illustrate the types of agencies and procedures that may be involved. In Brazil the authorization for contracting or guaranteeing foreign loans by the federal government or a governmental agency is the responsibility of the executive branch of the federal government acting through the Secretariat of Planning and the Central Bank of Brazil.[51] External loan proposals and requests for federal guaranties are first reviewed and passed on by the minister of planning with the participation of the Central Bank. Previously, this function had been fulfilled by the Comisão de Emprestimos Externos (CEMPEX)—Commission on External Loans. Under the current practices of CEMPEX, major syndicated governmental loans are scheduled according to priorities set by the government so that no more than one governmental loan is being marketed at a time, thereby avoiding competition among governmental borrowers.

In Colombia the principal approval required for an external loan to a governmental borrower is that of the Ministry of Finance. Nevertheless, there are a number of other governmental authorizations or actions that are required before a loan has been duly authorized. These include approvals or opinions from the National Council on Economic and Social Policy, the Monetary Board, the Interparliamentary Commission on Public Credit, the Council of Ministers, and the National Department of Planning and the due registration with the Office of Foreign Exchange of the Central Bank and the Office of the Comptroller General of the Republic. All of these approvals, opinions, and registrations are important to obtain and the failure to do so may adversely affect the validity and enforceability of a loan.

Enforceability of a Loan against a Borrower
Not Duly Empowered or Authorized to Contract the Loan

Is a loan enforceable if the borrower did not have the power or was not authorized to incur it? This, of course, is the critical question concerning the borrower's power and authority to borrow, and it is not easy to answer. The consequences may be that the loan is void, with the result that the loan may be treated as unenforceable and uncollectible or, alternatively, that the lender can rescind the agreement and recover the loan proceeds in order to be returned to the status quo prior to the making of the loan. The loan may also be treated as voidable, with the parties being given the opportunity to cure the defects and continue with the loan. Unfortunately, the applicable laws are seldom clear as to what the consequences of a particular lack of authorization or power may be, so that the banker and his counsel must rely on an informed judgment or sense as to what the consequences might be. Of course, to the extent there has been political change or upheaval, the consequences of a lack of power or authorization may well be more grave than would ordinarily be the case.

In Colombia, Article 189 of Decree 150 of 1976 provides that a contract celebrated with the nation or a governmental agency is "absolutely null and void" if it was executed by persons who lacked authority, if it was not authorized by law, if it was the result of improper conduct by the government officials involved, or if the costs associated with it were not provided for in the national budget. Article 190 provides that a governmental contract that suffers from any other defects or omissions shall be "relatively null and void" and its performance is prohibited until the defects are cured. Although it is doubtful whether a loan agreement's "absolute nullity" would prevent the lender from being repaid at least the principal of its loan, there are several provisions of Decree 150 that might support a tenuous argument that the lender was not entitled to have the loan proceeds returned to it.[52] The agreement can, however, be made effective and valid in spite of such absolute nullity, pursuant to Article 46 of Decree 150, if the approval of the National Congress is obtained.

In Venezuela the constitution provides that the nation will only recognize those obligations assumed by authorized representatives of the public sector in accordance with the applicable law, with the consequence that obligations that do not satisfy those requirements are invalid and without legal effect.[53] Whether this means that the lender is unable to recover its loan or could treat the loan as rescinded and recover it on grounds of unjust enrichment is not clear. The Venezuelan Civil Code fortunately does contain a provision designed to prevent unjust enrichment.[54]

The foregoing illustrations, together with the reference made earlier to Article 141 of the new Peruvian Constitution, underscore the potentially serious consequences that may flow from a loan that has not been properly authorized and the importance of ensuring that all requisite authorizations have been obtained. Whether a sovereign borrower will challenge the validity and enforceability of a loan that was not properly authorized will often depend upon the prevailing political climate and the extent to which a successor government may be antagonistic to its predecessor that incurred the loan. In Venezuela, for example, although President Herrera Campins denounced certain irregularities in the incurring of loans by governmental agencies from foreign banks during his predecessor's administration, there has been no mention that Venezuela will refuse to recognize such faultily contracted loans. If the antagonism of the successor government toward its predecessor were greater or the political turmoil were as pronounced as in Iran or Nicaragua, the risk that unlawful loans would not be honored, even though the borrower, in fact, received the funds, is of course much greater.

Foreign Exchange Control Approvals

Many Latin American countries have established foreign exchange controls in order to regulate and conserve the use of their foreign exchange. As a result, in order to ensure that a borrower will be able to obtain the necessary foreign exchange to repay an external loan, such loan may have to be registered and approved by the appropriate foreign exchange office, which is ordinarily part of the central bank.[55] As a practical matter, foreign exchange registration of a loan does not necessarily guarantee that the central bank will make available to the borrower the foreign exchange necessary to service the loan, since the country (and, therefore, the bank) may, at the time the exchange is sought, have a foreign exchange shortage that prevents it from providing the exchange. Nevertheless, having the appropriate foreign exchange approvals will, under ordinary circumstances, ensure that exchange will be made available.

In certain countries, a single approval of the foreign exchange authorities for remittance of loan payments may not cover all payments to be made under the agreement. For example, in Colombia the separate approval of the Foreign Exchange Office of the Central Bank is required for each payment to be remitted and is obtainable only at the time of such remittance. Accordingly, it is not possible to obtain a single, all-encompassing approval prior to the making of the loan. Moreover, the Colombian Foreign Exchange Office has taken the position in correspondence with counsel for certain lenders that it will not authorize a remittance until it has been established that the proceeds of the loan were used for the proper purposes for which the loan was intended. This can be troublesome to a lender, which, ordinarily, has little control over a borrower's use of proceeds once a loan is disbursed.

Foreign exchange registration or approval of an external loan may not cover the remittance of foreign exchange for an accelerated prepayment required by a default or for a voluntary prepayment. For example, Argentine Central Bank approval only applies to scheduled payments on the dates set forth in the agreement so that any prepayments may require additional Central Bank approval. Thus, lenders should be aware that the elaborate clauses providing for accelerated prepayment in the event of default may be difficult to effect in practice if a new approval to remit foreign exchange is needed and the country is suffering from a shortage of foreign exchange.

USURY

The defense of usury to an action to enforce a loan seldom rears its ugly head in the context of external loans made to Latin American governmental borrowers. This is fortunate since usury is generally considered a matter of public order and the resultant penalties may be severe: unenforceability of the loan or, at a minimum, uncollectability of interest; fines; and even criminal sanctions. Furthermore, the usury laws of the borrower's country are generally applicable even if the loan is executed abroad or the loan agreement is, by its terms, governed by the laws of the lender's country. Nevertheless, in spite of the infrequency with which usury problems arise, because of the serious consequences of a usury violation, lenders should examine carefully whether a proposed loan could be considered usurious.

In Latin American countries usury laws and regulations tend to be applied in such a way as to distinguish between local currency loans and foreign currency loans received from abroad. Such a distinction is especially likely to occur if the local currency tends to depreciate rapidly against the U.S. dollar and, therefore, domestic interest rates are substantially higher than interest rates on dollar loans. For this reason, the application of the same usury limits to domestic loans and to external loans usually is inappropriate and the rates on dollar-denominated or other external loans are subject instead to guidelines determined by the borrower's central bank or ministry of finance.

In Brazil, for example, interest rates on external loans are subject to the approval of CEMPEX and the Central Bank, and the usury laws governing domestic loans apparently are not applicable. Similarly, in Colombia, although the domestic usury rate is double the current bank rate of interest of 18 percent (36 percent), this rate is not applied to external loans.[56] External loans to private sector, as distinguished from public sector, borrowers are subject to the limits fixed by the Monetary Board since the Office of Foreign Exchange of the Central Bank will not register an external loan and permit the remittance of foreign exchange in respect to a loan that exceeds such limits. External loans to public sector borrowers are not subject to any predetermined limits on interest rates, but the terms of the loan must be approved by the Ministry of Finance.

Since domestic interest rates in most Latin American countries have generally been substantially higher than LIBORs for U.S. dollars, the question of the applicability of the usury laws to dollar loans is usually academic. But would these laws be applied if interest rates on external loans exceeded the usury rates? This very question has arisen recently in Venezuela and created considerable uncertainty. The usury limit is fixed at 12 percent in Venezuela, considerably below current LIBOR levels irrespective of the spread that might be added to the LIBOR.[57] The Venezuelan usury law is a matter of public order and a loan that violates it may not only be unenforceable but also may subject the lender to criminal sanctions of up to two years imprisonment and a fine. This law, dating from 1946, has never been expressly derogated, although exceptions have been made for loans by Venezuelan financial institutions pursuant to the authority of the Venezuelan Central Bank to fix rates for the banking system. Such authority, however, does not cover foreign banks and, therefore, their loans do not benefit from such exception. In spite of the usury statute, SIEX continues to approve the making of external loans at rates in excess of 12 percent and foreign lenders continue to lend, albeit perhaps uneasily. Although there are reasons why the Venezuelan usury statute should not apply to external loans made to governmental borrowers or other substantial borrowers, nevertheless there apparently is no judicial precedent establishing its inapplicability. As a result, the issue is currently clouded by uncertainty. Most foreign lenders have continued to lend, however, thereby implicitly concluding that the risk of the usury laws being applied to such loans is acceptably small.

CONTROVERSIAL LOAN-AGREEMENT COVENANTS AND OTHER PROVISIONS

Certain loan-agreement provisions tend to generate more heated negotiation than others. Sometimes the issues are important and the heat is, therefore, justified; other times the disputes seem to be more in the nature of tempests in a teapot. Several provisions that may have considerable effect on the enforceability or administration of a loan are touched on briefly below.

Purpose Clause

The purpose clause sets forth the manner in which the borrower promises it will use the proceeds of the loan. Some loan agreements, surprisingly, contain no purpose clause; others contain only very general clauses such as "to finance economic development programs." Borrowers generally seek to avoid limiting the purpose for which they will use the loan proceeds, and lenders generally acquiesce unless a borrower is in financial difficulty. In spite of this tendency, there are reasons why more specific purpose clauses would be desirable. First, a clear and specific purpose clause forces the borrower to examine carefully how it will use the loan and, as a result, it is hoped, to employ such funds more productively in its business. Second, such a clause forces the lender to evaluate the borrower's financing program and to determine whether the proposed use of the funds will help the borrower generate the capability to repay the loan. Thus, a specific and thoughtful purpose serves to impose discipline on both the borrower and lender to make sure that the loan will be a sound one from both parties' points of view.

Finally, and most important, an effective purpose clause enables the lender to exert some pressure on the borrower to ensure

that the loan proceeds are not siphoned off improperly by officers of
the borrower or otherwise diverted to illicit or frivolous purposes.
Of course, once the loan is disbursed, the lender cannot force the
borrower to use the proceeds for a particular purpose, although the
lender should be in a position, assuming the loan agreement is
drafted properly, to call a default and accelerate the loan if the purpose clause has been breached. However, if the lender does not attempt to encourage the sound use of the loan proceeds through a meaningful purpose clause or, worse yet, has reason to know that the proceeds may be diverted to purposes that clearly are not in the best interests of the borrower's country, a risk exists that a subsequent
government may repudiate the loan on the grounds that the lender con-
spired or otherwise cooperated in a loan that benefited a privileged
few and not the country as a whole. Such a risk would ordinarily appear to be quite small except for the fact that this was apparently
one of the arguments used by the revolutionary junta in Nicaragua in
considering repudiating certain of Nicaragua's external indebtedness.

Events of Default

The Events of Default section of a loan agreement is instrumen-
tal to the lender's right to accelerate the payment of all amounts due
under the agreement prior to their scheduled maturities. If certain
events occur that give rise to a significant risk that the borrower will
be unable to repay the loan, the lender will want the right, even if it
chooses not to exercise it, to move quickly to enforce its rights
against the borrower. Some of the most controversial of the events
of default clauses are the cross-default, political upheaval, and representation default provisions.

The cross-default provision permits the lender, in general, to
accelerate the loan if the borrower is in default under another loan
agreement. Borrowers, of course, seek to avoid the inclusion of any
such clauses in any form since they create the risk that a default on
one loan, even if minor, may result in all other loans being accelerated. A lender wants to be assured that if other lenders are taking
steps to enforce their loans it will not be left behind to pick up the
pieces. Compromises that are reached include requirements that a
cross default will not occur unless (1) another lender has actually accelerated its loan as a result of a default; (2) the default that has occurred, although the loan has not been accelerated, is for nonpayment
of principal or interest (rather than a so-called technical default) and
is in excess of a certain amount; and/or (3) the default, absent acceleration, has not been remedied for a specified number of days. A
lender may be willing to accept greater or lesser limitations on its

right to accelerate by reason of a cross default depending upon the nature of the default and upon the lender's perception of the political and financial stability of the borrower's country (and, hence, the likelihood that prompt action may be necessary to enforce the loan).

Some loan agreements contain an event of default provision permitting acceleration in the event of political, military, or economic disturbances of a national or international nature that in the opinion of the lender or lenders may imperil or prevent the borrower from fulfilling its obligations. Provisions such as this, especially those involving a subjective determination by the lender, are usually resisted by the lender. Nevertheless, it may be reasonable for a lender to require some form of disaster or upheaval default, especially in light of recent events in Nicaragua and Iran.

Loan agreements usually contain a long series of representations of fact and covenants that, if breached or not fulfilled, give rise to an event of default and a right to accelerate. Certain of these representations and covenants may be drafted so strictly that it may be difficult for the borrower to avoid being in default as soon as the agreement is executed. This problem is aggravated by the fact that cross-default clauses in other agreements may permit other lenders to accelerate their loans. Ordinarily, lenders overlook minor, technical breaches of representations and covenants and do not accelerate their loans on such account. Nevertheless, if the default exists, then a right to accelerate also exists, thereby creating a potentially unstable lender-borrower relationship. To avoid this risk, lenders and borrowers should cooperate closely to ensure that the representations and covenants made by borrowers are accurate and reasonable under the circumstances.

Some Lessons from the Iranian Situation

The recent political and financial upheaval in Iran, the U.S. Treasury's Iranian Assets Control Regulations, and the resultant efforts by many lenders to set off against deposits held by them amounts owed to them by Iranian borrowers or to attach assets of such borrowers have focused attention on a number of loan-agreement provisions, including consents or waivers relating to setoff and attachment, events of default of the type noted above, the lender's right to assign its interest in the loan, and a lender's obligation to share payments received from the borrower with other members of a lending syndicate.

A lender's right to exercise a setoff against assets it holds belonging to a borrower and its ability to obtain an effective attachment on a borrower's assets and, ultimately, to execute on such assets will be enhanced and may even be dependent on an express provision or waiver to this effect in its loan agreement. Some banks that have lent to Iranian borrowers are realizing that their loan agreements do not give them the explicit rights or waivers they may need to make an effective setoff or attachment. This problem can be avoided in the future by careful drafting of loan documentation, but borrowers may understandably object to provisions that subject their assets to the risks of setoff and attachment.

Syndicated loan agreements ordinarily permit a member bank of the lending syndicate to assign its interest in the loan to the borrower only with the consent of the borrower. Such consent requirement may prevent a lending bank from being able to sell or assign its loan. In the context of the Iranian problem, such a clause could prevent a lender from assigning its loan to another bank that was in a better position to set off the loan against assets of the borrower. The borrower, on the other hand, has an interest in ensuring that its lenders are known to it and are not changed without its consent. A compromise might be to permit assignability of loan interests among the members of the same banking syndicate without the consent of the borrower.

Syndicated loan agreements sometimes contain a provision requiring a member bank to share with other banks in the syndicate any payments made to it by the borrower in excess of such bank's pro rata share. Disputes have arisen in the Iranian situation as to whether banks that have exercised setoffs or obtained attachments are required to share the proceeds with the other syndicate members. Careful drafting of these provisions should eliminate these uncertainties, although lead banks and member banks will undoubtedly have differing views as to how these pro rata sharing provisions should function. The borrower may also have an interest in how such provisions will be drafted as a result of the Iranian experience.

CONCLUSION

Lending to Latin American governmental borrowers is a challenge for lender and borrower alike, and the structuring and legal documentation aspects of such transactions are no exception. Whether a borrower will be legally able or willing as a matter of policy to agree to a foreign governing law provision, submit to the jurisdiction of foreign courts, or waive its immunity to jurisdiction and execution will vary from country to country and even within the same country, depending upon the type of governmental borrower. If a lender is unable to negotiate its own law as governing, or the borrower's submission to the jurisdiction of the lender's courts, or an effective waiver of the borrower's sovereign immunity, the lender must examine the legal risks to enforceability that will result. The acceptability of these risks will depend upon the laws and judicial system of the borrower's country, the nature of the borrower, the political and economic stability of the borrower, and the perceived possibility of a default.

A lender should evaluate the procedures for enforcing a loan in the borrower's country and how such enforcement may be expedited through the use of promissory notes that qualify for executive action. Although the basic principles underlying the right to executive action may be similar in most Latin American countries, a form of promissory note that qualifies as an executive instrument in one country may not qualify in another.

Lenders sometimes take for granted the nature and legal status of their borrowing customers and fail to examine carefully the effect of such nature and status on the likelihood of repayment and the legal risks involved. The nature, function, and legal status of a borrower will also affect the optimal structure, both from a credit and legal standpoint, of a loan and the necessity or benefit of having it guaranteed.

The process of assuring that a borrower has full power and has obtained all required authorizations to undertake a loan has become increasingly complex and oftentimes burdensome. Nonetheless, such assurances must be obtained, especially since the consequences of a borrower's lacking due power and authority may render the loan null and void.

The economic and political instability of a particular country or region imposes an even greater burden on bankers and their counsel to structure a loan thoughtfully, to provide that the loan proceeds are used for the nation's benefit, and to make sure that the loan is legal and valid. Political and economic turmoil impose perhaps the greatest stress on the effectiveness of a loan's structure and documentation. The greater the risk of turmoil, of course, the greater the need for care.

Although the difficulties of, and necessity for care in, structuring and documenting a loan have perhaps never been greater, at the same time the pressures of syndicated loan marketing have created a counterproductive tendency toward competitive laxity in the documenting of loans. Thus, banks may compete with each other in convincing prospective borrowers that their loan documentation and legal review will be briefer and less onerous than that of their competitors. Such pressures may yield benefits in the form of simpler documentation; they also may lead to a weakening of the documentation—and, ultimately, the enforceability—of the loan. Bankers and lawyers should be sensitive to the fact that sound loan documentation requires that certain minimum standards be preserved and that, although these standards may properly vary depending upon the borrower or country involved, they should not be subject to the same competitive pressures affecting interest margins or management fees.

NOTES

1. See Chile, Decree Law 2349 of 1978 and the discussion in the sections on governing law and procedural issues.

2. Colombia, Decree 150 of 1976, Art. 115.

3. Colombia, Law 63 of 1978, Art. 5.

4. Colombia, Commercial Code, Arts. 3 and 7.

5. Chile, Decree Law 2349 of October 13, 1978, Art. 1. (Diario oficial, October 28, 1978.)

6. Ibid., Art. 3.

7. Ibid., Art. 4. The Banco Central and Banco del Estado de Chile are excempt from this requirement. Chile, Decree 1009 of December 13, 1978. (Diario oficial, December 23, 1978.)

8. In the case of Argentina, see Civil Code §§ 1209, 1210, and 1212; the National Code of Civil and Commercial Procedure § 1; and the Preliminary Title of the Commercial Code § 5.

9. Diario de Caracas, November 7, 1979, pp. 16–17.

10. Memoria de la procuradoría, 1977.

11. New York Civil Practice Law and Rules (CPLR) §§ 301 and 302(a).

12. Colombia, Law 63 of 1978, Art. 5. See the earlier discussion of governing law.

13. Bidart Campos, Derecho constitucional del poder 2: 380.

14. Longines-Wittnauer Watch Co. v. Barnes & Reinecke, Inc., 15 N.Y. 2d 443, 209 N.E. 2d 68, 261 N.Y.S. 2d 8 (1965).

15. Chemical Bank v. Major Realty Corp., 439 F. Supp. 181 (S.D.N.Y. 1977); National Iranian Oil Co. v. Commercial Union Insurance Co., 363 F. Supp. 129 (S.D.N.Y. 1973).

16. Carbon Black Export v. The S.S. Monrosa, 254 F 2d 297 (5th Cir. 1958); cert. dismissed, 359 U.S. 180 (1959); Kyler v. United States Trotting Ass'n., 12 A.D. 2d 874, 210 N.Y.S. 2d 25 (4th Dept.), appeal denied, 12 A.D. 2d 1004, 212 N.Y.S. 2d 1022 (4th Dept. 1961).

17. Bremen v. Zapata Off-Shore Co., 407 U.S. 1 (1972). Restatement (Second) of the Conflict of Laws § 80 (1971) provides that "the parties' agreement as to the place of the action cannot oust a state of judicial jurisdiction, but such an agreement will be given effect unless it is unfair or unreasonable."

18. For a useful discussion of the unjust and unreasonable standard, see Lars O. Lagerman, "Choice of Forum Clauses in International Contracts: What Is Unjust and Unreasonable?" International Lawyer 12 (1978): 779.

19. See Delaume, "Public Debt and Sovereign Immunity: The Sovereign Immunities Act of 1976," American Journal of International Law 71 (1977): 399; von Mehren, "The Foreign Sovereign Immunities Act of 1976," Columbia Journal of Transnational Law 17 (1978): 33.

20. Foreign Sovereign Immunities Act of 1976 § 1605(a)(1) and (2).

21. Ibid., § 1610(a)(1) and (2).

22. Decree 150 of 1976, Art. 115, implicitly precludes a waiver of immunity from jurisdiction by providing that loan agreements shall be submitted to the courts of Colombia.

23. H.R. Rep. no. 1487, 94th Cong., 2d sess., at 16.

24. Colombia, Code of Civil Procedure, Arts. 336, 497, and 498.

25. Colombia, Commercial Code, Art. 619.

26. Ibid., Arts. 621 and 709.

27. Ibid., Arts. 673 and 711.

28. Colombia, Code of Civil Procedure, Art. 488.

29. Colombia, Commercial Code, Art. 902.

30. Ibid., Art. 672.

31. Ibid., Art. 673(3).

32. Opinion of the Colombian Superintendent of Banks, Oficio O.J.409, December 10, 1976.

33. Colombia, Commercial Code, Art. 646.

34. See Colombia, Decree 150 of 1976, Art. 54, which provides that payment of a contractual obligation is subordinated to the appropriations made for such payment in the appropriate budget.

35. Argentina, Law 3952 § 7, as amended by Law 19,549.

36. Argentina, Constitution (1853), Art. 1.

37. J. G. Starke, An Introduction to International Law (London: Butterworths, 1977), chap. 10, pp. 364-65. Under the principle of continuity, a state continues to be bound by its rights and obligations under international law, including treaty rights and obligations, notwithstanding alterations in the organization or constitutional structure of the state.

38. Argentina, Constitution (1853), Art. 35, provides the following:

> The different names used from 1810 to the present, viz. United Provinces of the River Plate, Argentine Republic, Argentine Confederation, will be official names used without differentiation to designate the government and territory of the provinces, the words "Argentine Nation" being used in the sanction and enactment of laws.

39. See, for example, Colombia, Constitution, Arts. 1, 2, and 4 (nación) and Ar5s. 8, 11, 202, and 203 (república).

40. Ibid., Arts. 203 and 204.

41. Ibid., Art. 57.

42. Decision of the Corte Federal de Casación of May 30, 1945, quoted from Allan R. Brewer-Carias, Jurisprudencia de la Corte Suprema 1930-74 y estudios de derecho administrativo (Caracas: Universidad Central de Venezuela, 1975), 1: 293.

43. Colombia, Commercial Code, Arts. 632-36.

44. Argentine Central Bank, Charter, Law 20,539 § 1.

45. Banco de la Nación Argentina, Charter, Law 21,799 § 2; and Banco Nacional de Desarrollo, Charter, Law 21,629 § 2.

46. Argentina, Commercial Code, Title X § 34, enacted by Decree 5965 and ratified by Law 16,478.

47. The Central Bank of Argentina, for example, is expressly forbidden by its charter from guaranteeing or endorsing obligations of the national government, political subdivisions, decentralized agencies, and similar institutions. Law 20,539 § 19(c).

48. Peru, Decree Law 17,063 of October 3, 1968, Art. 5.

49. Colombia, Constitution, Art. 76.

50. Ibid., Art. 203.

51. Brazil, Decree 84,128 of October 29, 1979. This decree abolished CEMPEX.

52. Colombia, Decree 150 of 1976, Arts. 54,190 and 54,194.

53. Venezuela, Constitution, Art. 232. See also Venezuela, Organic Law of Public Credit, Art. 60.

54. See Venezuela, Civil Code, Art. 1184, concerning unjust enrichment; and Opinion of the Legal Counsel of the Ministry of Justice, dated October 2, 1961, quoted from Brewer-Carias, Jurisprudencia, 2: 638.

55. See, for example, in respect to Brazil, Law 4131 of September 3, 1962; and, in respect to Colombia, Decree 444 of 1967.

56. Article 884 of the Colombian Commercial Code sets forth the domestic usury rate.

57. Venezuela, Decree Law 247 of 1946.

18
SOURCES OF INFORMATION
FOR APPRAISING COUNTRY RISK

Leila Jenkins

Obtaining up-to-date economic, political, and social information on foreign nations can be one of the most critical aspects of assessing country risk. The potential for sudden change is such that a
fine tuning of the evaluation process is advisable, and gaining access
to reliable information is an integral part of that process. This chapter is an attempt to identify and comment on a number of sources of
information available to the public. It is, however, essential to set
the scope and limitations of this treatise: it is a selected, annotated
list of business periodicals and reference sources, with an emphasis
on current material. The selections are derived from a bibliography
employed by a number of practicing international economists, and the
intent is to be descriptive rather than analytical. It is the task of the
researcher to perceive the biases of the various publications and to
weigh that into the analytical process.

The first step in country evaluation is the adaptation to a global
mentality, and it is through this framework that international information should be synthesized. The relative importance of what can be
gleaned through quantitative and qualitative insights must be kept in
mind, and appropriate conclusions from sources must include an appreciation for the size and level of development of a country.

Another consideration is the frequency with which the material
is updated. This varies from country to country and, in reporting
statistical data, is directly related to the priority level assigned to
the task by the individual government. Certain economic data, such
as gross domestic product (GDP), population, balance of payments,
and debt figures, will always lag by varying amounts of time owing
to efficiency of tabulation and input.

Never to be omitted from a search for country information are
the human resources around the world. Of course it is optimal to

travel to the country being researched, where indigenous governments and public and private institutions may be consulted, but that is not always possible. However, there are a number of institutions in the United States that can be of assistance in providing accurate and recent data as well as an intuitive interpretation. The federal government, with its many departments that maintain libraries, offers a pool of knowledge. The Department of Commerce and the Treasury are extensive resources. The export information room at the Department of Commerce has excellent files of country data supplied by international organizations. The Department of State has staff members assigned to each country with which the United States has diplomatic relations and maintains a wealth of printed economic and political information. The Central Intelligence Agency occasionally publishes reports that are relevant to country-risk assessments. The international agencies such as the World Bank (IBRD) and the International Monetary Fund (IMF) not only have country desk officers but also support staff solely assigned to technical analyses and projections of internal and external situations. Private research groups such as the Brookings Institution and the Conference Board are available as resources, as are many independent consulting firms around the United States. Larger commercial banks maintain libraries and analytical staffs (usually in an economics department) that assess country risk, and much of this information can be obtained through either a client or correspondent relationship. More informally, there exist across the continent international committees and lunch clubs that bring in knowledgeable speakers and entertain informative discussions. Pertinent printed material for assessing country risk comes in the usual variety of forms: magazines, newspapers, newsletters, books, and independent studies. For the purpose of brevity, mentioned are those publications that I have found most useful. Assuredly many more are available, but in considering efficient allocation of staff time, a decision must be made as to what information and depth of analysis is appropriate to the firm. No annotation will be made where the resource is of a more general nature covering the topic specifically indicated by the title. Also, it should be remembered that in much published information an editorial bias exists that sometimes should be discounted to better assess a particular situation.

MAGAZINES

Business Week. New York: McGraw-Hill.

Covers all aspects of business, domestic and abroad. Weekly.

<u>Economist</u>. London: Economist Newspaper.

Covers the international economic scene and business world with emphasis on the United Kingdom and the United States. Weekly.

<u>Euromoney</u>. London: Euromoney Publications.

Captures most relevant issues in international banking, accounting, currencies, commodities, politics, and economies with statistics on Eurodollar and interest rates. Monthly.

<u>Fortune</u>. Chicago: Time.

Covers all aspects of the business world in the United States and abroad. Biweekly.

<u>Institutional Investor</u>. International ed. New York: Institutional Investor.

Covers international banking, currency and money management, markets, deals, takeovers, economies, and so on. Monthly.

<u>World Business Weekly</u>. London: Financial Times.

New international periodical covering many aspects of international business. Weekly.

NEWSPAPERS

<u>American Banker</u>.

Covers news about bank developments, U.S. regulations, international monetary affairs, and the like. Five days a week.

<u>Christian Science Monitor</u>.

General daily newspaper with excellent international coverage. Five days a week.

<u>Journal of Commerce</u>.

Covers international business and world trade. Daily.

London <u>Financial Times</u>. Frankfurt: Financial Times (Europe).

General news including international business and country surveys. Daily.

New York Times.

Excellent business and finance section in addition to overall news coverage. Daily.

Wall Street Journal.

Emphasis on economic and business happenings. Daily.

NEWSLETTERS AND MISCELLANEOUS PERIODICALS

Banco do Brasil. Monthly Letter. Brasilia.

Covers Brazil's economy, politics, banking regulations, commodities, and the like, and includes statistics. Monthly.

Banco Lar Brasileiro. Trends and Perspectives of the Brazilian Economy.

Covers current economic trends and policies. Quarterly.

Banco Real. Economic Letter. São Paulo.

Covers Brazilian economy. Monthly.

Business International, New York.

Business International is a publishing company that prints weekly and biweekly regional management reports containing information on companies, economies, developments in currencies, taxes, licensing, capital sources, politics, and some statistical tables. These include Business Asia, Business Europe, Business Latin America, Business China, Eastern Europe Report, and Business International Money Report. Also, Business International publishes extensive reports on individual countries and loose-leaf supplemented reports on investing, licensing, and trading conditions abroad and financing foreign operations. In addition, a Master Key Index is published to locate information and include all other publications.

Chase Manhattan Bank. International Finance. New York.

Information on countries, commodities, money markets, world regions, international rates, and the like. Biweekly.

Conference Board, New York.

Publishes a number of studies on international economics and management.

Economist Intelligence Unit. Quarterly Economic Reviews. London.

The EIU publishes 77 separate quarterly reviews covering economic and business conditions, with outlooks for approximately 150 countries.

Ernst and Ernst. International Business Series. New York.

Separate booklets on a number of countries summarizing factors that affect trade and investment for each country.

First National Bank of Boston. Newsletter Argentina. Boston.

_____. Newsletter Brazil. Boston.

Cover economic and political situations. Weekly.

First National Bank of Chicago. First Chicago World Report. Chicago.

Covers pertinent international banking and economic issues. Bimonthly.

Institute for International Research. International Accounting and Financial Report. London.

Covers international accounting, tax, and currency issues. Biweekly.

Inter-American Development Bank. IDB News. Washington, D.C.

Covers news of the organization and information on countries where projects are ongoing. Monthly.

International Monetary Fund. Balance of Payments Yearbook. Washington, D.C.

_____. Direction of Trade. Washington, D.C.

_____. Finance and Development. Washington, D.C.

_____. IMF Survey. Washington, D.C.

_____. International Financial Statistics. Washington, D.C.

Cover fund activities and international economies and include excellent statistics on all member nations.

International Reports. International Reports. New York.

Up-to-date weekly advisory service in all fields of international finance.

Latin America Newsletters. <u>Latin America Commodities Report</u>. London.

_____. <u>Latin America Weekly Report</u>. London.

Cover once weekly the main economic and political issues arising in the Latin American countries.

Lloyds Bank International. <u>Bank of London and South America Review</u>. London.

Survey articles on Latin American countries plus Spain and Portugal; includes commodities and statistics. Monthly.

Merrill Lynch Economics. <u>Planning Report: International Review</u>. New York.

Monthly report of economic situation in a number of industrialized countries.

Morgan Guaranty Trust Company. <u>World Financial Markets</u>. New York.

Up-to-date statistics by country and rates for new bond issues, Eurodollar deposits, treasury bills, and so on. Monthly.

National Foreign Trade Council. <u>Breve</u>. New York. (Weekly digest of European reports.)

_____. <u>Noticias</u>. New York. (Weekly digest of hemisphere reports.)

_____. <u>Pacific-Asia Report</u>. New York. (Biweekly digest.)

Short synopses on countries' pertinent week-to-week political and economic information.

Organization for Economic Cooperation and Development, Paris.

Publishes economic pamphlets on member countries and a monthly bulletin of economic indicators.

Peat, Marwick, Mitchell. <u>International Tax and Business Notes</u>. New York.

Reports on changes in international taxes and implications in business.

Price Waterhouse. <u>Information Guide for Doing Business in [name of country]</u>. New York.

Separate booklets on many countries reporting on accounting practices, taxes, labor legislation, investment laws, and so on.

Standard Chartered Bank Limited. Standard Chartered Review. London.

> Review of economic, political, banking, and investment situations in many countries. Monthly.

U.S., Central Intelligence Agency. Economic Indicators Weekly Review. Washington, D.C.: Government Printing Office.

> Provides up-to-date information on changes in the domestic and external economic activities of the major noncommunist developed countries.

U.S., Department of Commerce. International Economic Indicators. Washington, D.C.: Government Printing Office.

> Economic indicators for a group of industrialized countries. Monthly.

U.S., Department of State. Background Notes. Washington, D.C.: Government Printing Office.

> On each country with which the United States has diplomatic relations, giving background of history, government, politics, economics, and overall internal and external situation.

World Bank, also known as International Bank for Reconstruction and Development (IBRD), Washington, D.C.

> Publishes "grey cover" reports on countries that contain excellent economic and political information and staff working papers, which cover many aspects of international economies.

BOOKS

Avramovic, Dragoslav. Economic Growth and External Debt. Baltimore: Johns Hopkins Press, 1964.

> A sound framework for evaluating country risk. It starts with economic development and ensuing need for debt, including a statistical presentation and following with essays on report fluctuations, debt-servicing problems over the long term, and conditions of debt failure.

Kindleberger, Charles P. International Economics. 5th ed. Home-
wood, Ill.: Irwin, 1973.

Classic text on workings of international economics: micro and
macro subjects, balance of payments, currency markets, international monetary arrangements, and the like.

Nagy, P. J. Country Risk. London: Euromoney, 1979.

How to assess, quantify, and monitor country risk.

Vernon, Raymond. The Economic Environment of International Business. Englewood Cliffs, N.J.: Prentice-Hall, 1972.

Textbook focusing on international trades payments and investments.

Zenoff, David B., and Jack Zwick. International Financial Management. Englewood Cliffs, N.J.: Prentice-Hall, 1969.

Theory and practice of international financial management with
an emphasis on the environmental forces of a country that affect international transactions.

Last but not least are computer resources. The International
Monetary Fund has on computer tapes all of the International Financial Statistics. This information can be obtained through most of the
major computer-time-sharing companies. The computer proves to
be a marvelous tool when analyzing country risk, as ratios may be
calculated and graphed for cross-country comparisons, moving averages of indicators can be followed historically to show trends, the
international accounts may be dissected and reported—a host of applications could be mentioned. Many firms have taken this information,
sometimes adding supplements, to create a country ranking to be used
as a quantitative tool for senior management. However, because of
the time lags in reporting much of this economic data, a reference
should always be made to the corresponding dates. It must also be
remembered that statistics alone do not summarize country risk. A
qualitative opinion should accompany all quantitative assessments of
foreign nations and their markets.

INDEX

ADELA (Atlantic Community Development Group for Latin America), 31
Adua, Shehu yar', 224
Aemi, Koichi, 81-82
Africa, 269; and cultural and political factors in trade with Latin America, 229-31; and expanding economic ties with Latin America, 222-33; financing of trade in, 231-33; and growth of trade with Latin America, 223-28
African Development Bank, 223
African Development Fund, 223
Agency for International Development (AID), ix, 36
agricultural lending projects, viii
Algeria, 224
allocation of savings, 77; and capital markets, 77-80; and fiscal policy, 81-83
American Banker, 338
American Institute of Certified Public Accountants, 251
Andean Development Corporation (ADC), ix
Angola, 227
Arab-Latin American Bank, ix
Argentina, vii, 9, 10, 22, 28-29, 45, 244, 287, 292; debt servicing in, 40; Eurocurrency lending to, 270-72; exchange rate experience in, 62-67; industrial financing in, 115-23; inflation rate in, 65, 70; law governing loans to, 299-300, 313, 333; sources of funds of industrial corporations in, 119-21; sources of funds in manufacturing enterprises in, 116; and trade with Gabon, 227

Asia, 269
Avramovic, Dragoslav, 342

Background Notes, 342
Bahamas, 62; exchange rate experience in the, 62-64
Balance of Payments Yearbook, 340
Banco do Brasil, 339
Banco Lar Brasileiro, 339
Banco Real, 339
Bank for International Settlements (BIS), 268
Bank of London and South America, 195
Bank of London and South America Review, 341
Bank of Tokyo, 195
Bankers Trust, 195
Barbados, ix; exchange rate experience in, 62-64
Barbosa, Mario Gibson, 223
Beagle Island, 10
BLADEX (Latin American Export Bank), ix
Bolivia, ix, 17, 270; exchange rate experience in, 62-64
Brazil, vii, ix, 18, 19, 20, 22, 29-30, 45, 61, 70-74, 224, 244; on contracting foreign loans by, 323-24, 327; debt servicing in, 41-42; development and financing of small-scale industry in, 141-75; economic setting in, 141-43; economic situation and outlook in, 179-90; Eurocurrency lending to, 270-72; exchange rate experience in, 62-65; financing small and medium-sized industries in, 160-67; growth of small

344

ABOUT THE EDITORS
AND CONTRIBUTORS

JEAN-CLAUDE GARCIA-ZAMOR is President of the International Development Group, a Washington, D.C., consulting firm and a Vice-President of the International Institute of Public Management. Since 1971 he has also been associated with the Department of Political Science at Howard University. Formerly, Dr. Garcia-Zamor taught at the Brazilian School of Public Administration in Rio de Janeiro and at the University of Texas at Austin; served as Senior Specialist in Public Administration at the Organization of American States; and was Controller of the Inter-American Development Bank. He holds B.A. and M.A. degrees from the University of Puerto Rico, as well as a Ph.D. in public administration from New York University. Dr. Garcia-Zamor has published three books in the field of public administration, edited a fourth one, and authored several articles in various academic journals.

STEWARD E. SUTIN is Executive Vice-President and Chief Executive Officer of Banco de Boston Dominicano, an affiliate of the First National Bank of Boston. Prior to this assignment, Dr. Sutin was the First National Bank of Boston's Regional Coordinator for Argentina, Chile, and Uruguay; a loan officer covering Caribbean and Andean Pact countries for the Marine Midland Bank; and a Latin American specialist for the Library of Congress. He is the recipient of research fellowships from the Organization of American States and the University of Texas and holds a Ph.D. in Latin American history and government from the University of Texas at Austin. Dr. Sutin has lectured on Latin America before several universities and business groups and has published several articles in newspapers, magazines, and professional journals.

STEVEN H. ARNOLD is Associate Professor of Government and Director of the International Development Program at the American University. He is a graduate of Occidental College and the holder of M.A. and Ph.D. degrees from Johns Hopkins University. Dr. Arnold has published several studies in the field of international relations.

RODRIGO K. BRIONES is Senior Currency Analyst at the Chase Manhattan Bank and, as such, follows events in various Latin American countries. Previously, Mr. Briones was an economist specializing in Latin America with the New York Office of Bank of America. He has also served in various capacities with agencies of the United Nations (such as United Nations International Children's Emergency Fund, Food and Agriculture Organization, and the Economic Commission for Latin America) as well as with Chilean private and government corporations. Mr. Briones holds B.A. and M.A. degrees in economics from the University of Chile and an M.B.A. from New York University.

SHELDON J. GITELMAN is Executive Vice-President of Marine Midland Bank and the head of its domestic banking activities. He was formerly chief of Marine Midland's Latin American Division and, prior to joining the bank, he served as Senior Director of Finance for Africa, the Middle East, and South Asia at the Overseas Private Investment Corporation. Mr. Gitelman is the recipient of a law degree from the University of Minnesota, an L.L.M. from Georgetown University, and an M.A. in African Studies from Howard University. He has published articles in various law, business, and banking journals.

ROBERT HAMPTON III is a partner of Price Waterhouse and Company. He serves in the Accounting and Auditing Services Department and is the U.S. representative on the Accounting Standards Group of Price Waterhouse International. A graduate of Princeton University, Mr. Hampton holds an M.B.A. from the Harvard Business School and is a Certified Public Accountant in New York and other states. He is a frequent public speaker on international accounting issues and has published various technical studies on accounting.

LEILA JENKINS is an Officer of the Credit Division of the Chemical Bank and, as such, is involved in the assessment of risk on bankwide exposure. Miss Jenkins, a graduate of Boston College, served with the New England Merchants National Bank and the First National Bank of Boston.

WHITMAN E. KNAPP is Vice-President and General Manager of the Paris Branch of the First National Bank of Boston. Until recently, Mr. Knapp was Managing Director of the First National Boston Limited, in London. Formerly a professor of history, he holds B.A. and M.A. degrees from Yale University.

JOSEPH M. MARTIN is Vice-President of Chemical Bank and a banking officer within its Latin American Division. He also serves as a Director of Sociedad Financiera Exterior, of Venezuela. Mr. Martin is a graduate of the University of Florida and is the recipient of an M.B.A. from Northwestern University.

AIDA M. PARDEE is currently Vice-President and International Economist with the Money Management Division of Marine Midland Bank. Previously, she held posts with Bankers Trust, the Central Bank of the Dominican Republic, and Puerto Rico's Corporation for the Economic Development of the Caribbean. She is a graduate of the Autonomous University of Santo Domingo, in the Dominican Republic, and has attended seminars at the International Monetary Fund and the Center for Latin American Monetary Studies.

ARTURO C. PORZECANSKI is presently Associate Economist with the Morgan Guaranty Trust Company of New York, where he acts as an adviser on Latin American economic and political affairs. He is the recipient of a B.A. in economics from Whittier College, as well as of M.A. and Ph.D. degrees in economics from the University of Pittsburgh. Dr. Porzecanski has served previously with the International Monetary Fund and the Center for Latin American Monetary Studies. He has published three books and approximately a dozen articles on Latin American economics and politics.

ANDREW C. QUALE, JR., is a Member of the New York law firm of Coudert Brothers and a Member of the Bars of the State of New York and the Commonwealth of Massachusetts. He is also a lecturer on international and domestic banking law at the University of Virginia. Mr. Quale is a graduate of Harvard College and the recipient of an LL.B. degree from Harvard University. He is a member of the Inter-American Affairs Committee of the Association of the Bar of the City of New York and of the Latin American Law Committee of the American Bar Association.

JUAN RADA is currently Director of FINCONSULTA and Senior Partner of Rada, Bosch y Asociados, a leading Venezuelan consulting firm in the field of cash and asset management. A founding officer of Venezuela's first operating money desk and a member of the National Banking Council's Commission on Money Desks, Mr. Rada serves as an adviser to the investment committees of several local and foreign corporations. He contributes frequently to Venezuelan and international business publications.

ROBERT S. REITZES is Manager of International Economic Analysis at the International Paper Company. He has earlier served as an international economist with E. I. Dupont and the Library of Congress and has lectured at the University of Delaware, Georgetown University, and Howard University. Dr. Reitzes's graduate degrees (M.A. and Ph.D.) are from Georgetown University.

353

HUGH H. SCHWARTZ is Senior Economist and Industrial Specialist at the Inter-American Development Bank. Previously, he taught economics at Case Western Reserve University, the University of Kansas, and at Yale University. Dr. Schwartz is the author of several articles in various economics journals and the coeditor of a volume published by the Inter-American Development Bank. He received his B.A. degree from Cornell University and M.A. and Ph.D. degrees from Yale University.

VITO TANZI is Chief of the Tax Policy Division in the Fiscal Affairs Department of the International Monetary Fund. He is a graduate of George Washington University and holds M.A. and Ph.D. degrees in economics from Harvard University. Dr. Tanzi was formerly on the faculty of American University. He is a well-known expert on tax policy in Latin America and the author of many articles on taxation issues published in leading professional journals.

JAMES B. THORNBLADE is Assistant Vice-President in the Economics Department of the First National Bank of Boston, where his responsibilities include the assessment of sovereign risk in international lending. He is a graduate of Oberlin College and a recipient of a Ph.D. degree in economics from the Massachusetts Institute of Technology. Prior to joining the First National Bank of Boston, Dr. Thornblade taught at Syracuse University and served as an economist in Washington, D.C., with the Executive Office of the President.

WILLIAM G. TYLER is Associate Professor of Economics at the University of Florida (Gainesville). He has previously carried out research at the Kiel Institute of World Economics and at the Brazilian School of Public Administration. A graduate of Dickinson College, he was awarded M.A., M.A.L.D., and Ph.D. degrees at the Fletcher School of Law and Diplomacy. Dr. Tyler is the author of numerous publications, many of which deal with Brazil's industrial development.